D1413287

EDUCATIONAL MEDIA AND TECHNOLOGY YEARBOOK

EDUCATIONAL MEDIA AND TECHNOLOGY YEARBOOK

Robert Maribe Branch and Mary Ann Fitzgerald, Editors

1998 VOLUME 23

Published in Cooperation with the
ERIC® Clearinghouse on Information & Technology
and the
Association for Educational Communications
and Technology

Libraries Unlimited, Inc. • Englewood, Colorado

LIBRARIES UNLIMITED, INC.
P.O. Box 6633
Englewood, CO 80155-6633
1-800-237-6124
www.lu.com

Library of Congress Cataloging-in-Publication Data

Suggested Cataloging:

Educational media and technology yearbook,
     1998 volume 23 / Robert Maribe Branch and Mary Ann Fitzgerald, editors --
Englewood, Colo.: Libraries Unlimited, 1998.
     xii, 296 p. 17x25 cm.
     ISBN 1-56308-591-7
     ISSN 8755-2094
     Published in cooperation with the ERIC Clearinghouse on Information
& Technology and the Association for Educational Communications and
Technology.
     1. Educational technology--yearbooks. 2. Instructional materials
centers--yearbooks. I. ERIC Clearinghouse on Information & Technology.
II. Association for Educational Communications and Technology.
III. Branch, Robert Maribe. IV. Mary Ann Fitzgerald.
LB 1028.3.E372   1998   370.778

Contents

Part Four
LEADERSHIP PROFILES

Part Five
ORGANIZATIONS AND ASSOCIATIONS
IN NORTH AMERICA

Part Six
GRADUATE PROGRAMS

Part Seven
MEDIAGRAPHY
Print and Nonprint Resources

Preface

The purpose of the 23d volume of *Educational Media and Technology Yearbook* is to present the multifaceted perceptions people have about educational communications. This volume of the *Yearbook* continues to provide information to help media professionals practice their craft in a changing, expanding field. This volume also maintains the philosophy of its senior editor for several years, Professor Emeritus Donald P. Ely, that "the definition of the field of *instructional* technology has evolved over the years, and this publication has been the chronicle of its development." It is hoped that readers of this *Yearbook* will become better informed about the purposes, activities, programs of study, and accomplishments of the organizations and associations dedicated to the advancement of educational communications and technology.

Technology is being defined more broadly than in the past. It is referred to as techniques and procedures derived from scientific research about methods for promoting change in human performance. Technology is *not* restricted to machines and hardware, but is perceived as a way of organizing thought, science, art, and human values. The evolution of educational media and advancements in information delivery technology are requiring educators to reconsider the traditional concept of audiovisual aids and to consider the concept of multimedia applications. This volume of the *Yearbook* reflects current thinking by including essays from respected authors about technology trends in education and training, teaching methods and curricular issues, electronic publishing and the state of the profession, and Internet resources.

Educational Media and Technology Yearbook has become a standard reference in many libraries and professional collections. This volume of the *Yearbook* contains sections devoted to Trends and Issues, The Profession, Current Developments, Leadership Profiles, Organizations and Associations in North America, Graduate Programs, and a Mediagraphy (of print and nonprint resources).

The editors, publishers, and professionals dedicated to the field believe it is important to record the events associated with educational technology through reviews of the profession, generations of leadership, and the influence of culture relative to the utilization of educational media and technology.

ROBERT MARIBE BRANCH

Contributors to
Educational Media and Technology
Yearbook 1998

Saada Al-Ghafry, Teaching Assistant
Instructional Technology
University of Georgia
Athens, Georgia 30602
e-mail: alghafry@coe.uga.edu

Lisa T. Bennett, Teaching Assistant
Instructional Technology
University of Georgia
Athens, Georgia 30602
e-mail: lbennet@coe.uga.edu

Robert Maribe Branch, Ed.D., Associate
    Professor
Instructional Technology
University of Georgia
Athens, Georgia 30602
e-mail: rbranch@coe.uga.edu

John Childs, Professor Emeritus
Wayne State University
Childs Consulting Associates, Inc.
29516 Southfield Road
Southfield, MI 48076

Rodney Earle, Ph.D., Associate Professor
College of Education
210Q MCKB
Brigham Young University
Provo, Utah 84602
e-mail: rodney-earle@byu.edu

John D. Emerson, Professor
Department of Mathematics and Computer
    Science
Middlebury College
Middlebury, Vermont 05753
e-mail: jemerson@panther.middlebury.edu

Mary Ann Fitzgerald, Co-editor
Instructional Technology
University of Georgia
Athens, Georgia 30602
e-mail: mfitzger@coe.uga.edu

Kent Gustafson, Ph.D., Professor
Instructional Technology
University of Georgia
Athens, Georgia 30602
e-mail: kgustafs@coe.uga.edu

R. David Lankes, Associate Director
ERIC Information & Technology
4-194 Science & Technology
Syracuse University
Syracuse, New York 13244-4100
e-mail: rdlankes@ericir.syr.edu

Michael Molenda, Ph.D., Professor
Instructional Systems Technology
Education 2234
Indiana University
Bloomington, Indiana 47405
e-mail: molenda@indiana.edu

Nancy A. Morgan, AskERIC Coordinator
ERIC Information & Technology
4-194 Science & Technology
Syracuse University
Syracuse, New York 13244-4100
e-mail: nmorgan@ericir.syr.edu

Frederick Mosteller, Professor Emeritus
Harvard Statistics Department
Science Center 603
One Oxford Street
Cambridge, Massachusetts 02138

Robert Muffoletto, Ph.D., Professor
School of Education
University of Northern Iowa
Cedar Falls, Iowa 50614
e-mail: robert.muffoletto@uni.edu

Ann Watts Pailliotet, Ph.D., Assistant
    Professor
Education
Whitman College
Walla Walla, Washington 99362
e-mail: pailliaw@whitman.edu

Lloyd P. Rieber, Ph.D., Associate Professor
Instructional Technology
University of Georgia
Athens, Georgia 30602
e-mail: lrieber@coe.uga.edu

James D. Russell, Ph.D., Professor
School of Education
Purdue University
West Lafayette, Indiana 47909
e-mail: jrussell@purdue.edu

Sharon Smaldino, Ph.D., Associate
    Professor
College of Education
University of Northern Iowa
Cedar Falls, Iowa 50614
e-mail: sharon.smaldino@uni.edu

Kenneth J. Smith, Ph.D., Professor
Educational Psychology
The University of Arizona
Tucson, Arizona 85721
e-mail: kjsmith@ccit.arizona.edu

Roy Tennant, Project Manager
Digital Library Research & Development
385 Doe Library, #6000
University of California, Berkeley
Berkeley, California 94720-6000
e-mail: rtennant@library.berkeley.edu

Gene L. Wilkinson, Ph.D., Associate
    Professor
Instructional Technology
University of Georgia
Athens, Georgia 30602
e-mail: gwilk@coe.uga.edu

Darryl Yorke
3330 Templeton Gap #25
Colorado Springs, Colorado 80907

Part One
Trends and Issues

Introduction

Technological innovations and applications of educational media are often predicated on previous occurrences—trends. There is some logic in tracing the trends of educational media and technology to determine *indicators* for the future of the field. Trends do not necessarily predict the future, nor is predicting the future the intent of trends. Soothsaying notwithstanding, Mike Molenda, Jim Russell, and Sharon Smaldino have provided an examination of the trends related to media and technology that are now affecting the fields of formal education and corporate training and development. Bob Muffoletto shares a wonderful narrative about how teachers and students can ask critical and reflective questions concerning the mediated experiences they receive in school as part of the official curriculum. A group of scholars at the University of Georgia's Department of Instructional Technology offer a case in action that describes how the Internet can be used to create a virtual community of professionals who interact and create information electronically.

Trends in Media and Technology in Education and Training

Michael Molenda
Indiana University

James D. Russell
Purdue University

Sharon Smaldino
University of Northern Iowa

Accurately predicting the future has never been easy, especially when it involves new technologies. A century ago, Western Union, the telegraph company, decided that "This 'telephone' has too many shortcomings to be seriously considered as means of communication. The device is inherently of no value to us" (*Time*, July 15, 1996, p. 54). As chancy as predictions were a century ago, they're even riskier today in light of the increasingly rapid pace of technological change.

What we attempt here is an examination of the trends related to media and technology that are now affecting the fields of formal education and corporate training and development. We define technology broadly to include "soft" technologies such as instructional systems design processes and problem-based learning systems.

We have organized the discussion of trends around a "Top Ten" list of key issues. The ranking within the list is not meant to imply order of importance. Nor are these really separate issues; they are intertwined with each other. The sequencing is only for the thematic flow of the discussion.

There is a large degree of subjectivity in designating these 10 issues as more prominent than others, of course. But we do have a basis in the research literature on trends in educational technology in formal education and corporate training. In the realm of formal education, Don Ely and his cohorts prepare an annual assessment of trends for the Clearinghouse on Information and Technology at Syracuse University. Their assessments are based on content analysis of the literature that enters the Clearinghouse, revealing what people are talking about, if not necessarily what is happening. We have referred to the most recent of their studies as a beginning point for our analysis (Ely, 1996). More recent data on the availability and use of telecommunications media in public schools is provided by the U.S. Department of Education (NCES, 1997)

In the realm of corporate training we also have access to a recent, authoritative analysis of trends (Bassi et al., 1996). The Bassi report is based primarily on data provided by training managers of the largest U.S. corporations—ASTD's Benchmarking Forum—but it also draws on a number of other surveys, market analyses, and government research reports. Another major source of data on corporate training is the annual Industry Report published by *Training*.

There is a pronounced local bias in this analysis. The issues and trends we discuss are most pertinent to the United States unless otherwise indicated. This local bias is more applicable to schools than to businesses. As agencies of national governments, schools and their instructional patterns tend to take on a national coloration. On the other hand, with the globalization of business it is increasingly difficult to label any company as American, Canadian, Japanese, or any other nationality. Companies of the Fortune 500 size tend to have operations in many different countries. The corporate training literature we cite is largely of U.S. origin, but in our experience the trends discussed here can be noted in large organizations in Korea and Finland as much as in the United States.

With each issue, we discuss the trends that appear to be operating in the corporate and formal education realms. We often find highly contrasting trends in the two realms. Certain issues are worked out differently in schools as opposed to universities or businesses. So we see trends moving in different directions at different speeds. Because of the complexity of forces at work, both direction and speed may also change without prior notice. Who knows whether any of these trends will suddenly take off at an accelerated pace, slow and diminish, or be overtaken by other forces that are not even over the horizon of our vision today?

TRENDS 1997

Issue 1. Incorporation of traditional audiovisual media into the instructional mainstream

Although traditional audiovisual media do not attract the attention that the newer computer-based media do, they are still used far more often than computer-based media, both in the corporate and the school realm, but they are used less than print-based media. However, use still runs far behind availability, and complete integration into lessons is rarer still.

Trends in Corporate Education

Instructor presentation/demonstration is still the most universally applied method of training, being used in 91 percent of companies (Industry report, 1996). Videotapes and printed workbooks and manuals are used in about 80 percent of companies, while overhead transparencies and audiocassettes are employed in about half and slides in about 30 percent of the organizations surveyed. The combination of instructor plus overhead and printed materials accounts for about one-half of all the training given (Industry report, 1996). Overall, videotapes, transparencies, and slides seem to be receding slowly as they are replaced by computer-based display media. Films have virtually disappeared, replaced by videotapes.

Trends in Formal Education

Even in countries in which access to audiovisual technology is nearly universal, its use by teachers is limited. In the United States, for example, printed material is the dominant media format, according to teacher self-reports (Association of American Publishers, 1996). Seven times as many teachers use textbooks every day (41%) as use audio (6%) or video materials (1%). Textbooks and other printed materials are the most common tools throughout the world, although even these are frequently unavailable or poor in quality. Both in the United States and in other countries, access to media is highly correlated with economic levels, with richer school districts consistently reporting greater supply of hardware and materials.

Issue 2. Incorporation of computer-based media into the instructional mainstream.

Trends in Corporate Education

Computer-based training (including interactive multimedia) is used at less than half the companies surveyed (Industry report, 1996). At only 25 percent of all companies does CBT account for more than a quarter of all training. Bassi et al. (1996) estimate that "traditional CBT" accounts for 7 percent of all training time, with "interactive/multimedia CBT" adding another 4 percent. The two delivery systems that are growing rapidly are CD-ROM and wired networks (LANs and intranets); thus, we find trends toward both decentralization and centralization in terms of distribution. Overall, use of computer-based media is on the rise as more proven off-the-shelf courseware becomes available and as attractive multimedia features are incorporated.

Trends in Formal Education

In the economically advanced nations, computers are found in virtually every school although greater numbers are found at the secondary level, with a ratio of about one computer to every fifteen students. About 10 percent of all teachers employ computers in their teaching. International surveys of computer use (Pelgrum et al., 1993) indicate that the major application was "learning about computers," but that utilization in traditional subjects was slowly increasing. They note that

> it is quite obvious from the data that computers are far from being a tool for regular use in the daily school lives of students; not only are very small numbers of students using computers regularly, but also (especially in secondary education) computers tend to be used mostly for "office" applications like word processing and hardly for learning new material. (p. 47)

In schools where computers are used, Becker (1993), using data from the international survey of computer use by Pelgrum et al. (1993), has noted an evolutionary pattern. At first, computers are housed in computer labs, are employed within a narrow range of the curriculum (typically in "computer literacy" or mathematics), and teachers have a low level of involvement in decision-making and a low sense of ownership. Over time, computers tend to migrate into classrooms, where they are employed across a wider range of the curricula and are embraced by more teachers, who subsequently take a larger role in technology decision-making. This evolutionary trend toward wider and deeper use is probably the most notable trend in the realm of computer-based instruction.

Issue 3. Incorporation of telecommunications-based media into the instructional mainstream

Trends in Corporate Education

There has been steady growth in communication networks, particularly among companies with more than 10,000 employees; about half of such businesses currently operate networks (Industry report, 1996). These networks—satellites for video communication or wired for digital communication—are typically established for other purposes but then are borrowed for delivery of distance learning. Videoconferencing allows real-time (synchronous) interaction among participants at widely dispersed locations, justified by savings in travel expense.

The development that has been attracting the most notice in the training and development literature in recent years is the steep rise in use of the World Wide Web (WWW) and intranets (WWW-type systems internal to one company) for delivery of training and information (Filipczak, 1996). The potential advantages include a huge reduction in printing costs and simplified updating of stored material. By 1996 about half of all companies were using either the WWW or their own intranet for delivery of training (Industry report, 1996). Bassi et al. (1996) report that about 2 percent of all training time was spent in using such Web-based learning. Concepts become quite blurry in this area. Because most Web-based learning is done by individuals interacting with text material (asynchronous sessions) stored on the net, it is difficult to estimate the time being spent this way. Likewise, it is increasingly difficult to distinguish training material from reference information.

Trends in Formal Education

About 75 percent of schools in the United States have cable TV service, and about half the teachers use some cable TV programming, the most popular being "Cable in the Classroom," a noncommercial service aimed at in-school audiences (Ely, 1996, p. 28). About one-quarter of schools have satellite reception antennas, which provide a wireless path for television reception. This path is used both for reception of directly instructional programs, such as those of TI-IN network, and for live videoconferences, providing professional development for teachers and administrators.

In general, distance learning courses are of limited importance to U.S. public schools. Because schools are inherently *local* in structure, they have little need to share courses across long distances (unlike a large business that might have branches all across the country). Whole courses are sought only in cases where the local school cannot afford to maintain a teacher in a given subject and that subject is vital to the mission of the school.

Colleges and universities follow a similar pattern. Universities that have multiple campuses are more likely to send and receive courses through telecommunications in the synchronous mode, emulating a regular classroom as closely as possible.

More newsworthy is the rapid pace at which schools have become connected to the Internet, which in turn carries the World Wide Web. In the United States, 65 percent of all public schools had access to the Internet in fall 1996 (NCES, 1997). This represented a 15 percent increase each year since 1994, and 95 percent of survey respondents expected to have Internet access by the year 2000. Among all schools, 20 percent of teachers used the Internet in connection with their teaching (NCES, 1997). Their primary application is to allow students to search the Internet and the WWW for information to be used for reports, papers, and discussions. As with the video-based telecommunications media, there is little interest in the delivery of whole courses or even intact units, such as is done with computer-assisted instruction.

Typically, only one room in a given school had access to the Internet, usually a computer lab or library media center. In some schools this development has spurred a new vision of the library media center as a dynamic hub of an inquiry-based curriculum.

At the college and university level, connection to Internet is virtually universal. There is little use of intranets as such, but there has been a rush to offer "correspondence"-type (asynchronous) courses to off-campus students via the WWW.

Issue 4. Application of advanced interactive technologies (e.g., multimedia, hypermedia, virtual reality)

Trends in Corporate Education

Interactive multimedia formats are beginning to gain a foothold in corporate training, primarily as part of efforts to deliver basic courses across multiple sites with standardization. They currently account for about 4 percent of the total hours of training (Bassi et al., 1996). Lack of hardware and software compatibility has restricted the availability of off-the-shelf courseware. Organizations are beginning to incorporate more multimedia courseware into their training programs as compatibility improves, thus increasing the supply of less-expensive off-the-shelf materials.

At the upper end of sophistication, and still largely experimental, is the virtual reality (VR) class of technologies, defined as computer-controlled multisensory systems in which users are immersed in an environment with which they can interact in an intuitive ("transparent") way. The most visible applications have been high-fidelity simulators for airplane and space shuttle flight training and tank warfare training. VR has also found successful applications in medicine, architecture, interior design, city planning, product design, and all sort of scientific visualization (McLellan, 1996).

Trends in Formal Education

Multimedia CD-ROM products are commonly found in school library media centers, primarily in the form of encyclopedias or other reference databases. There is still relatively little application of multimedia and hypermedia to core instruction in schools. In higher education there is large-scale experimentation with locally produced multimedia and hypermedia, but little in the way of standardized formats or acceptance across institutions.

VR is still largely experimental in formal education. It is beginning to be used in professional training in fields such as architecture, the sciences, and medicine. An application found at the school level is the "virtual field trip." Adaptive technologies for special education are being developed and tested.

Issue 5. Acceptance and support of the concept of Educational Technology

Trends in Corporate Education

Although the term *educational technology* is not necessarily growing in recognition in corporate training, the concepts of multimedia training and distance learning have become widely accepted. Expertise in the design of these technologies is respected more than for the earlier audiovisual technologies.

Trends in Formal Education

Widespread adoption of computers and computer-based technologies has led to a rebirth of interest in and commitment to educational technology in formal education. In the United States there is now an Office of Educational Technology in the Department of Education, which has proposed a national plan for development in this area. Ely (1996) points out that in 1995 the National Education Association, the largest teachers' union in the United States, adopted policy statements strongly supporting educational technology, reversing 25 years of opposition or neutrality.

Technology planning is required by state education departments, and technology costs are being integrated into school and university budgets to an extent unparalleled in the past.

Issue 6. The home as locus of technology-based learning

Trends in Corporate Education

In the 1970s the concept of telecommuting entered our vocabulary, strongly promoted by information technology companies. The current preferred name for this phenomenon is *telework*, defined as a method of working in which the employee works away from the office, perhaps at home, using a computer and telecommunications technology to communicate with a work site. Nearly half of all U.S. households now posses some form of home office. With personal computers, fax devices, cellular phones, and Internet connection, many people have the infrastructure to do information work in their own homes. Corporations have a strong motivation to move employees out of the company's quarters in order to reduce the huge overhead costs of acquiring and maintaining office space.

A national survey found that more than eight million Americans described themselves as teleworkers (ETRG, 1996), a number growing at a rate of about 20 percent annually. It is estimated that about 5 percent of the total workforce in the United States and Europe spends at least one day a week working at home. The likelihood of continued growth in telework is virtually certain because it is favored by both corporate and government policies in the major industrialized nations.

Just as organizations are encouraging workers to carry out their work at home, so are they quietly shifting their expectations about the time and place of learning. Because of the high cost of using paid time on the job for training, companies are increasingly expecting employees to undertake job-related learning at home through independent study by means of CD-ROMs and floppy disks that can be used on home or laptop computers. This trend has not received much public attention, but industry monitors have begun to detect it and report it (Trends to track, 1995). It can only grow, riding the waves of the growth of telework and the increasing portability of electronic technologies.

Trends in Formal Education

The growth of home offices has also provided the means for schooling to shift to the home as well. In a 1995 survey, parents estimated that their children spend 12 to 14 hours a week on learning activities at home (ETRG, 1995). The larger part of this is assigned homework from school, but a growing part of this is "information exploring" done on home computers, especially using the WWW. Indeed, Perelman (1992) argued that technology-based ("hyper-learning") at-home study offered an affordable and feasible *alternative* to public schools, and he advocated an end to public schooling as we know it.

Coming from a completely different direction but supporting the same goal is the home schooling movement. Originally rooted in religious objection to public schools, home school-ing has grown to encompass a wide variety of families who choose to teach their children at home. Estimates of students being educated at home range from 1 percent to 4 percent of the school-age population in the United States (Weston, 1996).

The home market for computer-based, education-oriented software is exploding. CD-ROMs aimed at home use now occupy major shelf space in bookstores and discount department stores. Studies of home schooling families indicate that they are heavy users of materials of this sort, with the average family purchasing several thousand dollars of instructional materials annu-ally. On the other end of the spectrum, those who use these materials in a less structured, often recreational way have created a huge market for "edutainment" products. The Disney multi-media conglomerate is now probably the leading purveyor of both educational and entertain-ment materials (Sullivan, 1997). There is no visible reason to expect a slowing of this trend.

Issue 7. Restructuring/Reengineering of basic organizational processes

Trends in Corporate Education

Training and development processes are undergoing rapid and major reengineering in the directions of a) downsizing, b) focusing on performance improvement, and c) demonstrating business impact (Bassi et al., 1996). Technology-based training is compatible with all these new demands. The case is stated succinctly by Shandler (1996): "Technology has emerged as a critical component of systems thinking, as well as a critical driver of the process of reengineering the training function" (p. 173).

In the late 1990s another driver of reengineering has emerged: integrated information systems (sometimes referred to as SAP [Systems, Applications, and Products], the name of a specific software program for business information integration). SAP software, which inte-grates all the information systems used within a business, has been adopted at 90 percent of the Fortune 500 companies (Filipczak, 1997). It not only ties together all the previously separate information systems, but it also incorporates proven "best practices." Adoption of SAP requires that virtually *all* employees need training on the new ways of doing their work. This is creating unprecedented demand for training, a demand that can only be met efficiently and effectively through technology.

Trends in Formal Education

Restructuring is much discussed, but the great majority of public schools still operate as they traditionally have. However, pressure for restructuring is mounting because of the growth of—and perceived success of—such developments as charter schools and home schooling. There is evidence that between 1994 and 1997 there was a substantial increase in the number of schools undergoing comprehensive and systemic reform; further, "those schools that have implemented changes to the greatest extent . . . have shown the greatest gains in state assessment and national standardized tests . . . " (Cawelti, 1997). Many, including Ely (1996) and Perelman (1992), have pointed out the obvious role of technology as a driver of and vehicle for school restructuring.

Issue 8. Updating paradigms and procedures for instructional systems design

Trends in Corporate Education

The forces described in Issue 7 are forcing training and development people to find ways of reducing instructional development cycle time and overall costs of designed training. These trends are particularly seen in technology-based training, where a significant amount of automation of design is taking place. As of 1997, off-the-shelf authoring software accessible to novice designers was available for computer-based training and Web-based course design. Theoretical and practical problems remain, but Tennyson (1995) and others see a bright future for the automation of instructional design by employing advancements from cognitive science.

Besides automation of design processes, another approach to the reform of instructional systems design has been advocated by Molenda, Pershing, and Reigeluth (1996)—a design model that places "business impact" at the center. Their argument is that the time and energy expended on instructional design can be reduced and rationalized by assuring that all design activities are justified in light of the ultimate goal of affecting organizational performance. The model shows how nontraining interventions and change-management interventions can be integrated with the phases of instructional design to produce greater impact for the dollar.

Trends in Formal Education

In the relative absence of competition, there is little external pressure to reform instructional design (ID) processes in formal education. In fact, ID is little applied to school or university course design. However, there is a strong and growing trend to reconsider ID processes in light of the growing knowledge base about how learning can be facilitated and about the rapidly changing organizational setting for instruction. Reigeluth and Nelson (1997) and Reigeluth (in press) argue two main points: a) contemporary cognitivist and constructivist perspectives on learning demand an ID process that involves users in the design process and yields a customized—rather than standardized—product; and b) a systemic change perspective requires an iterative rather than linear progression of steps and the addition of elements into the model so that the designed instruction is compatible with the overall system and is accepted by users.

Issue 9. Growing interest in learner-centered, inquiry-based instruction

This issue has arisen primarily out of the constructivist movement in education in the 1990s. Various voices have made various claims, but the central claim is that because learners construct their own meanings out of their experiences, instructional environments ought to allow greater learner control and encourage learners to explore, ask questions, and encounter multiple perspectives on problems. Grabinger has coined the term "rich environments for active learning (REAL)" to encompass the common ideas found in the various instructional configurations that have evolved from this movement.

Trends in Corporate Education

Corporate interest in REALs stems from a demand to make training more productive, particularly to increase transfer-of-training. To achieve this, many corporations are shifting to instruction that is more problem-based or "situated." Examples are high-fidelity simulations of business problems, referred to as "goal-based scenarios," used in training at Andersen Consulting (Rao, 1995) and on-site consultation with working teams at Apple Computer (Keegan and Jacobson, 1995). Perelman (1995) views this as shrinking the loop between learning and working—getting the learning as close to the work environment as possible. It is a trend that can only grow as pressures for productivity increase.

Trends in Formal Education

In schools, REALs are found only as local experiments, although there is growing discussion and acceptance of "constructivist learning environments" as an ideal. In universities, a significant number of professional schools—particularly medical and business—have been completely restructured around problem-based learning models. The upward slope of this trend is still low but could accelerate as educational institutions are held more accountable for the transferability of student learning to the world of work.

Issue 10. Commitment to increasingly authentic assessment

Trends in Corporate Education

Driven by competitive pressures, businesses have adopted Total Quality Management (TQM) and other reengineering programs that require more accurate measurement of the business impact of all expenditures. This has pushed more corporate training programs to consider assessing outcomes beyond mere learner satisfaction. Kirkpatrick (1994) proposed four levels of evaluation: 1) learner satisfaction, 2) skill demonstration, 3) transfer to the job, and 4) impact on business goals. Surveys of corporate trainers over the past few years show a marked increase in claims to be evaluating at levels 3 and 4. In 1996, fully 65 percent claimed to be applying level 3 evaluation to at least some of their courses, and nearly half claimed to be doing level 4 evaluation (Industry report, 1996).

Trends in Formal Education

In schools there is rising interest in authentic assessment, driven by commitment to competency-based instruction and to constructivist pedagogy. Some states have instituted more authentic forms of assessment in their state examination systems; some individual schools have experimented with means such as portfolio assessment. Although these practices are still far from being the norm, they do constitute a trend. This trend is important to educational technology because assessment has long been understood to be the driver for the rest of the instructional system, including media and methods. If assessment increasingly focuses on demonstration of mastery and ability to transfer new knowledge, it could become a driver for instructional systems design processes and for methods such as REALs. This trend has already led to the development of portfolio assessment, which has fueled interest in student production of media and even the compilation of electronic portfolios (Lankes, 1997).

REFERENCES

AAP (Association of American Publishers). (1996). *Instructional Materials Survey.* New York: AAP.

Bassi, Laurie J., Benson, George, and Cheney, Scott. (1996, November). The top ten trends. *Training & Development 50*(1), 28-42.

Becker H. J. (1993). Computer experience, patterns of computer use, and effectiveness—an inevitable sequence or divergent national cultures? *Studies in Educational Evaluation 19*, 127-48.

Buchmann, Anna. (1997, April 29). Finding footing on the web. *San Jose Mercury News.* Posted at www.sjmercury.com/news/local/tlesson30.htm.

Cawelti, Gordon. (1997). *Effects of High School Restructuring: Ten Schools at Work.* Arlington, VA: Educational Research Service.

Ely, Donald P. (1996). *Trends in Educational Technology 1995.* ERIC Clearinghouse on Information and Technology, Syracuse University.

Emerging Technologies Research Group (ETRG). (1995). *Children's Learning at Home.* New York: FIND/SVP.

Emerging Technologies Research Group (ETRG). (1996, October). *Telecommuting Report.* New York: FIND/SVP.

Filipczak, Bob. (1996, September). Training on intranets: The hope and the hype. *Training* 24-32.

Filipczak, Bob. (1997, March). Are you getting SAPped? *Training 34*(3), 40-50.

Grabinger, Scott. (1996). Rich environments for active learning. In *Handbook of Research for Educational Communications and Technology*, ed. D. Jonassen. New York: Simon & Schuster.

Industry report 1996. (1996, October). *Training 33*(10), 37-79.

Keegan, Linda, and Jacobson, Betsy. (1995, July). Training goes mod(ular) at Apple. *Training & Development*, 38-40.

Kirkpatrick, Donald. (1994). *Evaluating Training Programs: The Four Levels.* San Francisco: Berrett-Koehler.

Lankes, Anna Maria D. (1997). Electronic portfolios: A new idea in assessment. In *Educational Media and Technology Yearbook,* Vol. 22, ed. R. Branch and B. Minor. Englewood, CO: Libraries Unlimited.

McLellan, Hilary. (1996). Virtual realities. In *Handbook of Research for Educational Communications and Technology*, ed. D. Jonassen. New York: Simon & Schuster.

Molenda, Michael. (1996). Educational technology in elementary and secondary education. In *International Encyclopedia of Educational Technology*, 2d ed., ed. Plomp and Ely. Oxford, England: Pergamon.

Molenda, Michael, Pershing, James, and Reigeluth, Charles. (1996). Designing instructional systems. In *ASTD Training and Development Handbook*, 4th ed., ed. R. Craig. New York: McGraw-Hill.

Multimedia training in the Fortune 1000. (1996, September). *Training 33*(9), 53-60.

National Center for Educational Statistics (NCES). (1997). *Advanced Telecommunications in U.S. Public Elementary and Secondary Schools, Fall 1996.* Washington, DC: U.S. Department of Education.

Pelgrum, W. J., Janssen Reinen, I. A. M., and Plomp, Tj. (1993). *Schools, Teachers, Students and Computers: A Cross-National Perspective.* The Hague: International Association for the Evaluation of Educational Achievement.

Perelman, Lewis J. (1992). *School's Out.* New York: Avon Books.

Perelman, Lewis J. (1995). Kanban to Kanbrain. *Forbes ASAP 153*(12), 85-95.

Rao, Srikumar S. (1995). Putting fun back into learning. *Training 32*(8), 44-48.

Reigeluth, Charles M. (in press). What is instructional-design theory and how is it changing? In *Instructional-Design Theories and Models: A New Paradigm of Instructional Theories*, ed. C. M. Reigeluth. Hillsdale, NJ: Lawrence Erlbaum.

Reigeluth, Charles M., and Nelson, Laurie Miller. (1997). A new paradigm of ISD? In *Educational Media and Technology Yearbook*, Vol. 22, ed. R. Branch and B. Minor. Englewood, CO: Libraries Unlimited.

Shandler, Donald. (1996). *Reengineering the Training Function.* Delray Beach, FL: St. Lucie Press.

Sullivan, Michael. (1997, March). Remarks at IST Colloquium, Indiana University.

Tennyson, R. D. (1995). Four Generations of Instructional Systems Development. *Journal of Structural Learning and Intelligent Systems 12*, 149-64.

Trends to track. (1995). In *The Lakewood Report on Technology for Learning*. Minneapolis: Lakewood.

Weston, Mark. (1996, April). Reformers should take a look at home schools. *Education Week 15*(28), 22.

Quest for Knowing
Educational Media and Curricular Representations

Robert Muffoletto

College of Education, University of Northern Iowa

Sitting with my sixth graders, we began to look at a collection of photographs of the Midwest wheat farming belt. I asked my students what they saw and what they thought the photographs meant. I then asked them to work within their groups and formulate three research questions they wished to ask concerning wheat farming in the Midwest. The students began to discuss and formulate their questions. They were then directed to search the Internet, read books and reports in their school and community libraries, watch videotapes on the topic, and locate and interview someone on the Internet who lives in the Midwest. Their assignment was to construct a multimedia presentation displaying what they had learned. I also provided a few focus questions that they were to answer in their exploration of wheat farming in the Midwest.

How did my students learn about the world they explored as part of their school curriculum? How did I teach them "how" to know?

If we set aside the various mediated forms through which we know the world, they would settle into three primary groups: pictures, written text (words), and audio stories. My students look at pictures, moving and still; they read the accounts of others (fiction and nonfiction) who tell their stories through the printed word; and they listen to stories told by perceived experts (teachers, authors, and narrators). In their collection of information the data provided tell them—so they and we may think—about wheat farming in the Midwest. Because the resources they used were found in the library, at preselected sites on the Web, or in a collection of documentaries and fictional works on the Midwest, my students never questioned the truthfulness of the images, the biases of the authors, or the memory of the storytellers. I, as their teacher, did not ask them to consider those questions. I never question the legitimized curriculum materials I use in my classroom. Unless, that is, I stop and think about the stories not being told, pictures never shown, and histories never written.

- Has a photograph ever lied?

- Do authors, especially historians, write their stories from a certain perspective?

- Do storytellers ever forget what they never knew?

The commonsense answer to the above questions is "yes" to all of them. After all, photographic images, moving and still, two- and three-dimensional, are usually considered to be the products of machines that recorded what was before them, not the product of science and human intervention and decision. Historians, so it may seem, only provide the facts, not the political and economic perspective that exists within and outside their paradigm. Storytellers tell us the way it was and is, leaving out the stories that don't tell it the way it is or that have not entered into their understanding. From this perspective, (my perspective—after all, I am the storyteller, and you are my reader), all visuals, accounts, and stories are fictions. They are products of a social consciousness, a sense of truth and rightness. It does not matter if the audience is sixth graders working on a school project or their parents watching the news; what we all get are constructed fictions of mediated experiences.

My purpose in this essay is to explore the need for teachers and students to ask critical and reflective questions concerning the mediated experiences they receive in school as part of the official curriculum (Apple, 1988). After all, it is the curriculum that re-presents the world and what we know about it to students and teachers (Muffoletto, 1987). The curriculum, the legitimized "way of knowing," not only constructs the world and our experience of it, but also places us in it. We are, after all, constructed subjects of our own experiences. To accomplish my purpose, we need to consider the following:

1. mediated experiences in all forms are representations;

2. media and the technologies of storage and delivery are not neutral devices; and

3. the notions surrounding the autonomous individual are false.

REPRESENTATIONS

Representations are historically encoded, with their meanings found within the hegemonic actions of struggling and competing ideological frameworks. The curriculum; the architecture of schools; the physical arrangements of classrooms; the power relationships between parents, students, teachers, and administrators; the monitoring and controlling technologies; the use of newer forms for the storage and delivery of the curriculum—these are all representations. They refer to power and knowledge, who has it, what is done with it, and who or what does it benefit.

Representations stand in place of, or refer to, the "things" they represent. It is more complex than the sign-signifier relationship commonly referred to in a semiotic structuralist model. Postsemiotics, poststructuralism, and postmodernism provide us with different ways of understanding the nature of representation. The meanings of a representation are the products of a socially and historically encoded gesture as read by a "reader" of the representation or "text" (the text is a postmodernist notion where the phenomenology of the experience is understood not as a natural but as a social construction). The nature of meaning is critical to understanding the sign and its usage. As I have argued elsewhere (Muffoletto, 1991; 1994b; 1997), meanings that emerge from the correspondence between readers of produced "texts" are formed within a social, linguistic, and historical context. Meanings on multiple levels emerge out of, and are the results of, paradigmatic and symbolic social relationships. As Stanley Fish suggests, meanings emerge out of interpretative communities bringing with them their histories, their world views, their languages, and their struggles (Fish, 1980). In this manner, meaning speaks to more than gender relations, race relations, and class relations. Meaning refers to the power relations set within a history of occurrences and usage.

The power of representations comes from many sources. On the surface, at a common-sense level, realist representations are understood as being neutral and objective, as mirrors or windows on the world. They are understood as discrete objects or practices, not as collective ideological discourses. The reification of the text and the naturalization of the discourse position the "reader of the text" as a consumer of normalized meanings. The normalization of meanings does not refer to the most common understandings, but to internalized and legitimized understandings. To legitimate ways of knowing, the socialization of the individual is not natural or neutral but social and historical. Through the reification of the sign, the meanings of the curriculum, its architecture, its power relationships, become normalized and natural. The power of the realist representation is not in its mirror- or window-like function, but in the invisibility of the glass surface.

Behind the reification of the image and the word is found the constructive nature of language (Cherryholmes, 1988; Belsey, 1980). The ideology of the representation, as Ellsworth and Whatley (1990) and Nicholas (1981) suggest, needs to be unpacked and contextualized within a discourse of struggle and social justice. Ellsworth and Whatley (1990) state that the "conventions of film, video, and photographic representation are not neutral carriers of content. Rather, they are ideological forms that inflect content with particular meanings. Likewise, educational media are not neutral carries of educational content, and they too are knowledge forms that inflect curricular content with particular meanings and interests." (p. 3)

THE NEED FOR
REFLECTIVE THOUGHT

Schooling in the United States, both as a process and as an institution, serves various interests, holding different visions for different people and representing various social, economic, and political interests. Educational media, as a form for the delivery of the "legitimized" curriculum, needs to be contextualized within a discourse that is representative of an ideology of conformity or resistance. In either case, if schooling is the carrier and disseminator of democratic visions, educational media needs to be unpacked and then repackaged in light of social justice and democratic goals (Muffoletto, 1994a, 1997).

Educators, students, and parents need to be reflective not only about teaching practices, but also about the knowledge and representations they legitimize. In this sense, reflective acts, reflective teaching, and reflective communities work to enable people to develop an awareness that contextualizes schooling in different ways. From this perspective, reflection is an enabling process, empowering the individual and the community to see themselves within historical, social, and political contexts. Being a reflective member of a community enables one to ask questions concerning why things are the way they are, and who benefits from the current arrangements of ways of knowing and legitimatized knowledge (Freire, 1970; Harbermas, 1968).

I don't believe that anyone would resist the idea that teachers need to be reflective about their routine actions in classrooms and their workings with students. We want teachers who can reflect on what they are doing and why. Reflective work removes individuals from a passive relationship to their actions and the actions of others, to a relationship that frees them from impulse and patterned actions, allowing them to plan and move in a desired direction. The challenge for teachers, administrators, parents, and students is to problematize the curriculum and its representations—to understand that educational media and its various products not only articulate particular ways of knowing and understanding but also act as a vehicle for the dissemination of technical control over what teachers and students do (Apple, 1988).

NON-NEUTRALITY

Analyzing educational media (form and message) from a reflective perspective raises questions concerning objectivity and knowledge, as well as intent. If the intent of educational media is to store and disseminate the curriculum, we need to consider the various curricula of educational media. As Marshall McLuhan (1964) pointed out to us three decades ago, "the medium is the message"; we now need to consider what curriculums, what messages, the medium gives. At one level, the medium and the message are representative of the technology as a system. Neither the educational television program nor the instructional kit as individual objects are important; rather, their systemic existence is the crucial factor. The technology of instruction positions teachers, students, communities, and schools in various power and epistemological relationships.

At another level, we need to consider the experienced representations, the messages, the overt curriculum. As discussed earlier, the veracity of the image—its iconic, realist re-presentation of the world—needs to be unpacked and repositioned. Educational media's re-presentation of the world and of ways of knowing need to be understood for what they are: frameworks of understandings that exist within paradigmatic, symbolic, and discursive structures (structures that are historical, social, and political). These structures not only define boundaries by what we know but also provide the borders that define us and others. Remember that these borders are not natural but are constructed from a social position within the world. Similar to photographs, which are the result of where the photographer stands and the tools used, educational media refers to where producers ideologically stand.

THE INDIVIDUAL

Educational media not only defines and abstracts the individual but also defines the relationship between that individual and others. Rarely do we see in mediated educational messages the individual constructed as a member of a community—a community existing within a set of structural relationships to other communities, which may be defined by class, gender, or race. In this manner, the producers of educational media programs, through their discursive practices, construct their user in various ways to form a sense of self and of others. The individual program does not construct the subjectivity of the user; what does is the full array of messages, the discourses delivered through educational media that beckon users to position themselves within one of many possible worlds. The school curriculum works to conform students to a world view through this continuous positioning of the individual. This world view occasionally conflicts with the reality outside the classroom's walls.

Thus, ideas and concepts concerning the individual and the community are shaped by the curricular experiences and the daily discourses found in classrooms. The power relationships found between classes, gender, race, sexual preference, and the like are what defines this shaping. My focus on school discourse is not meant to ignore the impact of the mass media, particularly television, on the subjective perceptions of individuals and communities. How we come to understand our private and public identities is a complex social and historical process.

Developments in educational media and technology, particularly in areas of publication and the Internet, have provided possibilities to counter the hegemonic actions of schooling and the mass media. Desktop publishing allows marginalized students and communities to have a voice. Underground presses in schools and communities have opened the door for alternative or oppositional voices to be heard. The Internet has taken this further. By decentralizing the control of information and its access, the Internet has provided an environment where the silent may now have a voice and at the same moment hear the voices of others from the margins as well as the center.

The presence of the Internet has made it critical for teachers to know how to decode or unpack the social and cultural messages of the school curriculum. With more information available to everyone, integrating the Internet into the life of the school and community becomes more than just an opportunity and a challenge. The real challenge may lie in the deconstruction of the messages delivered through the expanded schooling experience. The Internet, as part of the curriculum, offers the potential of challenging the status quo, the controlled nature of the traditional educational media curricular package, and the routine nature of the classroom.

TEACHER EDUCATION AND
CRITICAL THEORY

The Internet can, perhaps, expand the traditional school curriculum in ways that were once historically impossible. In the past, students could only communicate with others via traditional mail systems where exchanges would take weeks or months to be completed. Now with electronic mail, file transfer programs, and simplified Web production tools, students, teachers, and communities can exchange information at blinding speed. Participants in exchange projects can now encounter various ideological frameworks. In doing so, both ends of the exchange are open to new understandings of the human condition. With this potential comes the responsibility of teachers and the community to look within their own paradigms of knowing, to reflect upon and unpack their frameworks, and to realize that their way of understanding conditions is not "the" way, just one way.

Critical theory and critical thinking then become a major component of every teacher education program. The ability to apply social, historical, and cultural theories to the understanding of curriculum, to question the normality of routine practice, and to question the nature of the relationship between schooling, communities, social justice, and democracy, is a skill not easily taught in such programs. The first step may be to teach future teachers to think critically about the educational media and technologies that enter their classrooms. In order to reach this step, a rethinking of the relationship of teachers, students, and the community to media and technology will be necessary.

Teachers will be expected to question the legitimized mediated "text" of the school. They will need to recognize differing ideological frameworks, and as teachers they must place various instructional moments in the context of the community and democratic ideals. Teachers and communities will need to work against the reification of any text, in light of equity and social ideals.

To address the representational nature of schooling and the curriculum as mediated by educational media, teachers will first need the tools of critique and action. Not only will teachers continually need to unpack . . . but also repack the curriculum in light of social justice. If programs in educational media and technology (especially those within teacher education programs) wish to engage their students as active participants in the construction of knowledge, they will need to offer and model reflective action throughout their program. Faculty will need to step from behind the mask of neutrality, of nonpolitical discourse, and enter into the debate and struggle.

REFERENCES

Apple, M. (1988). *Teachers and texts: A political economy of class and gender relations in education.* New York: Routledge.

Belsey, C. (1980). *Critical practice.* London: Methuen.

Cherryholmes, C. (1988). *Power and criticism: Poststructural investigations in education.* New York: Teachers College Press.

Ellsworth, E., and Whatley, M. (1990). *The ideology of images in educational media: Hidden curriculums in the classroom.* New York: Teachers College Press.

Fish, S. (1980). *Is there a text in this class?* Cambridge, MA: Harvard University Press.

Freire, P. (1970). *Pedagogy of the oppressed.* New York: Herder and Herder.

Harbermas, J. (1968). *Knowledge and human interests.* Boston: Beacon Press.

McLuhan, M. (1964). *Understanding media: Extensions of man.* New York: Signet Book.

Muffoletto, R. (1987). The third person. In *Claremont reading conference 51st yearbook*, ed. M. Douglas. Claremont, CA: Claremont Graduate School.

Muffoletto, R. (1991). Technology and texts: Breaking the window. In *Paradigms redefined: The uses of illuminative, semiotic and post-modern criticism as modes of inquiry in educational technology*, ed. D. Hlynka and J. Belland. Englewood Cliffs, NJ: Educational Technology Publications.

Muffoletto, R. (1994a). Schools and technology in a democratic society: Equity and social justice, ed. A. Yeaman. *Educational technology 34*(2).

Muffoletto, R. (1994b). Thinking about diversity: Paradigms, meanings, and representations. In *Practicing what we teach: Confronting diversity in teacher education*, ed. R. Martin. Albany, NY: State University of New York Press.

Muffoletto, R. (1997). Technology, curriculum, and knowledge. In *Review journal of philosophy & social science 22*(2).

Nicholas, B. (1981). *Ideology and the image.* Bloomington, IN: Indiana University Press.

ITForum
An Alternative Approach to Academic Publishing

Lloyd P. Rieber
Gene L. Wilkinson
Lisa T. Bennett
Saada Al-Ghafry
The University of Georgia

Just as the development of television, particularly such programming services as CNN, has had a major impact on newspaper publishing, the Internet is having a major impact on academic publishing. The Internet is changing the way researchers and practitioners develop and share information. Electronic publishing via the World Wide Web is generally considered a more rapid, inexpensive, and widely available alternative to traditional academic publishing (Schauder, 1994). There are, however, many challenges to Web-based publications, such as questions of copyright and quality control. Other issues go well beyond the Internet as a mere publishing medium, such as how the Internet can be used to create a virtual community of professionals, interacting and creating information electronically.

ACADEMIC PUBLISHING AND THE INTERNET

The rapid growth of scholarship on the World Wide Web is almost overwhelming (Machovec, 1996). The most recent directory published by the Association of Research Libraries (Mogge, 1996) lists more than 3,000 academic and professional discussion lists and 1,688 electronic journals, many of which are peer-reviewed and maintain standards of quality that are as rigorous as those of print journals. Developments in electronic publishing are causing a reexamination of the role and format of more traditional scholarly publications (Okerson & O'Donnell, 1995; Shoaf, 1995) and are leading to defensive actions on the part of some publishers, such as the American Psychological Association's (APA's) recent statement that manuscripts posted on the Internet (e.g., an author's personal website) risk exclusion from consideration in an APA publication (Publishing papers on the Internet, 1996).

The Internet is having a major impact on the way in which scholars interact with each other and on the way publications are developed (Harper, 1995; Tompkins, 1995). Some of these efforts have been on a relatively small scale with clearly defined goals. For example, during the development of the March/April, 1997 issue of *Educational Technology* (which focused on Web-based learning) drafts of the articles were collected and posted on a website for review and comment by the other authors in order to enable cross-referencing, prevent overlap, and foster collaboration. On a much larger scale is H-NET: Humanities and Social Sciences Online (http://h-net2.msu.edu), a group of listservs that tie together more than 51,000 scholars in 70 countries (Guernsey, 1997). Through H-NET, subscribers share ideas, solve problems, and work together on collaborative projects.

A listserv is one of the most common discussion formats on the Internet. A listserv is a computer-mediated discussion venue whereby users can contribute information and opinions ("posts") on a variety of topics at their leisure to be read by the other participants either immediately upon receipt or at a time convenient for them. Replies can be sent either to the list (for replies of general interest) or privately to individuals. Listservs differ from bulletin board services (BBSs) and newsgroups (e.g., those on Usenet) in that each post to a listserv is sent as an E-mail message to each subscriber (Ferrara, Brunner, and Whittenmore, 1991).

A large number of listservs have been developed that are dedicated to various aspects of instructional technology (IT). LM_NET is focused on school library media at the K-12 level. EDTECH is aimed at students, faculty, and others interested in educational technology. EDNET explores the potential of using the Internet in education. Other listservs focus on such topics as educational gaming, distance education, artificial intelligence, and so on. The development of these electronic communities is changing the ways in which academics develop and share information and raises a number of issues that need to be addressed by the academic community. We will discuss and illustrate these issues in the context of our experiences with the listserv ITForum.

The ITForum Model

ITForum is an electronic listserv that discusses theories, research, new paradigms, and practices in the field of instructional technology. ITForum is affiliated with AECT's Division of Learning and Performance Environments (DLPE) and the Department of Instructional Technology at the University of Georgia (UGA). The list is open to anyone interested in instructional technology (a special invitation is extended to graduate students in IT programs).[1] The first ITForum discussion featured a paper by David Jonassen (1994) in which 84 subscribers participated. As of April 1, 1997, ITForum consists of a total of 790 subscribers representing 29 countries. ITForum will have hosted a total of 20 discussions by the end of May 1997.

ITForum began in May 1994 with little worry about success or failure, largely as an experiment in creating a virtual community where educational technology professionals could get together to discuss important issues raised by leading scholars in the field. ITForum was the brainchild of Cindy Leshin, then President of the Association for the Development of Computer-based Instructional Systems (ADCIS). ITForum was designed to be a professional service to ADCIS members. Lloyd Rieber, a faculty member in the Department of Instructional Technology at UGA, established the list at UGA and has remained the person largely responsible for maintaining both the technical and professional aspects of the list. Lisa Bennett and Saada Al-Ghafry, two doctoral students at UGA, have worked with Lloyd as moderators and managers for the list. (The plan is to provide similar opportunities to other graduate students in the future.) Recently, Gene Wilkinson, another UGA faculty member, has joined the collaboration, especially to help with current efforts to make past discussions accessible to the professional community using the World Wide Web.

After the dissolution of ADCIS in 1994, active members petitioned AECT to form DLPE. The professional affiliation of ITForum was then shared by DLPE and the Department of Instructional Technology at UGA. Interestingly, ITForum has yet to receive any external funding to operate and charges no fee for participation. Instead, it relies completely on the volunteer efforts of the moderators, authors, and subscribers. (It is important to recognize the technical support provided by the University of Georgia Computing and Networking Services. Though costs to maintain a listserv are real, these are absorbed by UGA.)

As previously mentioned, several other listservs dedicated to instructional technology issues were already operating at that time; however, ITForum took on a mission and operating plan unique in at least two ways. First, ITForum is more structured than other listservs in that specific discussions are organized throughout the year. From September to May, leading scholars in the instructional technology field are invited to submit short papers or essays that are posted on the list. Second, and most important, subscribers then have the opportunity to discuss the paper and its ideas directly with the author. Subscribers post comments or questions directly to the list. The author then responds to these each day for one week, either addressing specific comments and questions or general themes.

Dealing with an Iterative Mission and Purpose

There has been no attempt to establish formal policies and procedures for ITForum beyond the goal of soliciting papers or essays from leaders in the field and offering a discussion forum with subscribers. Papers are solicited solely at the discretion of Lloyd Rieber. Of course, he tries to carefully consider the recommendations of the subscribers. In a sense, ITForum has been shaped by its subscribers. We have likened ITForum discussions to the informal conversations that occur among colleagues after a particularly good keynote presentation at a conference. We have tried to make ITForum a place where people feel free to make casual comments about issues confronting the field. Again, one important distinction between ITForum and these "hallway chats" is that everyone has the chance to discuss the talk with the speaker as well as with colleagues from around the world.

A variety of *implicit* operating procedures have developed over time. As already noted, the authors are selected on an invitation-only basis, and they are free to choose their own topic. ITForum does not accept unsolicited papers nor has plans to do so. There has also been a deliberate effort to identify authors from different countries. So far, seven different countries have been represented by the authors of the 20 discussions held or scheduled to date. There has also been an effort recently to solicit participation from established scholars who are already subscribers to ITForum. At least half of the authors, however, were not aware of ITForum before they were invited to participate.

One open question remains about whether we should formalize ITForum's operating policies and procedures. So far, we have decided to keep the procedures loosely organized, so as not to fall into an established routine prematurely or unnecessarily. Part of the attraction of ITForum is its ability to improve continually its operating methods. We expect the purpose and mission of ITForum to change and grow as warranted by the membership.

PUBLISHING AS A PROCESS RATHER THAN A PRODUCT

The interactive nature of ITForum has some unique benefits for both subscribers and authors. Unlike traditional journals or books, ITForum provides subscribers with direct access to authors. They can pose questions and make comments for the author to respond to during the discussion week. How many times have you read an article and wished to be able to talk with the author? Perhaps you've even tried to contact some authors through phone or E-mail. ITForum provides subscribers with the opportunity to engage not only in a scholar's work, but also with the scholar directly in a way that few other media are able.

The number of ITForum subscribers has been increasing at a steady pace since it began, although the number of new subscribers closely matches the number signing off. (Like all listservs, there is a high rate of attrition among subscribers—people come and go frequently.) Why do people subscribe to ITForum? Although it may be a required activity for some graduate students, the greatest appeal simply remains the opportunity to read and discuss the scheduled papers. Many other reasons exist as well. For example, many subscribers report that there are few other educational professionals besides themselves at their workplaces. Hence, they often feel isolated from the profession and struggle to remain current with the latest ideas. ITForum provides many subscribers with a daily link to the profession.

ITForum also offers authors with unique opportunities. The reason authors write, of course, is to be read. A strong motivation for engaging in scholarly work in written form is the possibility that people will find one's work interesting and relevant. Most authors are grateful to hear from readers and enjoy the opportunity to engage in a dialogue about their work. Most authors would find much satisfaction in knowing that about 800 professionals around the world are setting aside time in any one week to read and discuss one of their papers or essays. Participation in ITForum means just that.

Another opportunity for authors goes well beyond motivation or the personal satisfaction of knowing that there are people reading their finished works. Although riskier than submitting a finished paper, ITForum provides authors with the chance to engage readers *during* the writing process and before a work is completed. Unlike traditional print media, such as professional journals and books, authors can use ITForum to solicit reactions and feedback from readers. This has particular advantages if the author is trying to develop new ideas. While it is common for an author to get feedback from colleagues or students, ITForum gives authors a chance to informally discuss their ideas with people with a wide range of experiences, backgrounds, and even cultures. Of course, not all authors have been willing to use ITForum in this way, and not all subscribers are equally open to reacting to works in progress. But the potential to provide a free exchange between scholars and readers while a project is in its formative stages is one of the most exciting prospects for the future of ITForum.

Access to People with Different Backgrounds, Perspectives, and Cultures

Professional papers go through an expert review process before being published. In the past, the expert reviewers were mainly from the country where the books or journals were published. International reviews, if any, were not the norm, probably because of the time it takes for postal mail to travel between countries, problems involved with international coordination, and possibly the costs involved too.

With the advent of the Internet it is possible to get international expert review. On ITForum, authors get instantaneous feedback from professionals of varied cultural backgrounds. Though few of the articles have dealt specifically with cultural matters, many argue that cognition itself is largely a cultural process. An author writes from his/her own perspective, mostly oblivious of how readers from other cultures will perceive the article. The advantage on ITForum is that the author gets feedback from people with very different international perspectives. Some authors accept the input and rethink their ideas, whereas others are less willing to accept viewpoints different from their own. Whatever the result, in one week of discussion the author and subscribers are "forced" to see alternative viewpoints and confront their own biases, prejudices, and ethnocentrism.

Promoting this kind of reflection is difficult without the global connectivity afforded by the Internet. ITForum encourages authors and subscribers to think in truly "global village" terms. It makes little sense to describe the ITForum schedule with terms such as "fall, winter, and spring," for example, because climatic seasons are not identical around the world (as subscribers in Australia quickly reminded the moderators early on!). The process of thinking beyond one's own cultural borders might be difficult, but the result can be a significant step towards developing intercultural understanding, empathy, and tolerance to views that differ from one's own.

Developing a Research Community

Through ITForum, subscribers become members of a larger academic community that is spread over the world. It doesn't matter whether they are active participants in the discussions or passive "lurkers" who silently follow the thread of the conversation. Even without subscribers meeting face-to-face, friendships and active collaborations often develop through the listserv. The informal exchange of opinions, experiences, and arguments during the discussions provides a much more personal element to academic discussions than can be derived from more formal forms of publishing. The spontaneous give-and-take of electronic communications exposes the character, the strengths, and the weaknesses of the participants and their arguments, and allows the development of mental and emotional ties without the need for physical proximity.

The existence of an electronic community can be demonstrated through the establishment of accepted rules of behavior (i.e., "netiquette") and through the development of shared values and experiences (Rheingold, 1993). Many examples of collaborative research and development projects or jointly authored scholarly publications that grew out of initial contacts over ITForum can be cited. The development of a community is probably best illustrated, however, by a few personal examples. Lloyd Rieber commented that when he visited Edith Cowan University and Curtin University of Technology in Perth, Australia, in 1995, he felt as though he was renewing friendships that had already been established through ITForum even though he had never actually met many of the people beforehand. The recent death of longtime ITForum participant Jeff Oliver of the United Kingdom was felt as a personal loss by many of us who had never met him face-to-face but felt that we knew him through his postings to the list.

POTENTIALS AND PITFALLS OF COMPUTER-MEDIATED COMMUNICATION (CMC)

Although the various forms of CMC differ, the asynchronous types of CMC (personal E-mail, listservs, bulletin boards, newsgroups) have some important characteristics in common. Each message is rendered in visual text only, without the usual conversational cues of body language, changes in vocal tone or pitch, or other paralinguistic clues. This lack of cues can lead quite easily to misunderstandings between users. For example, sarcasm is not conveyed well via E-mail (Newby, 1993). Users of CMC, however, have developed some norms unique to CMC in order to minimize misunderstandings. These include "emoticons" (emotion icons) such as the standard "smiley" typed as :-) that resembles a smile if you tilt your head to the left. The smiley is usually added after a line to indicate "I'm only kidding, don't take what I'm saying too seriously" (Murray, 1988).

Besides removing the barrier of time, CMC also removes the barrier of distance, allowing conversations between people separated physically and/or temporally. On ITForum, this has allowed scholars and IT professionals from all over the world to participate in discussions without consideration of geography or time zones.

Netiquette: Reliance on Self-Moderation

Since the inception of E-mail, users have been struggling to develop a set of standards of use, known as "netiquette." Some of the "rules" are to post only replies of general interest to the list (items of personal interest should be sent off-list) and to avoid sending any E-mail when angry or upset. Some list owners have had trouble getting their members to abide by these rules and have therefore begun "moderating" the list discussions. In a formally moderated list, all posts must first be sent to the moderator, who clears the ones deemed appropriate and posts them to the list. Personal, off-topic, or inflammatory posts are rejected. Because ITForum allows subscribers to post notes directly to the list without first getting them cleared by a moderator, it relies heavily on subscribers carefully considering what they decide to send. One of the most remarkable things of ITForum is the natural tendency of the list to moderate itself. With few exceptions, ITForum has largely been able to avoid problems of other lists, such as flaming and junk mail.

Achieving Critical Mass: Avoiding the Negative Side of Growth

ITForum exists by the very fact that people are willing to participate by sending their comments to the list. Participation defines the very nature of ITForum. On one hand, the number of subscribers (and the rate of increase/decrease in subscriptions) can be perceived as a measure of the value of ITForum to the profession. On the other hand, growth also holds several potential problems for the future of a listserv like ITForum. The first simply relates to the volume of mail that would be generated if even a small percentage of the subscribers were to post something to the list every day. Our subscribers are busy professionals who do not have the time to sort through a large number of messages. The second problem concerns the ratio of "fluff to stuff" in the daily ITForum postings. As the subscriber pool increases, there is a greater tendency for people to post notes or questions that have little relevancy to the majority of the subscribers.

In addressing the second problem, we have asked subscribers to keep all postings during scheduled discussion weeks directed toward the topic and to hold off sending other postings until the discussion has ended. Problems still arise when too many notes are received, even if they all are relevant to the topic. As already mentioned, we have tried to invite casual comments from subscribers, yet if more subscribers accepted our invitation the number of messages would be overwhelming. This dilemma does not have an easy resolution. Again, we rely on the membership for self-moderation. So far, we have been fortunate that membership interests and discussion topics vary widely, hence just a small proportion of the subscribers contribute to the discussion on any given topic.

When Viewpoints Conflict: Dancing on the Lip of the Volcano

ITForum offers subscribers an uncensored exchange of ideas and perspectives. Not surprisingly, viewpoints among subscribers often conflict. Fortunately, this usually results in our best discussions. ITForum subscribers have shown their willingness to listen and respect all viewpoints. Occasionally, however, emotions begin to take control of a discussion. It is interesting to watch how a discussion can quickly grow more intense within a short period of time. The immediacy of E-mail permits people to post and respond at will. The ease of pressing the "send" button sometimes leads to remarks that would probably not have been made in another medium. Although we feel that subscribers have rarely, if ever, crossed the proverbial "line in the sand" into unprofessional behavior, such dangers remain a constant presence in a medium such as this.

Providing Access to Past Discussions: Can You Catch the Wind?

The papers presented over ITForum are a rich resource of ideas related to many of the major issues of concern to students, practitioners, researchers, and scholars in the field of instructional technology. Questions related to developmental strategies and processes; research methodology, questions, and ethics; theories of knowledge development; and techniques of enhancing student learning have all be explored in recent discussions. Many of the papers presented have made their way into more traditional forms of publishing, and efforts have been made to provide access to the papers on the Internet by means of the DLPE homepage (http://dlpe.base.org) and InTRO (Instructional Technology Research Online) (http://intro. base.org). In many cases, however, the paper has been primarily a point of departure, and the value of the forum has been in the discussion that grew out of the paper. Capturing and presenting the ebb and flow of an ongoing discussion is like trying to take a snapshot of the wind.

Like almost all listservs, past ITForum discussions are preserved for a limited time and can be accessed through the listserv archives. The process of locating and downloading the appropriate files, however, is confusing and cumbersome. Once the file has been located, the individual postings that develop the thread of the argument are often lost in a tapestry of competing threads. In order to provide easier access to past discussions, an ITForum World Wide Web site is being established at the University of Georgia. The site is still under development, but you are invited to visit and provide us with comments or suggestions (http://itech1.coe.uga.edu/ITForum/home.html).

The discussions are presented virtually verbatim as they occurred, although minor editing has been done for stylistic and grammatical consistency and to improve the flow of the discussion. Messages that consisted primarily of "cheering" (voting for or against postings by other contributors) have been eliminated, as have messages that are clearly off the thread of the discussion. Only those messages that contributed to the development of issues raised in the papers have been kept. In addition, some minor rewording of some posts was done to clarify the intent of messages, but efforts have been made to preserve the feel of a give-and-take discussion.

Copyright: Who Owns the Discussion?

Making the ITForum discussions easily and widely available through the Internet raises a number of questions regarding such issues as rights of privacy, intellectual property rights, ethical treatment of participants, and copyright protection (Oakley, 1993; Lichtenberg, 1995; Schrum, 1995). Some of these problem areas are relatively easy to handle. For example, E-mail messages often have grammatical or spelling errors that would not normally be committed by the author in a more formal communication. In such circumstances, we view our function much like that of an editor or proofreader in a traditional publishing house, making those corrections that should be made while preserving the intent of the author.

On questions of copyright and intellectual property rights, however, we take a fairly restricted view. Following the lead of H-NET (Lawrence, 1995), we feel that although posting a message to ITForum gives ITForum the right to publish the message over the Internet, the ideas and words of the message remain the intellectual property of the subscriber, and publication on ITForum does not place the material in the public domain. Use or publication of such material by other writers requires citation of the source and, in the case of publication in any other arena than ITForum, permission of the writer. When messages in the discussions quote previous postings, common practice within the ITForum community has been for the source of the quote to be cited. On the Web site, we take this a step further: the wording of all quoted messages is verified, and the date and author of the original message are cited. The only exceptions to this are those few cases where questions of privacy rights come into conflict with intellectual property rights. A personal revelation is sometimes made in the heat of a listserv discussion that advances the discussion but that, given time to reflect, may be too revealing to be kept available in a more permanent and public form. In such cases, the author is consulted and the name deleted from the message, unless the editor is otherwise instructed.

SUMMARY

ITForum is a unique and thriving community of instructional technology scholars and professionals. By offering a schedule of papers and the opportunity to discuss them with the author, ITForum makes a valuable contribution to the professional community. Students, faculty members, and IT professionals alike have an equal opportunity to ask questions and make observations. The authors of the papers receive immediate feedback from a large pool of interested and knowledgeable professionals from around the world. Consequently, listservs like ITForum offer the opportunity for scholarly work to become a much more interactive process between authors and readers than is currently the case in traditional publications. Furthermore, listservs like ITForum truly bring the professional community into a global perspective. Colleagues from different countries can share ideas and experiences as if they worked on the same floor. Unanswered questions remain, such as those surrounding copyright. These will take time to resolve as the medium matures.

FOOTNOTE

1. To subscribe to ITForum, simply send the E-mail message "subscribe itforum firstname lastname" (e.g. subscribe itforum Pat Jones) to the address: listserv@uga.cc.uga.edu.

REFERENCES

Ferrara, K., Brunner, H., and Whittenmore, G. (1991). Interactive written discourse as an emergent register. *Written Communication 8*(1), 8-34.

Guernsey, L. (1997). A humanities network considers what lies beyond e-mail. *The Chronicle of Higher Education*, January 24, A23-A24.

Harper, D. (1995). Communities of scholarship in the electronic age. In *The politics and processes of scholarship*, ed. J. M. Moxley and L. T. Lenker (Westport, CT: Greenwood Press), 133-42.

Jonassen, D. H. (1994). Technology as cognitive tools: Learners as designers. *ITForum* [electronic listserv]. Athens, GA: University of Georgia. URL: http://itech1.coe.uga.edu/ITForum/home.html.

Lawrence, J. (1995). Virtual publication and the fair use concept. In *Filling the pipe line and paying the piper*, ed. A. Okerson (Washington, DC: Association of Research Libraries), 219-28.

Lichtenberg, J. (1995). Academic publishing and new technologies: Protecting intellectual property is the key. In *The politics and processes of scholarship*, ed. J. M. Moxley and L. T. Lenker (Westport, CT: Greenwood Press), 89-95.

Machovec, G. S. (1996). Electronic journals: Trends in World Wide Web (WWW) Internet access. *Online Libraries and Microcomputer 14*(4), 1-6.

Mogge, D., ed. (1996). *Directory of electronic journals, newsletters and academic discussion lists*, 6th ed. Washington, DC: Association of Research Libraries.

Murray, D. E. (1988). Computer-mediated communication: Implications for ESP. *English for Specific Purposes 7*(1), 3-18.

Newby, G. B. (1993). The maturation of norms for computer-mediated communication. *Internet Research 3*(4), 30-38.

Oakley, R. L. (1993). Copyright and electronic publishing. In *Scholarly publishing on the electronic networks. The new generation: Visions and opportunities in not-for-profit publishing*, ed. A. Okerson (Washington, DC: Association of Research Libraries), 91-100.

Okerson, A. S., and O'Donnell, J. J., eds. (1995). *Scholarly journals at the crossroads: A subversive proposal for electronic publishing*. Washington, DC: Association of Research Libraries.

Publishing papers on the Internet can pose problems. (December, 1996). *Monitor 27*(12), 15.

Rheingold, H. (1993). *The virtual community: Homesteading on the electronic frontier*. Reading, MA: Addison-Wesley.

Schauder, D. (1994). Electronic publishing of professional articles: Attitudes of academics and implications for the scholarly communication industry. *Journal of the American Society for Information Science 45*(2), 73-100.

Schrum, L. (1995). Framing the debate: Ethical research in the information age. *Qualitative Inquiry 1*(3), 311-26.

Shoaf, R. A. (1995). All information is already in formation: The Internet and the future of learned journals. In *The politics and processes of scholarship*, ed. J. M. Moxley and L. T. Lenker (Westport, CT: Greenwood Press), 97-104.

Tompkins, P. (1995). Homesteading on the outskirts of the Gutenberg Galaxy. *Community & Junior College Libraries 8*(1), 87-92.

Part Two
The Profession

Introduction

Ken Smith at the University of Arizona has selected the *Yearbook* to publish the results of his recent small airplane excursion across the United States and Canada to survey graduate programs in educational technology. Rodney Earle of Brigham Young University has selected the *Yearbook* to publish the results of a review of emerging perspectives about instructional design and teacher planning routines. Both Dr. Smith and Dr. Earle offer reflections about the field of educational media and technology that will allow those in the profession who construct formal programs of study to do so from an informed position.

Robert Maribe Branch

The State of Programs of Instructional Technologies in the United States and Canada
An Aerial View

Kenneth J. Smith
Professor, Educational Psychology
University of Arizona

As the person responsible for the development of graduate offerings in educational technologies at the University of Arizona, what is being done in that area at other universities in the United States and Canada is of great interest to me. Fortunately, I was granted a sabbatical leave for the fall semester of 1996-97 to travel to selected universities and see first hand what they were doing and what they were thinking about in order to make recommendations for our own graduate programs and their development. My wife, Dr. Barbara D. Smith, having taken early retirement, was able to accompany me and cooperate in the effort. Because we are both pilots and fly our own plane, it was feasible to visit 12 universities over a period of two months. We made arrangements to visit all of those universities, developed an interview guide, got the plane ready for a long trip, and hit the airways.

There certainly was no scientific basis for our selection of universities to visit, except that we did choose schools known to have made contributions to the field. Readers might wonder why some were omitted. Some were left out only because we had visited them fairly recently. Others were not included for reasons having to do with geography or weather. And some doubtless were missed due to our own ignorance. The fact that a particular university was not included does not mean that it wasn't considered worthy of a visit. We do believe that we got a fair sample of the active instructional technologies programs. Those visited included, in order, Utah State University, Western Washington University, the University of Alberta, Michigan State University, Indiana University, Penn State University, the University of Virginia, the University of Georgia, Florida State University, Vanderbilt University, the University of Houston, and the University of Texas (Austin).

PURPOSES

1. Because I have no responsibility for undergraduate offerings (except that two of our courses are available to seniors with high grade point averages who do not need those courses for graduation) our primary concern was with graduate programs. However, we did look at the undergraduate requirements, particularly as they had implications for the graduate programs. 2. Our own offerings are available as concentrations in the Department of Educational Psychology, but the organization of educational programs varies widely. We wanted to see how programs were organized and what the implications were for instructional technologies. 3. A major concern in program development, of course, is what markets shall be served by instructional technologies programs. We wished to determine the markets being served by these universities and what the implications were for their faculty and curricula. 4. Programs vary greatly in size, and we wished to determine what the size and make-up of a faculty needed to be in order to provide a sufficient critical mass and necessary competencies for an instructional technologies program. 5. Programs cannot be successful without support, and we wanted to determine the adequacy, sources, and dependability of such support. 6. Because ours is not a large program, we needed to know what was necessary to constitute a credible graduate program. 7. We were in a good position to get at least an impression of the general state of instructional technologies preparation, including concerns and potential for the future.

FINDINGS

Undergraduate requirements: Almost all of the universities require at least one course in instructional technologies. Two were attempting to meet those responsibilities by dispersing competencies through various methods courses. Indications from those involved were that this endeavor was not very successful, due to varying competencies and interests of faculty involved in those methods courses and the administrative difficulty of assuring that competencies were achieved in an efficient manner. In general, graduate programs had the advantage of having students who had a basic introduction to instructional technologies upon entry into the graduate program.

Graduate degree programs and organization: With the single exception of Western Washington University, all of the universities visited offered a doctorate, sometimes directly in instructional technologies, sometimes as an emphasis area under a degree program such as educational psychology. The educational specialist degree was offered in some universities, but it had a substantial enrollment only at the University of Georgia, where a state requirement for an instructional technologies coordinator in every school had built up that degree program.

The number of credit hours for master's and doctoral programs did not vary greatly, but the content did. The mix of technical and theoretical courses varied. Further, the amount and source of support in such areas as learning/development theory, measurement, and research design varied substantially. Where the educational psychology courses were in a separate department, or even college, the support sometimes seemed lacking. Some instructional technologies programs attempted, with varying degrees of success, to supply that support by including it in their own courses. Instructional technologies curricula are clearly works in progress, for nearly every program was reported to be undergoing substantial study and change.

Markets served: While some programs concentrated on a traditional education market, most were serving both the education market and the business/military market. Interestingly, it seemed that more than half of the graduates of instructional technologies programs were subsequently employed by business or the military.

Size of programs: It sometimes was difficult to count the number of core faculty devoted to instructional technologies graduate programs, for some had part-time assignments, some participated in both the graduate and the undergraduate programs, and others had duties in faculty development or materials development. Also, some had faculty in other areas who were quite active in instructional technologies. At Vanderbilt, for instance, it was difficult to tell who was in instructional technologies and who was not, a situation which we judged to be quite desirable. While some of the programs visited had as few as three or four faculty members, others had as many as 10, or even 18, according to how one counted them.

Student populations varied greatly, not necessarily in proportion to the size of the faculty. Master's degree programs ranged in size from 12 to over 200 active candidates, while doctoral programs had a few as three or as many as 166 students.

Program support: Some, but not all, of program support is financial. Some programs, particularly those with a long track record, have been very successful at obtaining external funding. Georgia even gets funding from the state lottery. (One wonders what happens to the money from other state lotteries that are supposed to support education!) Others are supported almost entirely by their own institutions. Some have a strong association with university faculty development, which can provide substantial student support, and others have students involved in materials development.

One matter that became quite evident was that support was sometimes inconsistent as a result of changes in administration. It takes some time to build a program. Yet, a good program can be destroyed in a very short time by an unsympathetic administrator, and the average tenure of deans is reported to be less than five years.

OBSERVATIONS

Undergraduate requirements: It seems that the most productive pattern is to have at least one required course in instructional technologies for undergraduates, with specialized applications taking place in methods courses. Of course, consistent modeling in all classes really helps.

Program organization: One can have a successful instructional technologies program with any of a variety of organizational schemes. However, instructional technologies is clearly driven by educational psychology theory, both learning/development and measurement/ research. Therefore, it seems to improve the quality of programs if instructional technologies is closely allied with educational psychology.

Markets served: The education market is the traditional market, and it would seem that it is one that we have a commitment to serve. The needs in that market are great, and the need for training in instructional technologies for the schools is one that has not yet been met. However, the business/military market is also appropriate and has apparently recognized its needs. It also is an important source of financial support. There is overlap in the kinds of program/faculty/resources needed for education and for business/military, but they are not identical.

Size: It is clear that a program need not be large in order to have high quality. Indeed, a possible caution is that a program can become so large, at least in terms of students, that it can become depersonalized and that supervision can become very difficult. However, it seems that a program needs a certain critical mass, so that people can talk and work together, and that certain subspecialties need to be present for a credible program.

Support: Support is needed for faculty and staff, for hardware and software, for operations, and for students. That support varies a lot from program to program, as might be expected, but an essential aspect is the consistency of support, and we are not speaking solely of finances. One necessity is that a program develop enough community and business respect and support to insulate it to some degree from the vagaries resulting from administrative changes.

Necessary size and make-up of a credible graduate program: As stated earlier, a program need not be large to be effective and credible. However, it does have some minimum requirements. It is our observation that a program dedicated to the education market needs to have at least three faculty members; one specializing in instructional design, one specializing in distance education, including the Internet; one specializing in K-12 applications. At least one of these needs to have substantial programming/engineering competence. obviously, these subspecialties are not mutually exclusive, and should not be, for communication would not be possible if each knew nothing of the others' subspecialities. For the business/military market, a faculty of three seems to be a minimum, with a specialist in business applications instead of one in K-12 applications. Because there is substantial overlap, it would be possible to serve both markets with a faculty of four, including both a K-12 and a business applications specialist.

Laboratory facilities need to be dedicated to the needs of the program. Some try to use open-access, drop-in labs for instructional purposes, but the needs are too different for that to be successful. It is feasible for an instructional lab to be used for open-access purposes when not being used for instruction, but the reverse does not seem workable. Further, separate lab facilities for advanced production are a necessity.

A program needs support for students. In many ways, assistantships or other employment that uses students' competencies in instructional technologies are superior to fellowships, for the former provide practical application of student abilities. Student participation in faculty development efforts seem an ideal way to provide student support.

The state of instructional technologies preparation: There of course are always external forces that can help us or do us harm. Sometimes those are beyond our control. The internal matter that may be of most danger is an inability or unwillingness to accept as legitimate and valuable the contributions of those with different theoretical positions from our own. My wife and I both received our initial training in the field of reading and were active in that area for many years. Reading education, in our judgment, damaged the profession and, in the process, millions of children through the polarization into the whole language and direct instruction (often misidentified as phonics) camps. The notion that to be my friend you must agree with me on all matters; that if you don't agree with me wholeheartedly, you are my enemy; that to recognize a contribution from someone in the other "camp" merely weakens one's position is really destructive. It happened in reading. There are signs of it in instructional technologies. Constructivists and systematic instruction designers both have made and will make contributions. Let's not allow what happened in reading happen to instructional technology.

We frankly were very impressed with the quality of the preparation programs that we saw. Most notable was the enthusiasm seen among both faculty and students. People with common goals, even though with different notions of how best to achieve them, were achieving a lot. Students were of very high quality. We're very optimistic about the future of instructional technologies and its contribution to education.

Instructional Design and Teacher Planning
Reflections and Perspectives

Rodney Earle
Brigham Young University

You are never given a dream without also
being given the power to make it true. . . .
You may have to work for it, however.

Richard Bach

One professional dream in the hearts of instructional designers has centered on the desire to make meaningful contributions to the quality of human learning, to have an impact on public schools, and to facilitate and improve the practices of teachers and learners. As a field we have witnessed and participated in tremendous developments in instructional design (ID) and technology in a variety of settings—business, industry, the military, health services, and education. In fact, experiences in these settings have influenced, developed, refined, modified, and expanded our professional theories and practices.

Despite these achievements, we face an unexpected setback, a frustrating disappointment, a major challenge to the field of instructional design: our apparent inability to influence in meaningful ways the one area with which we are most closely related and with which we share common roots—the public schools and their teachers, and ultimately the children in those schools. Of course, we *have* contributed a variety of instructional products and programs that have benefited teachers and children in classrooms across the nation and throughout the world. I do not in any way deny the impact of these materials. These activities continue to represent the major contribution of the ID field to education. However, the deficiency exists in our seeming incapacity to affect the planning and delivery practices of classroom teachers. We have been unable not only to connect our best practices with what teachers do and how they plan, but also to learn from their experiences and practices.

Is our dream "an impossible dream," similar to the quest in the theme song from *Man of La Mancha?* Are we "fight[ing] an unbeatable foe" and trying to "reach [an] unreachable star"? Personally, I believe firmly that this dream is achievable. I recognize the challenges related to its fruition. As a field we have begun to work for it and will need to continue to do so. Like Don Quixote, I believe that as we follow this quest—this dream to influence teaching and learning through teacher planning processes—the world of the classroom will be better, even if, at times, we find ourselves running where "the brave dare not go" and following "that star, no matter how far."

So how did we get into this predicament? Is there a history to our current situation? Let's reflect a little on our professional past in order to see more clearly in which directions we need to move.

REFLECTIONS: ROOTS AND SHOOTS

A naive outsider looking at the writings and practices of teacher education and instructional design might reasonably assume that practitioners, researchers, and theorists from these two closely related fields would be working collaboratively to exchange ideas, concerns, and challenges about the improvement of teaching and learning. However, in reality, over four decades, the gap between both fields has widened, even though their journeys have run fairly parallel with only minimal connections. The tendency has been for teacher educators and instructional designers to remain aloof from each other, reading, writing, implementing, investigating, and theorizing in their respective backyards, generally ignoring the synergistic contributions possible through collaborative ventures. Just like two siblings who grew up in the same neighborhood and then separated without contact for many years—a common heritage, but two district and separate branches of the same family tree. Is a reunion possible? I think so, but first we need to seek to understand each other because we've been comparative strangers for so long.

A look back over the development of the field of instruction design and technology reveals a rich heritage and a priceless legacy bestowed by many education pioneers (Anglin, 1995; Saettler, 1968, 1991). It's a journey each of us needs to relive by spending time reviewing these pivotal historical assessments.

Shrock (1995), in attempting to define instructional development, takes us through a seven-decade overview of ID history. The early decades found us very much a part of the education scene. Her mention of Tyler's (1949) rational model for developing curriculum and planning instruction as "work that in retrospect advanced the evolution of instruction development" (p. 14) illustrates that ID is firmly rooted in education. Both teacher educators and instructional designers would lay claim to Tyler's model as a direct ancestor.

Winn (1997) advances the notion that "any discipline is based on another more general, abstract and underlying discipline from which it draws" and that "any successful practitioner or researcher needs to be thoroughly versed in at least the immediately underlying discipline to his or her own" (p. 37). He identifies these roots as psychology and theories of human learning—a common heritage shared by teachers and designers.

Perhaps our shoots began to move in different directions as instructional design becomes more closely aligned with instructional technology, which Heinich (1995) feels is better viewed as "a subset of technology in general rather then as a subset of education or psychology" (p. 61). He further describes the separation by stressing that "when [instructional technology] moved as a field from a device to support a lesson to the design of instruction systems, we also moved from the side of labor [teacher] to that of management" (ibid., p. 72). In other words, we distanced ourselves from classroom teachers and their planning.

So, for instructional designers, who are very much a part of the broader field of instructional technology, was this guilt by association? Although I agree with Heinich's assertion that teachers are definitely the education professionals most directly affected by instructional technology, I hesitate to widen the gap by supporting the notion that "instructional technology can take over most of what teachers traditionally do" (ibid., p. 75). It's probably the "taking over" approach rather than a partnering perspective that causes me concern.

Well, even if Heinich's assessment of the split is accurate (and it makes good sense to me), being a subset of technology in general does not need to isolate us from the classroom, as demonstrated by Engler (1972):

> If we view the ecology of education as the web of relationships between and among learners, teachers, and the environment in which they operate [*including instructional designers, perhaps?*], then it becomes apparent that these relationships are largely defined by the prevailing technology of instruction [*including ID principles?*] (p. 62, my comments in italics).

Earlier, Engler (1972) had defined instructional technology not only as hardware but also, more significantly, as "a process by means of which we apply the research findings of the behavioral sciences to the problems of instruction" (p. 59). This sounds similar to the plea by Winn (1997) for ID to consider underlying disciplines as we approach instructional challenges.

Our perceptions of each other have certainly affected our relationships over time, further distancing designers from teachers and teachers from designers. In a recent study of ID culture over time through content analysis of articles from leading professional journals, Taguchi (1992) revealed a variety of images of teachers apparently supported by the field. Traditional perspectives describe teachers as nonprofessionals who have been perceived as consumers, delivery systems, and managers. Fortunately, recent shifts in perception to a posttraditionalist perspective view teachers as designers, partners, decision-makers, reflective practitioners, and sense-makers. Although teachers have certainly been reluctant to implement ID principles in their instruction and hesitant to collaborate with instructional designers, I wonder if our ID attitude developed a flavor of superiority, of having all the answers that we were ready to dispense to solve teacher problems. Perhaps our images of teachers in limited roles erected barriers to communication.

Whatever the causes of our separation, let's begin the process of understanding each other by taking a moment to look closely at developments in each field in an attempt to recognize the differences, note the similarities, and consider possible connections.

Teacher Cognition: Thinking and Planning

Two research threads have woven their way through studies of teacher practices. They are inextricably connected, yet one (planning) is clearly viewed as subset of the other (thinking). The formation of the International Study Association of Teacher Thinking is evidence of the significance of this field of study. Clark (1983) explained that while teacher effectiveness researchers have been primarily concerned with understanding the observable behaviors of effective teachers, researchers on teacher thinking have pursued inquiries into how teachers' minds function as they plan, make decisions, teach, and reflect on their practices.

Teacher Thinking

Researchers have found difficulty in separating teacher planning from teacher thinking (Clark & Yinger, 1977), noting in the 1970s that teachers did not appear to follow the rational model (the common ground with ID) prescribed in teacher education and curriculum planning (Tyler, 1949). Instead, they focused on content as well as considerations of the setting in which they taught (Clark & Yinger, 1978).

In the past decade, inquiries into how teachers think have centered on debating the possible contributions of research on teacher thinking (Floden & Klinzing, 1990; Lampert & Clark, 1990); exploring models of teachers' interactive thinking and connections with class-room practice (Mitchell & Marland, 1989); asking better research questions (Clark, 1988); making sense of teacher cognition and mental processes (Peterson & Comeaux, 1987; Moallem, 1994a, 1994b, 1996); and enabling teachers to understand classroom practice (Clark & Lampert, 1986; Morine-Dershimer, 1991; Udvari-Solner, 1996).

Teacher Planning

Teaching is a complex process in which teachers make and implement decisions that affect children and their learning. These decisions involve planning, developing, managing, implementing, and evaluating the instructional process to enhance student learning. Teachers make decisions before, during, and after instruction (Hunter, 1979). Clark and Yinger (1979) found that rather than linear in nature, teacher planning was incremental, interactive, and reflective.

A careful review of the teacher planning literature illustrates clearly that teachers rely on mental planning to guide what occurs in their classrooms. Morine-Dershimer (1978-1979) defined a teacher plan as a "detailed and comprehensive mental image or set of expectations for the lesson" (p. 85), noting that teachers carry this mental plan into interactive planning routines implemented in their classrooms. This mental planning, or reflective mental dialog, not only precedes written planning but also occurs throughout the design, implementation, and evaluation phases of instruction. It is a key element in planning *prior* to teaching; in reflection, monitoring, and adjustment *during* teaching; and in reflective evaluation and revision *following* teaching. McCutcheon (1980) described this reflective mental dialogue as a lesson rehearsal, "an envisioning of what would happen in the classroom," in her estimation "the richest form of teacher planning" (pp. 7-8).

Kerr's (1981) reflections on teacher design practices conclude that even though "teachers' thinking is not 'systematic' according to ID canons, it does have a system of its own" (p. 364). His review of the research on teacher thinking and teacher planning indicated that "teachers rarely seem to proceed in practice . . . from precisely defined objectives, through lesson design and materials selection, to instruction and evaluation" (p. 364). Teachers use "an approach that is more intuitive, and as the teachers see it, more 'practical' than Tyler's model . . . rarely ask[ing] "What am I trying to '*accomplish*'? . . . instead try[ing] to determine, 'What am I going to *do*'? It is in terms of doing that teachers define purposes and accomplishments" (ibid., p. 365). McCutcheon (1980) viewed teacher planning as a complex, simultaneous juggling of the dynamic elements of the instructional environment and culture, with a special emphasis on mental planning as a "rich and complex part of the professional life of teachers" (p. 20).

There exists a rich pool of research and reflections on teacher planning, largely conducted in the late 1970s and early 1980s (Clark & Peterson, 1986). This research has posed questions in three areas: the types and functions of teacher planning, the models used to describe the planning processes, and the relationships between teacher planning and teacher practices in the classroom. "Planning is challenging to study because it is both a psychological process and a practical activity" (ibid., p. 260).

Nevertheless, the range of research outcomes has been significant. Studies have considered teacher routines (Yinger, 1977); different types and functions of planning (Crosswhite, 1970; Clark & Yinger, 1979; Morine-Dershimer, 1977, 1978-1979; McCutcheon, 1980); planning models (Sardo-Brown, 1988; Borko, 1990; Neale, Pace, & Case, 1983; Sardo, 1982; Yinger, 1977; Zahorik, 1975); and connections between planning and teaching behaviors (Peterson, Marx, & Clark, 1978; Carnahan, 1980).

The research has shown that thinking plays a significant role in teaching; that teachers "plan in a rich variety of ways [which] have real consequences in the classroom"; that teachers "make planning decisions frequently during interactive teaching"; and that teacher theories and belief systems "influence their perceptions, plans, and actions" (Clark & Peterson, 1986, p. 292).

Common Ground

As teachers plan, they prepare learning experiences to meet the needs of the children in their classrooms. There seems to be no question that they are designing instruction, even if they do not adhere to classical ID principles, and even if they don't consider what they do to be instructional design (Clark & Angert, 1980). Even the casual observer perceives the similarities between Zahorik's (1975) classification of planning decisions by teachers and Andrews and Goodson's (1980) common elements of ID models (see Table 1)—not that I'm suggesting an exact match, but merely noting the similarities and potential connections.

Another content analysis of ID models (Darwazeh, Branch, & El-Hindi, 1991) identified common elements in the instructional activities of teachers and instructional designers. It seems that the practices of both include planning, designing lesson and unit plans, designing test items, stating objectives, implementing, managing, evaluating, and consulting. Differences center on the designer focus on analysis, sequencing, and production and the teacher focus on teaching and evaluating.

Table 1
Teacher Decisions and Instructional Design Elements

Zahorik (1975)	*Andrews and Goodson* (1980)
Objectives	Outcomes
Content	Analysis, Sequencing
Activities	Strategies
Materials	Media Selection, Materials Development
Diagnosis	Needs Assessment, Learner Attributes
Evaluation	Tests, Formative Evaluation
Instruction	Strategies
Organization	Constraints, Installation Costs, Maintenance

ID models and teacher planning. If, as the research in both ID and teacher planning indicates, teachers design instruction without adhering strictly to the rational or systematic approach, then perhaps a joint effort to describe teacher planning processes would be beneficial. Dick (1993) cautions us to remember that ID models represent a collection of design processes and were "not intended as a model for classroom teachers to use as they plan their instruction" (p. 13). Richey (1993) echoed this warning by calling for "new models and new theory stemming from new databases, such as those related to teacher decision-making" (p. 18). She based her call on Martin and Clemente's (1990) examination of the "inconsistencies between ISD theory and practice on the one hand and teacher needs, wants, and practices on the other" (p. 61). Gustafson (1993) issued a blunt challenge to the ID field by noting that we need "alternative ID paradigms that more closely match the goals and purposes of K-12 education and the reality of how it is organized and functions," because it is obvious that "our present ID paradigm [see Cooper, 1993; Reigeluth, 1996] is generally not workable in public education as it is presently constituted . . . and will not see widespread application" in its current form (p.29).

In a recent study, Moallem and Applefield (1997) suggested that "applications of instructional design for teachers be carefully modified to achieve models that better account for the ecology of the classroom environment " (p. 9). They also assert other necessary changes:

> ID models must also acknowledge the natural tendency of teachers to move quickly in their mental planning to selecting activities that will grab their students' attention, imagination, and interest. Finally, it is important that ID models more effectively incorporate principles of constructivist views of the teaching-learning process if they are to achieve the promise of having significant utility for improving the planning, teaching, and evaluation roles of teachers (ibid., p. 94).

A layers-of-necessity approach (Tessmer & Wedman, 1990); model development (Morse, 1997; Jonassen, 1994; Willis, 1995); constructivist reflections (Tessmer & Richey, 1997; Jonassen, 1994; Duffy & Jonassen, 1992; Wilson, 1997a); and theoretical discussions (Seels, 1997; Winn, 1997; Wilson, 1997b; Jonassen, et al., 1997; Reigeluth, 1997; Richey, 1997) certainly lead us in the right directions, but the bottom line is that we'll fail in our endeavor to develop a model that describes teacher planning practices and related ID skills unless we work together, share what we've found in our independent spheres, and learn from each other.

INSTRUCTIONAL DESIGN PERSPECTIVES

Following the rapid explosion of the field in the 1960s and a growing sense of identity (Shrock, 1995), several instructional designers began asking questions in an effort to reconnect with teaching and teachers. Beilby (1974), despite the prevalent assumption that ID "is too complex and time-consuming for teachers to deal with without help" (p. 12), reflected on the evolution of the teacher to teacher-designer. He argued that training teachers in the ID process might discourage conflicts between teachers and educational technologists who had exclusively claimed the ID role—might even bridge the gap already noticeable as competitive or territorial. In fact, Beilby warned that such territorial confrontations could seriously affect not only our field but also the quality of human learning—almost prophetic in the light of our current status.

Beilby's questions seemed to go unanswered for a while. Stolovitch (1980) heralded a renewed interest in the 1980s by discussing the challenges offered to teacher training by instructional technology. Yelon (1980) followed suit by suggesting ID principles for designing and implementing teacher training courses.

Perhaps spurred on by the "nation at risk" label attached to our public schools (National Commission on Excellence in Education, 1983), several instructional designers expressed opinions, shared insights and strategies, and described model programs that would hopefully allow the two fields to reconnect as the effectual door opened. These were meaningful contributions and attempts to have an impact on teachers and children in their classroom (Earle, 1985; Burkman, 1987; Snelbecker, 1987; Shrock & Byrd, 1987; Schiffman, 1987; Branson, 1987; Reigeluth, 1987, Reiser, 1988; Kerr, 1989). However, the optimism expressed by Shrock and Byrd (1987) has continued to pervade the field:

> [ID] provides the schema that the teaching effectiveness approach has lacked, and therefore provides the support for thinking about teaching. . . . If carefully communicated, instructional design could be seen as a logical extension of the teaching effectiveness movement (p. 52).

The interventions proposed included preservice teacher preparation, in-service professional development, and systems redesign. Reiser (1988) noted, with a sense of frustration shared by the entire field, that despite this spurt of activity, instructional designers continue in their struggle to play significant roles in public education.

The decade of the 1990s reflected two major thrusts by ID to influence education: a close look at teacher planning processes and a focus on school reform and systemic restructuring. The formation of the Change Division of AECT indicated the commitment of the systemic researchers, practitioners, and theorists (Reigeluth, 1992; Frick, 1991; Gabehart, 1992; Fishman & Duffy, 1992; Banathy, 1991; Salisbury, 1992; Reigeluth & Garfinkle, 1992; Jenlink et al., 1997).

Because my emphasis in this chapter is on teacher planning processes, I'll recommend that interested readers engage in a study of systemic change at another time, while we look closely here at research aimed at connecting teacher planning and instructional design. A small cadre of interested instructional designers has spent several years researching the similarities between the practices of classroom teachers and instructional designers. What are the needs of teachers? What aspects of their practices reflect ID principles? How can classical ID theory complement, supplement, or improve classroom teaching and learning? What are the barriers to collaboration? Do our ID models need adjustments to fit teacher thinking? How can ID practitioners make a difference for teachers and their students?

> *What is education but a process by which a person begins to learn how to learn.*
>
> Peter Ustinov

We don't have definitive answers to these questions yet. The work is still in progress. Let me attempt to summarize some thinking generated by our research efforts.

- Systems approach principles can be taught effectively to preservice teachers (Earle, 1985, 1992b; Klein, 1991; Reiser, 1994; Moallem & Applefield, 1997; Applefield, 1992; Reiser & Radford, 1990), but one course is insufficient for successful ongoing use in classrooms (Reiser, Branch, & Earle, 1995; Reiser & Dick, 1996).

- Differences exist between ID models and teacher models of thinking and learning (Moallem, 1994a).

- Teachers implicitly apply ID practices when planning to teach (Branch, 1994; Earle, 1992a, 1996; Reiser & Mory, 1991; Branch, Darwazeh, & El-Hindi, 1992; Branch, 1996).

- Teachers think and talk about instructional planning in different ways. A common technical language of instruction is necessary to generate understanding (Driscoll, Klein, & Sherman, 1994; Branch, 1994; Earle, 1994b).

- Mental planning and imagery play key roles in teacher planning (Earle, 1992b, 1995; Reiser, 1994; Reiser & Dick, 1996).

- Teachers have a skimpy knowledge of learning theory as an underlying framework for instruction and are unable to see instruction from a systems or ID perspective (Kennedy, 1994). Teachers do not employ a systematic planning model (i.e. a classical ID model) (Reiser, 1997).

- The scientific bases of teaching need to be validated as essential precursors of the art of teaching (Earle, 1994b).

- ID models need to be modified in the light of teacher practice (Earle, 1994b; Moallem & Applefield, 1997). "If instructional designers hope to have any input on teacher education, they face the challenge of modifying strict instructional design principles and theory into models that will be helpful to the practice of teaching" (Earle & Sheffield, 1995, p. 215; Martin, 1990; Reiser & Radford, 1990).

- Experienced teachers work from plans that are much sketchier than the detailed plans prepared by novice teachers (Reiser, 1995).

- Teachers' written objectives are very brief and often obtained from existing sources (Reiser, 1995). They are early considerations in teacher planning (Branch, Rahardjo, & Randall, 1995; Earle, 1992a, 1996, 1997). They do not play a major role in teacher planning (Reiser, 1997). Teachers often plan instructional activities without thinking about objectives first (Reiser, 1995).

- Planning is important to teachers. It is driven more by content and learner characteristics than objectives. It does not occur in a linear fashion (Reiser, 1997; Earle, 1996).

- Introducing ID principles to preservice teachers results in enhanced perceptions about what is important in teacher planning routines (Branch, Rahardjo, & Randall, 1995).

- The crucial elements of planning included goals, learner analysis, objectives, activities and strategies. These aspects are addressed formally and in written plans (Earle, 1996).

- Initial planning decisions center around content and objectives, while most planning time is spent on content, materials, and activities (Earle, 1996).

- Training teachers in ID competencies enhances their planning routines and student academic achievement (Darwazeh, 1995).

- Teachers use modified ID principles in their planning processes (Reiser, Branch, & Earle, 1995; Earle 1994a).

- Teachers who receive formal training in the use of a systematic planning model are likely to employ it as they engage in written and planning activities (Reiser & Mory, 1991).

This summary of research outcomes on ID and teacher planning is intended to generate questions as well as, perhaps, provide answers and suggest future directions. I've tried to be comprehensive in reflecting on ID inquiries into teacher planning, but I've probably over-looked some related studies addressing these issues. However, this overview should provide a flavor of what is happening in current research efforts.

THE BOTTOM LINE: SYNERGISM

What are the needs of teachers? What contributions can classical ID theory and practice make to teacher planning and student learning? How can we complement, supplement, or improve the processes recorded in the teacher planning literature? What can we learn from teachers and the processes they implement to facilitate learning? As you can see from the preceding summary of research outcomes, we've only just begun to scratch the surface of these questions—often with ambiguous results. Where do we proceed from here? Instead of strug-gling with the diverse aspects of our relationship, we should, as in the case of siblings separated in infancy, focus on reuniting the "family" in the common vision we share to enhance the quality of teaching and learning.

Almost making it, or coming close enough, won't work here. My childhood friends and I enjoyed swinging on a rope across a creek. It was thrilling to make it across to the other side. Occasionally, however, we didn't quite make it to the other side and splashed into the water below. It didn't matter whether we were inches or feet short of the other bank; almost wasn't close enough to avoid the soaking. Complete collaboration between ID and teacher education is essential; otherwise we face an outcome where "almost" is still dysfunctional.

Synergism occurs through the "cooperative action of discrete agencies such that the total effect is greater than the sum of the two or more effects taken independently" (Gove et al., 1986). For example, in framing a house, an 8' vertical 2" x 4" stud will support a load of 615 lbs. However, if two such studs are bonded together, the combined load able to be borne is 2,460 lbs.—an exponential effect. Thus could be the effect with the bonding of instructional design and teacher planning.

While many teacher educators view instructional design skills as important, few teacher education programs offer courses that would provide opportunities for preservice teachers to develop ID competencies (Snelbecker, 1987). Our challenge is to connect with teacher education programs and teachers so together we will bridge the gap between the theory of instructional design and the practice of teaching, developing practical models and principles to reach our common goal of enhancing teaching and learning.

For a successful venture into the area of teacher preparation and professional develop-ment, we need to first seek to understand what's happening in schools and teacher education, then develop a common language and understanding, and finally seek to be understood in order to overcome the perceptions of teachers about the low credibility of ID interventions. It is crucial that ID skills be merged with teacher planning practices as essential elements in the preservice and in-service preparation of classroom teachers, because, as our experiences indicate, teachers teach the way they're taught. As a field we have the power to make this synergistic dream come true.

Discovery is seeing what everybody else has seen,
and thinking what nobody else has thought.

Albert Szent-Gyorgi

REFERENCES

Andrews, D. H., and Goodson, L. A. (1980). Comparative analysis of models of instructional design. *Journal of Instructional Development 3*(4), 2-16.

Anglin, G. J., ed. (1995). *Instructional technology: Past, present, and future.* Englewood, CO: Libraries Unlimited.

Applefield, J. M. (1992). Knowledge structure, lesson planning, and teacher performance. *The 14th Annual Proceeding of Selected Research and Development Presentations.* Washington, DC: AECT Publications.

Banathy, B. H. (1991). *Educational systems design: A journey to create the future.* Englewood Cliffs, NJ: Educational Technology Publications.

Beilby, A. E. (1974). Instructional development in the public schools—whose job? *Educational Technology 24*(1), 11-16.

Borko, H. (1990). Teachers' thinking about instruction. *Remedial and Special Education 11*(8), 40-49, 53.

Branch, R. C. (1994). Common instructional design practices employed by secondary school teachers. *Educational Technology 34*(3), 25-33.

Branch, R. C. (1996). Validating instructional design in schools: A teacher planning inventory. Paper presented at the annual meeting of the Association for Educational Communications and Technology, Indianapolis, IN.

Branch, R. C., Darwazeh, A., and El-Hindi, A. E. (1992). Instructional design practices and teacher planning routines. *The 14th Annual Proceeding of Selected Research and Development Presentations.* Washington, DC: AECT Publications.

Branch, R. C., Rahardjo, S., and Randall, J. P. (1995). Perceptions of preservice teachers as instructional designers. Paper presented at the annual meeting of the Association for Educational Communications and Technology, Anaheim, CA.

Branson, R. K. (1987). Why schools can't improve: The upper-limit hypothesis. *Journal of Instructional Development 10*(4), 15-26.

Burkman, E. (1987). Prospects for instructional systems design in the public schools. *Journal of Instructional Development 10*(4), 27-32.

Carnahan, R. S. (1980). *The effects of teacher planning on classroom processes.* (Technical Report No. 541). Madison, WI: Wisconsin Research and Development Center for Individualized Schooling.

Clark, C., and Lampert, M. (1986). The study of teacher thinking: Implications for teacher education. *Journal of Teacher Education 37*(5), 27-31.

Clark, C. M. (1983). Research on teacher planning: An inventory of the knowledge base. In *Essential knowledge for beginning educators,* ed. D. C. Smith. Washington, DC: American Association of Colleges of Teacher Education.

Clark, C. M. (1988). Asking the right questions about teacher preparation: Contributions of research on teacher thinking. *Educational Research 17*(2), 5-12.

Clark, C. M., and Peterson, P. L. (1986). Teachers' thought processes. In *Handbook of research on teaching,* ed. M. C. Wittrock. New York: Macmillan.

Clark, C. M., and Yinger, R. J. (1977). Research on teacher thinking. *Curriculum Inquiry 7*(4), 279-304.

Clark, C. M., and Yinger, R. J. (1978). *Research on teacher thinking.* (Research Series No. 12). East Lansing, MI: Michigan State University.

Clark, C. M., and Yinger, R. J. (1979). *Three studies of teacher planning.* (Research Series No. 55). East Lansing, MI: Michigan State University.

Clark, F. E., and Angert, J. F. (1980). Instructional design and research on teacher education. Paper presented at the annual meeting of the Southwest Educational Research Association, San Antonio, TX.

Cooper, P.A. (1993). Paradigm shifts in designed instruction. *Educational Technology 33*(5), 12-19.

Crosswhite, F. J. (1970). Implications for teacher planning. *National Council of Teachers of Mathematics Yearbook.* Washington, DC: NCTM, 313-36.

Darwazeh, A. (1995). The effect of training in instructional designer competencies on teachers' planning routines and their students' academic achievement. *14th Annual Proceedings of Selected Research and Development Presentations.* Washington, DC: AECT Publications.

Darwazeh, A., Branch, R. C., and El-Hindi, A. E. (1991). The influence of instructional designer competencies on teacher planning routines. Paper presented at the annual conference of the Association for Educational Communications and Technology, Orlando, FL.

Dick. W. (1993). Enhanced ISD: A response to changing environments for learning and performance. *Educational Technology 33*(2), 12-16.

Driscoll, M. P., Klein, J. D., and Sherman, G. P. (1994). Perspectives on instructional planning: How do teachers and instructional designers conceive of ISD planning practices? *Educational Technology 34*(3), 34-42.

Duffy, T. M., and Jonassen, D. H. (1992). *Constructivism and the technology of instruction: A conversation.* Hillsdale, NJ: Lawrence Erlbaum.

Earle, R. S. (1985). Teachers as instructional developers. *Educational Technology 25*(8),15-18.

Earle, R. S. (1992a). The use of instructional design skills in the mental and written planning processes of teachers. *The 1992 Proceedings of Selected Research and Development Presentations.* Washington, DC: AECT Publications.

Earle, R. S. (1992b). Talk about teaching: Fingers in the dike or bridge to reform? *Educational Technology 32*(12), 23-35.

Earle, R. S. (1994a). Spontaneously systematic or systematically spontaneous? The application of instructional design, mental imagery, and metaphors in the planning and delivery practices of elementary school teachers. Paper presented at the annual meeting of the Association for Educational Communications and Technology, Nashville, TN.

Earle, R. S. (1994b). Instructional design and the classroom teacher: Looking back and moving ahead. *Educational Technology 34*(3), 6-10.

Earle, R. S. (1995). Imagery and metaphors: Windows to teaching and learning. *Educational Technology 35*(4) 52-59.

Earle, R. S. (1996). Instructional design fundamentals as elements of teacher planning processes: Perspectives and practices from two studies. *Eighteenth Proceedings of Selected Research and Development Presentations.* Washington, DC: Association for Educational Communications and Technology.

Earle, R. S. (1997). Teacher planning and instructional design: Distant relatives or kissing cousins? Paper presented at the annual meeting of the Association for Educational Communications and Technology, Albuquerque, NM.

Earle, R. S., and Sheffield, C. J. (1995). Changes in ID fundamentals: Implications for teacher education. In *Instructional design fundamentals: A reconsideration,* ed. B. B. Seels. Englewood Cliffs, NJ: Educational Technology Publications.

Engler, D. (1972). Instructional technology and the curriculum. In *Technology in education: Challenge and change,* ed. F. J. Pula and R. J. Goff. Worthington, OH: Charles A. Jones.

Fishman, B. J., and Duffy, T. M. (1992). Classroom restructuring: What do teachers really need? *Educational Technology Research and Development 40*(3), 95-111.

Floden, R. E., and Klinzing, H. G. (1990). What can research on teacher thinking contribute to teacher preparation? A second opinion. *Educational Research 19*(5), 15-20.

Frick, J. W. (1991). A systems view of restructuring education. In *Comprehensive systems design: A new educational technology,* ed. C. M. Reigeluth. Berlin: Springer-Verlag.

Gabehart, M. E. (1992). A systemic and systematic approach to public school restructuring. Paper presented at the annual conference of the Association for Educational Communications and Technology, Washington, DC.

Gove, P. B., et al., eds. (1986). *Webster's third new international dictionary.* Springfield, MA: Merriam-Webster.

Gustafson, K. L. (1993). Instructional design fundamentals: Clouds on the horizon. *Educational Technology 33*(2), 27-32.

Heinich, R. (1995). The proper study of instructional technology. In *Instructional technology: Past, present, and future*, ed. G. A. Anglin. Englewood, CO: Libraries Unlimited.

Hunter, M. (1979). Teaching is decision making. *Educational Leadership 37*(1), 62-67.

Jenlink, P., Reigeluth, C., Carr, A., and Nelson, L. (1997). Guidance for the systemic change process. Paper presented at the annual meeting of the Association for Educational Communications and Technology, Albuquerque, NM.

Jonassen, D. H. (1994). Toward a constructivist design model. *Educational Technology 34*(4), 34-37.

Jonassen, D. H., et al. (1997). Certainty, determinism, and predictability in theories of instructional design: Lessons from science. *Educational Technology 37*(1), 27-34.

Kennedy, M. F. (1994). Instructional design or personal heuristics in classroom instructional planning. *Educational Technology 34*(3), 17-24.

Kerr, S. T. (1981). How teachers design their materials: Implications for instructional design. *Instructional Science 10*, 363-78.

Kerr, S. T. (1989). Technology, teachers, and the search for school reform. *Educational Technology Research and Development 37*(4), 5-17.

Klein, J. D. (1991). Preservice teacher use of learning and instructional design principles. *Educational Technology Research and Development 39*(3), 83-89.

Lampert, M., and Clark, C. M. (1990). Expert knowledge and expert thinking on teaching: A response to Floden and Klinzing. *Educational Research 19*(5), 21-23, 42.

Martin, B. L. (1990). Teachers' planning processes: Does ISD make a difference? *Performance Improvement Quarterly 3*(4), 53-73.

Martin, B. L., and Clemente, R. (1990). Instructional systems design and public schools. *Educational Technology Research and Development 38*(2), 61-75.

McCutcheon, G. (1980). How do elementary school teachers plan? The nature of planning and influences on it. *The Elementary School Journal 81*(1), 4-23.

Mitchell, J., and Marland, P. (1989). Research on teacher thinking: The next phase. *Teaching and Teacher Education 5*(2), 115-28.

Moallem, M. (1994a). An experienced teacher's model of thinking and teaching: An ethnographic study on teacher cognition. Paper presented at the annual meeting of the Association for Educational Communications and Technology, Nashville, TN.

Moallem, M. (1994b). On the social construction of an experienced teacher. Paper presented at the annual meeting of the American Educational Research Association, New Orleans, LA.

Moallem, M. (1996). Instructional design models and research in teacher thinking: Toward a new conceptual model for research and development. Paper presented at the annual meeting of the Association for Educational Communications and Technology, Indianapolis, IN.

Moallem, M., and Applefield, J. (1997). Instructional systems design and preservice teachers' processes of thinking, teaching, and planning: What do they learn and how do they change? Paper presented at the annual meeting of the Association for Educational Communication and Technology. Albuquerque, NM.

Morine-Dershimer, G. (1977). What's in a plan? Stated and unstated plans for lessons. Paper presented at the annual meeting of the American Educational Research Association, New York.

Morine-Dershimer, G. (1978-1979). Planning and classroom reality: An in-depth look. *Educational Research Quarterly 3*(4), 83-99.

Morine-Dershimer, G. (1991). Learning to think like a teacher. *Teaching and Teacher Education 7*(2), 159-68.

Morse, R. (1977). Non-linear instructional design models. Paper presented at the annual meeting of the Association for Educational Communications and Technology, Albuquerque, NM.

National Commission for Excellence in Education. (1983). *A nation at risk: The imperative for educational reform*. Washington, DC: U.S. Department of Education.

40 / The Profession

Neale, D. C., Pace, A. J., and Case, A. B. (1983). The influence of training, experience, and organizational environment on teachers' use of the systematic planning model. Paper presented at the annual meeting of the American Educational Research Association, Montreal.

Peterson, P. L., and Comeaux, M. A. (1987). Teachers schemata for classroom events: The mental scaffolding of teachers' thinking during classroom instruction. *Teaching and Teacher Education* 3(4), 319-31.

Peterson, P. L., Marx, R. W., and Clark, C. M. (1978). Teacher planning, teacher behavior, and student achievement. *American Educational Research Journal 15*, 417-32.

Reigeluth, C. M. (1987). The search for meaningful reform: A third-wave educational system. *Journal of Instructional Development 10*(4), 3-14.

Reigeluth, C. M. (1992). The imperative for systematic change. *Educational Technology 22*(11), 9-13.

Reigeluth, C. M. (1996). A new paradigm of ISD? *Educational Technology 36*(3), 13-20.

Reigeluth, C. M. (1997). Instructional theory, practitioner needs, and new directions: Some reflections. *Educational Technology 37*(1), 42-47.

Reigeluth, C. M., and Garfinkle, R. J. (1992). Envisioning a new system of education. *Educational Technology 32*(11), 17-23.

Reiser, R. A. (1988). Instructional designers in public schools and higher education. *Journal of Instructional Development 11*(3), 3-6.

Reiser, R. A. (1994). Examining the planning practices of teachers: Reflections on three years of research. *Educational Technology 34*(3), 11-16.

Reiser, R. A. (1995). Teacher planning research: Findings and implications. Paper presented at the annual meeting of the Association for Educational Communications and Technology, Anaheim, CA.

Reiser, R. A. (1997). Do "expert" teachers employ systematic instructional planning procedures? Paper presented at the annual meeting of the Association for Educational Communications and Technology, Albuquerque, NM.

Reiser, R. A., and Dick, W. (1996). Teacher planning and instructional design. Paper presented at the annual meeting of the Association for Educational Communications and Technology, Indianapolis, IN.

Reiser, R. A., and Mory, E. H. (1991). An examination of the systematic planning techniques of two experienced teachers. *Educational Technology Research and Development 39*(3), 71-82.

Reiser, R. A., and Radford, J. M. (1990). Preparing preservice teachers to use the systems approach. *Performance Improvement Quarterly 3*(4), 40-52.

Reiser, R. A., Branch, R. C., and Earle, R. S. (1995). Teaching, planning and instructional design: Do teachers use ID principles? Symposium presented at the annual meeting of the Association for Educational Communications and Technology, Anaheim, CA.

Reiser, R. A., Branch, R. C., and Earle, R. S. (1996). A symposium on teacher use of instructional design principles. Presented at the annual conference of the Association for Educational Communications and Technology, Indianapolis, IN.

Richey, R. C. (1993). Instructional design theory and a changing field. *Educational Technology 33*(2), 16-21.

Richey, R. C. (1997). Agenda-building and its implications for theory construction. *Educational Technology 37*(1), 5-11.

Saettler, P. (1968). *A history of instructional technology.* New York: McGraw-Hill.

Saettler, P. (1991). *The evaluation of American educational technology.* Englewood, CO: Libraries Unlimited.

Salisbury, D. J. (1992). Designing and implementing new models of schooling. *International Journal of Educational Research 19*(2), 133-143.

Sardo, D. (1982). Teacher planning styles in the middle school. Paper presented to the Eastern Educational Research Association, Ellenville, NY.

Sardo-Brown, D. (1988). Twelve middle school teachers' planning. *Elementary School Journal 89*(1), 69-89.

Schiffman, S. S. (1987). Influencing public education: A "window of opportunity" through school library media centers. *Journal of Instructional Development 10*(4), 41-44.

Seels, B. B. (1997). Taxonomic issues and the development of theory in instructional technology. *Educational Technology 37*(1), 12-21.

Shrock, S. A. (1995). A brief history of instructional development. In *Instructional technology. Past, present, and future*, ed. G. A. Anglin. Englewood, CO: Libraries Unlimited.

Shrock, S. A., and Byrd, D. M. (1987). An instructional development look at staff development in the public schools. *Journal of Instructional Development 10*(4), 45-53.

Snelbecker, G. E. (1987). Instructional design skills for classroom teachers. *Journal of Instructional Development 10*(4), 33-40.

Stolovitch, H. D. (1980). Instructional technology and its challenge to teacher training. *NSPI Journal 20*(6), 17-19.

Taguchi, M. (1992). Images of teachers in the instructional systems design literature over time. Unpublished doctoral dissertation, Florida State University.

Tessmer, M., and Richey, R. C. (1997). The role of context in learning and instructional design. Paper presented at the annual meeting of the Association for Educational Communications and Technology, Albuquerque, NM.

Tessmer, M., and Wedman, J. F. (1990). A layers of necessity model of instructional development model. *Educational Technology Research and Development 38*(2), 77-85.

Tyler, R. W. (1949). *Basic principles of curriculum and instruction.* Chicago: University of Chicago Press.

Udvari-Solner, A. (1996). Examining teacher thinking: Constructing a process to design curricular adaptations. *Remedial and Special Education 17*(4), 245-54.

Willis, J. (1995). A recursive, reflective instructional design model based on constructivist-interpretivist theory. *Educational Technology 35*(6), 5-23.

Wilson, B. G. (1997a). *Constructivist learning environments.* Englewood Cliffs, NJ: Educational Technology Publications.

Wilson, B. G. (1997b). Thoughts on theory in educational technology. *Educational Technology 37*(1), 22-27.

Winn, W. (1997). Advantages of a theory-based curriculum in instructional technology. *Educational Technology 37*(1), 34-41.

Yelon, S. L. (1980). Instructional technology and teacher training courses. *NSPI Journal 20*(6), 20-25.

Yinger, R. J. (1977). A study of teacher planning: Description and theory development using ethnographic and information processing methods. Unpublished doctoral dissertation, Michigan State University.

Zahorik, J. A. (1975). Teachers' planning models. *Educational Leadership 33*(2), 134-39.

Part Three
Current Developments

Introduction

One of the goals of the *Educational Media and Technology Yearbook* is to present up-to-date information on new developments in the field. This year's volume focuses on developing media as tools for learning science reading and Internet basics. While this section attempts to be comprehensive in its review of current developments, the range of topics is not exhaustive. A most illustrative example of current developments in educational media and technology is the propagation of the World Wide Web and the vast amount of information available via the Internet.

This section features reviews of interactive multimedia reviews (a type of metaanalysis), lessons learned from the sciences about interactive multimedia, technology tools for literacy learning, and the bread and butter of the Internet. The authors for this part represent teachers, students, professors, network information specialists, virtual librarians, and administrators from all levels of educational institutions. They are as follows:

John D. Emerson

Frederick Mosteller

Ann Watts Pailliotet

Nancy Morgan

Roy Tennant

Dave Lankes

The topics presented in Part 3 clearly indicate the way educational media and *technology* can be used as tools to support learning. Furthermore, while *instructional* technology and *educational* technology may connote different meanings, the *Educational Media and Technology Yearbook* serves as a forum where all such issues and innovations are discussed.

Robert Maribe Branch

Interactive Multimedia in College Teaching. Part I
A Ten-Year Review of Reviews

John D. Emerson
Department of Mathematics and Computer Science, Middlebury College

Frederick Mosteller
Professor Emeritus, Department of Statistics, Harvard University

ABSTRACT

Rapid technological change has led to new generations of computer software offering convenient user access and powerful features that create an interactive learning environment. Reviews and research syntheses published from 1987 through 1996 provide the raw material for this report.

This paper addresses two main questions:

1. Does using interactive multimedia technologies lead to increased learning by college students?

2. Which uses of these technologies hold the greatest promise for college teachers?

Empirical findings answer "yes" to the first question; the evidence indicates that multimedia technology can help teachers achieve modest yet valuable gains in student learning. As yet, computers have delivered no great breakthrough in college instruction. Only now has research begun to address the second question. The findings thus far suggest that software with the following characteristics has a good chance of enhancing knowledge acquisition and improving retention of what is learned. Such software:

encourages the user to be an active participant, not just a passive observer;

invites the user to make choices about a learning sequence, and informs the learner about choices made by the program;

simultaneously engages the learner's multiple senses with video, sound, or animation; and

creates or supports collaboration among learners.

INTRODUCTION

This paper focuses on empirical research about college-level instruction that uses interactive multimedia programs. It acknowledges the further rapid advances in technology since the mid-1980s by concentrating on reviews and research syntheses that have appeared since 1987. It organizes and integrates research findings, and it gives special attention to findings based on syntheses of carefully designed empirical studies carried out as an integral part of college courses. Finally, it interprets these research findings so as to offer advice for college teachers.

Multimedia teaching programs combine the use of some of these features: sound, color graphics, animation, excerpts from movies, traditional text display, and active participation by the user. Often the learner has much control over the path taken through the software program.

Some colleges and universities deliver (or promise to deliver) access to campus-wide, and indeed worldwide, computing resources in each dormitory room. In principle, at least, these developments can assist in providing computer-based instruction to students on an individual basis. Thus, they offer the potential for substantial changes in the delivery of collegiate instruction. Yet similar past promises for emerging technologies, including audio-visual and computer equipment, have led to disappointment.

We ought to ask: What is being delivered to students, and how good is it? When does instruction using modern microcomputers work better than traditional classroom instruction? Does highly interactive software enhance learning more than did the forms of computer-assisted instruction that disappointed us in the 1970s? Can computer-driven multimedia, with its use of video, sound, animation, and nearly instantaneous access to information, fulfill its promise to improve college instruction? Or will we again face disappointments?

COMPUTER TERMINOLOGY AND BACKGROUND

This section assembles the computer terminology and abbreviations used throughout this paper. It also reviews the statistical concept of an "effect size" for measuring the typical change associated with the use of a new teaching method.

A List of Computer Terminology and Related Abbreviations

We list abbreviations used in this report in discussing applications of computer technology in teaching.

Terminology and Acronyms for Computer Instruction

AI: artificial intelligence
   the computer program "learns" from its prior interaction with the user and modifies its response accordingly

CAI: computer-assisted instruction
   any instruction that uses computers in teaching

CBI: computer-based instruction
   CAI in which the computer has a principal role in delivering the lesson

CEI: computer-enriched instruction
   CAI in which software uses simulation, artificial intelligence, etc., for higher-level intellectual tasks

CMI: computer-managed instruction
   CAI in which the computer keeps records about the instruction, administers tests, and records data

Hypermedia: combination of multimedia technology with flexible pathways through the instructional program.

IMI: interactive multimedia instruction
   CAI that uses two or more different media (text, sound, video, movies), and where what happens along the way helps determine the sequence of steps that follow

IV: interactive video
   CAI in which the learner can manipulate and respond to static or dynamic graphical images

---

Effect Size

Primary research studies that assess the effectiveness of an innovative teaching method typically compare the achievement of two or more groups of students who were instructed using different forms of instruction. Investigators ask whether the groups differ in how much and how well they have learned, so they need a reliable common examination on what is to be learned as a yardstick for making comparisons. Familiar statistics like t-tests and F-tests can tell us whether differences in average test scores are statistically significant, or whether the observed differences could have arisen by chance. Statistics can provide confidence limits for the differences of two means. Such tools, although important in answering questions about scientific hypotheses and in drawing other inferences from empirical data, do not provide easily interpreted measures of the differences seen among groups that got different forms of instruction.

Another statistic, called an "effect size," offers a way of comparing that is sometimes more practical; it may help us begin to address the issue of "practical effect," just as t-tests address "statistical significance." An effect size is not a statistical test but one way to report a difference in outcome between two groups or treatments being compared. Although the concept of an effect size is rather general, we describe it as it applies to averages of scores on examinations.

Effect Size

To calculate an effect size for a new teaching method, we begin by finding the difference between the average examination score for the students in the group that received the innovative instruction, and the average score for the students in the control group (or in some other comparison group). The effect size is then obtained by dividing this difference in averages by the standard deviation of the scores from the control group. Thus, an effect size is a measure of the average gain (or loss, when the difference is negative) associated with the innovative teaching method, with the measure reported relative to the natural variability of the test scores from students getting the regular form of instruction. The effect size is an average gain measured in standard deviation units of the scores in the control group.

Here is an example to illustrate how we interpret an effect size. Suppose that a teaching program using hypermedia technology gives an average gain of 4 points. Suppose also that the group taught in the traditional way has a standard deviation of 8. The effect size (ES) for the new instructional program is then:

$$ES = 4/8 = .5$$

This means that the average student in the group getting the new form of instruction scored .5 standard deviation units above the middle student in the traditional group. For the kinds of distributions usually met in practice, the average student in the experimental group scored higher on the examination than did 69 percent of the students in the traditional group. The new instruction enabled the average student to score at the 69th percentile, whereas the average student would have been at the 50th percentile when instructed in the traditional way.

Study Design and Materials

We searched systematically for research articles and review articles about college-level instruction that uses interactive software and computer-driven multimedia. Appendix I describes our search strategies and inclusion criteria and the materials that they produced.

Our searches provided more than 500 potentially relevant research articles, reports, and books that have appeared since 1990. Altogether, we read and abstracted information from 130 articles, reports, and chapters, with 126 of these appearing since 1990. We summarize in the box below the categories of articles used; Appendix I provides the details and the rationale for the classification.

Results from Searches for Literature About Computers and College Teaching

Description	Number of Articles
Articles identified by searches and other means	500+
Articles identified for reading and extraction of information	130
Mutually exclusive categories of articles:	
Research syntheses and review articles since 1987	22
Primary controlled research in classroom setting since 1990	47
Primary controlled research not in classroom setting	33
Computing environments, learning environments	14
Descriptive, theoretical, philosophical, advocacy	12
Statistical methods and methods for research synthesis	2
Subtotal	130

PRINCIPLE FINDINGS FOR COMPUTER-ASSISTED INSTRUCTION (CAI)

Most review articles and quantitative research syntheses (meta-analyses) since the late 1960s consider instruction at different levels and do not restrict their attention to college-level teaching. Niemiec and Walberg (1987) published a synthesis of these studies through 1985, and as our point of departure we summarize their findings about traditional computer uses in college teaching. The following section turns to findings from research synthesis and review articles that are specific for interactive video and interactive multimedia.

Synthesis by Niemiec and Walberg

Niemiec and Walberg (1987) located 16 reviews, and five of these concentrated on the college level. Although most of the reviews considered primary research from many disciplines, a few focused on a particular area (e.g., the sciences). By integrating findings from the 16 reviews they estimate the average effect size for computer-assisted college teaching as .26. This value means that the typical student taught using CAI would achieve at a level that outperforms 60 percent of the college students (instead of 50 percent) who are conventionally taught.

Niemiec and Walberg found that CAI tended to give larger positive effects at lower educational levels (average ES=.32 at high school level; ES=.46 at the elementary level; and ES=.56 in special education settings for handicapped students). Kulik and Kulik (1991) interpret these findings as indicating that CAI has been "less successful in teaching the higher order skills emphasized at higher educational levels." Later in this section we discuss recent research findings that may challenge this interpretation.

Niemiec and Walberg also note that for microcomputer-based studies at the college level, the average effect size is larger, at .43 (equivalent to the 67th percentile). They speculate that this difference in the effects may mean that microcomputers are more effective in bringing about achievement or alternatively that it may be attributable to their novelty in the early and mid 1980s.

Meta-Analyses of Kulik and Kulik

James Kulik, Chen-Lin Kulik, and their colleagues conducted many meta-analyses of CBI. Their 1987 report integrated the findings from 199 primary research studies that had been the focus of four meta-analyses already conducted by their team. They updated this report in 1991 by expanding it to 254 studies meeting their inclusion criteria, and we rely on this more recent study.

Kulik and Kulik (1991) found that the average effect for computer-based instruction at all educational levels was to raise examination scores by .30 standard deviations, or equivalently, for the middle student, from the 50th to the 62d percentile. They further report that students who used CBI liked their classes better (average ES=.28 based on N=22 effect sizes) and had more positive attitudes toward computers (ES=.34, N=19), but that their attitudes toward subject matter differed little from those of the students in the traditional classes (ES=.05, N=34).

An especially noteworthy finding was that the CBI groups needed less instructional time; on the average, students in 32 investigations of this point used only 70 percent as much instructional time as students in conventional classes. All of these studies were at the college level.

Kulik and Kulik examined the impact of study characteristics on their findings. Effects were larger in published than in unpublished studies, possibly because reviewers, journal editors, and authors like to publish statistically significant results. Effects were larger in studies where different teachers taught experimental and control classes; perhaps the more effective teachers tend to teach the classes with the innovative computer instruction. Effects were larger in studies of short duration, possibly because the learning outcomes measured in these studies are more readily influenced by computer intervention than are the outcomes measured at the end of an entire course or year of study. An alternate explanation is that shorter studies are subject to greater variability in their measured effects. Of course, other explanations are worth considering.

The findings of Kulik and Kulik did not confirm earlier suggestions that using microcomputers gives larger gains than using mainframe computers. Similarly, they did not corroborate findings that the effects of CBI are improving over time.

Some of the Kuliks's work used primary research reports that addressed a wide range of disciplines at the college level; the sciences, social sciences, mathematics, and technical areas were well represented. Based on 101 studies of achievement gains in college instruction, they found an average effect size of .26, a finding that coincided with that of Niemiec and Walberg (1987). When they considered a subcategory of CEI (which includes uses of the computer as a calculator, as a programming tool, and in simulation), they found that college students and adults experience larger achievement gains (ES=.34, N=35) than do school children (ES=.10, N=18). This finding might mean that older learners benefit more than younger learners from computer uses involving relatively complex intellectual activities. It could also mean simply that people who go to college are better at this kind of learning than those who haven't attended college. In either event, the gains for college students from CEI (ES=.34, N=35) were not different from the gains when CMI (ES=.43, N=17) or CAI (ES=.27, N=97) were used to aid instruction in college courses.

In sum, Kulik and Kulik (1986) characterize CAI in college-level courses as giving "moderate positive contributions to student learning." They conclude, "It is clear that the computer can teach satisfactorily while reducing time spent in instruction." (pp. 90-91)

Summary of Findings for Traditional Computer-Assisted Instruction

We summarize some recent findings about traditional computer-assisted instruction. In addition to drawing on the reports already cited, we rely on other research studies, including research syntheses, for additional findings about features of computer-assisted instruction that enhance its effectiveness.

Findings from Research Synthesis

1. Traditional computer-assisted instruction gives modest, yet valuable, gains in achievement as measured on course examinations.

This finding seems widely accepted (Niemiec and Walberg, 1987; Kulik and Kulik, 1991; Cohen and Dacanay, 1992), and it holds for CAI both in general and in college-level teaching. Cohen and Dacanay report an average effect size of .41 for 37 studies of CAI in college-level courses in the health professions. Fletcher-Flinn and Gravatt report effect sizes of .24 using 120 studies at all educational levels, and .20 for 48 studies in all fields of college-level instruction. Their report finds no learning benefit for CAI when the control group used manual instruments or a paper-and-pencil version of CAI materials; they conclude that what accounts for learning gains for CAI is the better quality of instruction provided by the CAI materials rather than the use of computers per se.

2. Students at all levels who experience traditional computer-assisted instruction have positive attitudes about their instruction (and possibly about computers).

The average effect sizes and numbers of effects for this comparison are: ES=.28, N=22 (Kulik and Kulik, 1991); ES=.30, N=34 (Cohen and Dacanay, 1992); ES=.50, N=10 (Fletcher-Flinn and Gravatt, 1995); and not reported (Niemiec and Walberg, 1987). Kulik and Kulik also report that attitudes about computers may be enhanced by CAI (ES=.34, N=19), but here the recent research synthesis of Fletcher-Flinn and Gravatt finds a positive effect size of only .07 (N=7).

3. Students who receive computer-assisted instruction may need less instructional time.

As noted already, Kulik and Kulik (1991) report that CAI requires 70 percent as much time as does traditional classroom learning for similar learning tasks. Cohen and Dacanay (1992) examine time efficiency and report no statistically significant benefit for CBI based on nine studies. They mention that those CBI-instructed groups needing substantially more instructional time were those whose teachers paced the instruction; we note that this finding need not imply criticism of teachers, because good teachers may use the added time in ways that encourage deeper or broader understanding.

Goforth (1994) found a positive relationship between increased learner control over an instructional sequence and efficiency gains in learning times; see item 5 in this list.

4. Providing feedback to the learner is valuable. Diagnostic and prescriptive management strategies for computer-assisted instruction provide effective feedback.

Azevedo and Bernard (1995) published a research synthesis of 22 studies at all education levels about the effects of feedback in CAI. They found that when a posttest is given immediately after instruction the effect size gain for computer feedback is substantial, at .80. They also found that it is important that the computer program report to the student both the correctness of the user's answer and the underlying causes of error.

In a meta-analysis of 58 effect sizes from 40 reports, Bangert-Drowns et al. (1991) found that error correction is a primary benefit of feedback and that feedback may be more important when the content is more complex. Kulik and Kulik (1988) found that immediate feedback is superior to delayed feedback when performance is measured by actual classroom tests (ES=.28, N=11). Clariana (1993) also reported on a research synthesis whose findings (ES=.56, N=16) support the importance of feedback as a valuable feature of CAI. Cohen and Dacaney (1992) found that two studies in the health sciences with the largest effect sizes (ES 2) were those in which students received immediate computer feedback with a correct answer and an explanation of the answer.

5. Providing the learner with some level of control in a computer-learning environment, along with clear information and advice about choices to be made, can support successful learning outcomes.

Goforth (1994) reported on a research synthesis of 44 studies of learner control in CAI. He found that some amount of learner control in a computing environment is beneficial, and that there is value in communicating explicitly to the learner about program control. The learner benefits from knowing where the control and decisions rest—that is, whether the learner or the program has control at a particular point in the program.

Goforth's findings do not suggest placing unlimited program control in the user's hands; rather, they indicate that the learner can benefit by receiving adaptive advice from the program and a clear explanation of alternatives. Goforth concludes, "Control decisions need to be informed ones." (p. 20)

Goforth also asked about possible gains in learning efficiency. Among the 44 papers in his research synthesis, 19 studies examined time on task for learners, and 11 of the 19 found a statistically significant reduction in learning time from increased learner control of the instruction sequence (Goforth, 1994). Only one primary study found that providing learner control over the instructional sequence led to increased instructional time needed for successful learning, but that study indicated that times can improve when the decisions about learner control are made explicit.

6. In college-level learning, computer-assisted instruction may afford greater learning gains when higher-order and more complex intellectual tasks are taught.

In their meta-analysis of computer-based instruction in the health professions, Cohen and Dacanay (1992) found that "computer-enriched instruction," which is defined to include simulation, artificial intelligence software, and other forms of software that require high levels of student reasoning, led to an effect size of .65 in 19 studies and .79 in 15 published studies of CEI; other types of software that involve drill and practice and tutoring produced an effect size of .15 (N=16).

Grimes and Ray (1993) reviewed the use of microcomputers in college economics courses; they reported that computerized instruction is most effective when simulation programs are used, but they also found benefits from computer drills. However, Fletcher-Flinn and Gravatt (1995), whose research synthesis includes primary research at all educational levels, found almost the same effect size for simulation programs (ES=.25, N=25) as for drill and practice (ES=.23, N=46).

> 7. *Mastery learning is an effective method of instruction, and it can take good advantage of computer-assisted instruction.*

Mastery learning requires the learner to attain a prespecified level of mastery of the contents of each unit of instruction before proceeding to the next unit. For example, a teaching program might permit a student to go on to the next chapter only after scoring 85 percent or more on an end-of-chapter quiz.

The literature on mastery learning is extensive; we refer to the classic works by Gagné (1985) and Torshen (1977) for detailed background and discussion of mastery learning. Walberg (1984) observed that separate syntheses of mastery programs in science show an average effect of 0.8. Kulik, Kulik, and Bangert-Drowns (1990) reported a meta-analysis for mastery learning in which they found an average effect size of .4 when mastery is set at 70 to 85 percent, and an average effect size of .8 when mastery is set at 100 percent. (With complicated learning tasks, we wonder whether most students can achieve 100 percent mastery and thus have a chance to achieve these impressive gains.) Spencer (1991, p. 18) summarized findings from research and meta-analysis about mastery learning: "These methods are certainly producing significant educational effects. . . ."

PRINCIPLE FINDINGS FOR INTERACTIVE MULTIMEDIA INSTRUCTION

The body of research about interactive multimedia technology is somewhat limited by its relative newness. Fletcher-Flinn and Gravatt (1995, p. 232), whose meta-analysis of CAI research included primary research published from 1987 through 1992, remarked that " . . . unfortunately our data do not include the new multimedia technology because so few studies of this type were found." This section summarizes some limited and tentative findings from research syntheses about IMI.

Potential Advantages of IMI

The apparent benefits of feedback and learner control enumerated above suggest that interactivity is a desirable attribute in educational software. Cognitive learning theory and related empirical research suggest that learning is enhanced when two or more forms of stimulus (e.g., visual and auditory) are used to convey information (Spencer, 1991).

A review article by Miech, Nave, and Mosteller (1997) found that computer-assisted [second] language learning (CALL) is more effective when two or more channels are used together. In particular, they reported that the use of captions in the language to be learned, along with voice and drama in the videos, produced substantial gains in second language learning for adults. The effectiveness of CEI using simulation programs and artificial intelligence also suggests potential gains for software that combines two or more media that interact with the user.

In her discussion of multimedia in higher education, Lamb (1992, p. 33) is optimistic:

> Multimedia classrooms can provide a stimulating environment for teaching and learning. The most obvious benefit is that a virtually limitless array of resources can be incorporated into the lesson plan, providing learning experiences that would otherwise be unavailable to students. Because multiple channels are involved, instructors can address individual learning styles. Multimedia encourages exploration, self-expression, and a feeling of ownership by allowing students to manipulate its components. Active multimedia learning environments foster communication, cooperation, and collaboration among instructor and students. Multimedia makes learning stimulating, engaging, and fun.

Lamb supports her position by citing specific benefits offered by interactive multimedia (Lamb attributes many of these items to Miller, 1990, pp. 15 and 17). We enumerate in a box those benefits that seem to apply specifically to interactive CAI and to IMI, rather than to computer-assisted instruction more generally.

Benefits for Interactive CAI and IMI

1. Multimedia learning environments offer flexibility and ease of use.

2. Instructional materials are more engaging, so learners spend more time learning.

3. Student motivation is increased because students share some of the control.

4. Feedback and involvement motivates learners.

5. Use of multiple sensory channels is more effective than the use of single channels.

6. Information has multiple links rather than being presented in a linear fashion.

7. Interaction with materials provides increased information retention.

8. Interactive environments help support mastery learning.

9. Interactive technologies can reduce learning time.

The claims for interactive multimedia instruction seem impressive, but they are rather tentative. Some (including items 3, 4, and 9) are supported by empirical research already summarized. A few other research syntheses and review articles give further support for some of these claims for IMI; we turn next to these.

Meta-Analysis of McNeil and Nelson for IVI

McNeil and Nelson (1991) synthesized the findings of 63 primary research studies of interactive video instruction (IVI) from 1978 through 1988. They defined IV as a video program in which sequence and selection of content is determined by the learner's response. Although this research predated educational uses of the newer hypermedia technology now widely available in HyperCard applications for the Macintosh environment and in parallel applications for the Windows 95 environment, it examined applications of videotape and videodisc technology that take advantage of the interactivity supported by these media.

The meta-analysis of McNeil and Nelson found studies in two main categories: studies of instructional design that explore and compare the effectiveness of different characteristics of the teaching programs; and studies that compare IVI to other, more traditional, forms of CAI. McNeil and Nelson searched for research that considered student cognitive gains, and they excluded studies that focused exclusively on such issues as student attitude, cost, and time efficiency. Their report considered instruction for students at all levels, and did not report separate findings for college-level instruction.

McNeil and Nelson found that the mean of 89 effect sizes for achievement, after correcting for some other studies, was .53 (corresponding to a gain to the 70th percentile for the median student). This result is stronger than that previously reported for traditional CAI, and McNeil and Nelson (p. 4) speculated that "Perhaps the video capabilities of IV, such as the ability to depict real-life situations, may account in part for differences in size of the effects between CAI and IV." However, McNeil and Nelson were careful not to overstate the benefits found for IVI; in the abstract of their report, they summarize the synthesis by saying, "IV can be an effective form of instruction. The effect is similar to that of computer-assisted instruction."

McNeil and Nelson found a substantial amount of variation among the effect sizes of primary studies, and they interpreted this variation as a result of the influence of "a myriad of variables that are difficult or impossible to account for in a single meta-analysis." However, their synthesis did manage to account for some sources of variability in effect sizes.

Factors that influenced the magnitude of effects from IVI included:

1. *Source of publication.* Effect sizes from published studies were larger (average ES=.74, N=40) than those from unpublished reports and dissertations (ES=.40, N=41); this finding for IVI corroborates the findings from meta-analyses of other forms of CAI (Kulik and Kulik, 1991; Cohen and Dacanay, 1992).

2. *Supplement versus replacement of instruction.* One particularly noteworthy finding was that studies using IV for supplementing instruction averaged significantly higher achievement effects (ES=.77, N=29) than did studies for which IV replaced traditional forms of instruction (ES=.36, N=64). Although IVI may not replace good teachers, it may help teachers be more effective.

3. *Type of learner control.* Program control of the instructional sequence in lessons gave significantly higher achievement effects (ES=1.20, N=12) than did learner-controlled studies (ES=.44, N=29). Similarly, when the program guided the control of review and lessons, achievement effects were higher (ES=1.09, N=8) than when the learner controlled these aspects of instruction. McNeil and Nelson (1991) concluded that after incorrectly responding to embedded questions learners benefited more from guidance or suggestions on what to review.

These findings about learner control deserve amplification. Few researchers would contest a claim that active learner involvement in the instructional process through learner interaction with the instructional program enhances learning. The findings by McNeil and Nelson suggest that there are limits to the extent of student involvement. Control that rests with the program itself, and feedback that explicitly guides the learner in choosing what to do next, appear to be more effective than giving exclusive control of the instructional sequence to the learner.

Some control by the learner may help maintain the learner's attention and active involvement; for example, the learner may be invited to choose whether to start a lesson over again, review the lesson, receive additional drill, or take a quiz that reassesses the learner's progress in that lesson. However, the program may retain control over when and under what circumstances the learner moves ahead to a new lesson. It seems wise for the program to communicate to the learner when it makes such a choice, and to convey the assessment of the learner's progress that led to that choice. McNeil and Nelson's meta-analysis suggests that such communication by the program to the learner aids the effectiveness of the interactive instruction.

Findings of Cronin and Cronin for IVI in "Soft-Skill" Areas

Cronin and Cronin (1992) reviewed and critically synthesized primary research since 1984 about interactive video instruction in "soft skills" areas; they defined these as the humanities and social sciences. They reported that IVI appears to produce significantly greater learning than linear video—videotape instruction that offers no active participation in the learning process and no feedback concerning the acquisition of new skills and knowledge. However, they acknowledged that the benefits of IVI may be attributable to the greater "time on task" sometimes associated with interactive video when learners become caught up with the video and are free to explore ideas that relate to the presentation. Thus, the medium itself may not be responsible for the additional learning gains when comparing IVI to linear video. Cronin and Cronin found that studies that control for time-on-task reveal a potential advantage of IVI:

> This technology allows learners to work at their own pace. Most studies reported that students enjoy IVI more than conventional instruction. The active participation required by well-designed interactive video instruction may motivate learners to devote more time to learning. (p. 67)

Cronin and Cronin also asked about comparisons of IVI with conventional instruction in soft skill areas. Here they were less equivocal in reporting gains for IVI. They pointed to a body of research that controlled for instructional time differences and still found significant learning gains for IVI over conventional instruction. They also found research that focused on the delivery itself by keeping the content nearly identical for two delivery systems being compared. The findings still supported the superiority of IVI, and thus they support a belief that apparent gains for IVI come from the instructional media, not from differences in content material.

Summary of Findings for Interactive Multimedia Instruction

1. Interactive multimedia instruction may promote achievement by college students somewhat more than does traditional computer-assisted instruction.

This finding is supported, at least to an extent, by the reports of McNeil and Nelson (1991), Cronin and Cronin (1992), Cronin (1993), and Fletcher (1992).

Some writers are more ambivalent in their views and their interpretations of the research literature on the benefits to learning of multimedia instruction. Burton, Moore, and Holmes (1995) presented a review in which they cite an unpublished report by Ragan, Boyce, Redwine, Savenye, and McMichael (1993); this review of 139 research studies of multimedia, mostly concerned with adult learners, concluded that multimedia is at least as effective and often more effective than traditional forms of instruction. However, Burton and his coauthors mentioned that few of the published reports were experiments, and that (in 1994) there existed little useful (randomized and controlled) research on multimedia (1995).

Slee (1989) presented a literature review in which she concluded that learning gains associated with interactive video instruction are not attributable to the medium itself, but rather to other instructional variables. This finding is at odds with the findings of Cronin and Cronin summarized above. Bosco (1990) reviewed 29 primary research studies of IV instruction; eight of these were at the college level. He was critical of the body of research; he noted that most studies were of limited duration and that, whereas gains for attitude toward IV instruction were commonplace, the assessment of *learning* gains gave mixed results.

We are cautiously optimistic in our own views about the value of multimedia instruction; research findings to date seem to indicate that interactive learning using multimedia may be effective for some learning tasks. Taking the findings as a whole, we are encouraged to believe that multimedia instruction is sometimes an improvement on traditional instruction. Although we do not find evidence for a major breakthrough in college teaching based on multimedia instruction, we think that there are indications of some benefits from this form of instruction. In particular, its flexibility sometimes encourages teachers to rethink their pedagogy and to develop new and more effective presentations of their subject material. Whether measured gains for learning derive from the new presentation of material or from the medium itself seems not important.

The empirical evidence in support of our "cautious optimism" is rather weak: it is based mainly on the opinions of researchers with few randomized controlled experiments and, indeed, few compelling studies. Thus, while there seems to be an emerging consensus of belief in the effectiveness of multimedia instruction at the college level, there is not a strong body of trustworthy experimental evidence to give high confidence in those beliefs.

> 2. *Higher levels of interactivity between the learner and the IVI computer*
> *program often are associated with improved learning outcomes.*

We note that feedback and learner control imply at least some level of interactivity. Fletcher (1992) reviewed findings both for CAI and IVI, and he examined the role of interactivity in IVI. Based on 14 primary studies of IVI in higher education, he reported an effect size of .69 (gain from 50th to 75th percentile). He identified six studies that compared different levels of activity within the same IVI materials, and found that all six studies "suggest that interactivity contributes to student achievement in interactive videodisc instruction (p. 10)." Slee (1989) also suggested that interactivity between the program and the user enhances learning, but questioned whether it does so sufficiently to warrant the frequently increased time associated with interactivity.

> 3. *The use of interactive multimedia instruction can sometimes reduce the*
> *time needed to achieve a learning goal, and it thus offers gains in efficiency.*
> *However, learners may sometimes be motivated to spend more time in a*
> *multimedia learning environment.*

Burton, Moore, and Holmes (1995) summarize research about efficiency gains for IMI, and their findings support this claim. Ragan, Boyce, Redwine, Savenye, and McMichael (1993, as cited in Burton, Jones, and Holmes, 1995) report efficiency gains of around 30 percent for instructional programs that use hypermedia technology. The meta-analysis by Cronin and Cronin (1992) also lends considerable support for this claim for IMI.

FINDINGS FOR COLLEGE TEACHERS

We conclude this review by summarizing a few practical findings that may be useful to college teachers who want to use computer technology in their own teaching.

1. Computer software can support good teaching and the efforts by teachers to further strengthen their teaching (McNeil and Nelson, 1991; Cronin and Cronin, 1992; Cronin, 1993; Fletcher, 1992). The evidence thus far does not demonstrate that computer software is a viable replacement for creative and dedicated teachers (Fletcher, 1992; McNeil and Nelson, 1991).

2. Interactive computer-assisted instruction is often more effective when it requires the learner to be an active participant in the educational process (Fletcher, 1992). Research suggests that interactive programs, when they use a well-thought-out combination of learner control, feedback to the learner, and program control, achieve their successes by helping learners become active participants in the learning process. Learner control with broad constraints on the learning sequence and ample feedback for the learner seem an ideal combination (McNeil and Nelson, 1991; Cronin and Cronin, 1991; Goforth, 1994).

3. Learning is often more successful when it uses two or more channels in engaging the student. Multimedia instruction may prove to have special advantages because it can involve multiple senses at once by combining two or more of these elements: text, dialogue, images, motion, sound, and touch (Spencer, 1991; Miech, Nave, and Mosteller, 1997).

4. Interactive computer-assisted instruction can accommodate the varying needs of individual students by letting them participate in choosing their progression through a lesson (Cronin and Cronin, 1992; Goforth, 1994).

5. Computer-assisted instruction can provide gains in learning efficiency. Successful learning can take place even when the total instructional time is reduced (Burton, Moore, and Holmes, 1995; see also Cronin and Cronin, 1992).

CONCLUSIONS

Is interactive multimedia instruction effective when used in college courses? The findings tell us that computers can help make teaching more effective in some settings and for parts of some college courses. It also reveals that students often enjoy learning interactively using multimedia technology. Although computing has often shown some gains in teaching specific things, we still do not have a great leap forward based on computer instruction, whereas in actually carrying out computations and in processing enormous amounts of data, such a leap has occurred. There is little evidence that derives from randomized and carefully controlled studies about the value of using multimedia in entire college courses. Research has yet to show us whether interactive multimedia instruction will achieve a significant breakthrough in enhancing student learning at the college level.

ACKNOWLEDGMENTS

The project was facilitated by a grant from the Andrew W. Mellon Foundation to the American Academy of Arts and Sciences in support of the Center for Evaluation of the Academy's project "Initiatives for Children."

We acknowledge gratefully the work of our research assistant, Ying Zhang, who assisted us with the computer searches and helped organize those source materials.

We appreciate receiving information, advice, and materials from the following: Jack Bookman; Cathy Crocker; Joan Garfield; Carolyn Kotlas; Carl Leinbach; David M. Mathews; George McCabe; Edward Miech; Bill Nave; Kent L. Norman; Marjorie Olson; Mary Parker; Allan J. Rossman; Richard Schaeffer; Keith E. Schwingendorf; David A. Smith; and Cleo Youtz. Bill Nave and Kathy Krystinik provided detailed and useful comments on earlier drafts of this manuscript.

APPENDIX I: SEARCHES, INCLUSION CRITERIA, AND MATERIALS

Literature Searches

Our computer search used three large library databases: Educational Resources Information Center (ERIC), Psychological Abstracts (PsycINF0), and the Harvard University Libraries catalog (HU). Initial searches used the keyword phrases "computer-assisted instruction" and "higher education." Later searches used various combinations of "multimedia," "hypermedia," "interactive video," "technology," and "meta-analysis."

We searched recent volumes of many journals by hand in order to include current work that may not already have been cataloged in standard computer databases. We also reviewed the reference lists of the articles we read, and these often led us to additional articles and reports.

Finally, we gained useful information and relevant source materials through personal contact with several investigators who are named in our acknowledgments.

Inclusion Criteria

Our literature search had two main targets—primary empirical research and reviews about computers in college teaching—and some secondary targets described below. We included unpublished reports based on presentations at conferences; ERIC documents provided many articles of this type.

We limited the searches to reports appearing since 1990, except for research syntheses. To obtain background information, we searched for research syntheses, meta-analyses, and reviews of the effectiveness of computer-assisted instruction. Lipsey and Wilson (1993) present an in-depth review and analysis of the role of meta-analysis in assessing the efficacy of psychological, educational, and behavioral treatments. We used Niemiec and Walberg (1987) and Kulik and Kulik (1987) as starting points, and we tried to locate review articles up to the present. We did not restrict attention to reviews of uses of technology in college courses, but each review we used included the college level as a part of its focus; some reviews did not subdivide their analyses by the level of students.

We also focused on primary research articles since 1990 that met each of the following criteria for inclusion:

Assesses uses of computers in delivering or aiding instruction

Uses subjects from postsecondary education

Uses learning by the subjects as a primary basis for evaluation

Provides data that enable comparison of two or more treatment groups

Evaluates instruction in the context of an actual college course

Reports on work done in the United States or Canada

This investigation included research carried out in a wide variety of academic areas because we wanted to look for patterns that cross disciplinary boundaries.

We sought to distinguish research about actual college courses from experimental research, typically carried out in a laboratory setting, using "one-shot" treatments. We also distinguished research that compared two or more interventions (often with one of the treatment groups being a noncomputer control group) from studies that simply described an experience with new educational uses for computers or new computing environments.

Research Materials and Methods

Our searches provided more than 500 potentially relevant research articles, reports, and books appearing since 1990; these articles are categorized in a table already shown.

Information in the abstracts, introductions, and tables of contents narrowed our focus to 130 articles, reports, and chapters; one of us read all of these and completed forms designed to extract essential information about each potential source. This information enabled us to decide whether each article met the inclusion criteria for primary research or for research syntheses (or for neither).

This paper relies on reviews and systematic syntheses of research about computers in education. We found 22 of these articles that were published since 1987.

Research articles that compare computer-based instruction with more traditional teaching in actual college courses, or that compare two or more ways of delivering computer-based instruction, were of special interest. We found 47 articles that report on such primary research. Our second paper focuses on our review of these articles.

We found 33 other articles similar to these except that their experimental research was carried out in a research laboratory setting that was not an integral part of a college course. Those articles provided additional useful background information, but we did not include them in our main category of primary research.

We read and extracted information from still other types of articles. These included 14 articles since 1990 about computing environments, computerized learning centers, and uncontrolled evaluations of software and technologies for teaching. They also included 12 articles since 1990 that were primarily philosophical, theoretical, descriptive, or advocates of a particular approach to teaching with computers. Finally, we included two articles that focused on statistical issues for synthesizing research. Altogether, we read and abstracted information from 130 articles, reports, and chapters, with 126 of these appearing since 1990.

REFERENCES

Azevedo, Roger, and Bernard, Robert M. (1995). A meta-analysis of the effects of feedback in computer-based instruction. *Journal of Computing Research 13*, 111-27.

Bangert-Drowns, Robert L., Kulik, Chen-Lin C., Kulik, James A., and Morgan, Mary Teresa. (1991). The instructional effect of feedback in test-like events. *Review of Educational Research 61*, 213-38.

Bosco, James. (1990). An analysis of evaluations of interactive video. Paper presented at the 5th International Conference of Computers and Education (Brussels, Belgium, March 20-22, 1990). (ED 326 208)

Burton, John K., Moore, D. Michael, and Holmes, Glen A. (1995). Hypermedia concepts and research: An overview. *Computers in Human Behavior 11*, 345-69.

Clariana, Roy B. (1993). A review of multiple-try feedback in traditional and computer-based instruction. *Journal of Computer-Based Instruction 20*, 67-74.

Cohen, Peter A., and Dacanay, Lakshmi S. (1992). Computer-based instruction and health professions education: A meta-analysis of outcomes. *Evaluation & the Health Professions 15*, 259-81.

Cronin, Michael W. (1993). Empirical measures of learning outcomes from oral communication across the curriculum. Paper presented at the 79th Annual Meeting of the Speech Communication Association (Miami Beach, FL, November 18-21, 1993). (ED 366 025)

Cronin, Michael W., and Cronin, Karen A. (1992). Recent empirical studies of pedagogical effects of interactive video instruction in "soft skill" areas. *Journal of Computing in Higher Education 3*, 53-85.

Dacanay, Lakshmi S., and Cohen, Peter A. (1992). A meta-analysis of individualized instruction in dental education. *Journal of Dental Education 56*, 183-89.

Emerson, John D., and Mosteller, Frederick. (1998). Interactive multimedia in college teaching. Part II: Lessons from research in the sciences. In *Educational Media and Technology Yearbook 1998*, ed. Robert M. Branch and Mary Ann Fitzgerald (Englewood, CO: Libraries Unlimited), 59-75.

Fletcher, J. Dexter. (1992). Cost-effectiveness of interactive courseware. *Institute for Defense Analyses*, Alexandria, VA. December 1992. (ED 355 914)

Fletcher-Flinn, Claire M., and Gravatt, Breon. (1995). *Journal of Educational Computing Research 12*, 219-42.

Gagné, Robert M. (1985). *The Conditions of Learning and Theories of Instruction* (4th ed.). New York: Holt, Reinhart and Winston.

Goforth, Dave. (1994). Learner control = decision making + information: a model and meta-analysis. *Journal of Educational and Computing Research 11*, 1-26.

Grimes, Paul W., and Ray, Margaret A. (1993). Economics: Microcomputers in the college classroom—a review of the academic literature. *Social Issues Computer Review 11*, 453-63.

Kulik, Chen-Lin C., and Kulik, James A. (1986). Effectiveness of computer-based education in colleges. *AEDS Journal 19*, 81-108.

Kulik, Chen-Lin C., and Kulik, James A. (1991). Effectiveness of computer-based instruction: An updated analysis. *Computers in Human Behavior 7*, 75-94.

Kulik, Chen-Lin C., Kulik, James A., and Bangert-Drowns, Robert L. (1990). Effectiveness of mastery learning programs: A meta-analysis. *Review of Educational Research 60*, 265-99.

Kulik, James A., and Kulik, Chen-Lin C. (1987). Review of recent literature on computer-based instruction. *Contemporary Educational Psychology 12*, 222-30.

Kulik, James A., and Kulik, Chen-Lin C. (1988). Timing of feedback and verbal learning. *Review of Educational Research 58*, 79-97.

Lamb, Annette C. (1992). Multimedia and the teaching-learning process in higher education. In *Teaching in the Information Age: The Role of Educational Technology,* ed. Michael J. Albright and David L. Graf. (New Directions for Teaching and Learning). San Francisco: Jossey Bass.

Lipsey, Mark W., and Wilson, David B. (1993). The efficacy of psychological, educational, and behavioral treatment. *American Psychologist 48*, 1181-1209.

McNeil, Barbara J., and Nelson, Karyn R. (1991). Meta-analysis of interactive video instruction: A 10-year review of achievement effects. *Journal of Computer-Based Instruction 18*, 1-6.

Miech, Edward, Nave, Bill, and Mosteller, Frederick. (1997). On CALL: A review of computer-assisted language learning in U.S. colleges and universities. In *Educational Media and Technology Yearbook 1997,* ed. Robert M. Branch and Barbara B. Minor (Englewood, CO: Libraries Unlimited), 61-84.

Miller, Rockley L. (1990). Learning benefits of interactive technologies. *Videodisc Monitor 8*, 15-17.

Niemiec, Richard, and Walberg, Herbert J. (1987). Comparative effects of computer-assisted instruction: A synthesis of reviews. *Journal of Educational Computing Research 3*, 19-37.

Ragan, T., Boyce, M., Redwine, D., Savenye, W. C., and McMichael, J. (1993). Is multimedia worth it? A review of the effectiveness of individualized multimedia instruction. Paper presented at the Association for Educational Communications and Technology Convention, New Orleans, LA.

Slee, Elisa J. (1989). A review of the research on interactive video. In *Proceedings of Selected Research Papers Presented at the Annual Meeting of the Association for Educational Communications and Technology* (Dallas, Texas, February 1-5, 1989). (ED 308 818)

Spencer, Ken. (1991). Modes, media and methods: The search for educational effectiveness. *British Journal of Educational Effectiveness 22*, 12-22.

Torshen, Kay P. (1977). *The Mastery Approach to Competency-Based Education.* New York: Academic Press.

Walberg. H. J. (1984). Improving the productivity of America's schools. *Educational Leadership*, May 19-27.

Interactive Multimedia in College Teaching. Part II
Lessons from Research in the Sciences

John D. Emerson
Department of Mathematics and Computer Science, Middlebury College

Frederick Mosteller
Professor Emeritus, Department of Statistics, Harvard University

ABSTRACT

Computer-assisted instruction is rapidly changing in ways that take advantage of highly visual windows-icon interfaces and of the color image, sound, and motion capabilities of today's computers. This report examines primary empirical research from 1990 through 1996 that evaluates uses of emerging computer technologies in college courses in the sciences and social sciences.

This second paper addresses the same questions as its companion paper:

1. Do uses of interactive multimedia technologies lead to increased learning by college students?

2. Which uses of these technologies hold the greatest promise for college teachers?

This paper focuses in detail on six controlled primary research studies of using interactive computing and multimedia in college classrooms. The six reports provide valuable insights about our current understandings of the effectiveness of computers in college-level teaching in the sciences. Although these studies do not constitute a representative sample of recent research on computer-assisted teaching, they do aid us in telling a story about what we learned from a systematic study of a much larger collection of research reports.

Uses of computer technologies that actively involve the student in the learning activities can be effective in college-level instruction; this may be especially true when the student participates in determining the learning activities and the instructional sequence. Collaboration among students in their computer work may enhance its value. Computer support of mastery learning programs appears promising. College teachers are good at identifying specific and focused aspects of their course where computer-supported instruction gives valuable gains. Although interactive multimedia instruction seems effective in aiding specific aspects of science instruction, there is not yet convincing evidence that this technology is ready to replace the college classroom teacher.

INTRODUCTION

This paper and its companion focus on primary empirical research about college-level instruction that uses interactive multimedia programs. It acknowledges the rapid advances in technology since the mid-1980s by concentrating on primary research in the newer technologies that has appeared since 1990. It organizes and interprets research findings, and it gives special attention to findings based on carefully designed empirical studies carried out as an integral part of college courses.

This report provides detailed reviews of six comparative primary research studies of computer uses in teaching in the sciences, social sciences, and mathematics. We selected the six studies as valuable illustrations of controlled studies of innovative teaching that uses interactive computing and multimedia. As the second of two papers reporting on a review of recent literature on computers in college-level instruction, this paper builds upon the foundation established in our report on research reviews and syntheses (see pp. 43-58).

This report complements the research by Miech, Nave, and Mosteller (1997) on using computer technology in teaching foreign languages in colleges and universities. They report on a few studies giving evidence for modest benefits of computerized instruction in language learning. Their findings indicate that when computer-controlled resources use more than a single medium—for example, using scenes with captions in the language being learned or video with sound—language acquisition and retention tend to improve. The present report addresses similar issues in the sciences, broadly defined.

STUDY DESIGN, METHODS, AND MATERIALS

Search Strategies and Inclusion Criteria

We searched systematically for articles about college-level instruction that uses interactive software and computer-driven multimedia. The companion paper gives further details of the search strategy used in this project.

This report focuses on primary research articles since 1990 that met each of the following criteria for inclusion:

- Assesses uses of computers in delivering or aiding instruction

- Uses subjects from postsecondary education

- Addresses the sciences or social sciences

- Uses learning by the subjects as a primary basis for evaluation

- Provides data that enable comparison of two or more treatment groups

- Evaluates instruction in the context of an actual college course

- Reports on empirical research carried out in the United States or Canada.

We sought to distinguish research about actual college courses from experimental research, typically carried out in a laboratory setting, using "one-shot" treatments.

Our investigation included research carried out in a wide variety of academic areas because we wanted to look for patterns that cross disciplinary boundaries. However, the present report emphasizes primary research in college courses in the sciences, social sciences, and mathematics.

SUMMARY OF SEARCHES FOR RECENT EMPIRICAL STUDIES

Searches provided more than 500 potentially relevant research articles, reports, and books appearing since 1990; our companion report gives further details. Research articles that compare computer-based instruction with more traditional teaching in actual college courses, or that compare two or more ways of delivering computer-based instruction, were of special interest. We found 47 articles published from 1990 through 1996 that report on such primary research.

We read and abstracted information from the 47 papers. Nearly all of these studies used computer software that offers at least some level of interaction between the learner and the program. Approximately 15 of these reports address interactive multimedia instruction specifically; others use hypertext technology to provide flexibility in interaction with learners; and still others use simulation software.

A boxed display shows the distribution of the 47 studies across academic areas. Among the studies, eight are in the biological and physical sciences; 16 are in the quantitative sciences and mathematics; 16 are in the business and social sciences; and the remaining seven are in other areas, including education and physical education. These results do not evenly represent the disciplines. Instead, they reflect the emphasis we placed on mathematics and statistics, both in our contacts with other colleagues and with professional organizations, and in our pursuit of recent literature cited in the bibliographies of the articles first identified through automated computer searches.

Fourteen of these studies randomly assigned students to treatments; in addition, a few studies randomly assigned the treatments to sections of courses. It is seldom possible to randomize the assignment of students to treatments in research on college teaching. Students cannot schedule the section of their course at a time that conflicts with other courses or important activities. Students often resist constraints on their freedom to choose their own schedules.

Primary Research Studies About CAI: Academic Disciplines

Discipline or Academic Area	Number of Studies	Discipline or Academic Area	Number of Studies
Biology	3½ *	Mathematics	10
Business and Management	5	Physics	1
Chemistry	2½ *	Political Science	1
Communications	1	Psychology	8
Computer Science/ Information	1	Physical Education	2
Economics	2	Statistics	5
Education	2	Writing/English as Second Lang.	2
Environmental Science	1		
		Total	47

* one study considered biology and chemistry courses together

When random assignment of students to experimental treatments is impossible, investigators may gather information about the students in each course section at the beginning of the course, so they can use this information to adjust their analyses for differences among the students in different sections. However, it is difficult to ensure comparability of the groups by using such adjustment because not all differences among students can be measured and known at the start of the experiment. Researchers therefore generally place greater confidence in randomized studies.

LESSONS FROM SIX EMPIRICAL
STUDIES IN THE SCIENCES

This section reviews and analyzes six primary studies of uses of interactive computing and/or multimedia instruction in college teaching. We selected these studies as instructive representatives of the 47 primary research articles described and categorized above. We also chose these articles for their value in amplifying and extending the general findings reported in our companion paper.

Six Primary Studies of Interactive Computing and Multimedia		
Study	**Area and Features**	**Findings**
Campbell et al. (1995)	Business, students randomly assigned, total N=26, examined six hours of instruction, computer instruction used interactive tutorial	Computer gave gains in learning efficiency, whereas control group did not learn well in reduced 6-hour time frame
Palmiter (1991)	Mathematics (calculus), students randomly assigned to computer algebra system and to control, total N=120, addressed first half of course	Students in computer group scored higher on both conceptual and computational exams; students in computer group had higher confidence in their own abilities; fewer students in computer group continued study of calculus
Leonard (1992)	Biology labs, sections randomly assigned, total N=142, computer treatment addressed 2 of 13 weekly labs using simulation of labs	Computer simulation of labs was as effective as traditional lab instruction; gains for computer group in efficiency
Williamson and Abraham (1995)	Chemistry, sections randomly assigned, total N=124, computer animation addressed two 2-week units of course	Groups that saw animation scored higher in their understanding of molecular structure in chemistry
Montazemi and Wang (1995)	Management information systems, previous year's class used for rough comparison, total N=333, hypermedia-based tutorial package for full semester course	More time invested yields higher exam grades; mastery learning does not speed the learning rate; external pressures reduce academic performance; hypermedia software may support mastery learning
Janda (1992)	Political science, sections assigned in a balanced "arbitrary" manner, total N=238, five interactive videos addressed full-semester course	Positive student attitudes; no measured learning gains from interactive video; possible gains in areas not assessed in study

We limit our attention to only six of the 47 primary research studies in order to focus on a few studies in depth. In doing so, we hope to give readers deeper insights into the current state of research about using interactive computing and multimedia in college teaching. We believe that the studies presented can together provide a useful perspective on the larger body of primary research on computer-assisted classroom teaching at the college level.

We review first those studies that used a randomized assignment of students to treatments or of classes to treatments. Then we turn to a study that was not randomized but that tried to achieve comparability among the student groups through statistical adjustment based on previously measured information about the students.

Campbell et al. (1995): IVI for Teaching Interpersonal Skills

J. Olin Campbell and his colleagues (1995) investigated whether computer and video technology can support expert human coaches in training undergraduates to facilitate others' interpersonal problem-solving. This randomized experiment compared two groups of under-graduate business students taking a course in organizational development. The students received training designed to help them improve their problem-solving and communication skills in addressing interpersonal conflict. The research included two studies: a pilot study and a more refined and carefully controlled experiment. We will discuss primarily the main experiment.

The control group with 11 students was divided into two teams. These students received three two-hour classes of instruction in lecture format, with the teacher serving as a model for the human interactions. The students were also coached in small group role-play sessions by the instructor and the graduate assistant throughout the six-hour period. Six hours of instruction was a reduction from nine hours previously used, and one question was whether this reduction would hurt student learning. The pilot study had assessed learning using nine hours of instruction, but that was for a different group of students.

The experimental group with 15 students was divided into three teams. These students received just two hours of instruction from the teacher. The other four hours used computer-based tutorials that included viewing two-person role-play exercises with evaluative feedback. The treatment group used video that presented concepts and modeled skills. In another part of the video instruction, students responded to statements made by a character on the computer screen by selecting from a list of responses. As pairs of students practiced the role-plays, other students in the group worked with a rating guide to assess each others' skill at interpersonal problem-solving.

The dependent variable was performance in a two-person role-play in which the student subject (the helper) responded to the person needing help (the helpee). In one example, the students tried to respond effectively to a hypothetical problem situation in which a domineering team leader rejected the ideas of the team members.

The skills used related to the following interaction. The helper is taught to look directly at the helpee, lean forward, and maintain eye contact. The helpee explains the problem in a way that conveys that person's emotions and frustration. Then the helper responds by reflecting back both the feeling and the content of what the helpee said. The helper tries to assist the helpee to "take ownership" of the situation—that is, to begin to analyze the problem and explore strategies for addressing it. Finally, the helper and the helpee try to agree on concrete actions to address the problem.

The rating guide used by independent reviewers (graduate students in counseling who did not know what treatment the students had received) was similar to one used by the subjects in assessing each other's skills. The two raters used the guide in their scoring of how well the helper was able to follow the steps outlined above. The helper's attentiveness to the helpee, the helper's initial response to the problem, the helper's effectiveness in personalizing the problem, and the initiation of steps to help the helpee form a specific strategy for addressing the problem all entered into the ratings. The ratings also measured the appropriateness of the sequence of steps used by the student helper in addressing the problem. In this way, the raters evaluated each stage of the interaction sequence in the role-plays.

Unlike most educational studies designed to compare student achievement, assessment in this study was not done through an objective paper-and-pencil or computer-administered test. Rather, the subjects (student helpers) were given both pretests and posttests in the form of role-plays that were videotaped for later scoring. Thus, the subjects were evaluated in their actual demonstrated skill, not their knowledge about the skill as might be measured in a more typical classroom setting.

The results of the assessments were unexpected. The experimental group improved substantially from pretest to posttest, but the group receiving conventional instruction did not improve at all. The test results were recorded on a scale from 0 (worst) to 1 (best). The mean of the pretests for the 11 students who had regular classroom instruction was .32, and their mean score on the posttest was .30. Thus, the six hours of classroom instruction were ineffective. Campbell and his coauthors suggest that the reduced opportunity for relevant practice may have been an important reason for the lack of success of the control group.

The mean pretest score was .32 for the 15 students who received instruction with computer video, whereas the mean posttest score was .63. Although we lack precise data for calculating an effect size for the gain by the computer group relative to the control group, it appears to have been at least 1.5. Computer assistance seemed to enable the reduced instructional time to work for the experimental group.

We note that the design of this study did not provide a direct comparison between the computer-assisted instruction when given in a six-hour time frame and either form of instruction when given in the traditional nine-hour time frame. The pilot study had compared computer instruction with the original classroom instruction, where each form of instruction was used for nine hours; it found them to be equivalent. We lack evidence about whether the computer instruction in the reduced time frame was equally effective. Thus, we cannot answer the question about whether the time reduction can work as well, although we know it did not work in the noncomputer group. The authors of the report believe that the students who used the computer module and received six hours of instruction did exhibit positive learning outcomes.

The report concluded that "computer- and video-supported methods have the potential to decrease instructor time and increase learner performance, even for complex interpersonal problem solving skills" (Campbell et al., 1995, p. 223).

The computer instruction used substantially less instructor time than conventional classroom instruction alone, and it enabled students to develop the interpersonal skills they need. This study also illustrates how computers can assist an instructor in teaching well; note that the instructor still maintained an important role in the computer-assisted instruction.

Palmiter (1991): A Computer Algebra System in Calculus

Over the past decade the mathematics community has given much attention to the reform of calculus courses. For example, professional study groups have recommended the use of computer algebra systems to allow less emphasis on calculations and more emphasis on the concepts of calculus. Computer algebra systems can address most calculus problems traditionally posed in undergraduate calculus textbooks using any of three approaches: symbolic, numerical, and graphical. Palmiter reported on a controlled, randomized experiment whose purpose was to determine whether using a computer algebra system improves (or perhaps hinders) conceptual performance in calculus.

Palmiter used the package MACSYMA with her experimental group of students in second semester calculus for engineers. She randomly assigned volunteer subjects to an experimental group (n=60) using MACSYMA and to a control group (n=60) that did not have access to the MACSYMA software. After attrition in both groups, she was able to compare the performances of 39 remaining students in the experimental group and 39 students in the control group. Palmiter characterizes the student attrition as normal for the course, but an attrition rate of one-third seems to us rather large for an introductory calculus-for-engineering course. Perhaps the college had different versions of second semester calculus from which a student could choose, and students could easily shift to different courses.

The groups had different instructors who were experienced in teaching integral calculus and who were thought to be equally effective teachers. The two teachers conferred with each other regularly to try to ensure that aspects of the course other than the use of computer software were as similar as possible. The two groups used the same textbook, were assigned common problem sets, were given the same examples, and took common examinations.

The experimental group attended a weekly one-hour lab in which they used MACSYMA to evaluate a limit, find an integral, evaluate a sum, or display a graph. An algebraic symbol manipulation package like MACSYMA can integrate functions commonly used in calculus and give an answer in algebraic form. For example, the indefinite integral of $f(x) = 1/x$ with $x > 0$ is $F(x) = \log(x) + C$ (the logarithm is in base e, and C is any constant). It can also carry out a related integral with definite limits, say as x ranges from 1 to 2, and express the result symbolically; here the integral of $f(x)$ as x ranges from 1 to 2 is $\log(2)$. A symbol manipulation package can also give the result of this integral problem numerically; for example, $\log(2)$ is .693147.

Finally, MACSYMA or a similar program can calculate approximations to this integral using geometric objects like rectangles or trapezoids. A student can specify a sum of areas of, say, 100 nonoverlapping rectangles, each having a width of .01, whose tops are very close to the graph of the curve $f(x)$. MACSYMA can quickly follow a student's directions, calculate the areas of all 100 rectangles, and add the areas to obtain a sum whose value is close to the true value of the integral.

To carry out these steps, students must understand calculus concepts well enough to frame the problems precisely and to ask MACSYMA for the desired results. Students also need to develop a working knowledge of the control language for MACSYMA. The software package does the needed calculations almost instantly, and it relieves students of the tedious work needed to carry out the calculations. At least in theory, it permits the student to focus on the concepts and the logical thinking involved in the problem, without being distracted by time-consuming and tedious calculations. For example, students can use MACSYMA to approximate an area under a curve using 10 rectangles, then 100 rectangles and 1000 rectangles. They can experience in a direct way the convergence of successive approximations, using the sum of areas of increasingly many rectangles, to the actual area under a curve. Thus MACSYMA may help beginning calculus students to better appreciate through hands-on experience the meaning of a definite integral as a limiting process—a concept that the course is trying to deliver.

Palmiter's experiment used the part of the course that covered techniques of integration. The traditional group covered the material in a 10-week quarter, whereas the experimental group covered the same material in only five weeks. The students in the computer group used MACSYMA to do all integrals, and thus these students did not learn until the second five weeks the techniques of integration that are traditionally an important component of second semester calculus.

Both groups of students took identical computational and conceptual exams, after five weeks for the MACSYMA group and after 10 weeks for the control group. Palmiter wanted to know whether the experimental group had as good (or better) an understanding of calculus concepts and of problem-solving as the control group, even though the first group had received no instruction in techniques of integration. For the computational part of the exam, students in the traditional group were given two hours to complete the exam, whereas the experimental group had just an hour to complete the same problems with assistance from MACSYMA.

Students in the MACSYMA group scored significantly higher both on the conceptual and computational examinations; their average examination scores were about 18 percent and 20 percent higher, respectively, than those for the traditional instruction. After the exams were administered, the MACSYMA students were given five weeks of instruction in (manual) techniques of integration because they would not always have access to the specialized computer software in their subsequent calculus courses.

At the end of the course Palmiter assessed and compared the attitudes of the students in the two groups. Generally, students in the experimental group had more confidence in their own abilities in calculus; 85 percent of the MACSYMA group said they were confident in continuing the calculus sequence, compared to 68 percent of the traditional group. Students in the MACSYMA group rated their learning of calculus higher than did the control group; 73 percent said they had learned more mathematics than in the usual mathematics course, whereas 48 percent of students in the traditional group said they had learned more.

Palmiter was also interested in the future progress of her students. She found that 43 percent of the MACSYMA students continued their calculus study, whereas 63 percent of the students taking traditional calculus continued the sequence. This empirical finding seems seriously at odds with the data gathered in the student surveys. (Palmiter reports that 40 percent of the MACSYMA students were in a major that required no further calculus, compared with 24 percent of students in the traditional group.) She tracked the performance of continuing students though the next two quarters of calculus and found that those who had been in the experimental group received higher grades, on the average, in both courses. Thus, gains in achievement for the MACSYMA group seem to have been sustained well after the end of the course on which the experiment was based.

Palmiter's findings about future progress raise some questions about interpretation because of the potential noncomparability of the groups. She obtained follow-up data for just 17 students who had used MACSYMA and for 24 students from the group that had received traditional instruction. Differences in the rates of continuation in mathematics mean that the two groups are no longer comparable even if the groups who completed Calculus II were still roughly comparable; the relatively few MACSYMA students who took the next two courses may have been especially strong students. We wonder also whether the lower number of students in the MACSYMA group who went on to further mathematics courses might be partly attributable to their calculus experience, and not just to the requirements of their academic programs.

Palmiter's study may suggest that computers can take over some of the mechanical manipulations and calculations of beginning calculus, so that students can focus on conceptual issues and other kinds of learning that lead to greater and more lasting insights about calculus. For example, learning lists of formulas for integrating common mathematical functions may not teach students as much about integration in calculus as does seeing the approximation of an area by a growing number of increasingly narrow rectangles. Understanding the geometric content of important calculus concepts may have special value for students, and computer software can support this goal.

We wonder, however, whether these hopes were realized for most students who participated in this experiment. The technical challenges to the students in learning effective use of a package like MACSYMA, and the time demands associated with use of the computer package, may have discouraged some students from continuing in calculus. The lower number of MACSYMA students in the subsequent mathematics course means that caution must be used in interpreting the group comparisons.

Leonard (1992): Computer-Simulated Biology Labs

Science teachers invariably believe that a hands-on laboratory experience is valuable and even essential for college students who are learning science. They sometimes summarize their case by saying, "The way to learn science is to *do* science." Laboratory components in science courses can be particularly expensive. They are messy and inconvenient, and they can pose risks for personal safety (e.g., chemistry experiments gone awry, toxic fumes in the lab) and concerns from advocacy groups (e.g., animal-rights groups may criticize biology labs).

Computer technology may provide an effective alternative to some traditional science labs using simulation programs supported by interactive multimedia.

William Leonard conducted an experiment that compared instruction using interactive videodiscs with conventional laboratory instruction. The experimental units were pairs of lab sections of about 20 students each, and the labs in each pair met weekly at the same hour. Four pairs of laboratory sections were assigned randomly to either interactive videodisc lessons or to conventional laboratory instruction for two of the laboratory experiments during the semester. Thus, four conventional laboratory sessions were paired with four interactive video sections. Altogether, 72 students participated in all aspects of the conventional laboratory treatment, and 70 students participated fully in the videodisc treatment. Each of four lab instructors was assigned to one videodisc section and one conventional section. The specific lab topics were biogeography (climate and life) and respiration in plants and animals; the contents of the lessons for the treatment group and control group were similar.

We focus here on the instruction about respiration. In both groups, students worked in pairs, and the reports "required systematic use of science process skills, especially observing; predicting; hypothesizing; deriving information from tables, graphs, and other visual aids; planning experiments; identifying and controlling for variables; experimenting; collecting and organizing data; and inferring and generalizing from data" (Leonard 1992, p. 98).

Students in the conventional lab sections planned their experiments, chose variables they wished to study, and gathered data. Students in the videodisc groups viewed television-quality videos of manipulation of the apparatus, and they viewed actual experimental results for three different organisms (pea seedling, frog, and mouse) under a wide range of temperatures. They were able to interact with the program and listen to or view the program's responses.

Leonard's research used five outcome measures: grades on student reports for the two laboratory investigations that compared videodisc "experiments" with conventional laboratory work; grades for quizzes given within two weeks of each laboratory investigation; and a grade on the laboratory final examination, a 100-question multiple-choice exam that covered all 13 weekly labs assigned during the semester. Note that in 11 of the 13 labs, the computer was not used for either group of students, so we might well expect any effect of the experimental treatments in two labs to be modest on the final examination.

No statistically significant differences were found between the two treatment groups (videodisc versus conventional) for any of these outcomes. The modest differences in group means favored the conventional group on the respiration lab report (ES=-.11) but favored the videodisc group on the climate and life lab report (ES=.19). The two group means were identical for the quiz on the respiration lab (ES=0.00), whereas the difference in means for the quizzes on respiration slightly favored the videodisc group (ES=.15). The difference in means for the laboratory final exam was also modest, with an effect size favoring the conventional group (ES=-.05). Students evidently learned as much of what is covered on the quizzes and the exam from the interactive videodisc simulations as from the hands-on laboratory experiences. Of course, there may well be other kinds of learning that takes place best in an actual lab experience, but Leonard's findings seem to suggest that some parts of laboratory instruction can be provided effectively using computer simulation.

Even though the learning outcomes were comparable for the two groups, an important difference in performance occurred. The videodisc group spent an average of 73 minutes of classroom time on the respiration experiment, and the conventional lab group spent an average of 143 minutes (ES=-1.00). For the biogeography (climate and life) activity, the videodisc group spent an average of 83 minutes, and the control group took an average of 128 minutes (ES=-.47). Both of these average time differences were statistically significant.

Leonard reports that the time savings for the videodisc group was time spent in waiting for things to happen in the laboratory and time spent in doing busy work. It is of course quite possible that some of the extra time used by the traditional lab group was well used and beneficial. For example, it may have provided students who were waiting for something to happen with extra chances for private conversations about science and biology with effective lab instructors; these conversations could have important benefits not measured on quizzes or tests. Some might even argue that the students who did not get the actual lab instruction did not learn how to do science.

Leonard's study is a controlled experiment in which preformed lab classes were randomized to treatments. It examines real college courses in which the computer-assisted instruction replaces a traditional form of instruction. Instead of the computer instruction using extra student time, it provided a savings in learning time without apparent losses in instructional effectiveness in those areas measured by the lab reports and quizzes.

Computer software was used in only two of 13 weekly laboratories, and these labs may have been the ones offering the best chance for efficiency gains using computers. The selection of lab topics for experimental comparison may have simply reflected the availability of software that had already been developed. Selection effects are possible, and we cannot conclude that videodisc instruction would have compared as favorably to traditional lab instruction in other laboratory units. The study does demonstrate that science teachers can identify at least some topics in a laboratory science course for which computer instruction can be as effective as traditional labs and also gain some time efficiencies.

Finally, although we have not seen the videodisc presentation, Leonard describes the quality and realism of the presentations in detail. The combination of movie-quality video with the benefits of interaction between the user and the program probably helps account for the success of the interactive video in simulating lab experiences.

Williamson and Abraham (1995): Animation in Science Teaching

Williamson and Abraham studied the use of interactive software with dynamic and three-dimensional animated models of particulate matter in introductory college chemistry. The belief that motivated their research was that the difficulties students have in understanding concepts at the level of particles are the source of many student misconceptions in chemistry. Thus, Williamson and Abraham wanted to know whether showing students a series of brief (two-minute) animated simulations could improve student conceptual understanding of particulate matter.

Williamson and Abraham used a quasiexperimental posttest design. The course sections were randomly assigned to three treatments: 1) a control group; 2) a group that saw animation (under the interactive control of the teacher who taught all three groups) at the level of particles and molecules; and 3) a group that saw the animation both during the lectures and also in the discussion sections where they could view them repeatedly and answer worksheet questions about them. In all other respects, the researchers tried to ensure that the three groups got identical instruction: the same teacher gave essentially the same lectures and used a common text, the same overhead displays, and the same chalk diagrams. The teacher trained the graduate student TAs for the 16 discussion/lab sections.

Students in the control group, like those in the experimental groups, had ample access to visual representations of particulate matter. The instructor who taught all lecture sections had a strong interest in visualization. Thus, all the students viewed many figures, overhead transparencies, and chalk diagrams depicting the particulate nature of the phenomena being studied. The control group was often given static figures of the same systems that were used in the animations. A central question of this research was whether the dynamic computer animations further enhanced students' conceptual understanding of particulate matter beyond the level achieved with ample use of static displays and diagrams.

The animation sequences covered two important topics in introductory chemistry: reaction chemistry and gases, liquids, and solids. Some animations were of fixed length; others were interactive and dynamic. For example, an animation called "Ideal Gas" allowed the instructor (and, in the lab, the student) to control the number of particles, pressure, temperature, and volume of the gas being depicted.

A total of 124 students qualified (by their near-perfect attendance) for inclusion in the study for the first unit on ideal gases; there were 48, 41, and 35 students in the three groups: control, animation only, and animation-with-lab, respectively. 124 students qualified for inclusion in the study for the second unit on reaction chemistry, with 54, 38, and 32 students in the respective treatment groups. The instruction in each of the two units lasted for around two weeks; we are unsure about how many other units there were in the course, perhaps seven altogether. The investigators asked whether the three groups differed with respect to conceptual understanding, course achievement on the final exam, and attitudes toward the instruction. Their analyses controlled for differences in students' reasoning ability as measured by pretests.

The results of a standardized pretest showed that the three groups were similar in their reasoning ability. The final course exam also showed no significant differences among the groups for either unit of study. Similarly, there were no statistically significant differences in attitudes among the groups for either study unit.

There were significant differences among the three treatment groups in student conceptual understanding for both units of instruction. This outcome was measured by a standardized test carefully designed to evaluate conceptual understanding of particulate matter for each of the instructional units. The test included questions that required students to make drawings, give written explanations, or choose from among multiple responses.

The two groups that saw the animation scored higher than the control group; there was no significant difference between the lecture animation group and the lecture/computer lab animation group. The results indicate that even brief exposure to dynamic animated simulations of particulate behavior can be effective in aiding students' conceptual understanding of basic concepts in chemistry. The benefits of dynamic animation presented by a computer seem to extend beyond whatever benefits are achieved by using the static forms of visual display viewed by the control group.

Williamson and Abraham provided detailed illustrations of the differences in the conceptual understanding between students who viewed the animation and those who did not. For example, students were asked to draw sketches showing the changes that occur when a substance melts. In these sketches, only 56 percent of students in the control group drew pictures depicting conservation of particles, whereas around 75 percent of students in the other two groups had pictures that exhibited conservation of particles. The authors commented that "The impact of an animation of short duration is again surprising" (Williamson and Abraham 1995, p. 532).

Like Leonard's investigation of computer presentations in chemistry labs, this research project chose two particular topics as the focus for comparing dynamic animation with traditional presentation of models for particulate matter. These areas—properties of gases, liquids, and solids; and reaction chemistry—may have been chosen because the investigators hoped that they offered the best chance of revealing the benefits of dynamic computer animation as a part of the instruction. We cannot conclude that the findings of this project would extend to other topics in the chemistry curriculum or to other science areas. The findings do, however, suggest that computer animations can enhance student visualization and conceptual learning in some important areas of college science instruction.

Montazemi and Wang (1995): Mastery Learning

Montazemi and Wang investigated the effectiveness of interactive CBI in support of mastery learning. Their subjects were 333 university students in a first course in Management Information Systems (MIS); their project used a tutorial software package called MIST (Management Information Systems Tutor). This package uses hypermedia technology to let learners control their paths through the materials in each learning lesson. Although the design of the learning environment encourages students to browse, it prevents students from moving to a new lesson until they have understood the current one.

The investigators followed the presentations in a standard textbook on MIS, and they specified the sequence of learning lessons in advance. They designed the course around 20 main chapters with a total of 87 sections, each with several learning lessons. Within each lesson, students used buttons on the computer screen to choose additional information about the present topic in the form of text, figures, graphs, and pictures. Offering the learner these choices within a learning lesson helped tailor the instructional sequence to the preferences and needs of the individual student.

Mastery learning seems ideally suited to students' differing needs, because different students can spend differing amounts of time in various areas of the course. Students achieve mastery of different subject areas at different rates, and mastery learning programs provide students with as little or as much time as they need to master each topic.

A commitment to mastery learning may appear inconsistent with the software design used by Montazemi and Wang, because the design seems to give students great flexibility in choosing what to do next. However, the wide range of choices was offered primarily within the individual lessons of the chapter sections. Mastery learning meant that all learning-lessons within a section had to be successfully completed before a student could go on to the next section.

Mastery of each lesson was tested through random selection from a set of questions about each section. When a response was incorrect, the program again presented the student with the related learning lesson, but it did not give the correct answer to the question missed. The student could always choose to leave the learning-lesson and answer another randomly generated question. Learning for the lesson continued in this way until the student attained sufficient mastery to give a correct response to the short-answer question. Although it is doubtful that a correct response to a single question can indicate mastery of a particular learning-lesson even when the lesson is brief and focused, perhaps successful responses to single questions in a succession of integrated learning-lessons within a chapter section can indicate mastery for that material.

The program also administered questions on all chapter sections after a student completed each chapter. Here the program gave the correct answers, and students used these "tests" as indicators of their preparation for weekly lab tests. The students knew that these lab tests counted 40 percent of the course grade.

As support for what learning theorists sometimes call "external motivation," students had access to icons at the bottom of the screen to determine: how much material they had covered: performance in each chapter; weekly test score; and class average. The final exam taken by all students consisted of 200 multiple-choice and true/false questions covering all 20 chapters. A class of 454 students who had taken the course (and the same exam) without MIST in the previous year served as an ad hoc control group for this study, although this comparison seems to have been a relatively minor part of the study.

Montazemi and Wang primarily asked whether student use of MIST was effective in supporting mastery learning; they seemed persuaded by earlier empirical research that mastery learning facilitated by human tutors is effective in college courses. They also asked how the time students spent in studying and reviewing a lesson ("time-on-task") related to their achievement as measured by test questions. MIST recorded and stored both the students' responses to questions and the amount of time they spent in each learning-lesson.

Among the findings of this project were these:

1. Learning is significantly influenced by the amount of time a student spends in learning. For 84 of the 87 chapter sections, there was significant positive correlation between the time students spent on the learning task and student performance for that section. The median correlation was just over .5.

2. Differences among students in the time spent on learning do not diminish as students progress through lessons, even with mastery learning. Apparently some students need more time than others to learn effectively, and students seem to recognize this difference in the ways they use their time.

3. Student differences in performance do not diminish as students progress through the learning sequence. This finding runs against a belief by some proponents of mastery learning that its use can eventually lead students to demonstrate similar levels of success in their learning. We suspect that as the material being studied becomes harder, learning differences among students will sometimes become greater.

4. External factors such as midterm exams in other courses and the assignment of major papers or projects near the end of the course had an adverse affect on academic performance; those labs given during the period when substantial assignments (or examinations) were given in other courses turned out to have the lowest student performance.

5. The MIST system may have enabled students to improve their academic performance, although the evidence about this has questionable reliability. The 333 students in the present study that used MIST had an average score of 81.8 percent on the comprehensive 200-question final exam, whereas 454 students in the previous year had an average of 71.4 percent on the same exam. The differences in average performance for the two years seem striking, but Montazemi and Wang do not discuss any steps taken to prevent this year's students from obtaining prior information about the examination.

The study by Montazemi and Wang supports a belief that hypermedia software can work well with mastery learning. This report illustrates the potential value of hypermedia software for offering instruction tailored to the needs and abilities of each learner. The software can demand some level of successful learning before it lets the student go on to a new topic, and it also invites the learner to choose paths through a learning sequence that can help the learner achieve mastery.

Janda (1992): Sobering Lessons from Multimedia in Political Science

Much of the research on CAI in college teaching has come in the physical and biological sciences and in mathematics. Kenneth Janda (1992) asked whether positive findings in those areas extend to the social sciences, particularly to political science. He carried out a nonrandomized experiment that compared multimedia instruction to a second form of computer instruction and to traditional instruction. His primary interest was in whether the special features of multimedia instruction give it advantages for providing effective instruction in political science at the introductory college level.

Janda used three different teaching techniques to supplement his lectures in a course on American government and politics. He lectured to the entire class of 238 students, mostly freshmen and sophomores, three times each week. All students had identical reading assignments from a common syllabus using the same text. The class was split into 12 discussion sections of around 20 students each. Although students were not randomly assigned to these sections, they chose their own discussion sections having knowledge only of the meeting times of the sections. Four experienced graduate TAs taught the 12 sections, and each TA used the three teaching techniques in their three sections—one technique to a section. This research design helped ensure that differences among the TAs would not contribute to any differences in outcomes measured for the three teaching techniques.

The three teaching methods were:

1. traditional discussion sections;

2. computer-assisted discussion sections using tutorial software (for the first week, in political ideology) and statistical software (for the remaining nine weeks, in cross-tabulation of data); and

3. multimedia discussion sections using hypermedia-based software and videodisc presentations of recent important historical topics in American politics.

The multimedia materials were built around five video units—the Watergate Affair; Ideology, Mass Media, and Participation; Presidential Popularity; Civil Rights and Equality; and the Vietnam War. For each unit, a video path contained from 17 to 36 computer screens keyed to between eight and 23 video segments. Altogether, there was approximately 130 minutes of viewing time in the multimedia presentations. In the Watergate unit, for example, one video clip showed press secretary Ziegler denying any presidential involvement in the break-in; other clips showed scenes from the subsequent Senate Select Committee hearings on Watergate. Each unit concluded with a computer screen posing questions designed to elicit student thought and opinions about the topic covered. For example, one question asked, "Did President Ford act in the best interests of the nation by pardoning Richard Nixon?"

Janda evaluated the results of his experiment in several ways. Students in the course were graded on four course components: a midterm examination, a seven-page term paper whose nature depended on the type of the section attended, attendance and participation at the discussion sections and a short quiz, and a 60-item multiple-choice final examination covering the entire course. None of these factors displayed statistically significant differences among the three teaching techniques. Students in the traditional discussion sections scored slightly higher on the 60-question final exam (mean=45.4) than did students in the multimedia sections (mean=43.4) and the computer sections (mean=43.1). Thus there were no measured learning gains observed for students in the multimedia sections, compared to those in other sections.

Seventy-eight students in the multimedia sections who responded to questions about their experiences indicated very positive attitudes toward the multimedia units. For example, 89 percent of these students agreed that they "enjoyed doing the computer and videodisc assignments," and 93 percent agreed that "the realism of the video segments helped [them] understand complex events more than only reading or hearing about them" (Janda 1992, p. 347). Student responses to several other statements added evidence that their attitudes toward the multimedia instruction were strongly positive.

Janda explored the relationship between student attitudes and student learning with the three instructional techniques. He compared students' responses to three questions posed at the end of the course to their responses on the first day of class to the same questions. These questions addressed: 1) self-rating of knowledge about American government and politics; 2) interest in American government and politics; and 3) plans to take another course in American government and politics. All three groups gave substantially more positive responses at the end of the course than they had given initially.

There were no statistically significant differences, however, in the sizes of these gains among the three instructional groups. Students in the traditional sections rated their own knowledge slightly higher than did the students in either of the two treatment groups. Although students in the multimedia section gave high marks to the multimedia units, their positive assessments did not translate to greater interest in, or a sense of greater knowledge of, American government and politics than did those of their peers in the other instructional groups.

Janda used randomly formed "focus groups" of four students from each of the 12 sections to probe the student assessments of the course and its instructional techniques. Twenty-five of the 48 students selected actually participated in one of three focus groups, one group for each method. These sessions were led by a professional interviewer and were openly tape-recorded.

From these sessions, Janda learned that students who liked the multimedia presentations nonetheless did not believe that the videos helped them "learn" as much as alternative techniques that they might not like as much. For example, one student who believed that the videos were "the highlight of the course" also reported, "I don't think it will help on the final and I don't think it helped on the midterm."

Even though the students were very positive about the videos, they did not believe that the videos helped them learn the material they believed they were expected to learn. The results from the multiple-choice final exam seemed to support their beliefs.

Although the use of videos may not have enhanced the kinds of learning that are evaluated on examinations, we believe that does not mean that the videos are without educational value. Most teachers would appreciate the impact of the videos on students in the affective realm. The apparent "interest, attention, and affect" gains for video has its own value even if they are not cognitively graded. We wonder whether or how to give credit for reinforcement received from videos when we evaluate student learning.

Janda (1992, pp. 349-50) formulated two "sobering lessons" from the experiment:

Lesson 1: Students distinguish between what they like doing and what they think helps them learn, and they hold a narrow view of learning.

Lesson 2: Multimedia produces other forms of learning that are not measured by performance in the course nor by expressions of interest, knowledge, or future course plans.

Janda based his second lesson on indications by students that the video clips in the multimedia units were "almost like experience" and were "the next best thing to being there." He noted, however, that further studies need to identify and demonstrate the benefits of multimedia instruction in American government. The last sentence in Janda's research report was candid, "My own effort to demonstrate these benefits in this experiment was disappointing" (p. 353).

We agree that researchers need to develop better ways to measure the other forms of learning referred to in Lesson 2, yet we are encouraged by the findings in Janda's research that lend support for this lesson.

SUMMARY OF FINDINGS FROM RECENT EMPIRICAL RESEARCH

We have examined six comparative empirical studies of interactive multimedia computing used in college courses. Two studies (Campbell et al., 1995; Palmiter, 1991) were randomized in that students were randomly assigned to instructional groups. Two studies (Leonard, 1992; Williamson and Abraham, 1995) were also experimental in that classes were randomly assigned to instructional groups. One study (Janda 1992) used pretest data in an attempt to determine whether instructional groups were roughly equivalent. Janda's study "arbitrarily" assigned teaching methods to sections after the students had already signed up for their sections. The study by Montazemi and Wang (1995) had no reliable control but used the same final examination given in the previous year for crude comparison.

Three of the reports (Campbell et al., 1995; Leonard, 1992; Williamson and Abraham, 1995) dealt with a very modest part of a semester course, perhaps a fifth of the course or less. One report (Palmiter, 1991) dealt with about half of a semester course. These four studies report reliable improvement in some aspects of a specific part of a college course. They demonstrate that in some college courses it may be possible to produce effective computer materials at least for some component of the course.

The other studies (Montazemi and Wang, 1995; Janda, 1992) each dealt with a full semester course. The study by Montazemi and Wang had no reliable control, but it did produce some instructive qualitative results: more time spent on learning led to better grades on exams; students did not speed up as they learned more, even when in mastery learning programs; variation among students in learning time needed did not diminish as the course went on; and outside pressure (exams, term papers) tended to reduce performance in a course. Janda's study had each of the four TAs use each teaching method for their three sections, and it gathered pretest data; thus, the controls were probably effective. Although Janda found positive student attitudes toward multimedia instruction, he found no positive learning gains for students who received multimedia instruction.

In two studies that found learning gains for computers, students collaborated with others in a group or in pairs (Campbell et al., 1995; Leonard, 1992). Students had at least some control over the learning sequence in all six studies; however, the software limited the extent of this control in at least one study (Montazemi and Wang, 1995), and the collaborative nature of some of the instructional programs necessarily limited a student's independence in controlling the learning sequence.

Findings from three of the studies (Campbell et al., 1995; Leonard, 1992; Palmiter, 1991) suggested that interactive computer instruction might, in some circumstances, be able to reduce either the instructional time needed from teachers or the learning time required of students. However, in other circumstances computers may also encourage students to spend more time on their course.

The findings for these studies seem to be rather narrow in that they apply to small parts of a course, or they are qualitative findings instead of findings that measure and compare the overall learning outcomes of a group that received computer instruction with the learning outcomes for a control group. Still, modest gains can be worthwhile and important.

FINDINGS FOR COLLEGE TEACHERS

We conclude this report by repeating the practical findings for teachers in our companion report. These findings emerge both from the reviews and research syntheses summarized in the companion paper, and from the primary studies discussed in some detail in this report. We refer to the earlier paper for details and references; here we indicate which of the six primary studies seem to give further support for each finding.

1. Computer technology can support good teaching and the efforts by teachers to further strengthen their teaching (Campbell et al., 1995; Williamson and Abraham, 1995; Palmiter, 1991). The evidence thus far does not demonstrate that computer software is a viable replacement for creative and dedicated teachers.

2. Interactive computer-assisted instruction is usually more effective when it requires the learner to be an active participant in the educational process. Some research suggests that interactive programs, when they use a well-thought-out combination of learner control, feedback to the learner, and program control, achieve their successes by helping learners become active participants in the learning process. Learner control with broad constraints on the learning sequence and ample feedback to the learner seem ideal.

3. Learning is often more successful when it uses two or more channels in engaging the student. Multimedia instruction may prove to have special advantages because it can involve multiple senses at once by combining two or more of these: text, dialogue, images, motion, sound, and touch. But even when students react positively to multimedia instructional programs, they may not always demonstrate measurable gains in their learning (Janda, 1992).

4. Interactive computer-assisted instruction can accommodate the varying needs of individual students by letting them choose their progression through a lesson. It can also aid individuals in achieving a level of mastery that helps them learn more successfully what comes next (Montazemi and Wang, 1995).

5. Computer-assisted instruction can provide gains in learning efficiency. Successful learning can take place even when the total instructional time is reduced (Campbell et al., 1995; Leonard, 1992).

CONCLUSIONS

Is interactive multimedia instruction effective when used in college courses? The findings tell us that computers can help make teaching more effective in some settings for parts of some college courses. They also reveal that students often enjoy learning interactively with multimedia. Although computing has often shown some gains in teaching specific things, we still do not have a great leap forward based on computer instruction, whereas in actually carrying out computations and in processing enormous amounts of data, such a leap has occurred.

There is little evidence that derives from randomized and controlled studies about the value of using multimedia in entire college courses. We think that further carefully controlled research is needed to determine whether interactive multimedia instruction will achieve a breakthrough in enhancing student learning in college.

ACKNOWLEDGMENTS

The project was facilitated by a grant from the Andrew W. Mellon Foundation to the American Academy of Arts and Sciences in support of the Center for Evaluation of the Academy's project "Initiatives for Children."

We acknowledge gratefully the work of our research assistant, Ying Zhang, who assisted us with many of the computer searches and helped organize those source materials.

We appreciate receiving information, advice, and materials from the following: Jack Bookman; Cathy Crocker; Joan Garfield; Carolyn Kotlas; Carl Leinbach; David M. Mathews; George McCabe; Edward Miech; Bill Nave; Kent L. Norman; Marjorie Olson; Mary Parker; Allan J. Rossman; Richard Schaeffer; Keith E. Schwingendorf; David A. Smith; and Cleo Youtz. Bill Nave and Kathy Krystinik provided detailed and useful comments on an earlier draft of this manuscript.

REFERENCES

Campbell, J. Olin, Lison, Cheryl A., Borsook, Terry K., Hoover, Jay A., and Arnold, Patricia H. (1995). Using computer and video technologies to develop interpersonal skills. *Computers in Human Behavior 11*, 223-39.

Emerson, John D., and Mosteller, Frederick. (1998). Interactive multimedia in college teaching. Part I: A ten-year review of reviews. In *Educational Media and Technology Yearbook 1998*, ed. Robert M. Branch and Mary Ann Fitzgerald (Englewood, CO: Libraries Unlimited), 43-58.

Janda, Kenneth. (1992). Multimedia in political science: Sobering lessons from a teaching experiment. *Journal of Educational Multimedia and Hypermedia 1*, 341-54.

Leonard, William H. (1992). A comparison of student performance following instruction by interactive videodisc versus conventional laboratory. *Journal of Research in Science Teaching 29*, 93-102.

Miech, Edward, Nave, Bill, and Mosteller, Frederick. (1997). On CALL: a review of computer-assisted language learning in U.S. colleges and universities. In *Educational Media and Technology Yearbook 1997*, ed. Robert M. Branch and Barbara B. Minor (Englewood, CO: Libraries Unlimited), 61-84.

Montazemi, Ali R., and Wang, Feng. (1995). An empirical investigation of CBI in support of mastery learning. *Journal of Computing in Educational Research 13*, 185-205.

Palmiter, Jeanette R. (1991). Effects of computer algebra systems on concept and skill acquisition in calculus. *Journal for Research in Mathematics Education 22*, 151-56.

Williamson, Vickie M., and Abraham, Michael R. (1995). The effects of computer animation on the particulate mental models of college chemistry students. *Journal of Research in Science Teaching 32, 521-34.*

Reading and Writing Across the Media
Using Diverse Educational Technologies for Literacy Learning

Ann Watts Pailliotet
Assistant Professor of Education
Whitman College Education Department

CHANGING CONDITIONS, CONCEPTIONS, AND PRACTICES OF LITERACY

New communications technologies have altered individuals (McLuhan, 1962), U.S. society (Lehtonen, 1988), and schools (Papert, 1993), but not all these changes have been positive (Cummins & Sayers, 1995). Callister (1994) points out, "If we are to develop a new and progressive educational technology that avoids . . . negative consequences, we need to start with the understanding that technology must be subservient to the educational questions it is employed to answer" (pp. 240-41). Perhaps the most important questions educators should ask concern literacy understandings and practices in increasingly technological contexts (Bolter, 1991; Edwards Jr., 1991; Reinking, 1995). If teachers, media specialists, and other educators are to prepare students to become literate citizens in the emerging global community, we must question our beliefs about literacy, educational texts, and instructional practices (Olson, 1996).

More than 60 years ago, William Gray, the originator of the *Dick and Jane* series, observed, "Every teacher is a teacher of reading" (in O'Brien & Stewart, 1990, p. 102). The core of Gray's assertion remains valid; all teachers implicitly or explicitly ask students to "read" texts in some way. However, Gray wrote and taught in a print-based culture where computers, mass media, and other modern technologies were in their infancy. Today, high school students spend more time watching television than in classrooms (Lutz, 1989) and countless hours interacting with videos, CD-ROMs, computer games, and other media. To better reflect current social conditions and student needs, educators must rethink understandings of what "reading" is, to encompass a broader notion: "Every teacher is a teacher of literacy."

This article first summarizes how current scholarship is redefining and extending literacy understanding, materials, and instruction to encompass far more than reading and writing print texts. Second, it demonstrates principles for applying these conceptions. By reading and writing across the media—using diverse educational technologies and literacy processes—educators may extend their instructional beliefs and frameworks. Last, it offers three lesson plans and an account of their recent use to demonstrate how educators may apply changing literacy ideas in their own classrooms.

RECONCEPTUALIZING AND REDEFINING READING AND WRITING: QUESTIONING AND EXTENDING LITERACY DEFINITIONS, TEXTS, AND INSTRUCTION

A growing number of researchers and educators recognize that new technologies require new definitions of literacy and literate behaviors. Reinking (1995) observes that we have entered a "post-typographic world" where we must "realign" reading research and literacy instruction. Selfe and Hilligoss (1994) believe changes in educational technology, particularly computers, require us to rethink writing and composing. Flood and Lapp (1995) propose a "broader conceptualization in which literacy is defined as the ability to function competently in the 'communicative arts' which include the language arts as well as the visual arts of drama, art, film, video, and television" (p. 1). Educators seeking to realign literacy understandings with practices use varied terms, like "new literacy" (Foster, 1979); "visual literacy" (Considine and Haley, 1992); "media literacy" (Lloyd-Kolkin and Tyner, 1991); "technological literacy" (Vacca and Vacca, 1996); "computer" or "television literacy" (Streibel, 1985); and "communications arts," "media arts" or "language arts" (Farstrup and Myers, 1996). Despite these disparate labels, recent conceptualizations share common beliefs about texts, learning, and teaching.

First, modern literacy involves much more than reading and writing print; it encompasses a myriad of competencies with diverse texts. For example, Levinson (1994) argues we must "identify and teach reading and writing as a processes applicable not only to print but to the messages in . . all media" (pp. 4-5). To be literate today, we must be able to understand many media—visual (Considine and Haley, 1992), oral (Goody, 1978), electronic (Bianculli, 1992), and combinations (Adams and Hamm, 1989), as well as print. Therefore, educators must extend ideas about appropriate texts beyond traditional author-generated print materials to include culturally situated events (Barthes, 1957), student-generated work (Bissex, 1980), popular mass media (Witkin, 1994), and computers (Reinking, 1987) in classrooms and curricula.

Second, literacy is now widely understood not as a single, isolated, linear act where a sole, passive individual receives meaning from a text in a conduit fashion (Mosenthal, 1988; Rosenblatt, 1978). Instead, it is an ongoing, recursive, interactive process among varied audiences and texts (Flower, 1989; Hairston, 1982; McLuhan, 1964). Neuman (1991) argues that we must understand literacy as "synergy" among media and processes; Sinatra (1986) defines it as complementary print, visual, and critical understandings. Current conceptions also stress that students are actively involved in meaning-making, constructing understandings of existing experiences, and generating new ones (Berger and Luckmann, 1963; Bloome and Eagan-Robertson, 1993). Kincheloe and Steinberg (1993) use the metaphor of a "dance between the student's experience and knowledge" (p. 308) to describe these active thinking processes. Literate behaviors involve dynamic "readerly" reception and "writerly" generation of meaning (Barthes, 1974). In the constructivist model, students become readers, writers, and authors when they engage with texts (Smith, 1984); texts become both "representation and production tools" (Newby, Stepich, Lehman, and Russell, 1996, p. 19).

There are several implications of constructivist views for literacy instruction. Active learning requires that teachers and students assume changing, flexible roles (Brophy, 1992). Teachers aren't the sole classroom questioners and don't have all the answers; students also generate questions and understandings. Constructing personal meanings implies that students need choices, are responsible for learning, and are capable of making decisions. Educators must employ a range of classroom methods and materials, teaching students multiple strategies for active interpretation and creation of texts. Because literacy learning is continually evolving, teachers and students must assess both processes and products through varied, authentic means (Wiggins, 1993).

Third, literacy acts are profoundly social in nature (Vygotsky, 1978). Even when students read or write individually, they are part of rich social systems and draw from what Emig (1983) calls "webs of meaning." Constructing texts and textual understandings involve diverse social interactions (Alvermann et al., 1996), dynamic connections among past and present personal and social experiences (Bhaktin, 1988; Considine and Haley, 1992), and integrating home, school, and social literacy environments (Heath, 1983; Hynds, 1990; McLuhan and McLuhan, 1988). To foster sound literacy learning, teachers and educational specialists must create social contexts where students may interact in meaningful, active ways.

Next, literacy involves multiple ways of knowing. Individuals construct meaning through emotions (Brand, 1987; Bruner, 1990; Ediger, 1993), intellectual responses (Herber and Herber, 1993; Lusted, 1991), representational processes (Eisner, 1997), and metacognitive strategies (Corkill, 1996). When engaging in literate behaviors, students also employ multiple intelligences (Gardner, 1985), learning styles (Glasgow, 1996), cultural perspectives (Banks and Banks, 1997), and modalities or senses (McLuhan and Fiore, 1967; Pike, Compain, and

Mumper, 1994). Increasingly, scholarship stresses the importance of visual elements, under-standings, and perceptions in literacy learning (e.g., Arnheim, 1993; Bolter, 1991; Bucking-ham, 1993; Cairney, 1997; Considine and Haley, 1992; Flood and Lapp, 1995; Lester, 1995; Messaris, 1994; Watts Pailliotet, 1994). Educators may create inclusive learning contexts where multiple ways of knowing are developed and valued through explicit teaching of visual elements in diverse media, varied response strategies, critical viewing of existing texts, and procedures for generating new ones.

Furthermore, all texts share common traits: narratives, genres, and structures (Frye, 1957; Lusted, 1991); expository patterns and comprehension levels (Herber and Herber, 1993; Kervin, 1985); signs, symbols, and signification (Barthes, 1957; Bopry, 1994; Saint-Martin, 1990); metaphors (Lakoff and Johnson, 1980); implicit and explicit origins, purposes and ideologies (Althusser, 1986; Giroux, 1993); and rhetorical devices (Lusted, 1991; Ohlgren and Berk, 1977). Teachers should use varied materials, so students may explore and make connections among experiences, people, processes, and texts.

Last, literacy development and modalities are connected (Atwell, 1985; Dyson, 1984; Elbow, 1985). Reading, writing, speaking, listening, and viewing are interdependent, interac-tive elements (Barthes, 1957; Considine and Haley, 1992; Dyson, 1984; Sinatra, 1986; Watts Pailliotet, 1997). Strategies and understandings fostered in one medium support others (Fiske and Hartley, 1978; Sinatra, 1990; Watts Pailliotet, Semali, Flood, Lapp, and Briggs, 1996). Because literacy involves complex, ongoing, and varied interactions with diverse texts in social environments, educators need to conceptualize and implement instruction that enables students to read and write across media and contexts. Principles to guide this instruction are detailed next.

READING AND WRITING ACROSS THE MEDIA: QUESTIONING AND EXTENDING INSTRUCTIONAL PRACTICES

Evolving conditions, definitions of literacy, and technologies require corresponding changes in teaching and learning. But what should these changes look like? Might educators implement new conceptions of literacy within their existing belief systems and instructional frameworks?

Varying forms of representation develop different cognitive skills (Eisner, 1997). Most educators recognize the importance of teaching diverse cognitive skills and already use a range of print texts to teach them; many also employ new educational technologies like video, computers, or CD-ROMs in their classrooms. But Callister (1994) points out that new technologies are often used to simply replicate existing instruction rather than in innovative or relevant ways. New technologies have expanded representational forms and responses to them. How we represent abstract or concrete experiences affects our understandings and actions (Messaris, 1994). Contemporary students employ diverse cognitive strategies to understand concrete and abstract experiences conveyed thorough varied symbol systems and representations. Therefore, educators must question what texts they use and how they use them. They must begin employ varied texts in new ways to reflect the multiplicities of representation, symbol systems, and responses made possible by electronic, print, and experiential texts (Adams and Hamm, 1989). One way to accomplish these goals is by teaching students how to read and write across the media.

Reading and writing across media involves "positioning media arts, instead of traditional language arts, at the heart of all disciplines in the curriculum. . . . Reading and writing is still about pencils and books, but it is also about the symbolic and visual languages of film, video, computers, and popular culture texts" (Leveranz and Tyner, 1996, p. 10). Within this instruc-tional framework, varied media are used in diverse, innovative ways, not as mere enrichment or add-ons, but as texts worthy of study. For example, teachers would not simply use television or videos as a way to convey educational content, but would teach students to critically "read" rhetoric, structures, ideologies, and processes presented through them and to "write" their own texts through print, oral, and electronic means.

Educators may successfully merge print-based instruction with new conceptions of literacy and texts. Reading and writing across media support and extend many educators' instructional goals, theories, models, and practices. Using varied educational technologies promotes literacy learning among diverse populations (Levinson, 1994), particularly for culturally marginalized students (Cummins and Sayers, 1995). Employing mass media in literacy instruction fosters multicultural appreciation (Sinatra, 1990); develops reading, writing, and critical thinking skills (Sinatra, 1986); helps students make personal connections among experiences (Lester, 1995); promotes comprehension of textual elements (Watts Pailliotet, 1997); deepens abstract understandings (Arnheim, 1993); and creates connections among social experiences (Stevenson, 1995). Teaching with varied technologies, mass media, and popular texts may further students' civic involvement and future professional success (Levinson, 1994); generate interest and active engagement (Witkin, 1994); and support multiple modalities, variations in academic ability and learning styles (Glasgow, 1996). Additionally, media literacy is compatible with print literacy theories like whole language (Fehlman, 1996) and transactional approaches (Reutzel and Cooter, 1996), enabling educators to forge a middle ground among competing reading paradigms (Lueker, 1996). Reading and writing across media also extends many prevailing instructional models—presentation, demonstration, discussion, problem solving, drill and practice (Newby et al., 1996)—and strengthens instructional practices like cooperative learning, use of multicultural texts, and teaching critical thinking (Considine and Haley, 1992).

In particular, computer use supports current literacy conceptions, goals, and practices. Creative teaching with computers promotes understandings of language purposes and varied symbolic forms (Labbo, 1996), by building on student strengths and individual needs (Schwartz, 1989). Students who compose with computers demonstrate increased investment in academic tasks, and many basic writers improve their skills (Zeni, 1990). Kearsley, Hunter, and Furlong (1992) identify additional benefits: computers help reluctant students with poor handwriting or vocabulary skills express ideas; they shift learning from lower-order memorization to higher-order problem-solving; and they foster meaningful communication. Computers also encourage students to spend more time thinking about writing and revising than when composing freehand (Kearsley et al., 1992; Zeni, 1990). Teamwork and cooperative learning may be employed in computer lessons to generate positive literacy environments and social interactions (Kearsley et al., 1992; Scrimshaw, 1993; Zeni, 1990). Because computers allow for options in writing, they make possible new student/teacher roles like coaching or mentoring; they encourage students to think about processes as well as products, thus alternative authentic assessments like writing improvement conferences, observation, and team evaluations become possible (Zeni, 1990, pp. 166-75). Last, computers help students develop competencies and connections across media and contexts (Adams and Hamm, 1989; Collins, 1985; Moore, 1989; Reinking, 1995).

The three lessons presented next reflect current literacy conceptions, principles, goals, and practices. All begin with traditional print lesson frameworks but employ varied print, electronic, and experiential texts. All engage students in varied literacy processes, develop diverse skills and competencies, encourage active constructions of meaning, and foster readerly/writerly connections among people, texts, and experiences. These lessons occur in highly social environments, employ multiple modalities, value diverse ways of knowing, and use varied instructional approaches. Throughout these activities, students and teachers also assume many roles and are actively involved in ongoing assessment.

READING AND WRITING ACROSS THE MEDIA: THREE LESSON PLANS FOR USING VARIED EDUCATIONAL TECHNOLOGIES FOR LITERACY LEARNING

Description of Students

These literacy activities have been used successfully with students ranging from fifth grade through high school and college. With younger students, more time, modeling, and active teacher monitoring may be necessary.

Overview

Each lesson uses the same text, but in different ways. All ideally take place in a computer lab but could be easily adapted for classrooms with one computer or a small number. If you do not have adequate computers, do this activity using scheduled writing times and multiple computer files, or even a round-robin station format where students move from poster texts on tables or desks. These activities will take a minimum of three days (Day One: Prewriting; Day Two: Drafting, Revising, Responding, and Editing; Day Three: Publishing) but are most easily extended to a five-day writing workshop. Adaptations for each are noted.

These lessons follow a traditional literacy lesson framework with Before, During, and After reading activities (Vacca and Vacca, 1996). Each also employs all stages in the writing process (Hairston, 1982). Procedures, teacher and student prompts, sample peer response questions, and assessment ideas are provided.

Materials

Materials will vary according to activity, but include computers, paper, text (*The Mysteries of Harris Burdick* [Van Allsburg, 1984]), disks, newspapers or newscast videos, poster paper for charts, thesauri, dictionaries, varied art materials, magazines for collages, scissors, colored pens for revisions, and video or audio taping equipment.

Initial Activity: Whole Group Oral Reading

All lessons begin with a whole group oral reading of *The Mysteries of Harris Burdick*. Written by award-winning author Chris Van Allsburg, the text consists of a series of titles and one-sentence story starters, each accompanied by unusual black-and-white drawings. Students of all ages love their eeriness and complexity.

Before Reading

Objectives:

Prepare and involve students for writing activities, activate interest, increase student confidence in personal responses, generate ideas for prewriting, model textual responses through teacher questioning.

Procedures:

Teacher shows title and cover illustration to whole group.
Ask students, "What do you think the book will be about?"
Students will give various replies, but most, if not all, will refer to a narrative or describe a story.

Teacher: "You're all right! This author allows you to create your own stories! He gives you pictures and a single sentence. It is up to you to write your own story. As we read and look at the pictures, think about the types of stories you might write. As we read, we'll share our ideas."

During Reading

Objectives:

Further preparation, activation of schema and interest, development of oral reading fluency, comprehension, vocabulary, and critical viewing, generate ideas for prewriting, model textual responses through teacher questioning.

Procedures:

Students and teacher take turns reading each title and sentence; teacher shows each illustration. Ask students to define vocabulary they may not be familiar with. Stop at each page to help students generate ideas and textual connections. Because there are no "right" or "wrong" answers, this activity is an excellent way to involve all students. For each page, ask multiple students for their responses. Suggested prompts include:

What is this about? (Students generate ideas after reading title.)

What is happening? (Students suggest plots based on pictures.)

What is the next line? (Students articulate the next sentence after reading the story starter.)

Who are these people? (Students describe a character.)

Where is this taking place? (Students brainstorm settings.)

What parts of the picture do you like best? (Students analyze content and artistic technique.)

What words best describe this picture? (Students use vivid verbs, adjectives, or adverbs to describe the mood or content.)

What is this picture like? (Students generate metaphors.)

If this picture were in a newspaper, what would be the headline? What would the caption say underneath?

If this picture were on the six o'clock news, what would the newscaster say to sum it up and capture your attention?

After Reading: Writing Process Activities

Objectives:

These activities span Bloom's objectives from level one through level six. They help students develop multiple literacy modalities; promote reading comprehension and oral and print fluency; foster competencies in writing process; increase computer skills; heighten enjoyment; develop knowledge of narrative structures through use of story grammars; further social skills and collaboration; deepen student vocabulary through use of figurative and colorful language; strengthen analytic understandings of expository patterns; encourage creation of meaningful, authentic texts; teach critiques and applications of structures used in popular newscasts; connect media and experiences; improve grammar and spelling; develop cognitive skills like comparing, contrasting, synthesizing, generating, and evaluating; and generate awareness of metacognitive strategies.

Option One: Writing Group Stories

Prewriting:

1. After reading and viewing the book, students brainstorm other scary story opening sentences and write them down (e.g., "It was a dark and stormy night. . . " "The clock struck midnight.").

2. Students select one sentence for each member of their group. They may use one from the book or an original one. They enter each on a separate computer or paper.

Drafting:

1. Round-robin writing.
   Teacher directions: "We will use a common story grammar format to develop our stories. Leave room between sections for revising and editing."
   Each group member sits at a computer (or station) and begins the story. Teacher calls time, and students move to next computer or text. Allow a minimum of 10 minutes per round. I have found that students quickly become engaged in this activity and are reluctant to stop writing (!). Stress that they are to get their ideas down and not worry about grammar or spelling at this point—they will have time to revise later.

   Round One: Establish characters and setting
   (Cinderella lives with her stepmother and stepsisters in a big house and
      is unhappy.)

   Round Two: Initiating event and internal response
   (The prince plans a ball and Cindy wants to go.)

   Rounds Three and Four: Goals, attempts, and blocks
   (Goal and attempt one: She tries to make a dress but has no shoes.
   Goal and attempt two: Fairy godmother helps her, but she has to leave the ball.
   Goal and attempt three: The prince finds her shoe and searches the land.)

   Round Five: Outcomes
   (The prince finds her and the slipper fits.)

2. Return students to their original stories to promote investment in text and writing.

   Round Six: Resolution
   (Cindy and the prince live happily ever after.)

3. Save on disk or server and print out these stories.

Revising and Editing:

1. Individual students read their stories silently.

2. Teacher reviews story grammar elements and criteria in the whole group. Connecting print narrative structures to films students have seen and enjoyed (*Star Wars* is a great one) fosters comprehension and involvement. Using guiding questions, teacher and students discuss narrative elements and identify examples of effective and ineffective narratives—whether they are conveyed through film or print text. Create a rubric with criteria for each part of the narrative. For example, under "Establishing characters and settings," criteria might include physical details of

setting, early character introduction through vivid descriptions, dialogue, creation of interest and curiosity, and strength of opening sentences. The rubric can be recorded on a piece of poster paper or overhead transparency using an intersected list model. An example of one entry might look like this:

ELEMENTS in NARRATIVES

	Excellent	**Good**	**Poor**
Establishing Characters and Setting			
Physical details	Uses strong images senses. May be unusual. Immediate action. Creates strong audience interest.	Some images. Present but is slow or predictable. Creates some interest.	Little detail or little opening action. Boring.

Post the rubric for student use.

3. Individually or in pairs, students circle and label each part of the story structure using colored pens.

4. Using the rubric as a guideline, students add to structures that are missing or need more development, writing on the hard copy or using the electronic copy. (It's easier to use the computer.)

5. Peer response: Students read stories aloud to one or more peers in pairs or teams. Peers listen and take notes on peer response form. (See Appendix 1 for sample peer response questions.) Author asks for feedback. Peers should also evaluate text for elements in rubric and offer specific suggestions for revision. Teachers will need to model response strategies if students are not familiar with them.

6. Students revise story based on peer feedback. At the end of writing, they should add a title and proof text for grammar, spelling, and punctuation. Remind them options include spellchecking, using dictionaries and other print resources, and checking mechanics with peers or teacher.

7. Print out revised final version.

Publishing Options:

Create an illustration or book jacket for your story using a computer program or other artistic medium.

Create a movie poster for your story. Cast actors for your story main characters and credit them on your poster.

Author's chair.

Class book.

Paired oral readings in or out of class.

Teacher Assessment Options:

Use rubric to evaluate strengths and weaknesses of narrative elements; pass/fail upon completion of all assignment parts; observations, anecdotal records, or checklists of on-task or cooperative behaviors; improvement from first to last draft.

Student Assessment Options:

Completion of peer response; conferencing report with teacher or peers to identify goals; oral or written summary of improvement or learning; evaluation of own or peers' final peer stories through reviews; editing final class book; use rubric to evaluate strengths and weaknesses of narrative elements through written means or oral conference; metaanalysis of changes made and why.

Option Two: Responding to Images

Prewriting:

1. Students look at the pictures in the text.

2. Students select a picture they particularly like.

3. In groups, students brainstorm and write a list of situations to explain the picture.

Drafting:

1. In pairs or individually, students write a story about the picture. They may write a traditional narrative, a letter to a friend, a poem, or a song, or use any other format they wish.

2. Students save the double-spaced document to disk and print it.

Revising and Editing:

In a whole-group or mini-lesson, students and teachers generate a list of words that evoke strong images or moods and those that do not. Teacher and students develop a hit list of words to avoid and think of more vivid ones. Teachers can model how to use computer or print thesauri and encourage students to recall effective language from recent readings or viewings of class texts. Record responses on a poster or transparency or in a computer file. Group words under parts of speech (nouns, verbs, adjectives, etc.), senses, or other categories depending on student need. An example is shown below.

IMAGES, SENSES, and MOOD WORDS

"Hit list" (Words to avoid)	Alternatives
Images	
nice	accommodating, amicable, congenial
beautiful	comely, alluring, captivating
bad	waggish, impish, roguish, disobedient
big	gargantuan, ample, stupendous, massive
Senses	
see	discern, witness, perceive, behold
sounds	clamor, din, bedlam, serenity, silence

Teachers and students can identify parts of speech on list. Teachers also need to discuss with students how words can convey multiple meanings and can be changed. For example, "witness" may be a verb or noun, depending on context, and may be changed to "witnessing." At this point, students and teachers may choose to set certain writing goals—identifying a number of words as "word bank" vocabulary for use in student writing, generating words for spelling tests, or focusing on a particular part of speech or sense. Post the chart for student use.

1. Students reread their texts individually and silently.

2. Students circle all verbs, nouns, adjectives, and adverbs. They also underline all vague "hit words." They may want to use different colored pens for each part of speech to reinforce understandings.

3. Using a print or computer thesaurus and referring to the "hit list," students replace nouns, verbs, adjectives, and adverbs on the computer text or hard copy so that their story conveys a particular mood (e.g., scary, angry, happy) and powerful images. Direct students to make sure they have words and sentences that evoke all senses, strong imagery, and/or discernible moods.

4. Peer conferencing: In pairs or teams, students orally read texts to peers. Listeners generate a written list of words and phrases they find effective and not effective. Peer listeners then read aloud their lists back to the author and identify the story's mood. Peer listeners should also fill out the response form. Teachers may ask peer respondents to identify words that evoke all the senses.

5. Student authors revise, based on feedback. At the end of writing, they should add a title and proof text for grammar, spelling, and punctuation. Remind them options include spellchecking, using dictionaries and other print resources, and checking mechanics with peers or teacher.

6. Print out the revised final copy.

Publishing Options:

Create an illustration that depicts the most vivid scene in your text.

Construct a collage from magazines that depicts the mood and tone of your writing.

Create an advertisement poster with an image and slogan that capture your story's mood.

Author's chair or choral reading

Class book edited by students.

Class thesaurus generated by students using computer or print.

Teacher Assessment Options:

Successful use of word bank or target words in text; informal assessment or checklist of on-task or collaborative behaviors; points or grade for completion of all parts of assignment; list of student-generated words spelled successfully in postwriting quiz; improvement through revisions.

Student Assessment Options:

Students complete peer response and identification of effective language; generate spelling words; rewrite another passage using effective language and imagery to change mood; identify mood or assessment of writing strengths and weaknesses during author's chair; student editors compile an accurate computerized thesaurus or edit class book correctly.

Option Three: Reporting "The Evening Ghouls": Adapting Literature to Other Media

Prewriting:

1. Students decide if they want to do a newscast or newspaper article.

2. After rereading the text, brainstorm topics that are scary or unusual or that deal with the occult (ghosts, vampires, UFOs, sightings of Elvis, etc.) and generate a written list.

3. Students pick a topic to write about.

Drafting:

1. In a group, in pairs, or individually, students write news stories. Include:

   Who (Who was involved? Who are they?)

   What (What happened?)

   Where (Where did it happen?)

   When (When did it happen?)

   How (How did it happen? What was the sequence of events?)

   Why (Why did it happen?)

2. Students save and print out this document.

Revising and Editing:

1. Students reread their texts individually and silently.

2. In whole-group or mini-lesson format, teacher and students identify the traits of an effective news story. Teacher may show a brief clip of a newscast and direct students in teams to record elements, purposes, and devices used. Or teachers can use a newspaper article and ask students in the whole group, in small groups, or in pairs to identify elements, purposes, and writing devices. For example, the teacher may direct students to circle and label the five Ws and how. Also ask students what is missing in terms of textual elements and information to increase critical thinking skills.

Students and teachers then compile a list using a poster, transparency, or computer:

NEWS STORIES

Element	Purposes	Writing Devices
Strong lead sentence	Establish context, evoke interest.	Use vivid words; ask a question; summarize; relate to a previous story.
Who	Helps audience relate to story; shows importance, provides information.	Use physical description; detail past and present actions; use pictures and quotes.
When	Creates immediacy and importance.	Inclusion of dates; images using verbs in present tense.
Evidence and detail	Provides information, increases reporter credibility, generates audience interest.	Quotes; using charts or graphs; citing experts; using statistics; use adjectives and adverbs.
Missing information	Reflects point of view; furthers story impact; creates credibility and cohesive story.	Using dialogue from only one person; camera angles; using certain facts or statistics and not reporting others.

Post this chart for student reference.

3. Students reread their texts, circle elements identified in chart, and note ones that are missing. At this point, teachers may want to incorporate a lesson on research strategies and resources. For example, teachers might introduce or review search, note taking, summarizing, or citation procedures, then model use of resources like electronic or print catalogs, books, newspapers, the Internet, CD-ROMs, videos, magazines, and class texts. Students may engage in research and then revise, or immediately write by making up facts, depending on lesson focus.

4. Students exchange papers at the "Editor's desk." In pairs or groups, they read news stories aloud to peers. Peers listen and take notes about each element. They will evaluate the story, based on the class-generated chart, identifying which parts are strong, weak, or missing. Peers fill out response form and, like news editors, make specific suggestions for final "publication" or "production."

5. Based on peer feedback, students revise again. They should add supporting evidence and detail, include media devices like statistics or quotes from experts and witnesses (made up or researched), use effective language, and generate descriptions of people, places, situations, etc.

6. Students proof and print out final story.

Publishing Options:

Create a "photograph," chart, newscast backdrop, or other visual that explains your story.

Find a chart, picture, or photograph on the World Wide Web and print it or incorporate it into your text.

Using a layout program, create a newspaper that reports all stories.

Using a video or audio recorder, tape news stories and present them to classmates.

Dramatic Reading: report "newscasts" or read "news articles" to the class.

Teacher Assessment Options:

Grade for quality of supporting evidence and detail; pass/fail for completion of all parts of assignment or 5 Ws and how; informal assessment of cooperative or on-task behaviors; speaking skills checklist or anecdotal records; pretest and posttest of vocabulary development or spelling; comments or conferences on effective language usage; notes or grades on student research skills and accuracy of resources; improvement from first to last draft.

Student Assessment Options:

Oral or written summary of principles and elements in news articles; process accounts; peer response; successful editing of peer work; compilation of class newspaper or newscast.

Cumulative student assessment might include the following: Students role-play reporters and describe orally or in written form what they need to consider and do to write an effective news story. Students become "sponsors" of newscasts or "advertisers" in newspapers using the chart to evaluate the effectiveness of peers' texts and decide if they want to give "stations" or "papers" their business.

AN EXAMPLE OF LITERACY INSTRUCTION: FROM "DO WE HAVE TO?" TO "CAN WE DO MORE?"

I define literacy broadly—as interactive, complex, social processes of "reading" and "writing" that occur across multiple media and contexts. I also believe literate acts should be meaningful and, ideally, enjoyable. My understandings are reflected in the preservice literacy methods courses I teach. My students are diligent undergraduates who complete dual majors in a rigorous liberal arts setting. While fulfilling numerous academic requirements, most also maintain jobs, community service commitments, and relationships. Many are currently completing senior theses, comprehensive orals, and written exams. My preservice teachers and I recently engaged in some of the activities presented here the week before spring break. When I announced we were going to the computer lab for a writing lesson, several groaned audibly. There was unanimous class consensus:

"Do we have to?"

"Yes," I replied. "Trust me. This will be fun."

They sluggishly rose, reluctantly hoisted overladen backpacks, trudged like arthritic 80-year-olds down the hall, and unenthusiastically slumped into chairs. Several sighed deeply or covertly glanced at their watches. One failed to mask a yawn.

Subtle transformations began to occur as we read *The Mysteries of Harris Burdick* aloud and generated ideas. Tense faces relaxed; smiles appeared; bodies leaned closer to the text and classmates; voices became excited; and responses grew in creativity and frequency. There was even laughter.

"This is pretty cool."

"This isn't your typical book."

"This isn't what I expected."

"What's next?" they asked, unprompted, after we had finished. I explained their options. All decided to write group stories and headed to the computers. They moved noticeably more quickly than they had earlier. I gave directions to begin. Gazes were intent upon computer screens; fingers flew; the click-clack of keyboarding was broken only by an occasional chuckle or head scratch. No one yawned or checked the time. At 10-minute intervals I directed them to change stations. Now the groans involved pleas for more time. With each change, the students became increasingly slow to leave their chairs and ever more reluctant to leave the texts they were creating.

"Do we have to?"

"Wait, I'm on a roll."

"Five more minutes—please?"

I couldn't help but make a few snide (but insightful) observations:

"Mmm, You're *asking* to write? You *want* to write *more*? You *want* to write *longer*?"

"Pretty interesting behavior for burned-out seniors who are tired of writing."

"Look at you! I could set off a bomb in here, and I bet you wouldn't even look up!"

I don't know how much they heard me—they were too involved.

Finally, it was time for them to return to the original stations, write conclusions, and print. All signs of former lethargy had disappeared. Now several fairly bolted across the lab to retrieve their papers from the printer. The noise level rose as they clustered about, reading their drafts to each other.

"Check this out! Excellent metaphor!"

"Who wrote this? Did you write this? You have really good descriptions! How do you do this?" An impromptu discussion of creative writing process and strategies ensued.

"Oh yeah—awesome twist in plot!"

"This would make the coolest *Twilight Zone* episode."

I gathered my students back together. Smiles abounded. It was hard to stop them from talking about their writing and reading to each other. I did the professor closure modeling thing. I pointed out the instructional approaches and literacy strategies we had used. They identified teaching principles and theories we had applied. We discussed their positive responses to the lesson. As time ran out, I asked them, "Any questions?"

They posed several:

"Can we do more?"

"Can we revise these? Can we read them to the class?"

"Could we change the format? Rewrite them like a movie?"

"Can I work on this over break?"

As class ended, there was again unanimous consensus, but it had a decidedly different focus:

"This was really fun, and we learned stuff too."

This account demonstrates how educators may apply current literacy reconceptualizations, principles, and practices—and the many positive outcomes that occur when they do. When my students return, we will continue this lesson, because I believe teachers and students learn much with varied educational technologies to read and write across media.

APPENDIX: PEER RESPONSE QUESTIONS

Directions: The reader will read the paper aloud to the listener. The listener should make notes and then discuss the following points with the reader. Exchange roles and repeat the process. DO NOT throw out these papers. Use them as you edit your draft and turn them in with your final paper. For each question, cite textual examples and identify your responses to them.

1. What do you like about this text?

2. What did you notice about it first?

3. How do you feel when you listen to this text? Are there parts that particularly interest you or that seem more "real" than others? What could the author do to make all parts interesting?

4. What is this text about? What confuses you about this text?

5. What questions do you still have about the text after listening to it?

6. What might the writer add or delete?

7. Ask the writer, "What do you think of this text? How does it sound to you? What problems are you having writing it?" Note the writer's observations and list possible solutions.

8. Ask the writer, "What can you do to make this text better?" List the remarks.

9. Offer suggestions to the writer.

10. List your plan for revision here.

REFERENCES

Adams, D. M., and Hamm, M. E. (1989). *Media and literacy: Learning in an electronic age.* Springfield, IL: Charles C. Thomas.

Althusser, L. (1986). Ideology and ideological state apparatuses. In *Critical theory since 1965,* ed. H. Adams and L. Searle (Tallahassee, FL: Florida State University Press), 239-51.

Alvermann, D. E., Young, J. P., Weaver, D., Hinchman, K. A., Moore, D. W., Phelps, S. F., Thrash, E. C., and Zalewski, P. (1996). Middle and high school students' perceptions of how they experience text-based discussion: A multicase study. *Reading Research Quarterly 31*(3), 244-67.

Arnheim, R. (1993). Learning by looking and thinking. *Educational Horizons 71*(2), 94-98.

Atwell, N. (1985). Writing and reading from the inside out. In *Breaking ground: Teachers relate reading and writing in the elementary school,* ed. J. Hansen, T. Newkirk, and D. Graves (Portsmouth, NH: Heinemann), 147-65.

Banks, J. A., and Banks, C. A., eds. (1997). *Multicultural education: Issues and perspectives.* Boston: Allyn and Bacon.

Barthes, R. (1957). *Mythologies.* Annette Lavers, trans. New York: Noonday Press/Farrar, Straus & Giroux.

Barthes, R. (1974). *S/Z.* Richard Miller, trans. New York: Hill and Wang/Noonday Press.

Berger, P. L., and Luckmann, T. (1963). *The social construction of reality.* Garden City, NY: Anchor.

Bhaktin, M. M. (1988). Intertextuality. In *Mikhail Bhaktin: The dialogical principle,* ed. T. Todorov. (Minneapolis: University of Minnesota Press), 60-74.

Bianculli, D. (1992). *Teleliteracy.* New York: Continuum.

Bissex, G. (1980). *Gnys at work.* Boston: Harvard University Press.

Bloome, D., and Eagan-Robertson, A. (1993). The social construction of intertextuality in classroom reading and writing lessons. *Reading Research Quarterly 28,* 304-33.

Bolter, J. D. (1991). *Writing space: The computer hypertext and the history of writing.* Hillsdale, NJ: Laurence Erlbaum.

Bopry, J. (1994). Visual literacy in education - A semiotic perspective. *Journal of Visual Literacy 14*(1), 35-49.

Brand, A. G. (1987). The why of cognition: Emotion and the writing process. *College Composition and Communication 38*(4), 436-43.

Brophy, J. (1992). Probing the subtleties of subject-matter teaching. *Educational Leadership 49*(7), 4-8.

Bruner, J. (1990). *Acts of meaning.* Cambridge, MA.: Harvard University Press.

Buckingham, D. (1993). Introduction: Young people and the media. In *Reading Audiences: Young people and the media*, ed. D. Buckingham (Manchester, England: Manchester University Press), 1-23.

Cairney, T. H. (1997). New avenues to literacy. *Educational Leadership 54*(6), 76-77.

Callister, T. A., Jr. (1994). Educational computing's new direction: Cautiously approaching an unpredictable future. *Educational Theory 44*(2), 239-56.

Collins, C. (1985). The interactive literacy: The connection between reading and writing and the computer. *Collegiate MicroComputer 3*(4), 333-38.

Considine, D. M., and Haley, G. E. (1992). *Visual messages: Integrating imagery into instruction.* Englewood, CO: Teacher Ideas Press.

Corkill, A. J. (1996). Individual differences in metacognition. *Learning and Individual Differences 8*(4), 275-89.

Cummins, J., and Sayers, D. (1995). *Brave new schools.* New York: St. Martin's Press.

Dyson, A. H. (1984). Reading, writing, and language: Young children solving the written language puzzle. In *Composing and comprehending*, ed. J. Jensen (Urbana, IL: National Council of Teachers of English), 165-74.

Ediger, M. (1993). The affective dimension in curriculum improvement. *Education 114*(1), 81-84.

Edwards, B. L., Jr. (1991). How computers change things: Literacy and the digitalized word. *Writing Instructor 10*(2), 68-76.

Eisner, E. W. (1997). Cognition and representation: A way to pursue the American dream? *Phi Delta Kappan 78*(5), 349-53.

Elbow, P. (1985). The shifting relationship between speech and writing. *College Composition and Communication 36*(3), 283-301.

Emig, J. (1983). *The web of meaning.* Upper Montclair, NJ: Boynton/Cook.

Farstrup, A. E., and Myers, M., eds. (1996). *Standards for the English language arts.* Urbana, IL: National Council of Teachers of English and Newark, DE: International Reading Association.

Fehlman, R. H. (1996). Viewing film and television as whole language instruction. *English Journal 85*(2), 43-50.

Fiske, J., and Hartley, J. (1978). *Reading television.* London: Methuen.

Flood, J., and Lapp, D. (1995). Broadening the lens: Toward an expanded conceptualization of literacy. In *Perspectives on literacy research and practice: Forty-fourth yearbook of the National Reading Conference*, ed. K. A. Hinchman, D. J. Leu, and C. K. Kinzer (Chicago: National Reading Conference), 1-16.

Flower, L. (1989). Cognition, context, and theory building. *College Composition and Communication 40*(3), 282-311.

Foster, H. M. (1979). *The new literacy: The language of film and television.* Urbana, IL: National Council of Teachers of English.

Frye, N. (1957). *Anatomy of criticism.* Princeton, NJ: Princeton University Press.

Gardner, H. (1985). *Frames of mind: The theory of multiple intelligences.* New York: Basic Books.

Giroux, H. A. (1993). Reclaiming the social: Pedagogy, resistance and politics in celluloid culture. In *Film theory goes to the movies*, ed. J. Collins, H. Radner, and A. P. Collins (New York: Routledge), 37-55.

Glasgow, J. N. (1996). Motivating the tech prep reader through learning styles and adolescent literature. *Journal of Adolescent and Adult Literacy 39*(5), 358-67.

Goody, E. N. (1978). Towards a theory of questions. In *Questions and politeness: Strategies in social interaction*, ed. E. N. Goody (New York: Cambridge University Press), 16-43.

Hairston, M. (1982). The winds of change: Thomas Kuhn and the revolution in the teaching of writing. *College Composition and Communication 33*(1), 76-88.

Heath, S. B. (1983). *Ways with words: Language life and work in communities and classrooms.* New York: Cambridge University Press.

Herber, H. L., and Herber, J. N. (1993). *Teaching in content areas with reading, writing, and reasoning.* Boston: Allyn & Bacon.

Hynds, S. (1990). Reading as a social event: Comprehension and response in the classroom, text, and world. In *Beyond communication: Reading comprehension and criticism*, ed. D. Bogdan and S. B. Straw (Plymouth, MA: Boynton/Cook/Heinemann), 237-56.

Kearsley, G., Hunter, B., and Furlong, M. (1992). *We teach with technology: New visions for education.* Wilsonville, OR: Franklin, Beedle.

Kervin, D. (1985). Reading images: Levels of meaning in television commercials. In *Readings from the 16th annual conference of the International Visual Literacy Association*, ed. N. Thayer and S. Clayton-Randolph (Bloomington, IN: Western Sun), 36-43.

Kincheloe, J. L., and Steinberg, S. R. (1993). A tentative description of post-formal thinking: The critical confrontation with cognitive theory. *Harvard Educational Review 63*(3), 296-320.

Labbo, L. D. (1996). A semiotic analysis of young children's symbol making in a classroom computer center. *Reading Research Quarterly 31*(4), 356-85.

Lakoff, G., and Johnson, M. (1980). *Metaphors we live by.* Chicago: Chicago University Press.

Lehtonen, J. (1988). The information society and the new competence. *American Behavioral Scientist 32*(2), 104-11.

Lester, P. M. (1995). *Visual communication: Images with messages.* Belmont, CA: Wadsworth Publishing.

Leveranz, D., and Tyner, K. (1996). What is media literacy? Two leading proponents offer an overview. *Media Spectrum 23*(1), 10.

Levinson, M. E. (1994). Needed: A new literacy. *The Humanist 54*(3), 3-5; 34.

Lloyd-Kolkin, D., and Tyner, K. R. (1991). *Media and you: An elementary media literacy curriculum.* Englewood Cliffs, NJ: Educational Technology Publications.

Lueker, D. H. (1996). Can technology help teach reading right? *Electronic Learning 16*(3), 32-39.

Lusted, D., ed. (1991). *The media studies book: A guide for teachers.* New York: Routledge.

Lutz, W. (1989). *DoubleSpeak.* New York: HarperPerrenial.

McLuhan, M. (1962). *The Gutenberg galaxy: The making of typographic man.* Toronto: University of Toronto Press.

McLuhan, M. (1964). *Understanding media: The extensions of man.* New York: McGraw-Hill.

McLuhan, M., and Fiore, Q. (1967). *The medium is the massage.* New York: Random House.

McLuhan, M., and McLuhan, E. (1988). *Laws of media: The new science.* Toronto: University of Toronto Press.

Messaris, P. (1994). *Visual literacy: Image mind and reality.* Boulder, CO: Westview Press.

Moore, M. A. (1989). Computers can enhance transactions between readers and writers. *The Reading Teacher 42*(8), 608-11.

Mosenthal, P. B. (1988). The conduit metaphor and the academic views of reading. *The Reading Teacher 41*(5), 448-49.

Neuman, S. B. (1991). *Literacy in the television age: The myth of the TV effect.* Norwood, NJ: Ablex Publishing.

Newby, T. J., Stepich, D. A., Lehman, J. D., and Russell, J. D. (1996). *Instructional technology for teaching and learning.* Englewood Cliffs, NJ: Merrill.

O'Brien, D. G., and Stewart, R. A. (1990). Preservice teachers' perspectives on why every teacher is not a teacher of reading: A qualitative analysis. *Journal of Reading Behavior 22*(2),101-29.

Ohlgren, T. H., and Berk, L. M. (1977). *The new languages: A rhetorical approach to mass media and popular culture.* Englewood Cliffs, NJ: Prentice-Hall.

Olson, G. A. (1996). Writing, literacy, and technology: Toward a cyborg writing. *JAC: A Journal of Composition Theory 16*(1), 1-26.

Papert, S. (1993). *The children's machine: Rethinking school in the age of computers.* New York: Basic Books.

Pike, K., Compain, R., and Mumper, J. (1994). *New connections: An integrated approach to literacy.* New York: HarperCollins.

Reinking, D., ed. (1987). *Reading and computers: Issues for theory and practice.* New York: Teachers College Press.

Reinking, D. (1995). Reading and writing with computers: Literacy research in a post-typographic world. In *Perspectives on literacy research and practice*, ed. K. A. Hinchman, D. J. Leu, and C. K. Kinzer (Chicago: National Reading Conference), 17-33.

Rosenblatt, L. (1978). *The reader, the text, the poem: The transactional theory of the literary work.* Carbondale, IL: Southern Illinois University Press.

Reutzel, R. D., and Cooter, R. B., Jr. (1996). *Teaching children to read.* Englewood Cliffs, NJ: Prentice Hall.

Saint-Martin, F. (1990). *Semiotics of visual language.* Indianapolis, IN: Indiana University Press.

Schwartz, H. J. (1989). Creating writing activities with the word processor. In *Computers in English and the language arts*, ed. C. L. Selfe, D. Rodrigues, and W. R. Oates (Urbana, IL: National Council of Teachers of English), 197-203.

Scrimshaw, P. (1993). Cooperative writing with computers. In *Language classrooms and computers*, ed. P. Scrimshaw (New York: Routledge), 100-110.

Selfe, C. L., and Hilligoss, S., eds. (1994). *Literacy and computers: The complications of teaching and learning with technology.* New York: Modern Language Association.

Sinatra, R. (1986). *Visual literacy connections to thinking reading and writing.* Springfield, IL: Charles C. Thomas.

Sinatra, R. (1990). Combining visual literacy, text understanding, and writing for culturally diverse students. *Journal of Reading 33*(8), 612-17.

Smith, F. (1984). Reading like a writer. In *Composing and comprehending*, ed. J. Jensen (Urbana, IL: National Council of Teachers of English), 47-56.

Stevenson, N., ed. (1995). *Understanding media cultures: Social theory and mass communication.* Thousand Oaks, CA: Sage.

Streibel, M. J. (1985). Visual literacy, television literacy, and computer Literacy: Some parallels and a synthesis. *Journal of Visual/Verbal Languaging 5*(2), 5-14.

Vacca, R. T., and Vacca, J. A. L. (1996). *Content area reading*, 5th ed. New York: HarperCollins.

Van Allsburg, C. (1984). *The mysteries of Harris Burdick.* Boston: Houghton Mifflin.

Vygotsky, L. S. (1978). *Mind in society.* Cambridge, MA: Harvard University Press.

Watts Pailliotet, A. (1994). Understanding visual information through deep viewing. In *Visual literacy in the digital age*, ed. D. G. Beauchamp, R. Braden A., and J. C. Baca (Blacksburg, VA: International Visual Literacy Association), 102-11.

Watts Pailliotet, A. (1997). Questing toward cohesion: Connecting advertisements and classroom reading through visual literacy. In *VisionQuest: Journeys toward visual literacy*, ed. R. E. Griffin, J. M. Hunter, C. B. Schiffman, and W. J. Gibbs (State College, PA: International Visual Literacy Association), 33-41.

Watts Pailliotet, A., Semali, L., Flood, J., Lapp, D., and Briggs, L. C. (1996). Reading, writing, and media viewing connections for teaching literacy. Workshop presentation at International Reading Association 41st Annual Convention. New Orleans, LA.

Wiggins, G. (1993). Assessment, authenticity, context and validity. *Phi Delta Kappan 75*(3), 200-213.

Witkin, M. (1994). A defense of using pop media in the middle school classroom. *English Journal 83*(1), 30-33.

Zeni, J. (1990). *WritingLands: Composing with old and new writing tools.* Urbana, IL: National Council of Teachers of English.

An Introduction to
Internet Resources for K–12 Educators
Part I: Information Resources, Update 1997*

Nancy A. Morgan

The Internet is an international computer network composed of thousands of smaller networks. Recently, through state and regional education networks and commercial providers, the vast resources of the Internet are increasingly available to administrators, school library media specialists, and classroom teachers. This digest lists a sample of no cost Internet resources of special interest to K–12 educators.

Readers should be aware that the resources and their Internet addresses below are subject to change.

GUIDES TO INTERNET RESOURCES

- **The Argus Clearinghouse:** A large collection of guides to Internet resources categorized by topic.

    http://www.clearinghouse.net/

- **AskERIC InfoGuides:** Topical guides to Internet, ERIC, and print resources.

    http://ericir.syr.edu/Virtual/InfoGuides/

LESSON PLANS

- **The AskERIC Virtual Library** contains hundreds of lesson plans, including, but not limited to, language arts, mathematics, social studies, and science. Also included are lesson plans from *School Library Media Activities Monthly*, *Newton's Apple Educators Guides*, and *Crossroads: K16 American History Curriculum*.

    http://ericir.syr.edu/Virtual/Lessons/

KEYPALS AND PENPALS

- **IECC—Intercultural E-mail Classroom Connections** maintains a suite of listservs that facilitate international and cross-cultural classroom exchanges via e-mail over the Internet. Archives and general information can be found on the St. Olaf's WWW server.

    http://www.stolaf.edu/network/iecc/

---

*This ERIC Digest was prepared by Nancy A. Morgan, AskERIC Coordinator for the ERIC Clearinghouse on Information & Technology at Syracuse University. nmorgan@ericir.syr.edu

ERIC Digests are in the public domain and may be freely reproduced and disseminated.

ERIC Clearinghouse on Information & Technology, 4-194 Center for Science & Technology, Syracuse University, Syracuse, NY 13244-4100; (315) 443-3640; FAX (315) 443-5448; e-mail: eric@ericir.syr.edu

This publication was prepared with funding from the Office of Educational Research and Improvement, U.S. Department of Education under contract no. RR93002009. The opinions expressed in this report do not necessarily reflect the positions of OERI or ED.

ACCEPTABLE USE POLICIES

Many schools which provide Internet access to students and staff have created policies and agreements for the appropriate use of Internet accounts. Samples of agreements, policies and opinion pieces have been collected at:

- **Armadillo's WWW Server:**

  http://chico.rice.edu/armadillo/Rice/Resources/acceptable.html

TECHNOLOGY PLANS FOR K–12 SCHOOLS

- **The National Center for Technology Planning** collects technology plans and makes them freely available over the Internet. Guidebooks and articles for developing technology plans are also included.

  http://www2.msstate.edu/~1sa1/nctp/index.html

INTERNET PROJECTS FOR THE CLASSROOM

Examples of telecommunication projects that incorporate the use of the Internet in the classroom can be found on the following sites:

- **Global SchoolNet Foundation:** Internet Projects Registry Archive Service.

  http://www.gsn.org/gsn/proj/index.html

- **Pitsco Online Collaborative Projects:**

  http://www.pitsco.com/pitsco/collab.html

GRANT INFORMATION

- **U.S. Department of Education Grants & Contracts Information:** Includes current Grant Application Announcements.

  http://gcs.ed.gov/
  Select "Grants Information"

- **Foundation Center:** Provides a searchable database of funding activities as well as links to private or corporate foundations' Web sites.

  http://fdncenter.org/

FEDERAL GOVERNMENT INFORMATION

- **Louisiana State University Libraries U.S. Federal Government Agencies Page:**

  http://www.lib.lsu.edu/gov/fedgov.html

- **The Federal Web Locator**, from the Villanova Center for Information Law and Policy.

  http://www.law.vill.edu/fed-agency/fedwebloc.html

STATE EDUCATION DEPARTMENTS

This is a sample list of state departments of education Internet sites.

- **California Department of Education:**

   http://goldmine.cde.ca.gov/

- **Michigan Department of Education:**

   http://www.mde.state.mi.us/

- **North Carolina Department of Public Instruction:**

   http://www.dpi.state.nc.us/

- **Vermont Department of Education:**

   http://www.state.vt.us/educ/

STANDARDS-BASED EDUCATION

- **The Mid-Continental Regional Educational Laboratory (McREL)** is recognized for its work in standards-based education. This WWW site includes several full-text online resources that will assist educators in developing their own standards-based curriculum.

   http://mcrel.org/standard.html

REFERENCE RESOURCES

- **The Libraries of Purdue University:** The Virtual Reference Desk: An extensive collection of online ready reference resources, such as dictionaries, thesauri, phone books and zip codes.

   http://thorplus.lib.purdue.edu/reference/index.html

LIBRARY CATALOGS

- **webCATS**, from the University of Saskatchewan Libraries is a directory of library catalogs which can be searched via the Web. webCATS is organized for searching geographically, by type of library, and by library catalog vendor.

   http://library.usask.ca/hywebcat/

- **Library of Congress:** Provides access to the holdings of the Library of Congress, U.S. Government copyright files, federal legislation, foreign law, and gateway access to many other library catalogs.

   http://lcweb.loc.gov/catalog/

OTHER RESOURCES

Hundreds of resources covering almost every subject imaginable exist on the Internet. Here are some additional ones that would be of special interest to K–12 educators.

- **ACCESS ERIC:** Gateway to the Internet sites of the Educational Resources Information Center (ERIC).

   http://www.aspensys.com/eric/index.html

- **Consortium for School Networking (CoSN):**

  http://www.cosn.org/

- **NASA Spacelink:** Information about NASA, including the space shuttle program, and science curriculum activities.

  http://spacelink.msfc.nasa.gov

  http://spacelink.msfc.nasa.gov/home.index.html

- **Roadmap: An Internet Training Workshop.**

  http://ualvm.ua.edu/~crispen/roadmap.html

- **Web 66:** A K–12 WWW Project from the University of Minnesota.

  http://web66.coled.umn.edu/

- **Yahoo:** A hierarchical subject-oriented catalog for the World Wide Web and Internet.

  http://www.yahoo.com/

REFERENCES AND READINGS

AskERIC Toolbox: Favorite resources of AskERIC's Question-Answering service: http://ericir.sys.edu/Qa/Toolbox/

Junion-Metz, G. (1996). *K–12 resources on the Internet: An instructional guide.* Internet workshop series, number 5. San Carlos, CA: Library Solutions Press. (ISBN-1-882208-14-5). (ED 389 316)

K–12 computer networking. (1995). *The ERIC Review, 4*(1). (ED 392 413)

Lankes, R. D. (1996). *Bread and butter of the Internet. ERIC Digest.* Syracuse, NY: ERIC Clearinghouse on Information & Technology. (ED number pending, IR-97-02)

Miller, E. B. (1996). *The Internet resource directory for K–12 teachers and librarians, 95/96 edition.* Englewood, CO: Libraries Unlimited. (ISBN-1-56308-366-3). (ED 389 330)

Serim, F. and Koch, M. (1996). *NetLearning: Why teachers use the Internet.* Sebastopol, CA: Songline Studios and O'Reilly & Associates. (ED 396 700)

Tennant, R. (1996). *Internet basics: Update 1996. ERIC Digest.* Syracuse, NY: ERIC Clearinghouse on Information & Technology. (ED 392 466)

Valauskas, E. J. and Ertel, M. (1996). *The Internet for teachers and school library media specialists: Today's applications, tomorrow's prospects.* New York: Schuman Publishers. (ISBN-1-55570-239-2). (ED 395 594)

An Introduction to
Internet Resources for K–12 Educators
Part II: Question Answering, Listservs,
Discussion Groups, Update 1997*

Nancy A. Morgan

The Internet is an international computer network composed of thousands of smaller networks. As K–12 schools connect to the Internet, a new method of communication opens up to educators and their students. This digest describes some sample services and resources that are available to the K–12 community by electronic mail over the Internet.

QUESTION ANSWERING

The number of services that use electronic mail to deliver information is increasing. Services that teachers will find on the Internet include:

- **AskERIC:** AskERIC is the Internet-based education information service of the Educational Resources Information Center (ERIC) system, headquartered at the ERIC Clearinghouse on Information & Technology at Syracuse University. Teachers, library media specialists, administrators, and others involved in education can send a message requesting education information to AskERIC. AskERIC information specialists will respond within 48 hours with ERIC database searches, ERIC Digests, and Internet resources. The benefit of the personalized service is that it allows AskERIC staff to interact with the user, and provide relevant education resources tailored to the user's needs.

    E-mail: askeric@ericir.syr.edu

- **AskERIC Virtual Library:** Resources developed from questions received at AskERIC are archived at the AskERIC Virtual Library.

    http://ericir.syr.edu

- **KidsConnect:** KidsConnect is a question-answering, help and referral service for K–12 students on the Internet. The goal of KidsConnect is to help students access and use the information available on the Internet effectively and efficiently. KidsConnect is a component of ICONnect, a technology initiative of AASL (American Association of School Librarians, a division of the American Library Association). Students use e-mail to contact KidsConnect and receive a response from a volunteer library media specialist within two school days.

    E-mail: AskKC@iconnect.syr.edu

    http://www.ala.org/ICONN/kidsconn.html

*This ERIC Digest was prepared by Nancy A. Morgan, AskERIC Coordinator for the ERIC Clearinghouse on Information & Technology. nmorgan@ericir.syr.edu

ERIC Digests are in the public domain and may be freely reproduced and disseminated.

ERIC Clearinghouse on Information & Technology, 4-194 Center for Science & Technology, Syracuse University, Syracuse, NY 13244-4100; (315) 443-3640; FAX (315) 443-5448; e-mail: eric@ericir.syr.edu

This publication was prepared with funding from the Office of Educational Research and Improvement, U.S. Department of Education under contract no. RR93002009. The opinions expressed in this report do not necessarily reflect the positions of OERI or ED.

- **Ask a Young Scientist:** A question answering service for students in grades 1–6 on scientific topics. Questions are researched and answered by advanced chemistry students at Christiansburg High School. Students are asked to limit their questions to five per message, but are encouraged to post as many times as they wish.

  E-mail: apscichs@pen.k12.va.us

- **Ask Dr. Math:** "Ask Dr. Math," a service for elementary, middle, and high school students, is administered by students and professors at Swarthmore College in Swarthmore, PA.

  E-mail: dr.math@forum.swarthmore.edu

  http://forum.swarthmore.edu/dr.math/dr-math.html

LISTSERVS

Listservs are automated programs that serve as distribution centers for mail messages. Listservs focus on a single topic that may be very broad or extremely narrow. People join a listserv by subscribing, then participate by reading messages, or actively contribute by sending messages to the listserv.

Below are listservs of special interest to K–12 educators:

ECENET-L: Early childhood education, to age 8.

—To subscribe, send a message to: listserv@postoffice.cso.uiuc.edu
—Leave the subject line blank.
—In the body of the message, write: subscribe ECENET-L your firstname lastname
  (Archives: http://ericir.syr.edu/Virtual/Listserv_Archives/)
For more information: http://ericps.crc.uiuc.edu/eece/listserv/ecenet-l.html

EDNET: Internet use in education.

—To subscribe, send a message to: listserv@lists.umass.edu
—Leave the subject line blank.
—In the body of the message, write: subscribe EDNET your firstname lastname
  (Archives: http://ericir.syr.edu/Virtual/Listserv_Archives/)

Edres-L: Educational Resources on the Internet.

—To subscribe, send a message to: listserv@listserv.unb.ca
—Leave the subject line blank.
—In the body of the message, write: subscribe Edres-L your firstname lastname

EdTech: Educational Technology.

—To subscribe, send a message to: listserv@msu.edu
—Leave the subject line blank.
—In the body of the message, write: subscribe Edtech your firstname lastname
  (Archives: http://h-net.msu.edu/~edweb)

GiftedNet: National science and language arts curriculum projects for high ability learners.

—To subscribe, send a message to: listserve@listserv.cc.wm.edu
—Leave the subject line blank.
—In the body of the message, write: subscribe GiftedNet your firstname lastname

K12ADMIN: K–12 educational administration.

—To subscribe, send a message to: listserv@listserv.syr.edu

—Leave the subject line blank.

—In the body of the message, write: subscribe K12 Admin your firstname lastname
(Archives: http://ericir.syr.edu/Virtual/Listserv_Archives/)

KIDLINK: Kidlink Society runs several listservs in support of a global dialog for 10–15 year old students. Subscribe to KIDLINK listserv to receive information about the other lists.

—To subscribe, send a message to: listserv@listserv.nodak.edu

—Leave the subject line blank.

—In the body of the message, write: sub Kidlink your firstname lastname

KIDSPHERE: Global network for K–12 children & teachers.

—To subscribe, send a message to: KIDSPHERE-request@vms.cis.pitt.edu

—Leave the subject line blank.

—In the body of the message, write: subscribe Kidsphere your firstname lastname
(Archives: http://ericir.syr.edu/Virtual/Listserv_Archives/)

LM_NET: School library/media services.

—To subscribe, send a message to: listserv@listserv.syr.edu

—Leave the subject line blank.

—In the body of the message, write: subscribe LM_NET your firstname lastname
(Archives: http://ericir.syr.edu/Virtual/Listserv_Archives/WWW:
http://ericir.syr.edu/LM_NET/)

MIDDLE-L: Education of children 10 to 14 years of age.

—To subscribe, send a message to: listserv@postoffice.sco.uiuc.edu

—Leave the subject line blank.

—In the body of the message, write: subscribe Middle-L your firstname lastname
(Archives: http://ericir.syr.edu/Virtual/Listserv_Archives/)

For more information: http://ericps.crc.uiuc.edu/eece/listserv/middle-l.html

MULTIAGE: Mixed-age grouping, mostly in elementary and middle schools.

—To subscribe, send a message to: listproc@mail.connect.more.net

—Leave the subject line blank.

—In the body of the message, write: subscribe Multiage your firstname lastname

NET-HAPPENINGS: Internet-related news and announcements.

—To subscribe, send a message to: listserv@lists.internic.net

—Leave the subject line blank.

—In the body of the message, write: subscribe Net-Happenings your firstname lastname

TAG-L: General discussion about all topics related to gifted children.

—To subscribe, send a message to: listserv@listserv.NODAK.EDU

—Leave the subject line blank.

—In the body of the message, write: subscribe Tag-L your firstname lastname

USENET NEWSGROUPS

Usenet Newsgroups are an electronic bulletin board system, accessible via the Internet, that consists of discussion forums on literally thousands of topics. Users should contact their system operator for instructions. Some of the Usenet Newsgroups are:

k12.chat.teacher—General discussion between K–12 Teachers

k12.ed.art—Arts and Crafts Education

k12.ed.business—Business Education

k12.ed.life-skills—Life Skills Education

k12.ed.math—Mathematics Education

k12.ed.music—Music and Performing Arts

k12.ed.science—Science Education

k12.ed.soc-studies—Social Studies Education

k12.ed.special—Educating students with special needs

k12.ed.tech—Technology Education

REFERENCES AND READINGS

Abilock, D. (1996). Integrating e-mail into the curriculum. *Technology Connection, 3*(5), 23-25. (EJ 531 026)

Hill, J. A., and Misic, M. M. (1996). Why you should establish a connection to the Internet. *TechTrends, 41*(2), 10-16. (EJ 520 228)

The Internet roadmap for educators. (1996). Arlington, VA: Educational Research Service. (ED 397 520)

Junion-Metz, G. (1996). *K–12 Resources on the Internet: An instructional guide.* Internet workshop series, number 5. San Carlos, CA: Library Solutions Press. (ISBN-1-882208-14-5). (ED 389 316)

K–12 computer networking. (1995). *The ERIC Review, 4*(1). (ED 392 413)

Lankes, R. D. (1996). *Bread and butter of the Internet. ERIC Digest.* Syracuse, NY: ERIC Clearinghouse on Information & Technology. (ED number pending, IR-97-02)

Laughon, S., and Kurshan, B. (1996). A monster of a job! *MultiMedia Schools, 3*(1), 12-18. (EJ 516 636)

Miller, E. B. (1996). *The Internet resource directory for K–12 teachers and librarians, 95/96 edition.* Englewood, CO: Libraries Unlimited. (ISBN-1-56308-366-3). (ED 389 330)

Tennant, R. (1996). *Internet basics: Update 1996. ERIC Digest.* Syracuse, NY: Eric Clearinghouse on Information & Technology. (ED 392 466)

Walter Shelby Group Ltd. *Tile.net/Lists: The reference to Internet discussion groups.* Internet WWW page, at URL: http://tile.net/ (copyright 1997).

Internet Basics
Update 1996*

Roy Tennant

This digest briefly describes the Internet computer network, the physical connections and logical agreements that make it possible, and the applications and information resources the network provides.

THE INTERNET

The Internet is a worldwide network of computer networks. It is comprised of thousands of separately administered networks of many sizes and types. Each of these networks is comprised of as many as tens of thousands of computers; the total number of individual users of the Internet is in the millions. This breadth of connectivity fosters an unparalleled opportunity for communication, collaboration, resource sharing, and information access.

PHYSICAL CONNECTIONS AND
LOGICAL AGREEMENTS

For the Internet to exist, there must be connections between computers and agreements on how they are to communicate. Connections can consist of a variety of communication media or methods: metal wires, microwave links, packet radio or fiber optic cables. These connections are usually established within areas or regions by the particular networking organization with authority or economic interest in that area. For example, a university academic department may use Ethernet cable to connect its personal computers and workstations into a local area network (LAN), which is then connected to the cables the campus uses to connect its buildings together. These cables are then linked to cables in a regional network, which itself ties into a national backbone which may be subsidized by the government. Therefore the path between any two points on the Internet often traverses physical connections that are administered by a variety of independent authorities.

For disparate computers (from personal computers to mainframes) to communicate over a network, there must be agreements on how that should occur. These agreements are called communication protocols. On the Internet, the Transmission Control Protocol/Internet Protocol (TCP/IP) suite of protocols defines communication at a machine-to-machine level. Application software for accomplishing specific tasks such as those outlined below is written to adhere to these standards and take advantage of the connectivity that they provide.

*This ERIC Digest was prepared by Roy Tennant, Digital Library Research & Development, The Library, University of California, Berkeley.

ERIC Digests are in the public domain and may be freely reproduced and disseminated.

ERIC Clearinghouse on Information & Technology, 4-194 Center for Science & Technology, Syracuse University, Syracuse, NY 13244-4100; (315) 443-3640; FAX (315) 443-5448; e-mail eric@ericir.syr.edu

This publication was prepared with funding from the Office of Educational Research and Improvement, U.S. Department of Education, under contract no. RR93002009. The opinions expressed in this report do not necessarily reflect the positions of OERI or ED.

ELECTRONIC MAIL

Electronic mail, or e-mail, is a fast, easy, and inexpensive way to communicate with other Internet users around the world. In addition, it is possible for Internet users to exchange e-mail with users of other networks such as America Online, CompuServe, Prodigy, and others. Internet users often find that the expanded capability to communicate with colleagues around the world leads to important new sources of information, collaboration, and professional development.

Besides basic correspondence between two network users, e-mail presents additional opportunities for communication. Through various methods of distributing e-mail messages to lists of subscribers, e-mail supports electronic discussions on a wide range of topics. These discussions bring together like-minded individuals who use such forums for discussing common problems, sharing solutions, and examining issues.

THE WORLD WIDE WEB

Presently one of the most widespread applications on the Internet besides electronic mail is the World Wide Web. By using a Web application program (often called a browser or client), Internet users can find information on a variety of topics hosted by a number of different kinds of Internet servers (computers that offer information to clients) around the world. Information on the Web is presented to the user as linked documents comprised of text, images, and links to other computer files. Online subject directories and searchable databases of Web resources provide basic methods for locating information. The future of the Web will likely include more sophisticated ways of interacting with online information, including virtual reality (depictions of three dimensional space), video conferencing, and other kinds of online interactivity and collaboration.

TELNET

Telnet allows an Internet user in one location to establish an online connection with a computer located elsewhere. Once a connection is established with a remote computer, users can use that remote system as if their computers were hard-wired terminals of that system. Utilizing Telnet, an Internet user can establish connections with a multitude of bibliographic databases (primarily library catalogs, full-text databases, data files [e.g., statistics, oceano-graphic data, meteorologic data, geographic data, etc.]), and other online services. Many of these systems are available for any Internet user to access and use without an account.

FILE TRANSFER (FTP)

Another application of the Internet is the ability to transfer files from one Internet-connected computer to another. This function is provided by the File Transfer Protocol (FTP) of the TCP/IP protocol suite. In a method similar to using Telnet, network users initiate an online connection with another Internet computer via FTP. But unlike Telnet, this online connection can perform only functions related to locating and transferring files. This includes the ability to change directories, list files, retrieve files, etc. Also, any World Wide Web client can download (get) files using FTP, but they generally cannot upload (put).

Types of files that can be transferred using FTP include virtually every kind of file that can be stored on a computer: text files, software programs, graphic images, sounds, files formatted for particular software programs (e.g., files with word processing formatting instruc-tions), and others. Many computer administrators have set aside portions of their machines to offer files for anyone on the Internet to retrieve. These archive sites support anonymous logins that do not require an account to access, and therefore are called anonymous FTP sites.

A PREMIER COMMUNICATIONS UTILITY

What makes the Internet truly remarkable is that ease and speed of access to information are not dependent upon proximity. An Internet user can connect to a system on the other side of the globe as easily as (and generally not much slower than) he or she can connect to a system in the next building. In addition, since many Internet users are not at present charged for their network use by their institutions, or at least are not charged by the level of their use, cost is often not a significant inhibitor of usage. Therefore the barriers of distance, time and cost, which are often significant when using other forms of electronic communication, are often less significant on the Internet.

GETTING CONNECTED

There are numerous ways to gain access to the Internet. Access options range from the low-end requirements of a computer, modem, and an account from an Internet access provider (the typical home configuration), to the high-end, which requires a computer equipped with a network card and access to an Ethernet network that is connected to the Internet (the typical business or organization configuration). Due to the relatively low cost for Internet access (often cheaper than cable TV), as well as the availability of inexpensive modems and free or inexpensive Internet software, virtually any computer user can afford to get access to the Internet and all that it provides. Those who have more money to spend on Internet access will soon see an array of fast connection options marketed to home users.

FUTURE POSSIBILITIES

The Internet constantly evolves through both formal standards development as well as individual and corporate software creation and enhancement. What began as a U.S. govern- ment-subsidized network to allow scholars and researchers to share supercomputer resources, has since become a mainstream production network tying together commercial companies, individuals, and organizations of all kinds. Commercial use of the Internet has spurred rapid development of new software, and it is a trend that is likely to continue. Some of the developments that are likely to help transform the Internet into a ubiquitous and full-featured information appliance include virtual reality, full-motion, realtime, high quality audio and video, and advanced scripting and programming capabilities.

FURTHER READING

Crumlish, C. (1996). *Internet for busy people.* Berkeley, CA: Osborne/McGraw-Hill.

Estrada, S. (1993). *Connecting to the Internet: An O'Reilly buyer's guide.* Sebastopol, CA: O'Reilly & Associates.

Hoffman, P., and Levine, J., eds. (1994). *The Internet.* Foster City, CA: IDG Books Worldwide.

Krol, E., and Hoffman, E. FYI on What is the Internet? Network Working Group, Request for Comments 1462 (FYI 20). Internet WWW page, at URL: http://ds.internic.net/fyi/fyi20.html (version current at May 1993).

LaQuey, T. (1994). *Internet companion: A beginner's guide to global networking,* 2nd ed. Reading, MA: Addison-Wesley.

Malkin, G., and Parker, T. L. (January 1993). Internet users glossary. Network Working Group, Request for Comments 1392 (FYI 18). Internet WWW page, at URL: http://ds.internic.net/fyi/fyi18.html (version current at January 1993).

Marine, A., Malkin, G., and Reynolds, J. (March 1994). FYI on questions and answers: Answers to commonly asked New Internet User questions. Network Working Group, Request for Comments 1594 (FYI 4). Internet WWW page, at URL: http://ds.internic.net/fyi/fyi4.html (version current at March 1994).

Tennant, R., Ober, J. and Lipow, A. G. (1994). *Crossing the Internet threshold: An instructional handbook,* 2nd ed. Berkeley, CA: Library Solutions Press. (ED 366 335)

The Bread and Butter of the Internet*

R. David Lankes

This Digest is based on the ERIC monograph,
The Bread and Butter of the Internet:
A Primer and Presentation Packet for Educators
R. David Lankes

INTRODUCTION

An increasing amount of national attention is focused on connecting K–12 schools to the Internet (Clinton, 1996), while at the same time, there is some debate on the benefits of using the Internet in the classroom. Most teachers know the Internet is a source of information, but they may not know how it works, or how to get it. The Internet is steeped in obscure acronyms and cute names. What other environment could brag about creating Veronica, to help Gopher users locate PDF files faster than FTP? By understanding the basics of how the Internet works, one can cut through the names, letters and numbers, and focus on using the Internet to improve teaching and learning.

THE INTERNET MODEL

Many teachers find the Internet and its terminology very confusing. A framework, or model is needed to put these concepts and terms into context. The Internet can be broken into four basics levels (Lankes, 1994):

- **Engineering Level**—The infrastructure that allows information to move from one computer to another.

- **Application Level**—The software that allows users to gather and share information.

- **Information Service Level**—The combination of information with hardware and software that allows users to meet their information needs.

- **Use Level**—The level where users use the information they find on the Internet.

*This digest was written by R. D. Lankes, Associate Director of the ERIC Clearinghouse on Information & Technology, Syracuse University, Syracuse, New York.

ERIC Digests are in the public domain and may be freely reproduced and disseminated.

ERIC Clearinghouse on Information & Technology. Syracuse University, 4-194 Center for Science and Technology, Syracuse, NY 13244-4100; (315) 443-3640; (800) 464-9107; Fax: (315) 443-5448; E-mail: eric@ericir.syr.edu; URL: http://ericir.syr.edu/ithome

Subscribe to our ITPUBS listserv for special announcements about ERIC/IT publications. Send an e-mail message to: listserv@listserv.syr.edu In the message type: subscribe itpubs (your firstname) (your lastname)

This publication was prepared with funding from the Office of Educational Research and Improvement, U.S. Department of Education, under contract no. RR93002009. The opinions expressed in this report do not necessarily reflect the positions of OERI or ED.

Educators can use this Internet model to help plan inservice agendas. For example, teacher training sessions can focus on the Information Service Level (finding lesson plans on the Internet) or on the Application Level ("Netscape Navigator: How to Use It"). Technology planning committees can use the model to help focus task forces—one to examine applications, another to determine appropriate use policies.

THE ENGINEERING LEVEL

The engineering level is the technical part of the Internet. It is the infrastructure, composed of hardware and software, that allows information to flow from one point to another. The engineering level includes:

- **Computers** to create messages (information) to be sent over the network;

- **Media** to transfer information over wires, fiber optics, infrared, etc.; and,

- **Protocols** to format the messages and send them to appropriate computer addresses. The protocol (or language being spoken) on the Internet is called TCP/IP (Transmission Control Protocol/Internet Protocol).

The engineering level includes modems, routers and protocols. If the engineering layer is working properly, it is transparent to the user. Using the "Information Superhighway" metaphor, the engineering level is the "road" the information travels on.

APPLICATION LEVEL

When teachers use the Internet to look for information, they are using the applications level. Applications level software such as Netscape *Navigator* or Microsoft's *Internet Explorer* don't contain any information in and of themselves, rather they are tools that allow teachers to link to Internet sites that contain the text, pictures, and other media that they can use in the classroom. Some basic Internet applications include:

- **Electronic mail** can be used to send memo-like messages to people connected to the Internet anywhere in the world. Mailing lists or Listservs can be used to send one e-mail message to hundreds of other users who share common interests.

- **Telnet** allows users to access and control programs on remote computers. With telnet, educators and students can use the most powerful computers in the world without leaving their classrooms.

- **FTP (File Transfer Protocol)** allows users to transfer files to and from a remote computer. A teacher can use FTP to get software and files from a vast collection of computer archives on the Internet. FTP can also be used to transfer World Wide Web files from a local computer to a remote server so that information can be shared with the world.

- **Gopher** allows users to navigate the Internet in a menu-like fashion. With Gopher, one can move through information systems easily by selecting numbers from a menu. Gophers combine information from a number of sources, often worldwide, and present it all together on one menu. A user can traverse the world and never realize it.

- **The World Wide Web** allows users to navigate the Internet in a hypermedia format. With Web browsers, a user can see information in a multimedia format. Text can be linked to pictures, pictures to animations, or animations to any digital information.

All Internet applications use the Client/Server model in one form or another. The user's computer is a client to a remote server. The client is responsible for formatting information, controlling user interaction, and managing all the resources on the user's computer. The server just holds information and sends it to the client when requested. The client/server paradigm gives the user control over the information being retrieved, and allows better use of the network and the user's computing resources.

In the "Information Superhighway" metaphor, the applications are the cars and trucks that travel the road.

INFORMATION SERVICES LEVEL

Teachers and students use the Internet to find information. In the Information Services Level, organizations (schools, publishers, businesses, etc.) use the Applications Level to provide information to end-users. Schools can become "Information Servers" by sharing their student works, and curriculum ideas with other educators on the Internet. One example of an information service on the net is AskERIC http://www.askeric.org.

Schools can use the same technology as Fortune 500 companies to build internal Internets, called intranets. Intranet technology is a hot topic in the corporate world, and schools can serve their communities by sharing what they know about this technology.

In the "Information Superhighway" metaphor, Information Services is the cargo in the cars and trucks that travel the road.

USE LEVEL

How educators apply information found on the Internet to the classroom constitutes the Use Level of the Internet. Security of information, acceptable use, and intellectual property are all Use Level issues. What works in one community may not work in another. For example, should schools allow free and open access to the Internet for all students, or should they restrict what students can see on the Internet?

In the "Information Superhighway" metaphor, the Use Level deals with why the cars and trucks are on the road, and what happens to their cargo when they reach their destinations.

CONCLUSION

The Internet is dynamic. New applications and new trends will make the Internet more real-time, more interactive, and more exciting. A constantly changing computer environment will present significant challenges to educators as they attempt to integrate revolutionary technology into an evolutionary teaching process. Teachers will learn about new software, and administrators will debate the merits of applying new technologies to the educational mission of the school. By understanding the basics of the Internet, educators will be better prepared to face the complexities that will surely follow.

REFERENCES

Clinton, W. J. (1996). State of the Union Address. Internet WWW page, at URL: http://www2.whitehouse.gov/WH/New/other/sotu.html (version current at January 1997).

Lankes, R. D. (1994). The Internet Model. *Information Searcher, 7*(1), 3-6.

Part Four
Leadership Profiles

Introduction

The purpose of this section is to profile individuals who have made significant contributions to the field of educational media and technology. There is no formal survey or popularity contest to determine the persons for whom the profiles are written, but those selected are usually emeritus faculty who may or may not be currently active in the field.

Leaders profiled in the *Yearbook* have either held prominent offices, written important works, or made significant contributions that have in some way influenced the contemporary vision of the field. They have often been directly responsible for mentoring individuals who have themselves become recognized for their contributions. The following are the people previously profiled in earlier volumes of the *Yearbook*:

James D. Finn	Robert Heinich
James W. Brown	Charles Francis Schuller
Wilbur Schramm	Harry Alleyn Johnson
Robert E. De Kieffer	Robert M. Morgan
Jean E. Lowrie	Paul Saettler
Robert Morris	Donald P. Ely
William Travers	James Okey
Robert Mills Gagné	Constance Dorothea Weinman

There are special reasons to feature people of national and international renown, and the editors of this volume of *Educational Media and Technology Yearbook* believe **Castelle (Cass) G. Gentry** is worthy of such distinction.

You are welcome to nominate individuals to be featured in this section. Your nomination must also be accompanied by the name of the person who will compose the leadership profile. Please direct any comments, questions, and suggestions about the selection process to the Senior Editor.

Robert Maribe Branch

Tribute to Castelle G. Gentry, Professor, Media and Technology, MSU

Darryl Yorke

Kent Gustafson
Instructional Technology
University of Georgia

John Childs

Castelle Gentry (1928-1996) was born in humble surroundings in southern Michigan and spent his early years working on a small family farm. During his professional years he often remarked that his early experiences provided him with a strong work ethic and the desire to help others of similar background to elevate their vision of what they might become. Thus, Cass was a tireless champion of education as a source of improvement for the human condition and the need to do whatever was necessary to help people succeed. However, this attitude coexisted with his belief that life should be enjoyable and that although education needed to be serious, it need not be grim. His sense of humor, especially his willingness to laugh at himself, was one of his most endearing traits.

Cass began his career in media, technology, and instructional development as one of the first five NDEA Media and Technology Fellows at Michigan State University (MSU) in the fall of 1962. Prior to that time, he had been teaching and engaging in curriculum development at the secondary level. He became an NDEA Fellow as the result of the work of Dr. Charles Schuller to create the program both nationally and at MSU. He was recommended and encouraged by Dr. Charles Blackman, MSU Professor of Curriculum and Instruction.

Throughout the three-year Fellowship program, Cass constantly encouraged his colleagues to make real applications of media and technology to K-12 schools. As the MSU Instructional Systems Development research project evolved, he challenged everyone involved with the project to "consider the real world of classroom teachers" working with large numbers of students.

Cass completed his Ph.D. at MSU in 1965. His first full-time higher education position was as assistant professor at the University of Maine, where he taught courses in media and technology. He subsequently held faculty positions at Syracuse University and the University of Toledo before returning to MSU to join the faculty. At first he worked part-time in the campus-wide media center for Dr. Schuller and taught in the College of Education Instructional Development and program coordinated by Dr. Paul W. F. Witt. In this dual role he both advised faculty campus wide on improving instruction through application of the instructional development process and taught about the process in the academic program. This period was one of the happiest of his professional life. Later, he became a full-time teacher and coordinator of the Academic Program in Instructional Development and Technology at MSU.

In his spare time, Cass bought a large farm, complete with a very old farmhouse, and returned to his roots by fixing up the house and doing a little farming. Nancy, his wife of many years, and his five children dubbed it the "funny farm," but they were glad that he had a hobby that satisfied him so much.

Cass's contributions to the field through scholarship, research, teaching, and the direction of doctoral students are extensive. He wrote and published continuously. His last professional book, *Introduction to Instructional Development*, was published by Wadsworth in 1994. In that book, he described his "dumbbell" model of instructional development—one of the few models that recognizes the importance of the management and logistical issues associated with successful projects. Ever the pragmatist, he also described and provided examples of numerous tools that could be used to apply the model in real instructional settings.

Upon retiring, Cass took up writing novels. In his first, *Metamorph Rising*, the main character was clearly autobiographical. He died in the story but returned to life. Darryl Yorke, knowing Cass had been battling cancer, recalls asking him, "Did you write this to prepare your family for your demise?" To which Cass enigmatically replied, "Ah, Yorke, my friend, you give me more credit than I am due."

Cass is remembered in many ways by his colleagues and students in the United States and around the world. Here is what they recall about him:

His sensitivity. Cass was an exceptionally empathic person. He could stand in your shoes and view your world. He not only saw your perspective, but he could also grasp your feelings. Each person who came in contact with Cass was encouraged and empowered by his strength and support. He was always there for others. You couldn't go unnoticed because he reached out and touched you. No matter your background, you would be immediately accepted by Cass.

His intellect. Cass was always a knowledge broker. He respected the products of others, and he respected his own thinking. Extremely well read, he loved learning, both for himself and others. He was a thinker, a writer, and a doer who would play with ideas in his mind but would ultimately want to test them in the real world.

His teaching. Cass was the consummate teacher. He presented complex ideas with great clarity and rigor. He challenged everyone, students and peers alike, to achieve mastery and superior performance. And he never gave up expecting students to do their best. He taught nearly everyone the synergistic effect. With probing questions and gentle prodding, he invited us to think more deeply, to get outside ourselves, and to stretch ourselves in identifying and solving problems.

While at MSU, Cass directed more than 20 doctoral dissertations of students from around the world and sat on the advising committees for countless others. He also advised a legion of Master's and Specialist students at the institutions where he taught.

His leadership. Cass made a lifelong study of leadership. He constantly talked about the principles of leadership (e.g., successive approximations, structure-induced practice, the cumulative feedback effect); but he differentiated between *good* leaders and *great* leaders. *Good* leaders made changes, helped their co-workers, and increased productivity, but when they left, the structure collapsed. *Great* leaders arranged things so that in their absence, the system (organization) would maintain itself.

Cass accepted the role of leader as described by the Chinese philosopher Lao-tzu, who said:

The best leaders go unnoticed and unknown.
The next best leaders are honored and revered;
The next are feared ...
The next, hated
And when the best leader's work is done, the people say, "We did it ourselves."

That was Cass personified! His associates felt his influence, often without knowing it, and they continued to improve. And because of the seeds he planted in all of us, we will continue to grow and improve in his absence.

Whether you knew Castelle G. Gentry through his work, as a professional colleague, as a student, or as a personal friend, he most likely had a strong and positive impact on you. His writings will continue to affect those who read them, and those who benefited so much from knowing him personally will carry on his rich heritage of ideas, idealism, and commitment to a better world. For the world is truly a better place, and we are better people, as a result of his having been among us.

Part Five
Organizations and Associations in North America

Introduction

Part Five includes annotated entries for associations and organizations headquartered in North America whose interests are in some manner significant to the fields of instructional technology and educational media. For the most part, these organizations are associations of professionals in the field or agencies which offer services to the educational media community. Entries are separated into sections for the United States and Canada. The US section begins with a classified list designed to facilitate location of organizations by their specialized interests or services. (The Canadian section is small enough not to need such a list.)

Information for this section was obtained by direct communication with each organization in early 1997. Five organizations (marked by an asterisk) did not provide updated information, and their entries contain information from the 1997 edition. Three organizations were deleted from the listing due to lack of response for two consecutive years. Two new organizations are listed as well. Readers are encouraged to contact the editors with names of unlisted media-related organizations for investigation and possible inclusion in the 1999 edition.

Figures quoted as dues refer to annual amounts unless stated otherwise.

United States

CLASSIFIED LIST

Adult and Continuing Education
(ALA Round Table) Continuing Library Education Network and Exchange (CLENERT)
Association for Continuing Higher Education (ACHE)
Association for Educational Communications and Technology (AECT)
ERIC Clearinghouse on Adult, Career, and Vocational Education (CE)
National Education Telecommunications Organization & Education Satellite Company (NETO/EDSAT)
National University Continuing Education Association (NUCEA)
Network for Continuing Medical Education (NCME)
PBS Adult Learning Service (ALS)
University Continuing Education Association (UCEA)

Children- and Youth-Related Organizations
Adjunct ERIC Clearinghouse for Child Care (ADJ/CC)
American Montessori Society
Association for Childhood Education International (ACEI)
Association for Library Service to Children (ALSC)
(CEC) Technology and Media Division (TAM)
Children's Television International, Inc.
Close Up Foundation
Council for Exceptional Children (CEC)
ERIC Clearinghouse on Disabilities and Gifted Education (EC)
ERIC Clearinghouse on Elementary and Early Childhood Education (PS)
National Association for the Education of Young Children (NAEYC)
National PTA
Young Adult Library Services Association (YALSA)

Communication
Association for Educational Communications and Technology (AECT)
ERIC Clearinghouse on Information & Technology (IR)
ERIC Clearinghouse on Languages and Linguistics (FL)
ERIC Clearinghouse on Reading, English, and Communication Skills (CS)
Health Science Communications Association (HeSCA)

International Association of Business Communicators (IABC)
Lister Hill National Center for Biomedical Communications of the National Library of Medicine
National Council of the Churches of Christ
Speech Communication Association (SCA)

Computers
(AECT) Division of Interactive Systems and Computers (DISC)
Association for the Advancement of Computing in Education (AACE)
Computer-Using Educators, Inc. (CUE)
International Society for Technology in Education (ISTE)
Online Computer Library Center (OCLC)
Society for Computer Simulation (SCS)

Copyright
Association of American Publishers (AAP)
Association of College and Research Libraries (ACRL)
Copyright Clearance Center (CCC)
Hollywood Film Archive
International Copyright Information Center (INCINC)
Library of Congress

Distance Education
Community College Satellite Network (CCSN)
International Society for Technology in Education (ISTE)
International Telecommunications Satellite Organization (INTELSAT)
National Education Telecommunications Organization & EDSAT Institute (NETO/EDSAT)

Education—General
American Society of Educators (ASE)
Association for Childhood Education International (ACEI)
Association for Experiential Education (AEE)
Council for Basic Education
Education Development Center, Inc.
ERIC Clearinghouse for Science, Mathematics, and Environmental Education (SE)
ERIC Clearinghouse for Social Studies/Social Science Education (ERIC/ChESS)
ERIC Clearinghouse on Counseling and Student Services (CG)
ERIC Clearinghouse on Disabilities and Gifted Education (EC)

ERIC Clearinghouse on Educational Management (EA)

ERIC Clearinghouse on Elementary and Early Childhood Education (PS)

ERIC Clearinghouse on Rural Education and Small Schools (RC)

ERIC Clearinghouse on Teaching and Teacher Education (SP)

ERIC Clearinghouse on Urban Education (UD)

Institute for Development of Educational Activities, Inc. (IIIDIEIAI)

Minorities in Media (MIM)

National Association of State Boards of Education (NASBE)

National Association of State Textbook Administrators (NASTA)

National Clearinghouse for Bilingual Education

National Council for Accreditation of Teacher Education (NCATE)

National Science Teachers Association (NSTA)

Education—Higher

American Association of Community Colleges (AACC)

American Association of State Colleges and Universities

Association for Continuing Higher Education (ACHE)

Association for Library and Information Science Education (ALISE)

Community College Association for Instruction and Technology (CCAIT)

Consortium of College and University Media Centers (CCUMC)

ERIC Clearinghouse for Community Colleges (JC)

ERIC Clearinghouse on Higher Education (HE)

Northwest College and University Council for the Management of Educational Technology

PBS Adult Learning Service

University Continuing Education Association (UCEA)

Equipment

Association for Childhood Education International (ACEI)

Educational Products Information Exchange (EPIE Institute)

ERIC Clearinghouse on Assessment and Evaluation (TM)

ITA

Library and Information Technology Association (LITA)

National School Supply and Equipment Association (NSSEA)

Society of Cable Television Engineers (SCTE)

ERIC

ACCESS ERIC

Adjunct ERIC Clearinghouse for Art Education (ADJ/AR)

Adjunct ERIC Clearinghouse for ESL Literacy Education (ADJ/LE)

Adjunct ERIC Clearinghouse for United States-Japan Studies (ADJ/JS)

Adjunct ERIC Clearinghouse on Chapter 1 (Compensatory Education) (ADJ/Chapter 1)

Adjunct ERIC Clearinghouse on Clinical Schools (ADJ/CL)

Adjunct ERIC Clearinghouse on Consumer Education (ADJ/CN)

ERIC (Educational Resources Information Center)

ERIC Clearinghouse on Adult, Career, and Vocational Education (CE)

ERIC Clearinghouse on Assessment and Evaluation (TM)

ERIC Clearinghouse for Community Colleges (JC)

ERIC Clearinghouse on Counseling and Student Services (CG)

ERIC Clearinghouse on Educational Management (EA)

ERIC Clearinghouse on Elementary and Early Childhood Education (PS)

ERIC Clearinghouse on Disabilities and Gifted Education (EC)

ERIC Clearinghouse on Higher Education (HE)

ERIC Clearinghouse on Information & Technology (IR)

ERIC Clearinghouse on Languages and Linguistics (FL)

ERIC Clearinghouse on Reading, English, and Communication Skills (CS)

ERIC Clearinghouse on Rural Education and Small Schools (RC)

ERIC Clearinghouse for Science, Mathematics, and Environmental Education (SE)

ERIC Clearinghouse for Social Studies/Social Science Education (SO)

ERIC Clearinghouse on Teaching and Teacher Education (SP)

ERIC Clearinghouse on Urban Education (UD)

ERIC Document Reproduction Service (EDRS)

ERIC Processing and Reference Facility

Film and Video

(AECT) Division of Telecommunications (DOT)

(AECT) Industrial Training and Education Division (ITED)

Academy of Motion Picture Arts and Sciences (AMPAS)

Agency for Instructional Technology (AIT)

American Society of Cinematographers

Anthropology Film Center (AFC)

Association for Educational Communications and Technology (AECT)

Association of Independent Video and Filmmakers/ Foundation for Independent Video and Film (AIVF/FIVF)

Cable in the Classroom

Central Educational Network (CEN)

Children's Television International, Inc.

Close Up Foundation
Community College Satellite Network
Council on International Non-theatrical Events
(CINE)
Film Advisory Board
Film Arts Foundation (FAF)
Film/Video Arts, Inc.
Great Plains National ITV Library (GPN)
Hollywood Film Archive
International Teleconferencing Association
(ITCA)
International Television Association (ITVA)
ITA
National Aeronautics and Space Administration
(NASA)
National Alliance for Media Arts and Culture
(NAMAC)
National Association of Broadcasters (NAB)
National Audiovisual Center (NAC)
National Education Telecommunications Organi-
zation & Education Satellite Company
(NETO/EDSAT)
National Endowment for the Humanities (NEH)
National Film Board of Canada (NFBC)
National Film Information Service (offered by
AMPAS)
National Information Center for Educational
Media (NICEM)
National ITFS Association (NIA/ITFS)
National Telemedia Council, Inc. (NTC)
The New York Festivals
Pacific Film Archive (PFA)
PCR: Films and Video in the Behavioral Sciences
Public Broadcasting Service (PBS)
PBS Adult Learning Service (ALS)
PBS VIDEO
Society of Cable Television Engineers (SCTE)

Games, Toys, Play, Simulation, Puppetry
Puppeteers of America, Inc. (POA)
Society for Computer Simulation (SCS)
USA-Toy Library Association (USA-TLA)

Health-Related Organizations
Health Science Communications Association
(HeSCA)
Lister Hill National Center for Biomedical
Communications
Medical Library Association (MLA)
National Association for Visually Handicapped
(NAVH)
Network for Continuing Medical Education
(NCME)

Information Science
Association for Library and Information Science
Education (ALISE)
ERIC Clearinghouse on Information and
Technology (IR)
Freedom of Information Center
International Information Management Congress
(IMC)

Library and Information Technology Association
(LITA)
Lister Hill National Center for Biomedical
Communications
National Commission on Libraries and Informa-
tion Science (NCLIS)

Innovation
Institute for Development of Educational
Activities, Inc. (I|I|D|E|A|)
Institute for the Future (IFTF)
World Future Society (WFS)

**Instructional Technology, Design, and
Development**
(AECT) Division of Educational Media Manage-
ment (DEMM)
(AECT) Division of Instructional Development
(DID)
Agency for Instructional Technology (AIT)
Association for Educational Communications and
Technology (AECT)
Community College Association for Instruction
and Technology (CCAIT)
ERIC Clearinghouse on Information &
Technology (IR)
International Society for Performance and
Instruction (ISPI)
Professors of Instructional Design and
Technology (PIDT)
Society for Applied Learning Technology (SALT)

International Education
Adjunct ERIC Clearinghouse for US-Japan
Studies (ADJ/JS)
(AECT) International Division (INTL)
East-West Center
International Association for Learning
Laboratories, Inc. (IALL)
International Visual Literacy Association, Inc.
(IVLA)
National Clearinghouse for Bilingual Education
(NCBE)

Language
ERIC Clearinghouse on Languages and
Linguistics (FL)
ERIC Clearinghouse on Reading, English, and
Communication (CS)
International Association for Learning
Laboratories, Inc. (IALL)
National Clearinghouse for Bilingual Education
(NCBE)

Libraries—Academic, Research
American Library Association (ALA)
Association of College and Research Libraries
(ACRL)
ERIC Clearinghouse on Information &
Technology (IR)

Libraries—Public

American Library Association (ALA)
Association for Library Service to Children
(ALSC)
ERIC Clearinghouse on Information &
Technology (IR)
Library Administration and Management
Association (LAMA)
Library and Information Technology Association
(LITA)
Public Library Association (PLA)
Young Adult Library Services Association
(YALSA)

Libraries and Media Centers—School

(ALA Round Table) Continuing Library Educa-
tion Network and Exchange (CLENERT)
(AECT) Division of School Media Specialists
(DSMS)
American Association of School Librarians
(AASL)
American Library Association (ALA)
American Library Trustee Association (ALTA)
Association for Educational Communications
and Technology (AECT)
Association for Library Collections and
Technical Services (ALCTS)
Association for Library Service to Children
(ALSC)
Catholic Library Association (CLA)
Consortium of College and University Media
Centers
ERIC Clearinghouse on Information &
Technology (IR)
International Association of School Librarianship
(IASL)
Library of Congress
National Alliance for Media Arts and Culture
(NAMAC)
National Association of Regional Media Centers
(NARMC)
National Commission on Libraries and Informa-
tion Science (NCLIS)
National Council of Teachers of English
(NCTE), Commission on Media
On-Line Audiovisual Catalogers (OLAC)
Southeastern Regional Media Leadership Coun-
cil (SRMLC)

Libraries—Special

American Library Association (ALA)
Association for Library Service to Children
(ALSC)
Association of Specialized and Cooperative
Library Agencies (ASCLA)
ERIC Clearinghouse on Information &
Technology (IR)
Medical Library Association (MLA)
Special Libraries Association
Theater Library Association
USA Toy Library Association (USA-TLA)

Media Production

American Society of Cinematographers (ASC)
Association for Educational Communications
and Technology (AECT)
(AECT) Media Design and Production Division
(MDPD)
Association of Independent Video and Filmmakers/
Foundation for Independent Video and
Film (AIVF/FIVF)
Film Arts Foundation (FAF)
International Graphics Arts Education
Association (IGAEA)

Museums and Archives

(AECT) Archives
Association of Systematics Collections
George Eastman House
Hollywood Film Archive
Library of Congress
Museum Computer Network (MCN)
Museum of Modern Art
National Gallery of Art (NGA)
National Public Broadcasting Archives (NPBA)
Pacific Film Archive (PFA)
Smithsonian Institution

Photography

George Eastman House
International Center of Photography (ICP)
National Press Photographers Association, Inc.
(NPPA)
Photographic Society of America (PSA)
Society for Photographic Education (SPE)
Society of Photo Technologists (SPT)

Publishing

Graphic Arts Technical Foundation (GATF)
International Graphics Arts Education
Association (IGAEA)
Magazine Publishers of America (MPA)
National Association of State Textbook
Administrators (NASTA)

Radio

(AECT) Division of Telecommunications (DOT)
American Women in Radio and Television
(AWRT)
Corporation for Public Broadcasting (CPB)
National Endowment for the Humanities (NEH)
National Federation of Community Broadcasters
(NFCB)
National Public Broadcasting Archives (NPBA)
National Religious Broadcasters (NRB)
Western Public Radio (WPR)

Religious Education

Catholic Library Association (CLA)
National Council of the Churches of Christ in the
USA
National Religious Broadcasters (NRB)

Research

(AECT) Research and Theory Division (RTD)
American Educational Research Association
(AERA)
Appalachia Educational Laboratory, Inc. (AEL)
Council for Educational Development and
Research (CEDaR)
ECT Foundation
Education Development Center, Inc.
ERIC Clearinghouses
Far West Laboratory for Educational Research
and Development (FWL) (see WestEd)
HOPE Reports
Mid-continent Regional Educational Laboratory
(McREL)
National Center for Improving Science Education
National Endowment for the Humanities (NEH)
National Science Foundation (NSF)
The NETWORK
North Central Regional Educational Laboratory
(NCREL)
Northwest Regional Educational Laboratory
(NWREL)
Pacific Regional Educational Laboratory
(PREL)
Research for Better Schools, Inc. (RBS)
SouthEastern Regional Vision for Education
(SERVE)
Southwest Educational Development Laboratory
(SEDL)
WestEd

Special Education

American Foundation for the Blind (AFB)
Association for Experiential Education (AEE)
Association of Specialized and Cooperative
Library Agencies (ASCLA)
Council for Exceptional Children (CEC)
ERIC Clearinghouse on Adult, Career, and
Vocational Education (CE)
ERIC Clearinghouse on Disabilities and Gifted
Education (EC)
National Association for Visually Handicapped
(NAVH)
National Center to Improve Practice (NCIP)
Recording for the Blind and Dyslexic
(RFB&D)

Telecommunications

(AECT) Division of Telecommunications (DOT)
Association for the Advancement of Computing
in Education (AACE)
Association of Independent Video and Filmmakers/
Foundation for Independent Video and
Film (AIVF/FIVF)
Community College Satellite Network (CCSN)
ERIC Clearinghouse on Information &
Technology (IR)
International Telecommunications Satellite
Organization (INTELSAT)
International Teleconferencing Association
(ITCA)
Library and Information Technology Association
(LITA)
National Education Telecommunications
Organization & Education Satellite
Company (NETO/EDSAT)
Research for Better Schools, Inc. (RBS)
Teachers and Writers Collaborative (T&W)

Television

American Women in Radio and Television
(AWRT)
Central Educational Network (CEN)
Children's Television International, Inc. (CTI)
Corporation for Public Broadcasting (CPB)
International Television Association (ITVA)
National Cable Television Institute (NCTI)
National Federation of Community Broadcasters
(NFCB)
Society of Cable Television Engineers (SCTE)

Training

(AECT) Industrial Training and Education
Division (ITED)
American Management Association (AMA)
American Society for Training and Development
(ASTD)
Association for Educational Communications and
Technology (AECT)
ERIC Clearinghouse on Adult, Career, and
Vocational Education (CE)
Federal Educational Technology Association
(FETA)
International Society for Performance
Improvement (ISPI)

ALPHABETICAL LIST

All dues are annual fees, unless stated otherwise.

Academy of Motion Picture Arts and Sciences (AMPAS). 8949 Wilshire Blvd., Beverly Hills, CA 90211. (310) 247-3000. Fax (310) 859-9351. Web site http://www.oscars.org. Bruce Davis, Exec. Dir. An honorary organization composed of outstanding individuals in all phases of motion pictures. Seeks to advance the arts and sciences of motion picture technology and artistry. Presents annual film awards; offers artist-in-residence programs; operates reference library and National Film Information Service. *Membership:* 6,000. *Publications: Annual Index to Motion Picture Credits; Academy Players Directory.*

Agency for Instructional Technology (AIT). Box A, Bloomington, IN 47402-0120. (812) 339-2203. Fax (812) 333-4218. E-mail ait@ait.net. Web site http://www.ait.net. Michael F. Sullivan, Exec. Dir. AIT is a nonprofit educational organization established in 1962 to develop, acquire, and distribute quality technology-based resources, providing leadership to the educational technology policy community. AIT fulfills this mission by being the largest single provider of instructional television programs and is a major player in the development of curriculum products. AIT has established a national model for contextual learning materials. AIT's strength lies in sound instructional design, early and continual involvement of classroom practitioners, formative evaluation, and creative production of video, videodisc, software, and print resources. AIT products have won many national and international awards, including the only Emmy and Peabody awards given to classroom television programs. Since 1970, 35 major curriculum packages have been developed by AIT through a process it pioneered. US state and Canadian provincial agencies have cooperatively funded and widely used these learning resources. Funding for other product development comes from state, provincial and local departments of education, federal and private institutions, corporations and private sponsors, and AIT's own resources. Currently, AIT offers 130 learning resource products, containing nearly 2,500 separate titles. Programming addresses pre-kindergarten through adult learners covering traditional curricular areas plus career development, early childhood, guidance, mental health, staff development, and vocational education. AIT programs account for 40 percent of the National Instructional Satellite Service (NISS) schedule, which is broadcast to K-12 classrooms across the country. AIT learning resources are used on six continents and teach nearly 34 million students in North America each year via electronic distribution and audio visual use. *Publications: TECHNOS: Quarterly for Education & Technology,* a forum for the discussion of ideas about the use of technology in education with a focus on reform ($28/yr., 4 issues). AIT is also the home of *TECHNOS Press,* publisher of *Final Exam* by Gerald W. Bracey. The Web site offers an online catalog, compete with program descriptions, ordering information, and direct links to AIT Customer Service.

American Association of Community Colleges (AACC). One Dupont Cir. NW, Suite 410, Washington, DC 20036. (202) 728-0200, (800) 250-6557. Fax (202) 833-2467. Web site http://www.aacc.nche.edu. David Pierce, Pres. AACC serves the nation's 1,100 community, technical, and junior colleges through advocacy, professional development, publications, and national networking. The annual convention draws more than 2,500 middle and top-level administrators of two-year colleges. Twenty-four councils and 8 commissions address priority areas for community colleges. AACC also operates the Community College Satellite Network, providing teleconferences and other programming and services to colleges. *Membership:* 1,110 institutions, 16 international, 5 foundations, 15 corporations, 157 individuals, and 70 educational associates. *Dues:* vary by category. *Meetings:* Annual Convention, spring. *Publications: Community College Journal* (bi-mo.); *Community College Times* (bi-weekly newspaper); *College Times*; Community College Press (books and monographs).

American Association of School Librarians (AASL). 50 E. Huron St., Chicago, IL 60611. (312) 280-4386. (800) 545-2433, ext. 4386. Fax (312) 664-7459. E-mail aasl@ala.org. Web page http://www.ala.org/aasl. Donald C. Adcock, Interim Exec. Dir. An affiliate of the American Library Association, AASL is interested in the general improvement and extension of school library media services for children and youth. Activities and projects of the association are divided among 55 committees and 3 sections. *Membership:* 7,690. *Dues:* Membership in ALA (1st yr., $48; 2nd yr., $71; 3rd and subsequent yrs., $95) plus $40; retired memberships and student membership rates available. *Publications: School Library Media Quarterly* (journal); *Hotline Connections* (newsletter, 4/yr.).

American Association of State Colleges and Universities (AASCU). One Dupont Cir. NW, Suite 700, Washington, DC 20036-1192. (202) 293-7070. Fax (202) 296-5819. James B. Appleberry, Pres. Membership is open to regionally accredited institutions of higher education (and those in the process of securing accreditation), that offer programs leading to the degree of Bachelor, Master, or Doctor, and that are wholly or partially state-supported and state-controlled. Organized and operated exclusively for educational, scientific, and literary purposes, its particular purposes are to improve higher education within its member institutions through cooperative planning, studies, and research on common educational problems and the development of a more unified program of action among its members; and to provide other needed and worthwhile educational services to the colleges and universities it may represent. *Membership:* 375 institutions (university), 28 systems, and 7 associates. *Dues:* based on current student enrollment at institution. *Publications: MEMO: To the President; The Center Associate; Office of Federal Program Reports; Office of Federal Program Deadlines.* (Catalogs of books and other publications available upon request.)

American Educational Research Association (AERA). 1230 17th St. NW, Washington, DC 20036. (202) 223-9485. Fax (202) 775-1824. E-mail aera@gmu.edu. Web site http://www.asu.edu/aera. William J. Russell, Exec. Dir. AERA is an international professional organization with the primary goal of advancing educational research and its practical application. Its members include educators and administrators; directors of research, testing, or evaluation in federal, state, and local agencies; counselors; evaluators; graduate students; and behavioral scientists. The broad range of disciplines represented includes education, psychology, statistics, sociology, history, economics, philosophy, anthropology, and political science. AERA has over 100 Special Interest Groups including Advanced Technologies for Learning, Computer Applications in Education, Electronic Networking, Information Technology and Library Resources, Instructional Technology, and Text, Technology and Learning Strategies. *Membership:* 23,000. *Dues:* vary by category, ranging from $20 for students to $45 for voting. *Meetings:* 1998 Annual Meeting, April 13-17, San Diego. *Publications: Educational Researcher; American Educational Research Journal; Journal of Educational Statistics; Educational Evaluation and Policy Analysis; Review of Research in Education; Review of Educational Research.*

American Foundation for the Blind (AFB). 11 Penn Plaza, Suite 300, New York, NY 10001. (212) 502-7600, (800) AFB-LINE. Fax (212) 502-7777. E-mail afbinfo@afb.org. Web site http://www.afb.org/afb. Carl R. Augusto, Pres.; Liz Greco, Vice Pres. of Communications. AFB is a leading national resource for people who are blind or visually impaired, the organizations that serve them, and the general public. A nonprofit organization founded in 1921 and recognized as Helen Keller's cause in the US, AFB's mission is to enable people who are blind or visually impaired to achieve equality of access and opportunity that will ensure freedom of choice in their lives. AFB is headquartered in New York City with offices in Atlanta, Chicago, Dallas, San Francisco, and Washington, DC. *Publications: AFB News* (free); *Journal of Visual Impairment & Blindness; AFB Press Catalog of Publications* (free).

American Library Association (ALA). 50 E. Huron St., Chicago, IL 60611. (312) 944-6780. Fax (312) 440-9374. Carol Henderson, Exec. Dir. The ALA is the oldest and largest national library association. Its 58,000 members represent all types of libraries: state, public, school, and academic, as well as special libraries serving persons in government, commerce, the armed services, hospitals, prisons, and other institutions. The ALA is the chief advocate of achievement and maintenance of high-quality library information services through protection of the right to read, educating librarians, improving services, and making information widely accessible. See separate entries for the following affiliated and subordinate organizations: American Association of School Librarians, American Library Trustee Association, Association for Library Collections and Technical Services, Association for Library Service to Children, Association of College and Research Libraries, Association of Specialized and Cooperative Library Agencies, Library Administration and Management Association, Library and Information Technology Association, Public Library Association, Reference and Adult Services Division, Young Adult Library Services Association, and Continuing Library Education Network and Exchange Round Table. *Membership:* 58,000. *Dues:* Basic dues $48 first year, $95 renewing members. *Meetings:* 1998 Midwinter Meeting, Jan 9-15, New Orleans; Annual Conference, Jun 25-Jul 2, Washington, DC. *Publications: American Libraries; Booklist; Choice; Book Links.*

American Library Trustee Association (ALTA). 50 E. Huron St., Chicago, IL 60611. (312) 280-2160. Fax (312) 280-3257. Susan Roman, Exec. Dir. An affiliate of the American Library Association, ALTA is interested in the development of effective library service for people in all types of communities and libraries. Members, as policymakers, are concerned with organizational patterns of service, the development of competent personnel, the provision of adequate financing, the passage of suitable legislation, and the encouragement of citizen support for libraries. *Membership:* 1,710. *Dues:* $50 plus membership in ALA. *Publications: Trustee Voice* (q. newsletter); professional monographs and pamphlets.

American Management Association (AMA). 1601 Broadway, New York, NY 10019-7420. (212) 586-8100. Fax (212) 903-8168. E-mail cust_serv@amanet.org. David Fagiano, Pres. and CEO. Founded in 1923, the AMA provides educational forums worldwide where members and their colleagues learn superior, practical business skills and explore best practices of world-class organizations through interaction with each other and expert faculty practitioners. AMA's publishing program provides tools individuals use to extend learning beyond the classroom in a process of life-long professional growth and development through education. The AMA operates management centers and offices in Atlanta, Boston (Watertown), Chicago, Hamilton (NY), Kansas City (Leawood), New York, San Francisco, Saranac Lake (NY), and Washington, DC and through AMA/International, in Brussels, Tokyo, Shanghai, Islamabad, and Buenos Aires. In addition, it has affiliated centers in Toronto, Mexico City, Sao Paulo, Taipei, Istanbul, Hong Kong, Singapore, Jakarta, Braamfontein, and Dubai. AMA offers conferences, seminars, and membership briefings where there is an interchange of information, ideas, and experience in a wide variety of management topics. Through its publication division, AMACOM, AMA publishes approximately 60 business-related books per year, as well as numerous surveys and management briefings. Other services offered by AMA include FYI Video; Extension Institute (self-study programs in both print and audio formats); *AMA Interactive Series* (self-paced learning on CD-ROM); Operation Enterprise (young adult program); AMA On-Site (video-conferences); the Information Resource Center (for AMA members only), a management information and library service; and six bookstores. It also cooperates with management associations around the world through correspondent association agreements. AMA, in conjunction with The American Society of Mechanical Engineers, annually awards the Henry Laurence Gantt Medal for "distinguished achievement in management as a service to the community." *Membership:* approx. 70,000. *Dues:* corporate, $550-1,495; growing company, $475-1,675; individual, $160 plus $40 per division. *Publications* (periodicals): *Management Review* (membership); *Compensation and Benefits Review; Organizational Dynamics; HR Focus; President; Getting Results...;* and *The Take Charge Assistant.*

American Montessori Society (AMS). 281 Park Ave. S, New York, NY 10010. (212) 358-1250. Fax (212) 358-1256. Michael N. Eanes, Natl. Dir. Dedicated to promoting better education for all children through teaching strategies consistent with the Montessori system. Membership is composed of schools in the private and public sectors employing this method, as well as individuals. It serves as a resource center and clearinghouse for information and data on Montessori affiliates, teacher training programs in different parts of the country, and conducts a consultation service and accreditation program for school members. *Dues:* teachers, schoolheads, $40; parents, $30; institutions, from $215 and up. *Meetings:* three regional and one national educational conference per year and four professional development symposia under the auspices of the AMS Teachers' Section. 38th Annual Conference, Mar 27-29, 1998, Boston. Annual Teacher's Section Touring Symposium: Feb 21, 1998, Delrey Beach, FL; Mar 18, 1998, Seattle. *Publications: AMS Montessori LIFE* (q); *Schoolheads* (newsletter); *Montessori in Contemporary American Culture*; *Authentic American Montessori School*; *The Montessori School Management Guide*; AMS position papers.

*American Society for Training and Development (ASTD). 1640 King St., Box 1443, Alexandria, VA 22313. (703) 683-8100. Fax (703) 683-8103. Curtis E. Plott, Pres. and CEO. Founded in 1944, ASTD is the world's premiere professional association in the field of workplace learning and performance. ASTD's membership includes more than 58,000 people in organizations from every level of the field of workplace performance in more than 100 countries. Its leadership and members work in more than 15,000 multinational corporations, small and medium sized businesses, government agencies, colleges, and universities. ASTD is the leading resource on workplace learning and performance issues, providing information, research, analysis, and practical information derived from its own research, the knowledge and experience of its members, its conferences and publications, and the coalitions and partnerships it has built through research and policy work. *Membership:* 58,000 National and Chapter members. *Dues:* $150, national. *Publications: Training & Development Magazine*; *Technical & Skills Training Magazine*; *Info-Line*; *The American Mosaic: An In-depth Report of Diversity on the Future of Diversity at Work*; *ASTD Video Directories*; *ASTD Directory of Academic Programs in T&D/HRD*; *Training and Development Handbook*; *Technical & Skills Training Handbook*. Quarterly publications: *National Report on Human Resources*; *Washington Policy Report*. ASTD also has recognized professional forums, most of which produce newsletters.

American Society of Cinematographers (ASC). 1782 N. Orange Dr., Hollywood, CA 90028. (213) 969-4333. Fax (213) 876-4973. Fax (213) 882-6391. E-mail ascmag@aol.com. Owen Roizman, Pres. ASC is an educational, cultural, and professional organization. *Membership:* 302. Membership is by invitation to those who are actively engaged as directors of photography and have demonstrated outstanding ability. Classifications are Active, Active Retired, Associates, and Honorary. *Meetings:* Book Bazaar (Open House) - December; Awards Open House, March 7, 1998; Annual ASC Awards, March 8, 1998, Beverly Hills, CA. *Publications: American Cinematographer Video Manual*; *American Cinematographer Film Manual* (7th ed.); *Anton Wilson's Cinema Workshop* (4th ed.); *The Cinema of Adventure, Romance, and Terror*; *The Light on Her Face*; and *American Cinematographers Magazine*.

American Society of Educators (ASE). 1429 Walnut St., 10th Fl., Philadelphia, PA 19102. (215) 563-6005. Fax (215) 587-9706. E-mail michelesok@aol.com. Web site http://www. media-methods.com. Michele Sokolof, Editorial Dir. ASE services the information needs of K-12 teachers, librarians, media specialists, curriculum directors, and administrators in evaluating the practical applications of today's multimedia and technology resources for teaching and learning purposes. *Membership:* 42,000. *Dues:* $33.50; $51.50 foreign. *Publications: Media and Methods*, bi.-mo. magazine.

American Women in Radio and Television (AWRT). 1650 Tyson Blvd., Suite 200, McLean, VA 22102-3915. (703) 506-3290. Fax (703) 506-3266. Mary McBride, Mgr. of Association Services. Terri Dickerson, Exec. Dir. Organization of professionals in the electronic media, including owners, managers, administrators, and those in creative positions in broadcasting, satellite, cable, advertising, and public relations. AWRT's objectives are to work worldwide to improve the quality of radio and television; to promote the entry, development, and advancement of women in the electronic media and allied fields; to serve as a medium of communication and idea exchange; and to become involved in community concerns. Organized in 1951. *Membership:* 40 chapters. Student memberships available. *Dues:* $125. *Publications:*

News and Views; *Resource Directory*; *Careers in the Electronic Media*; *Sexual Harassment* (pamphlet).

Anthropology Film Center (AFC). 1626 Upper Canyon Rd., Santa Fe, NM 87501-6138. (505) 983-4127. E-mail ziacine@ix.netcom.com, anthrofilm@nets.com, or anthrofilm@archaeology. com. Web site http://www.nets.com/anthrofilm. Carroll Williams, Dir. Offers the Ethnographic/ Documentary Film Program, a 30-week full-time course in 16mm film in CD production and theory. Summer workshops are offered as well. AFC also provides consultation, research facilities, and a specialized library.

Appalachia Educational Laboratory, Inc. (AEL). P.O. Box 1348, Charleston, WV 25325. (304) 347-0400, (800) 624-9120. Fax (304) 347-0487. E-mail aelinfo@ael.org. Terry L. Eidell, Exec. Dir. One of 10 Office of Educational Research and Improvement (OERI) regional educational laboratories designed to help educators and policymakers solve educational problems in their schools. Using the best available information and the experience and expertise of professionals, AEL seeks to identify solutions to education problems, tries new approaches, furnishes research results, and provides training to teachers and administrators. AEL serves Kentucky, Tennessee, Virginia, and West Virginia.

Association for Childhood Education International (ACEI). 11501 Georgia Ave., Suite 315, Wheaton, MD 20902. (301) 942-2443. Fax (301) 942-3012. E-mail ACEIHQ@aol.com. Anne W. Bauer, Ed. and Dir. of Publications. ACEI publications reflect careful research, broad-based views, and consideration of a wide range of issues affecting children from infancy through early adolescence. Many are media-related in nature. The journal (*Childhood Education*) is essential for teachers, teachers-in-training, teacher educators, day care workers, administrators, and parents. Articles focus on child development and emphasize practical application. Regular departments include book reviews (child and adult); film reviews, pamphlets, software, research, and classroom idea-sparkers. Five issues are published yearly, including a theme issue devoted to critical concerns. *Membership:* 12,000. *Dues:* $45, professional; $26, student; $23, retired; $80, institutional. *Meeting:* Annual International Conference and Exhibition, spring. *Publications: Childhood Education* (official journal) with *ACEI Exchange* (insert newsletter); *Journal of Research in Childhood Education*; professional division newsletters (*Focus on Infancy, Focus on Early Childhood*, and *Focus on Later Childhood/Early Adolescence*); *Celebrating Family Literacy Through Intergenerational Programming; Selecting Educational Equipment for School and Home; Developmental Continuity Across Preschool and Primary Grades; Implications for Teachers; Developmentally Appropriate Middle Level Schools; Common Bonds: Antibias Teaching in a Diverse Society; Childhood 1892-1992; Infants and Toddlers with Special Needs and Their Families* (position paper); and pamphlets.

Association for Continuing Higher Education (ACHE). Continuing Education, Trident Technical College, P.O. Box 118067, CE-P, Charleston, SC 29423-8067. (803) 722-5546. Fax (803) 722-5520. Wayne Whelan, Exec. Vice Pres. ACHE is an institution-based organization of colleges, universities, and individuals dedicated to the promotion of lifelong learning and excellence in continuing higher education. ACHE encourages professional networks, research, and exchange of information for its members and advocates continuing higher education as a means of enhancing and improving society. *Membership:* 1,622 individuals in 674 institutions. *Dues:* $60, professional; $240, institutional. *Meetings:* 1998 Annual Meeting, Oct 30-Nov 3, Fort Worth, TX. *Publications: Journal of Continuing Higher Education* (3/yr.); *Five Minutes with Ache* (newsletter, 10/yr.); *Proceedings* (annual).

Association for Educational Communications and Technology (AECT). 1025 Vermont Ave. NW, Suite 820, Washington, DC 20005. (202) 347-7834. Fax (202) 347-7839. Stanley Zenor, Exec. Dir; Franz Frederick, Pres. AECT is an international professional association concerned with the improvement of learning and instruction through media and technology. It serves as a central clearinghouse and communications center for its members, who include instructional technologists, library media specialists, religious educators, government media personnel, school administrators and specialists, and training media producers. AECT members also work in the armed forces, public libraries, museums, and other information agencies of many different kinds, including those related to the emerging fields of computer technology. Affiliated organizations include the Association for Media and Technology in Education in Canada (AMTEC), Community College Association for Instructional and Technology (CCAIT), Consortium of College and University Media Centers (CCUMC), Federal Educational Technology Association (FETA), Health Sciences Communications Association (HeSCA), International Association for Learning Laboratories (IALL), International Council for Educational Media (ICEM), International Visual Literacy Association (IVLA), Minorities in Media (MIM), National Association of Regional Media Centers (NARMC), National Council for Accreditation of Teacher Education (NCATE), National Instructional Television Fixed Service (ITFS), New England Educational Media Association (NEEMA), Northwest College and University Council for the Management of Educational Technology (NW/MET), and the Southeastern Regional Media Leadership Council (SRMLC). Each of these affiliated organizations has their own listing in the *Yearbook*. Two additional organizations, the AECT Archives and the ECT Foundation, are also related to the Association for Educational Communications and Technology and have independent listings. Divisions are listed below. *Membership:* 4,500, plus 9,000 additional subscribers, 11 divisions, 15 national affiliates, 46 state and territorial affiliates, and more than 30 national committees and task forces. *Dues:* $75, regular; $35, student and retired. *Meetings:* 1998 Annual Convention and InCITE Exposition, February 18-22, St. Louis; 1999 Annual Convention and InCITE Exposition, Feb 10-14, Houston. *Publications: TechTrends* (6/yr., free with membership; $36 nonmembers); *Report to Members* (6/yr., newsletter); *Educational Technology Research and Development* (q., $40 members; $55 nonmembers); various division publications; several books; videotapes.

Association for Educational Communications and Technology (AECT) Divisions:

(AECT) Division of Educational Media Management (DEMM). 1025 Vermont Ave. NW, Suite 820, Washington, DC 20005-3516. (202) 347-7834. Fax (202) 347-7839. E-mail aect@aect.org. Web site http://www.aect.org/Divisions/aectdiv.html and http://teams.lacoe.edu/demm/demm.html. Lisa Palchik, Pres. 1997-98 (lpalch@hobbes. kzoo.edu); Jay Harriman, Pres.-Elect (harriman@uga.cc.uga.edu). As leaders in the field of educational media, members of DEMM are actively involved in the design, production, and instructional applications of new and emerging multimedia technologies. DEMM members are proactive media managers who provide solutions, share information on common problems, and support the development of model media programs. *Membership:* 438. *Dues:* One division membership included in the basic AECT membership; additional division memberships $10. *Meetings:* DEMM meets in conjunction with the annual AECT National Convention. *Publication: DEMM Perspective* (newsletter, q.).

(AECT) Division of Instructional Development (DID). 1025 Vermont Ave. NW, Suite 820, Washington, DC 20005. (202) 347-7834. James Klein, Pres. DID is composed of individuals from business, government, and academic settings concerned with the systematic design of instruction and the development of solutions to performance problems. Members' interests include the study, evaluation, and refinement of design processes; the creation of new models of instructional development; the invention and improvement of techniques for managing the development of instruction; the development and application of professional ID competencies; the promotion of academic programs for preparation of ID professionals; and the dissemination of research and development work in ID. *Membership:* 726. *Dues:* One division membership included in the basic AECT membership; additional division memberships $10. *Meetings:* held in conjunction with the annual AECT Convention. *Publications: DID Newsletter;* occasional papers.

(AECT) Division of Interactive Systems and Computers (DISC). 1025 Vermont Ave. NW, Suite 820, Washington, DC 20005. (202) 347-7834. Zane Berge, Pres. Concerned with the generation, access, organization, storage, and delivery of all forms of information used in the processes of education and training. DISC promotes the networking of its members to facilitate sharing of expertise and interests. *Membership:* 883. *Dues:* One division membership included in the basic AECT membership; additional division memberships $10. *Meetings:* held in conjunction with the annual AECT Convention. *Publication:* Newsletter.

(AECT) Division of Learning and Performance Environments (DLPE). 1025 Vermont Ave. NW, Suite 820, Washington, DC 20005. (202) 347-7834. John Farquhar, Pres. Seeks to provide continuing education and leadership in the field of learning and human performance using computer-based technologies. The Division is composed of individuals from business, academic settings, and government who are looking for a forum for sophisticated discussions of the issues they face. Member interests include scholarly research, the application of theory to practice, design, development, evaluation, assessment, and implementation of learning and performance support systems for adults. *Dues:* One division membership included in the basic AECT membership; additional division memberships $10. *Meetings:* held in conjunction with the annual AECT Convention.

(AECT) Division of School Media Specialists (DSMS). 1025 Vermont Ave. NW, Suite 820, Washington, DC 20005. (202) 347-7834. E-mail smith@po.atlantic.county. lib.nj.us. Web site http://www.gnatnet.net/~paula/dsms1.htm./ Jim Smith, Pres. DSMS promotes communication among school media personnel who share a common concern in the development, implementation, and evaluation of school media programs, and strives to increase learning and improve instruction in the school setting through the utilization of educational media and technology. *Membership:* 902. *Dues:* One division membership included in the basic AECT membership; additional division memberships $10. *Meetings:* held in conjunction with the annual AECT Convention. *Publication:* Newsletter.

(AECT) Division of Telecommunications (DOT). 1025 Vermont Ave. NW, Suite 820, Washington, DC 20005. (202) 347-7834. Richard Hezel, Pres. Seeks to improve education through use of television and radio, video and audio recordings, and autotutorial devices and media. Aims to improve the design, production, evaluation, and use of telecommunications materials and equipment; to upgrade competencies of personnel engaged in the field; to investigate and report promising innovative practices and technological developments; to promote studies, experiments, and demonstrations; and to support research in telecommunications. Future plans call for working to establish a national entity representing instructional television. *Membership:* 607. *Dues:* one division membership included in the basic AECT membership; additional division memberships $10. *Meetings:* held in conjunction with annual AECT Convention. *Publication:* Newsletter.

(AECT) Industrial Training and Education Division (ITED). 1025 Vermont Ave. NW, Suite 820, Washington, DC 20005. (202) 347-7834. E-mail ayeaman@carbon. cudenver.edu. Mary Lou Shippe, Pres. ITED is involved with designing, planning, evaluating, and managing training and performance programs, and promoting appropriate uses of educational techniques and media. *Membership:* 273. *Dues:* one division membership included in the basic AECT membership; additional division memberships $10. *Meetings:* held in conjunction with annual AECT Convention. *Publication: ITED Newsletter.*

(AECT) International Division (INTL). 1025 Vermont Ave. NW, Suite 820, Washington, DC 20005. (202) 347-7834. Mei-Yan Lu, Pres. Seeks to improve international communications concerning existing methods of design; to pretest, use, produce, evaluate, and establish an approach through which these methods may be improved and adapted for maximum use and effectiveness; to develop a roster of qualified international leaders with experience and competence in the varied geographic and technical areas; and to encourage research in the application of communication processes to support present and future international social and economic development. *Membership:* 295. *Dues:* one division membership included in the basic AECT membership; additional division memberships $10. *Meetings:* held in conjunction with the annual AECT Convention. *Publication:* Newsletter.

(AECT) Media Design and Production Division (MDPD). 1025 Vermont Ave. NW, Suite 820, Washington, DC 20005. (202) 347-7834. Chuck Stoddard, Pres. Seeks to provide formal, organized procedures for promoting and facilitating interaction between commercial and noncommercial, nontheatrical filmmakers, and to provide a communications link for filmmakers with persons of similar interests. Also seeks to provide a connecting link between creative and technical professionals of the audiovisual industry. Advances the informational film producer's profession by providing scholarships and apprenticeships to experimenters and students and by providing a forum for discussion of local, national, and universal issues. Recognizes and presents awards for outstanding films produced and for contributions to the state of the art. *Membership:* 318. *Dues:* one division membership included in the basic AECT membership; additional division memberships $10. *Meetings:* held in conjunction with annual AECT Convention. *Publication:* Newsletter.

(AECT) Research and Theory Division (RTD). 1025 Vermont Ave. NW, Suite 820, Washington, DC 20005. (202) 3477834. Dennis Hlynka, Pres. Seeks to improve the design, execution, utilization, and evaluation of educational technology research; to improve the qualifications and effectiveness of personnel engaged in educational technology research; to advise the educational practitioner as to use of the research results; to improve research design, techniques, evaluation, and dissemination; to promote both applied and theoretical research on the systematic use of educational technology in the improvement of instruction; and to encourage the use of multiple research paradigms in examining issues related to technology in education. *Membership:* 452. *Dues:* one division membership included in the basic AECT membership; additional division memberships $10. *Meetings:* held in conjunction with annual AECT Convention. *Publication:* Newsletter.

(AECT) Systemic Change in Education Division (CHANGE). 1025 Vermont Ave. NW, Suite 820, Washington, DC 20005. (202) 347-7834. Atsusi Hirumi, Pres. Serves those who are interested in systemic change in a wide variety of settings, including public and private schools. Fosters the belief that systemic change is necessary in educational settings for meeting learners' needs and for dramatically improving the quality of education. *Dues:* one division membership included in the basic AECT membership; additional division memberships $10. *Meetings:* held in conjunction with the annual AECT Convention. *Publication:* Newsletter.

AECT Archives. University of Maryland at College Park, Hornbake Library, College Park, MD 20742. Thomas Connors, Archivist, National Public Broadcasting Archives. (301) 405-9255. Fax (301) 314-2634. A collection of media, manuscripts, and related materials representing important developments in visual and audiovisual education and in instructional technology. The collection is housed as part of the National Public Broadcasting Archives. Maintained by the University of Maryland at College Park in cooperation with AECT. Open to researchers and scholars.

Association for Experiential Education (AEE). 2305 Canyon Blvd., Suite 100, Boulder, CO 80302-5651. (303) 440-8844 ext. 3. Fax (303) 440-9581. E-mail info@aee.org. Web page http://www.princeton.edu/~rcurtis/aee.html. Sharon Heinlen, Exec. Dir. AEE is a nonprofit, international, professional organization with roots in adventure education, committed to the development, practice, and evaluation of experiential learning in all settings. AEE's vision is to be a leading international organization for the development and application of experiential education principles and methodologies with the intent to create a just and compassionate world by transforming education and promoting positive social change. *Membership:* more than 2,500 members in over 30 countries including individuals and organizations with affiliations in education, recreation, outdoor adventure programming, mental health, youth service, physical education, management development training, corrections, programming for people with disabilities, and environmental education. *Dues:* $55-$95, individual (depending on annual income); $110-$125, family; $200-$500, organizations and corporations. *Meetings:* Annual AEE International Conference, fall. Regional Conferences held in the Northwest, Heartland, Southeast, Mid-South, Mid-Atlantic, Northeast, West, and Rocky Mountains. *Publications: Jobs Clearinghouse* (m.); *The Journal of Experiential Education* (3/yr.); *Experience and the Curriculum*; *Adventure Education*; *Adventure Therapy*; *Therapeutic Applications of Adventure Programming*; *Experiential Education in High School*; *Manual of Accreditation Standards for Adventure Programs*; *The Theory of Experiential Education, Third Edition*; *Experiential Learning in Schools and Higher Education*; *Ethical Issues in Experiential Education, Second Edition*; *The K.E.Y. (Keep Exploring Yourself) Group: An Experiential Personal Growth Group Manual*; *Book of Metaphors, Volume II*; *Women's Voices in Experiential Education*; bibliographies, directories of programs and membership directory.

Association for Library and Information Science Education (ALISE). Sharon J. Rogers, Exec. Dir. P.O. Box 7640, Arlington, VA 22207. (703) 522-1899. E-mail srogers@gwis2. circ.gwu.edu. Web site http://www.si.umich.edu/ALISE/. Seeks to advance education for library and information science and produces annual *Library and Information Science Education Statistical Report.* Open to professional schools offering graduate programs in library and information science; personal memberships open to educators employed in such institutions; other memberships available to interested individuals. *Membership:* 650 individuals, 74 institutions. *Dues:* institutional, $250 full; $150 associate; $75 international; personal, $90 full-time; $50 part-time, $40 student, $50 retired. *Publications: Journal of Education for Library and Information Science*; directory; *Library and Information Science Education Statistical Report.*

Association for Library Collections and Technical Services (ALCTS). 50 E. Huron St., Chicago, IL 60611. (312) 944-6780. Fax: (312) 280-3257. E-mail alcts@ala.org. Karen Muller, Exec. Dir; Carol Chamberlain, Pres., July 1997-July 1998. An affiliate of the American Library Association, ALCTS is dedicated to acquisition, identification, cataloging, classification, and preservation of library materials, the development and coordination of the country's library resources, and aspects of selection and evaluation involved in acquiring and developing library materials and resources. Sections include Acquisitions, Cataloging and Classification, Collection Management and Development, Preservation and Reformatting, and Serials. *Membership:* 5,265. *Dues:* $45 plus membership in ALA. *Meetings:* 1998 ALA Midwinter Meeting Jan 9-15, New Orleans. 1998 ALA Annual Conference Jun 25-Jul 2, Washington, DC. *Publications: Library Resources & Technical Services* (q.); *ALCTS Newsletter* (6/yr.); *ALCTS Network News (AN2)*; *electronic newsletter issued irregularly.*

Association for Library Service to Children (ALSC). 50 E. Huron St., Chicago, IL 60611. (312) 280-2163. Fax (312) 280-3257. Susan Roman, Exec. Dir. An affiliate of the American Library Association, ALSC is interested in the improvement and extension of library services for children in all types of libraries, evaluation and selection of book and nonbook library materials, and improvement of techniques of library services for children from preschool through the eighth grade or junior high school age. Committee membership open to ALSC members. *Membership:* 3,600. *Dues:* $45 plus membership in ALA. *Meetings:* annual conference and midwinter meeting with ALA. *Publications: Journal of Youth Services in Libraries* (q.); *ALSC Newsletter* (q.).

Association for the Advancement of Computing in Education (AACE). P.O. Box 2966, Charlottesville, VA 22902. (804) 973-3987. Fax (804) 978-7449. E-mail aace@virginia.edu. Web site http://www.aace.org. Gary H. Marks, Exec. Dir.; April Ballard, contact person. AACE is an international educational professional organization whose purpose is to bring professionals from around the world to share knowledge and ideas on research, development, and application in information technology and education. It publishes major journals, books, and CD-ROMs on the subject, and organizes major conferences. Members include educators at all levels, technology center coordinators, and administrators in business and industry. *Membership:* 6,500. *Dues:* basic membership of $65 includes one journal. *Meetings:* SITE '98, April, Washington, DC; Ed-Media, June 1998, Europe; WebNet '98 in Oct or Nov. *Publications: Educational Technology Review* (3/yr.); *Journal of Educational Multimedia and Hypermedia* (q.); *International Journal of Educational Telecommunications* (q.); *Journal of Computers in Mathematics and Science Teaching* (q.); *Journal of Technology and Teacher Education* (q.); *Journal of Artificial Intelligence in Education* (q.); *Journal of Computing in Childhood Education* (q.). A catalog of books and CD-ROMs is available on request.

Association of American Publishers (AAP). 1718 Connecticut Ave. NW, Washington, DC 20009. (202) 232-3335. Fax (202) 745-0694. E-mail 250-5318@mcimail.com. 71 Fifth Ave., New York, NY 10003. (212) 255-0200. Fax (202) 255-7007. Nicholas A. Veliotes, Pres. (DC); Judith Platt, Dir., Communications and Public Affairs. AAP is the principal trade association of the book publishing industry. Association members publish hardcover and paperback books in every field, including general fiction and nonfiction; poetry; children's books; textbooks; Bibles and other religious books; reference works; scientific, medical, technical, professional and scholarly books and journals; and classroom instructional and testing materials. They also produce computer software and electronic products and services, such as online databases. AAP has five divisions: Trade, School (K-12), Higher Education, Professional and Scholarly Publishing, and International. The Association's highest priorities are expanding domestic and foreign markets for American books, journals, and electronic publishing products; promoting the status of publishing in the US and abroad; defending intellectual freedom at home and the freedom of written expression worldwide; keeping AAP members informed on legislative, regulatory, and policy issues that affect our industry and serving as the industry's voice on these issues; and protecting the rights of creators through ongoing efforts in defense of copyright. *Membership:* 200 corporate members. Membership categories are Regular, University Press Associate, Not-for-profit Associate, and Affiliate. *Meetings:* Annual Meetings, spring. For divisional annual meetings, contact Communications and Public Affairs Dept., (202) 232-3335, ext. 236. *Publications: Book Publishing and the First Amendment* (AAP DC); *Annual Industry Statistics* (NY office); *New Media Market Trends Survey* (AAP DC); *Copyright Management and the NII* (AAP DC). Contact Communications and Public Affairs for a current list of publications.

Association of College and Research Libraries (ACRL). 50 E. Huron St., Chicago, IL 60611-2795. (312) 280-3248. Fax (312) 280-2520. E-mail ajenkins@ala.org. Web site http://www.ala.org/acrl.html. Althea H. Jenkins, Exec. Dir. An affiliate of the American Library Association, ACRL provides leadership for development, promotion, and improvement of academic and research library resources and services to facilitate learning, research, and the scholarly communications process. It provides access to library standards for colleges, universities, and two-year institutions, and publishes statistics on academic libraries. Committees include Academic Status, Colleagues Committee, Copyright, Council of Liaisons, Government Relations, Professional Enhancement, Intellectual Freedom, International Relations, Media Resources, Professional Education, Publications, Racial and Ethnic Diversity, Research, Standards and Accreditation, and Statistics. The association administers 13 different awards, most of which are given annually. *Membership:* over 10,000. *Dues:* $35 (in addition to ALA membership). *Meetings*: 1999 National Conference, Apr 8-12, Detroit. *Publications: College & Research Libraries* (6/yr.); *College & Research Libraries News* (11/yr.); *Rare Books and Manuscripts Librarianship* (semi-annual); *CHOICE Magazine: Current Review for Academic Libraries* (11/yr.); *CLIP Notes* (current issues are #23-24). Recent titles include: *User*

Surveys in College Libraries; Reference Training in Academic Libraries; Environmental Studies Reviews; Directory of Curriculum Materials Centers; A Copyright Sampler; Bibliographic Control of Conference Proceedings, Papers, and Conference Materials; and *Continuity and Transformation: The Promise of Confluence,* proceedings of the 7th ACRL National Conference. A free list of materials is available. ACRL also sponsors an open discussion listserv, ACRL-FRM@ALA.ORG.

Association of Independent Video and Filmmakers/Foundation for Independent Video and Film (AIVF/FIVF). 304 Hudson St., 6th Floor, New York, NY 10013. (212) 807-1400. Fax (212) 463-8519. E-mail aivffivf@aol.com. Web site http://www.aivf.org. Ruby Lerner, Exec. Dir. AIVF/FIVF is the national trade association for independent video and filmmakers, representing their needs and goals to industry, government, and the public. Programs include screenings and seminars, insurance for members and groups, and information and referral services. Recent activities include advocacy for public funding of the arts, public access to new telecommunications systems, and monitoring censorship issues. *Dues:* $45, individual; $75, library; $100, nonprofit organization; $150, business/industry; $25, student. *Publications: The Independent Film and Video Monthly; The AIVF Guide to International Film and Video Festivals; The AIVF Guide to Film and Video Distributors; The Next Step: Distributing Independent Films and Videos; Alternative Visions: Distributing Independent Media in a Home Video World; Directory of Film and Video Production Resources in Latin America and the Caribbean.*

Association of Specialized and Cooperative Library Agencies (ASCLA). 50 E. Huron St., Chicago, IL 60611. (800) 545-2433, ext. 4399. Fax (312) 944-8085. Cathleen Bourdon, Exec. Dir. An affiliate of the American Library Association, ASCLA represents state library agencies, multitype library cooperatives, and libraries serving special clienteles to promote the development of coordinated library services with equal access to information and material for all persons. The activities and programs of the association are carried out by 21 committees, 3 sections, and various discussion groups. *Membership:* 1,300. *Dues:* (in addition to ALA membership) $40, personal; $50, organization; $500, state library agency. *Meetings:* 1998 Conference, Jun 25-Jul 2, Washington, DC. *Publications: Interface* (q.); *The Americans with Disabilities Act: Its Impact on Libraries; Deafness: An Annotated Bibliography and Guide to Basic Materials; Library Standards for Adult Correctional Institutions 1992.* Write for free checklist of materials.

Association of Systematics Collections (ASC). 1725 K St. NW, Suite 601, Washington, DC 20006. (202) 835-9050. Web site http://www.ascoll.org. K. Elaine Hoagland, Exec. Dir. Fosters the care, management, and improvement of biological collections and promotes their utilization. Institutional members include free-standing museums, botanical gardens, college and university museums, and public institutions, including state biological surveys, and agricultural research centers. The ASC also represents affiliate societies, keeps members informed about funding and legislative issues, and provides technical consulting about collection care and taxonomy. *Membership:* 82 institutions, 22 societies, 1,200 newsletter subscribers. *Dues:* depend on the size of collections. *Publications: ASC Newsletter* (for members and nonmember subscribers, bi-mo.); *Guidelines for Institutional Policies and Planning in Natural History Collections; Access to Genetic Resources; Collections of Frozen Tissues; Guidelines for Institutional Database Policies.*

Cable in the Classroom. 1900 N. Beauregard St., Suite 108, Alexandria, VA 22311. (703) 845-1400. Fax (703) 845-1409. E-mail cicofc@aol.com. Web site http://www.ciconline.com. Megan Hookey, Managing Dir. Cable in the Classroom is the cable industry's $420 million public service initiative to enrich education. It provides free cable connections to more than 75,000 public and private K-12 schools, reaching more than 82 percent of all US students with commercial-free, quality educational programming. It also provides curriculum-related support materials for its programming and conducts Teacher Training and Media Literacy workshops throughout the country. *Membership:* Cable in the Classroom is a consortium of more than 8,500 local cable companies and 34 national cable programming networks. *Meetings:*

Cable in the Classroom exhibited at 14 major education conferences in 1996. *Publications: Delivering the Future: Cable and Education Partnerships for the Information Age* (Dr. Bobbi Kamil); *Cable in the Classroom Magazine* (mo.); *Taking Charge of Your TV; A Guide to Critical Viewing for Parents and Children* (booklet, available on request).

Catholic Library Association (CLA). St. Joseph Central High School, 22 Maplewood Avenue, Pittsfield, MA 01201-4780. (413) 443-2CLA. Fax (413) 443-7020. Jean R. Bostley, SSJ, Past Pres. and Exec. Dir. Provides educational programs, services, and publications for Catholic libraries and librarians. *Membership:* approx. 1,000. *Dues:* $45, individual; special rates for students and retirees. *Meetings:* Meetings are held in conjunction with the National Catholic Educational Association: 1998, Apr 14-17, Los Angeles; 1999, Apr 6-9, New Orleans. *Publications: Catholic Library World* (q.); *Catholic Periodical and Literature Index* (q. with annual cumulations).

Central Educational Network (CEN). 1400 E. Touhy, Suite 260, Des Plaines, IL 60018-3305. (847) 390-8700. Fax (847) 390-9435. James A. Fellows, Pres. Provides general audience and instructional television programming and ITV services. *Membership:* PTV stations and educational agencies.

Children's Television International (CTI)/GLAD Productions, Inc. P.O. Box 220469, Chantilly, VA 20153-0469. 25451 Planting Field Drive, South Riding, VA 20152. (800) CTI-GLAD (284-4523). Fax (703) 327-6470. Ray Gladfelter, Pres. and Dir. of Customer Services. An educational organization that develops, produces, and distributes a wide variety of color television and video programming and related publications as a resource to aid the social, cultural, and intellectual development of children and young adults. Programs cover language arts, science, social studies, history, and art for home, school, and college viewing. *Publications:* teacher guides for instructional series; *The History Game: A Teacher's Guide*; complimentary catalog for educational videos.

Close Up Foundation. 44 Canal Center Plaza, Alexandria, VA 22314. (703) 706-3300. Fax (703) 706-0000. Stephen A. Janger, CEO; George Gold, Dir. of Publications. A nonprofit, nonpartisan civic education organization promoting informed citizen participation in public policy and community service. Programs reach more than a million participants each year. Close Up brings 25,000 secondary and middle school students and teachers and older Americans each year to Washington for week-long government studies programs, and produces television programs on the C-SPAN cable network for secondary school and home audiences. Meetings are scheduled most weeks during the academic year in Washington, DC, all with a government, history, or current issues focus.*Membership:* 25,000 participants. *Publications: Current Issues*; *The Bill of Rights: A User's Guide*; *Perspectives*; *International Relations*; *The American Economy*; documentary videotapes on domestic and foreign policy issues.

Community College Association for Instruction and Technology (CCAIT). New Mexico Military Institute, 101 W. College Blvd., Roswell, NM, 88201-5173. (505) 624-8382. Fax (505) 624-8390. E-mail klopfer@yogi.nmmi.cc.nm.us. Jerry Klopfer, Pres. A national association of community and junior college educators interested in the discovery and dissemination of information about problems and processes of teaching, media, and technology in community and junior colleges. Facilitates member exchange of data, reports, proceedings, personnel, and other resources; sponsors AECT convention sessions and social activities. *Membership:* 250. *Dues:* $20. *Meetings:* 1998, AECT National Convention, St. Louis, Feb 18-22. *Publications:* Regular newsletter; irregular topical papers.

(AACC) **Community College Satellite Network (CCSN)**. One Dupont Cir. NW, Suite 410, Washington, DC 20036. (202) 728-0200. Fax (202) 833-2467. E-mail CCSN@AACC. NCHE.EDU. Web site http://www.ancc.nche.edu. Monica W. Pilkey, Dir. An affiliate of the American Association of Community Colleges (AACC), CCSN provides leadership and facilitates distance education, teleconferencing, and satellite training to the nation's community colleges. CCSN offers discounted teleconferences, free program resources, and general informational assistance in telecommunications. CCSN meets with its members at various industry trade shows and is very active in the AACC annual convention held each spring. CCSN produces a directory of community college satellite downlink and videoconference facilities. *Membership:* 150. *Dues:* $400 for AACC members; $800 for non-AACC members. *Publications: Schedule of Programming* (2/yr.; contains listings of live and taped teleconferences for training and staff development); *CCSN Fall & Spring Program Schedule* (listing of live and taped teleconferences for training, community and staff development, business and industry training, and more); *Teleconferencing at US Community Colleges* (directory of contacts for community college satellite downlink facilities and videoconference capabilities). A free catalog is available.

Computer-Using Educators, Inc. (CUE). 1210 Marina Village Parkway, Suite 100, Alameda, CA 94501. (510) 814-6630. Fax (510) 814-0195. E-mail cueinc@aol.com. Web site http://www. cue.org. Gloria Gibson, Asst. Dir. CUE, a California nonprofit corporation, was founded in 1976 by a group of teachers interested in exploring the use of technology to improve learning in their classrooms. The organization has never lost sight of this mission. Today, CUE has an active membership of 11,000 professionals world-wide in schools, community colleges, and universities. CUE's 23 affiliates in California provide members with local year-round support through meetings, grants, events, and mini-conferences. Special Interest Groups (SIGs) support members interested in a variety of special topics. CUE's annual conferences, newsletter, advocacy, Web site, and other programs help the technology-using educator connect with other professionals. *Membership:* 11,000 individual, corporate, and institutional members. *Dues:* $30. *Meetings:* 1998 Spring CUE Conference, May 7-9, Palm Springs, CA; Fall CUE Conference, Oct 29-31, Santa Clara, CA. *Publication: CUE NewsLetter.*

Consortium of College and University Media Centers. 121 Pearson Hall-MRC, Iowa State University, Ames, IA 50011-2203. (515) 294-1811. Fax (515) 294-8089. E-mail donrieck@ iastate.edu; ccumc@ccumc.org. Don Rieck, Exec. Dir. CCUMC is a professional group of higher education media personnel whose purpose is to improve education and training through the effective use of educational media. Assists educational and training users in making films, video, and educational media more accessible. Fosters cooperative planning among university media centers. Gathers and disseminates information on improved procedures and new developments in instructional technology and media center management. *Membership:* 400. *Dues:* $160, constituent; $60, active; $160, sustaining (commercial); $25, student; $100, associate. *Meetings:* 1998, Oct, Santa Cruz, CA. *Publications: Leader* (newsletter to members); *University and College Media Review* (journal).

Continuing Library Education Network and Exchange Round Table (CLENERT). 50 E. Huron St., Chicago, IL 60611. (312) 280-4278. E-mail csullivan@ala.org. Web site http://www. ala.org. Amy Bernath, Pres.; Darlene Weingand, Pres.-Elect.; Coleen Sullivan, Staff Liaison. An affiliate of the American Library Association, CLENERT seeks to provide access to quality continuing education opportunities for librarians and information scientists and to create an awareness of the need for such education in helping individuals in the field to respond to societal and technological changes. *Membership:* 350. *Dues:* open to all ALA members; $15, individual; $50, organization. *Publication: CLENExchange* (q.), available to nonmembers by subscription at $20.

Copyright Clearance Center, Inc. (CCC). 222 Rosewood Dr., Danvers, MA 01923. (508) 750-8400. Fax (508) 750-4470. E-mail ihinds@copyright.com. Web site http://www.copyright. com/. Isabella Hinds, Vice President, Academic Licensing. CCC is a nonprofit corporation formed at the suggestion of Congress to facilitate compliance with US copyright law. CCC provides collective licensing systems involving the reproduction and distribution of copyrighted materials throughout the world. It currently provides licensing rights to over 8,000 corporations and their subsidiaries, as well as government agencies, law firms, document suppliers, libraries, academic institutions, copy shops, and bookstores within the U.S.

Corporation for Public Broadcasting (CPB). 901 E Street, NW, Washington, DC 20004-2037. (202) 879-9600. Fax (202) 783-1039. E-mail info@cpb.org. Web site http://www. cpb.org. Richard W. Carlson, Pres. and CEO. A private, nonprofit corporation created by Congress in 1967 to develop noncommercial television, radio, and online services for the American people. CPB created the Public Broadcasting Service (PBS) in 1969 and National Public Radio (NPR) in 1970. CPB distributes grants to over 1,000 local public television and radio stations that reach virtually every household in the country. The Corporation is the industry's largest single source of funds for national public television and radio program development and production. In addition to quality educational and informational programming, CPB and local public stations make important contributions in the areas of education, training, community service, and application of emerging technologies. *Publications: Annual Report*; *CPB Public Broadcasting Directory* ($15).

Council for Basic Education. 1319 F St. NW, Suite 900, Washington, DC 20004-1152. (202) 347-4171. Fax (202) 347-5047. E-mail info@c-b-e.org. Christopher T. Cross, Pres. CBE's mission is to strengthen teaching and learning of the basic subjects (English, history, government, geography, mathematics, the sciences, foreign languages, and the arts) in order to develop the capacity for lifelong learning and foster responsible citizenship. As an independent, critical voice for education reform, CBE champions the philosophy that all children can learn, and that the job of schools is to achieve this goal. CBE pursues this goal by publishing analytical periodicals and administering practical programs as examples to strengthen content in curriculum and teaching at the pre-college level. CBE is engaged in a multi-year project, Standards for Excellence in Education, to review academic standards across the disciplines. *Membership:* 2,500. *Dues:* $100, individual; $250, institution; $500, district; $40, subscription. *Publications: Basic Education* (monthly periodical on educational issues); *Perspective* (q.; treats current educational issues in depth).

Council for Educational Development and Research (CEDaR). 2000 L St. NW, Suite 601, Washington, DC 20036. (202) 223-1593. Fax (202) 785-3849. Web site http://www.cedar.org. Dena G. Stoner, Exec. Dir. The Council for Educational Development and Research is a nonprofit organization for institutions whose primary business is research, development, and related services. Its members use research knowledge to improve elementary and secondary education and engage in creating the new knowledge vital for improving education. The Council provides a forum for developing consensus among its membership about issues relating to the conduct of R&D and its application to education practice and policy. It synthesizes existing research and the wisdom from practice into discussions, forums, and documents that are designed to keep policymakers, education writers and other key groups and individuals abreast of the latest education research and development information. *Membership:* 16. *Publications: What We Know About Mathematics Teaching and Learning*; *What We Know About Science Teaching and Learning*; *Checking Up on Early Childhood Care and Education*; *Schools Along the Border: Education in the Age of NAFTA*; *Plugging In: Choosing and Using Educational Technology*; *What We Know About Reading Teaching and Learning*.

Council for Exceptional Children (CEC). 1920 Association Dr., Reston, VA 20191-1589. (703) 620-3660. TTY: (703) 264-9446. Fax (703) 264-9494. E-mail cec@cec.sped.org. Web site http://www.cec.sped.org. Nancy Safer, Interim Exec. Dir. CEC is the largest international professional organization dedicated to improving educational outcomes for individuals with exceptionalities (students with disabilities and the gifted). CEC advocates for appropriate governmental policies, sets professional standards, provides professional development, advocates for newly and historically underserved individuals with exceptionalities, and helps professionals obtain conditions and resources necessary for effective professional practice. Services include professional development opportunities and resources, 17 divisions for specialized information, public policy advocacy and information, conferences, and standards for the preparation and certification of special educators and professional practice. *Membership:* teachers, administrators, students, parents, related support service providers. *Publications:* journals and newsletters with information on new research findings, classroom practices that work, and special education publications. (*See also* the ERIC Clearinghouse on Disabilities and Gifted Education.)

(CEC) Technology and Media Division (TAM). Council for Exceptional Children. The Technology and Media Division (TAM) of The Council for Exceptional Children (CEC) encourages the development of new applications, technologies, and media for use as daily living tools by special populations. This information is disseminated through professional meetings, training programs, and publications. TAM members receive four issues annually of the *Journal of Special Education Technology* containing articles on specific technology programs and applications, and five issues of the TAM newsletter, providing news of current research, developments, products, conferences, and special programs information. *Membership:* 1,700. *Dues:* $10 in addition to CEC membership.

Council on International Non-Theatrical Events (CINE). 1001 Connecticut Ave. NW, Suite 638, Washington, DC 20036. (202) 785-1136. Fax (202) 785-4114. Donna Tschiffely, Exec. Dir. Coordinates the selection and placement of US documentary, television, short subject, and didactic films in more than 100 overseas film festivals annually. A Golden Eagle Certificate is awarded to each professional film considered most suitable to represent the U.S. in international competition and to winning films made by adults, amateurs, youths, and university students. Prizes and certificates won at overseas festivals are presented at an annual awards ceremony. CINE receives approximately 1300 entries annually for the competition. Deadlines for receipt of entry forms are Feb 1 and Aug 1. *Meeting:* 1998 Annual CINE Showcase and Awards, March, Washington, DC. *Publications: CINE Annual Yearbook of Film and Video Awards*; *Worldwide Directory of Film and Video Festivals and Events.*

East-West Center. 1777 East-West Rd., Honolulu, HI 96848. (808) 944-7666. Fax (808) 944-7333. E-mail culture@ewc. Kenji Sumida, Pres.; Grant Otoshi, Admin. Officer. The US Congress established the East-West Center in 1960 with a mandate to foster mutual understanding and cooperation among the governments and peoples of Asia, the Pacific, and the US. Officially known as the Center for Cultural and Technical Interchange Between East and West, it is a public, nonprofit institution with an international board of governors. Principal funding for the center comes from the US government, with additional support provided by private agencies, individuals, and corporations, and more than 20 Asian and Pacific governments, private agencies, individuals, and corporations. The center, through research, education, dialog, and outreach, provides a neutral meeting ground where people with a wide range of perspectives exchange views on topics of regional concern. Some 2,000 scholars, government and business leaders, educators, journalists, and other professionals from throughout the region annually work with Center staff to address issues of contemporary significance in such areas as international economics and politics, the environment, population, energy and mineral resources, cultural studies, communications, the media, and Pacific islands development.

ECT Foundation. c/o AECT, 1025 Vermont Ave. NW, Suite 820, Washington, DC 20005. Hans-Erik Wennberg, Pres. The ECT Foundation is a nonprofit organization whose purposes are charitable and educational in nature. Its operation is based on the conviction that improvement of instruction can be accomplished, in part, by the continued investigation and application of new systems for learning and by periodic assessment of current techniques for the communication of information. In addition to awarding scholarships, internships, and fellowships, the foundation develops and conducts leadership training programs for emerging professional leaders. Its operations are closely allied to AECT program goals, and the two organizations operate in close conjunction to each other.

Education Development Center, Inc. 55 Chapel St., Newton, MA 02160. (617) 969-7100. Fax (617) 244-3436. Janet Whitla, Pres. Seeks to improve education at all levels, in the US and abroad, through curriculum development, institutional development, and services to the school and the community. Produces videocassettes, primarily in connection with curriculum development and teacher training. *Publication: Annual Report.*

Educational Products Information Exchange (EPIE Institute). 103 W. Montauk Highway, Hampton Bays, NY 11946. (516) 728-9100. Fax (516) 728-9228. E-mail epieinst@aol.com. P. Kenneth Komoski, Exec. Dir. Involved primarily in assessing educational materials and providing product descriptions and citations of virtually all educational software. All of EPIE's services are available to schools and state agencies as well as individuals. *Publications: The Educational Software Selector Database (TESS)*, available to anyone. All publication material now available on CD-ROM.

Educational Resources Information Center (ERIC). National Library of Education (NLE), Office of Educational Research and Improvement (OERI), 555 New Jersey Ave. NW, Washington, DC 20208-5720. (202) 219-2289. Fax (202) 219-1817. Internet eric@inet.ed.gov. Keith Stubbs, Dir. ERIC is a federally-funded nationwide information network that provides access to the English-language education literature. The ERIC system consists of 16 Clearinghouses, 9 Adjunct Clearinghouses, and system support components that include ACCESS ERIC, the ERIC Document Reproduction Service (EDRS), and the ERIC Processing and Reference Facility. ERIC actively solicits papers, conference proceedings, literature reviews, and curriculum materials from researchers, practitioners, educational associations and institutions, and federal, state, and local agencies. These materials, along with articles from nearly 800 different journals, are indexed and abstracted for entry into the ERIC database. The ERIC database (the largest education database in the world) now contains more than 850,000 records of documents and journal articles. Users can access the ERIC database online, on CD-ROM, or through print and microfiche indexes. ERIC microfiche collections, which contain the full text of most ERIC documents, are available for public use at more than 1,000 locations worldwide. Reprints of ERIC documents, on microfiche or in paper copy, can also be ordered from EDRS. Copies of journal articles can be found in library periodical collections, through interlibrary loan, or from article reprint services. A list of the ERIC Clearinghouses, together with addresses, telephone numbers, and brief domain descriptions, follows here. *Publications: Resources in Education* (US Government Printing Office); *Current Index to Journals in Education* (Oryx Press).

ACCESS ERIC. Aspen Systems Corp., 1600 Research Blvd., Rockville, MD 20850-3172. 1-800-LET-ERIC [538-3742]. Fax (301) 309-2084. E-mail acceric@inet.ed.gov. Lynn Smarte, Project Dir. ACCESS ERIC coordinates ERIC's outreach and systemwide dissemination activities, develops new ERIC publications, and provides general reference and referral services. Its publications include several reference directories designed to help the public understand and use ERIC as well as provide information about current education-related issues, research, and practice. *Publications: A Pocket Guide to ERIC*; *All About ERIC*; *The ERIC Review*; the Parent Brochure series; *Catalog of ERIC Clearinghouse Publications*; *ERIC Calendar of Education-Related Conferences*; *ERIC Directory of Education-Related Information Centers; ERIC User's Interchange*; *Directory of ERIC Resource Collections. Databases*: ERIC Digests Online (EDO); Education-Related Information Centers; ERIC Resource Collections; ERIC Calendar of Education-Related Conferences. (The databases are available through the Internet: http://www.aspensys.com/eric.)

ERIC Clearinghouse for Community Colleges (JC) (formerly Junior Colleges). University of California at Los Angeles (UCLA), 3051 Moore Hall, P.O. Box 95121, Los Angeles, CA 90024-1521. (310) 825-3931, (800) 832-8256. Fax (310) 206-8095. E-mail ericcc@ucla.edu. Arthur M. Cohen, Dir. Development, administration, and evaluation of two-year public and private community and junior colleges, technical institutes, and two-year branch university campuses. Two-year college students, faculty, staff, curricula, programs, support services, libraries, and community services. Linkages between two-year colleges and business, industrial, and community organizations. Articulation of two-year colleges with secondary and four-year postsecondary institutions.

ERIC Clearinghouse for Social Studies/Social Science Education (SO). Indiana University, Social Studies Development Center, 2805 E. Tenth St., Suite 120, Bloomington, IN 47408-2698. (812) 855-3838, (800) 266-3815. Fax (812) 855-0455. E-mail ericso@indiana.edu. John Patrick, Dir. All levels of social studies and social science education; the contributions of history, geography, and other social science disciplines; applications of theory and research to social science education; education as a social science; comparative education (K-12); content and curriculum materials on social topics such as law-related education, ethnic studies, bias and discrimination, aging, and women's equity. Music and art education are also covered. Includes input from the Adjunct ERIC Clearinghouses for Law-Related Education, for U.S.-Japan Studies, and on Art Education.

> **Adjunct ERIC Clearinghouse for Art Education.** Indiana University, Social Studies Development Center, 2805 East 10th St., Suite 120, Bloomington, IN 47408-2698. (812) 855-3838, (800) 266-3815. Fax (812) 855-0455. E-mail clarkgil@indiana.edu; zimmerm@ucs.indiana.edu. Gilbert Clark and Enid Zimmerman, Co-Directors. Adjunct to the ERIC Clearinghouse on Social Studies/Social Science Education.

> **Adjunct ERIC Clearinghouse for Law-Related Education (ADJ/LR).** Indiana University, Social Studies Development Center, 2805 East 10th St., Suite 120, Bloomington, IN 47408-2698. (812) 855-3838, (800) 266-3815. Fax (812) 855-0455. E-mail patrick@indiana.edu, rleming@ucs.indiana.edu, temchkame@indiana.edu. John Patrick and Robert Leming, Co-Directors. Adjunct to the ERIC Clearinghouse on Social Studies/Social Sciences Education.

> **Adjunct ERIC Clearinghouse for United States-Japan Studies (ADJ/JS).** 2805 E. 10th St., Suite 120, Bloomington, IN 47408-2698. (812) 855-3838, (800) 266-3815. Fax (812) 855-0455. E-mail japan@indiana.edu. Marcia Johnson, Assoc. Dir. Provides information on topics concerning Japan and US-Japan relations. Adjunct to the ERIC Clearinghouse for Social Studies/Social Science Education. *Publications: Guide to Teaching Materials on Japan; Teaching About Japan: Lessons and Resources; The Constitution and Individual Rights in Japan: Lessons for Middle and High School Students; Internationalizing the US Classroom: Japan as a Model.*

ERIC Clearinghouse on Adult, Career, and Vocational Education (CE). The Ohio State University, Center on Education and Training for Employment, 1900 Kenny Rd., Columbus, OH 43210-1090. (614) 292-4353, (800) 848-4815. Fax (614) 292-1260. E-mail ericacve@magnus.acs.ohio-state.edu. Web site http://coe.ohio-state/cete/ericacve/index.htm. Susan Imel, Dir. All levels and settings of adult and continuing, career, and vocational/technical education. Adult education, from basic literacy training through professional skill upgrading. Career awareness, career decision making, career development, career change, and experience-based education. Vocational and technical education, including new subprofessional fields, industrial arts, corrections education, employment and training programs, youth employment, work experience programs, education and business partnerships, entrepreneurship, adult retraining, and vocational rehabilitation for individuals with disabilities. Includes input from the Adjunct ERIC Clearinghouse on Consumer Education.

> **Adjunct ERIC Clearinghouse for Consumer Education (ADJ/CN).** National Institute for Consumer Education, 207 Rackham Bldg., West Cir. Dr., Eastern Michigan University, Ypsilanti, MI 48197-2237. (313) 487-2292, (800) 336-6423. Fax (313) 487-7153. E-mail nice@emuvax.emich.edu. Rosella Bannister, Dir. Adjunct to the ERIC Clearinghouse on Adult, Career, and Vocational Education.

ERIC Clearinghouse on Assessment and Evaluation (formerly Tests, Measurement, and Evaluation). The Catholic University of America, 210 O'Boyle Hall, Washington, DC 20064-4035. (202) 319-5120, (800) 464-3742. Fax (202) 319-6692. E-mail eric_ae@cua.edu. Lawrence M. Rudner, Dir. Tests and other measurement devices; methodology of measurement and evaluation; application of tests, measurement, or evaluation in educational projects and programs; research design and methodology in the area of assessment and evaluation; and learning theory. Includes input from the Adjunct Test Collection Clearinghouse.

ERIC Clearinghouse on Counseling and Student Services (formerly Counseling and Personnel Services). University of North Carolina at Greensboro, School of Education, 101 Park Building, Greensboro, NC 27412-5001. (910) 334-4114, (800) 414-9769. Fax (910) 334-4116. E-mail ericcas2@dewey.uncg.edu. Web site http://www.uncg. edu/~ericcas2. Garry R. Walz, Dir. Preparation, practice, and supervision of counselors at all educational levels and in all settings; theoretical development of counseling and student services; personnel procedures such as testing and interviewing and the analysis and dissemination of the resultant information; group and case work; nature of pupil, student, and adult characteristics; and personnel workers and their relation to career planning, family consultations, and student services activities. *Meeting:* Assessment '98 Jan 16-18, St. Petersburg, FL. *Publications: Career Transitions in Turbulent Times*; *Exemplary Career Development Programs & Practices*; *Career Development*; *Counseling Employment Bound Youth*; *Internationalizing Career Planning*; *Saving the Native Son*; *Cultural and Diversity Issues in Counseling*; *Safe Schools, Safe Students*; many others. Call for catalog.

ERIC Clearinghouse on Disabilities and Gifted Education (EC). 1920 Association Dr., Reston, VA 20191-1589. (703) 264-9474, (800) 328-0272. TTY: (703) 264-9449. E-mail ericec@cec.sped.org. Web site http://www.cec.sped.org/ericec.htm. Sheila Mingo, Dir. Operated by The Council for Exceptional Children (see separate entry), ERIC/EC addresses prevention, identification and assessment, intervention and enrichment, both in special settings and within the mainstream. It responds to requests for information in special/gifted education and produces publications on current research, programs, and practices. Through the ERIC Clearinghouse, the ERIC/OSEP Special Project disseminates special education research through a variety of publications and conferences.

ERIC Clearinghouse on Educational Management (EA). University of Oregon (Dept. 5207), 1787 Agate St., Eugene, OR 97403-5207. (503) 346-5043, (800) 438-8841. Fax (503) 346-2334. E-mail ppiele@oregon.uoregon.edu. Philip K. Piele, Dir. The leadership, management, and structure of public and private education organizations; practice and theory of administration; preservice and inservice preparation of administrators; tasks and processes of administration; methods and varieties of organization and organizational change; and the social context of education organizations. Sites, buildings, equipment for education; planning, financing, constructing, renovating, equipping, maintaining, operating, insuring, utilizing, and evaluating educational facilities.

ERIC Clearinghouse on Elementary and Early Childhood Education (PS). University of Illinois, 805 W. Pennsylvania Ave., Urbana, IL 61801-4897. (217) 333-1386, (800) 583-4135. Fax (217) 333-3767. E-mail ericeece@uiuc.edu. Lilian G. Katz, Dir. The physical, cognitive, social, educational, and cultural development of children from birth through early adolescence; prenatal factors; parents, parenting, and family relationships that impinge on education; learning theory research and practice related to the development of young children, including the preparation of teachers for this educational level; interdisciplinary curriculum and mixed-age teaching and learning; educational, social, and cultural programs and services for children; the child in the context of the family and the family in the context of society; theoretical and philosophical issues pertaining to children's development and education. Includes input from the Adjunct ERIC Clearinghouse for Child Care.

Adjunct ERIC Clearinghouse for Child Care (ADJ/CC). Adjunct ERIC Clearinghouse for Child Care (ADJ/CC). National Child Care Information Center, 301 Maple Ave., Suite 602, Vienna, VA 22180. (703) 938-6555, (800) 616-2242. Fax (800) 716-2242. E-mail agoldstein@acf.dhhs.gov. Anne Goldstein, Proj. Dir. Adjunct to the ERIC Clearinghouse on Elementary and Early Childhood Education.

ERIC Clearinghouse on Higher Education (HE). George Washington University, One Dupont Cir. NW, Suite 630, Washington, DC 20036-1183. (202) 296-2597, (800) 773-3742. Fax (202) 296-8379. E-mail eriche@inet.ed.gov. Web site http://www.gwv. edu/~eriche. Jonathan D. Fife, Dir. Topics relating to college and university conditions, problems, programs, and students. Curricular and instructional programs, and institutional research at the college or university level. Federal programs, professional education (medicine, law, etc.), professional continuing education, collegiate computer-assisted learning and management, graduate education, university extension programs, teaching and learning, legal issues and legislation, planning, governance, finance, evaluation, interinstitutional arrangements, management of institutions of higher education, and business or industry educational programs leading to a degree. *Publications: Enriching College with Constructive Controversy*; *A Culture for Academic Excellence: Implementing the Quality Principles in Higher Education*; *From Discipline to Development: Rethinking Student Conduct in Higher Education*; *Proclaiming and Sustaining Excellence: Assessment as a Faculty Role*; *The Application of Customer Satisfaction Principles to Universities*; *Saving the Other Two-Thirds: Practices and Strategies for Improving the Retention and Graduation of African American Students in Predominately White Institutions*; *Enrollment Management: Change for the 21st Century*; *Faculty Workload: States Perspectives.*

ERIC Clearinghouse on Information & Technology (IR) (formerly Information Resources). Syracuse University, 4-194 Center for Science and Technology, Syracuse, NY 13244-4100. (315) 443-3640, (800) 464-9107. Fax (315) 443-5448. E-mail eric@ericir.syr.edu. AskERIC (question-answering service via Internet) askeric@ ericir.syr.edu. Michael B. Eisenberg, Dir. Educational technology and library and information science at all levels. Instructional design, development, and evaluation within educational technology, along with the media of educational communication: computers and microcomputers, telecommunications, audio and video recordings, film and other audiovisual materials as they pertain to teaching and learning. The focus is on the operation and management of information services for education-related organizations. Includes all aspects of information technology related to education.

ERIC Clearinghouse on Languages and Linguistics (FL). Center for Applied Linguistics, 1118 22nd St. NW, Washington, DC 20037-0037. (202) 429-9292, (800) 276-9834. Fax (202) 659-5641. E-mail eric@cal.org. Joy Peyton, Dir. Languages and language sciences. All aspects of second language instruction and learning in all commonly and uncommonly taught languages, including English as a second language. Bilingualism and bilingual education. Cultural education in the context of second language learning, including intercultural communication, study abroad, and international education exchange. All areas of linguistics, including theoretical and applied linguistics, socio-linguistics, and psycholinguistics. Includes input from the Adjunct ERIC Clearinghouse for Literacy Education.

Adjunct ERIC Clearinghouse for ESL Literacy Education (ADJ/LE). National Clearinghouse for Literacy Education, Center for Applied Linguistics (CAL), 1118 22nd St. NW, Washington, DC 20037-0037. (202) 429-9292, Ext. 200. Fax (202) 659-5641. E-mail ncle@cal.org. Joy Peyton, Dir. Adjunct to the ERIC Clearinghouse on Languages and Linguistics. *Publication: Literacy and*

Language Diversity in the United States by Terrence Wiley. McHenry, IL: Delta Systems.

ERIC Clearinghouse on Reading, English, and Communication (CS) (formerly Reading and Communication Skills). Indiana University, Smith Research Center, Suite 150, 2805 E. 10th St., Bloomington, IN 47408-2698. (812) 855-5847, (800) 759-4723. Fax (812) 855-4220. E-mail ericcs@ucs.indiana.edu. Carl B. Smith, Dir. Reading, English, and communication (verbal and nonverbal), preschool through college; research and instructional development in reading, writing, speaking, and listening; identification, diagnosis, and remediation of reading problems; speech communication (including forensics), mass communication, interpersonal and small group interaction, interpretation, rhetorical and communication theory, speech sciences, and theater. Preparation of instructional staff and related personnel. All aspects of reading behavior with emphasis on physiology, psychology, sociology, and teaching; instructional materials, curricula, tests and measurement, and methodology at all levels of reading; the role of libraries and other agencies in fostering and guiding reading; diagnostics and remedial reading services in schools and clinical settings. Preparation of reading teachers and specialists.

ERIC Clearinghouse on Rural Education and Small Schools (RC). Appalachia Educational Laboratory (AEL), 1031 Quarrier St., P.O. Box 1348, Charleston, WV 25325-1348. (304) 347-0465; (800) 624-9120. Fax (304) 347-0487. E-mail lanhamb@ael. org. Web page http://www.ael.org/erichp.htm. Craig Howley, Dir. Economic, cultural, social, or other factors related to educational programs and practices for rural residents; American Indians and Alaska Natives, Mexican Americans, and migrants; educational practices and programs in all small schools; and outdoor education. Check web site to subscribe to print newsletter, or call toll-free.

ERIC Clearinghouse on Science, Mathematics, and Environmental Education (SE). Ohio State University, 1929 Kenny Road, Columbus, OH 43210-1080. (614) 292-6717, (800) 276-0462. Fax (614) 292-0263. E-mail ericse@osu.edu. David L. Haury, Dir. Science, mathematics, and environmental education at all levels, and within these three broad subject areas, the following topics: development of curriculum and instruction materials; teachers and teacher education; learning theory and outcomes (including the impact of parameters such as interest level, intelligence, values, and concept development upon learning in these fields); educational programs; research and evaluative studies; media applications; computer applications.

ERIC Clearinghouse on Teaching and Teacher Education (SP) (formerly Teacher Education). American Association of Colleges for Teacher Education (AACTE), One Dupont Cir. NW, Suite 610, Washington, DC 20036-1186. (202) 293-2450, (800) 822-9229. Fax (202) 457-8095. E-mail ericsp@inet.ed.gov. Web site http://www. ericsp.org. Mary E. Dilworth, Dir. School personnel at all levels. Teacher recruitment, selection, licensing, certification, training, preservice and inservice preparation, evaluation, retention, and retirement. The theory, philosophy, and practice of teaching. Curricula and general education not specifically covered by other clearinghouses. Organization, administration, finance, and legal issues relating to teacher education programs and institutions. All aspects of health, physical, recreation, and dance education. Includes input from the Adjunct ERIC Clearinghouse on Clinical Schools.

Adjunct ERIC Clearinghouse on Clinical Schools (ADJ/CL). American Association of Colleges for Teacher Education, One Dupont Cir. NW, Suite 610, Washington, DC 20036-1186. (202) 293-2450, (800) 822-9229. Fax (202) 457-8095. E-mail iabdalha@inet.ed.gov. Ismat Abdal-Haqq, Coord. Adjunct to the ERIC Clearinghouse on Teaching and Teacher Education.

ERIC Clearinghouse on Urban Education. Teachers College, Columbia University, Institute for Urban and Minority Education, Main Hall, Rm. 303, Box 40, 525 W. 120th St., New York, NY 10027-6696. (212) 678-3433, (800) 601-4868. Fax (212) 678-4012. E-mail eric-cue@columbia.edu. Web site http://eric-web.tc.columbia.edu. Erwin Flaxman, Dir. Programs and practices in public, parochial, and private schools in urban areas and the education of particular ethnic minority children and youth in various settings; the theory and practice of educational equity; urban and minority experiences; and urban and minority social institutions and services.

> **Adjunct ERIC Clearinghouse on Chapter 1 (Compensatory Education) (ADJ/CHP1)**. Chapter 1 Technical Assistance Center, PRC Inc., 2601 Fortune Cir. E., One Park Fletcher Bldg., Suite 300-A, Indianapolis, IN 46241-2237. (317) 244-8160, (800) 456-2380. Fax (317) 244-7386. E-mail prcinc@delphi.com. Jean M. Williams, Coord. Adjunct to the ERIC Clearinghouse on Urban Education.

ERIC Document Reproduction Service (EDRS). 7420 Fullerton Rd., Suite 110, Springfield, VA 22153-2852. (703) 440-1400, (800) 443-ERIC (3742). Fax (703) 440-1408. E-mail service@edrs.com. Web site http://edrs.com. Peter M. Dagutis, Dir. Produces and sells microfiche and paper copies of documents abstracted in ERIC. Electronic delivery of recent documents in ERIC available. Delivery methods will include document fax-back and online delivery. Back collections of ERIC documents, annual subscriptions, cumulative indexes, and other ERIC-related materials are also available. ERIC documents can be ordered by toll-free phone call, fax, mail, or online through the EDRS web site. Document ordering also available from DIALOG and OCLC. Documents available for online delivery include all Level 1 and Level 2 documents with the appropriate copyright release from January 1996 forward, Level 1 documents from 1993 forward, and all public domain documents in ERIC.

ERIC Processing and Reference Facility. 1100 West Street, 2nd Floor, Laurel, MD 20707-3598. (301) 497-4080, (800) 799-ERIC (3742). Fax (301) 953-0263. E-mail ericfac@inet.ed.gov. Web page http://ericfac.piccard.csc.com. Ted Brandhorst, Dir. A central editorial and computer processing agency that coordinates document processing and database building activities for ERIC; performs acquisition, lexicographic, and reference functions; and maintains systemwide quality control standards. The ERIC Facility also prepares *Resources in Education (RIE), ERIC Processing Manual, Thesaurus of ERIC Descriptors, Identifier Authority,* ERIC Ready References, and other products.

Eisenhower National Clearinghouse for Mathematics and Science Education. 1929 Kenny Road, Columbus, OH 43210-1079. (800) 621-5785, (614) 292-7784. Fax (614) 292-2066. E-mail info@enc.org. Web site http://www.enc.org. Dr. Len Simutis, Dir. The Eisenhower National Clearinghouse for Mathematics and Science Education (ENC) is located at The Ohio State University and funded by the US Department of Education's Office of Educational Research and Improvement (OERI). ENC provides K-12 teachers and other educators a central source of information on mathematics and science curriculum materials, particularly those which support education reform. Among ENC's products and services are ENC Online, which is available through a toll-free number and the Internet; 12 demonstration sites located throughout the nation; and a variety of publications, including the *Guidebook of Federal Resources for K-12 Mathematics and Science,* which lists federal resources in mathematics and science education. In 1996, ENC produced CD-ROMs including curriculum resources and the *ENC Resource Finder,* which is the same searchable catalog of curriculum resources that is found through ENC Online. *Membership:* Users include K-12 teachers, other educators, policy makers, and parents. *Publications: ENC Update* (newsletter); *ENC Focus* (print catalog on selected topics); *ENC Online Brochure; Guidebook of Federal Resources for K-12 Mathematics and Science* (federal programs in mathematics and science education). ENC Online is available online (http://www.enc.org) or toll-free at (800)-362-4448.

Far West Laboratory for Educational Research and Development (FWL). See listing for WestEd.

Federal Educational Technology Association (FETA). FETA Membership, Sara Shick, P.O. Box 3412, McLean, VA 22103-3412. (703) 406-3040 (Clear Spring, Inc.). Beth Borko, Pres. An affiliate of AECT, FETA is dedicated to the improvement of education and training through research, communication, and practice. It encourages and welcomes members from all government agencies, federal, state, and local; from business and industry; and from all educational institutions and organizations. FETA encourages interaction among members to improve the quality of education and training in any arena, but with specific emphasis on government-related applications. *Membership:* 150. *Dues:* $20. *Meetings:* meets in conjunction with AECT InCITE, concurrently with SALT's Washington meeting in August, and periodically throughout the year in Washington, DC. *Publication:* Newsletter (occasional).

Film Arts Foundation (FAF). 346 9th St., 2nd Floor, San Francisco, CA 94103. (415) 552-8760. Fax (415) 552-0882. E-mail faf@igc.apc.org. Gail Silva, Dir. Daven Gee, Admin. Dir. Service organization that supports and promotes independent film and video production. Services include low-cost 16mm, Super-8, S-VHS, and AVID equipment rental, resource library, group legal and health plans, monthly magazine, seminars, grants program, annual film and video festival, nonprofit sponsorship, exhibition program, and advocacy. *Membership:* 3,200 plus. *Dues:* $45. *Publications: Release Print; AEIOU (Alternative Exhibition Information of the Universe); Media Catalog* (over 200 titles of independent media projects completed with FAF's nonprofit fiscal sponsorship).

Film/Video Arts (F/VA). 817 Broadway, New York, NY 10003. (212) 673-9361. Fax (212) 475-3467. Film/Video Arts is the largest nonprofit media arts center in the New York region. Dedicated to the advancement of emerging and established media artists of diverse backgrounds, F/VA is unique in providing a fertile environment where aspiring producers can obtain training, rent equipment, and edit their projects all under one roof. Every year over 2,500 individuals participate in F/VA's programs. There are over 50 courses offered each semester, covering topics such as rudimentary technical training in 16mm filmmaking and video production, advanced editing courses in online systems, history, cultural analysis, installation art, fundraising, grant writing, and distribution. F/VA is supported by the New York State Council on the Arts, the National Endowment for the Arts, and numerous foundations and corporations, and is therefore able to offer courses and production services at the lowest possible rates. Artists who got their start at F/VA include Jim Jarmusch, Mira Nair, Leslie Harris, Kevin Smith, and Cheryl Dunye. F/VA takes pride in meeting the needs of a broad range of filmmakers, working on features, documentaries, shorts, experimental pieces, industrials, cable shows, music videos and more by offering affordable services essential to the creation of their work and development of their careers. *Membership:* $40, individual, $70, organization.

Freedom of Information Center. 127 Neff Annex, University of Missouri, Columbia, MO 65211. (573) 882-4856. Fax (573) 884-4963. E-mail jourke@muccmail.missouri.edu. Kathleen Edwards, Manager. The Freedom of Information Center is a research library which maintains files documenting actions by governments, media, and society affecting the movement and content of information. Open 8:00 a.m. to 5:00 p.m., Monday through Friday, except holidays. Located at Missouri's School of Journalism. *Membership:* Research and referral services are available to all. *Publications: Access to Public Information: A Resource Guide to Government in Columbia and Boone County, Missouri.* Revised edition, 1990. Updated periodically by supplements. $10.00.

George Eastman House (formerly International Museum of Photography at George Eastman House). 900 East Ave., Rochester, NY 14607. (716) 271-3361. Fax (716) 271-3970. Web site http://www.it-rit.edu/~gehouse. Anthony Bannon, Dir. World-renowned museum of photography and cinematography established to preserve, collect, and exhibit photographic art and technology, film materials, and related literature, and to serve as a memorial to George

Eastman. Services include archives, traveling exhibitions, research library, school of film preservation, center for the conservation of photographic materials, and photographic print service. Educational programs, exhibitions, films, symposia, music events, tours, and internship stipends offered. Eastman's turn-of-the-century mansion and gardens have been restored to their original grandeur. *Dues:* $40, library; $50, family; $40, individual; $36, student; $30, senior citizen; $75, Contributor; $125, Sustainer; $250, Patron; $500, Benefactor; $1,000, George Eastman Society. *Publications: IMAGE; Microfiche Index to Collections; Newsletter; Annual Report: The George Eastman House and Gardens; Masterpieces of Photography from the George Eastman House Collections;* and exhibition catalogues.

The George Lucas Educational Foundation. P.O. Box 3494, San Rafael, CA 94912. (415) 662-1600. Fax (415) 662-1605. E-mail edutopia@glef.org; gopher glef.org. Web site http://glef.org. Patty Burness, Executive Dir. The Foundation promotes innovative efforts to improve education, especially those that integrate technology with teaching and learning, so all students will be prepared to learn and live in an increasingly complex world. Projects include a documentary film and resource book, a Web site, and bi-annual newsletter, all of which feature compelling education programs from around the country. The target audience is community and opinion leaders, parents, educators, media, corporate executives, and elected officials. The Foundation works to give these stakeholders useful tools to develop, make, and sustain changes in teaching and learning. The George Lucas Educational Foundation is a private operating foundation, not a grantmaking organization. *Publication: EDUTOPIA* (bi-annual newsletter).

Graphic Arts Technical Foundation (GATF). 200 Deer Run Road, Sewickley, PA 15143-2600. (412) 741-6860. Fax (412) 741-2311. George Ryan, Pres. GATF is a member-supported, nonprofit, scientific, technical, and educational organization dedicated to the advancement of graphic communications industries worldwide. For 73 years GATF has developed leading-edge technologies and practices for printing, and each year the Foundation develops new products, services, and training programs to meet the evolving needs of the industry. *Dues:* $40, teachers; $30, students; corporate dues based on percentage of sales (ranges from $350-$4,000). *Meetings:* Annual GATF/PIA Joint Fall Conference. *Publications: Professional Print Buying; Computer-to-Plate: Automating the Printing Industry; Understanding Electronic Communications: Printing in the Information Age; On-Demand Printing: The Revolution in Digital and Customized Printing.*

Great Plains National ITV Library (GPN). P.O. Box 80669, Lincoln, NE 68501-0669. (402) 472-2007, (800) 228-4630. Fax (402) 472-4076. E-mail gpn@unl.edu. Web page http://gpn.unl.edu. Lee Rockwell, Dir. Acquires, produces, promotes, and distributes educational media, videocassettes, videodiscs, and CD-ROMs. Offers more than 200 videotape (videocassette) courses and related teacher utilization materials. Available for purchase or, in some instances, lease. *Publications: GPN Educational Video Catalogs* by curriculum areas; periodic brochures.

Health Sciences Communications Association (HeSCA). One Wedgewood Dr., Suite 27, Jewett City, CT 06351-2428. (203) 376-5915. Fax (203) 376-6621. E-mail HeSCAOne@aol.com. Ronald Sokolowski, Exec. Dir. An affiliate of AECT, HeSCA is a nonprofit organization dedicated to the sharing of ideas, skills, resources, and techniques to enhance communications and educational technology in the health sciences. It seeks to nurture the professional growth of its members, to serve as a professional focal point for those engaged in health sciences communications, and to convey the concerns, issues, and concepts of health sciences communications to other organizations which influence and are affected by the profession. International in scope and diverse in membership, HeSCA is supported by medical and veterinary schools, hospitals, medical associations, and businesses where media is used to create and disseminate health information. *Membership:* 150. *Dues:* $150, individual; $195, institutional ($150 additional institutional dues); $60, retiree; $75, student; $1,000, sustaining. All include subscriptions to the journal and newsletter. *Meetings:* held in conjunction with annual AECT Convention.*Publications: Journal of Biocommunications*; *Feedback* (newsletter); *Patient Education Sourcebook Vol. II.*

Hollywood Film Archive. 8391 Beverly Blvd., #321, Hollywood, CA 90048. (213) 933-3345. D. Richard Baer, Dir. Archival organization for information about feature films produced worldwide, from the early silents to the present. *Publications:* comprehensive movie reference works for sale, including *Variety Film Reviews* (1907-94) and the *American Film Institute Catalogs* (1893-1910, 1911-20, 1921-30, 1931-40, 1941-50, 1961-70), as well as the *Film Superlist* (1894-1939, 1940-49, 1950-59) volumes, which provide information both on copyrights and on motion pictures in the public domain, and *Harrison's Reports and Film Reviews* (1919-62).

HOPE Reports, Inc. 58 Carverdale Dr., Rochester, NY 14618-4004. (716) 442-1310. Fax (716) 442-1725. Thomas W. Hope, Chairman and CEO; Mabeth S. Hope, Vice Pres. Supplies statistics, marketing information, trends, forecasts, and salary and media studies to the visual communications industries through printed reports, custom studies, consulting, and by telephone. Clients and users in the US and abroad include manufacturers, dealers, producers, and media users in business, government, health sciences, religion, education, and community agencies. *Publications: Hope Reports Presentation Media Events Calendar* (annual); *Contract Production for the '90s*; *Video Post-Production*; *Media Market Trends*; *Educational Media Trends through the 1990's*; *LCD Panels and Projectors*; *Overhead Projection System*; *Presentation Slides*; *Producer & Video Post Wages & Salaries*; *Noncommercial AV Wages & Salaries*; *Corporate Media Salaries*; *Digital Photography: Pictures of Tomorrow*; *Hope Reports Top 100 Contract Producers*; *Contract Production II*; *Executive Compensation*; *Media Production*; *Outsource or Insource.*

Institute for Development of Educational Activities, Inc. (|I|D|E|A|). 259 Regency Ridge, Dayton, OH 45459. (937) 434-6969. Fax (937) 434-5203. |I|D|E|A| is an action-oriented research and development organization originating from the Charles F. Kettering Foundation. It was established in 1965 to assist the educational community in bridging the gap that separates research and innovation from actual practice in the schools. Its goal is to design and test new responses to improve education and to create arrangements that support local application. Activities include developing new and improved processes, systems, and materials; training local facilitators to use the change processes; and providing information and services about improved methods and materials. |I|D|E|A| sponsors an annual fellowship program for administrators and conducts seminars for school administrators and teachers.

Institute for the Future (IFTF). 2744 Sand Hill Rd., Menlo Park, CA 94025-7020. (415) 854-6322. Fax (415) 854-7850. Web site http://www.iftf.org. Robert Johansen, Pres. The cross-disciplinary professionals at IFTF have been providing global and domestic businesses and organizations with research-based forecasts and action-oriented tools for strategic decision making since 1968. IFTF is a nonprofit applied research and consulting firm dedicated to understanding technological, economic, and societal changes and their long-range domestic and global consequences. Its work falls into 4 main areas: Forecasting and Strategic Planning, Emerging Information Technologies, Directions in Health Care, and Public Sector Initiatives. IFTF works with clients to think systematically about the future, identify socioeconomic trends and evaluate their long-term implications, identify potential leading-edge markets around the world, understand the global marketplace, track the implications of emerging technologies for business and society, leverage expert judgment and data resources, offer an independent view of the big picture, and facilitate strategic planning processes.

International Association for Learning Laboratories (IALL). IALL Business Manager, Malacester College, 1600 Grand Ave., St. Paul, MN 55105. (612) 696-6336. E-mail browne@macalstr.edu. Web site http://eleazar.dartmouth.edu/IALL/. Nina Garrett, Pres. Thomas Browne, Bus. Mgr. An affiliate of AECT, IALL is a professional organization working for the improvement of second language learning through technology in learning centers and classrooms. *Dues:* $40, regular; $15, student; $55 commercial. *Meetings*: Biennial IALL conferences treat the entire range of topics related to technology in language learning as well as management and planning. IALL also sponsors sessions at conferences of organizations with related interests, including AECT. *Publications: IALL Journal of Language Learning Technologies* (3 times annually); materials for labs, teaching, and technology.

International Association of Business Communicators (IABC). One Hallidie Plaza, Suite 600, San Francisco, CA 94102. (415) 433-3400. Fax (415) 362-8762. Elizabeth Allan, Pres. and CEO. IABC is the worldwide association for the communication and public relations profession. It is founded on the principle that the better an organization communicates with all its audiences, the more successful and effective it will be in meeting its objectives. IABC is dedicated to fostering communication excellence, contributing more effectively to organizations' goals worldwide, and being a model of communication effectiveness. *Membership:* 11,000 plus. *Dues:* $180 in addition to local and regional dues. *Meetings:* 1998, June 14-17, New Orleans, LA. *Publication: Communication World.*

International Association of School Librarianship (IASL). Box 34069, Dept. 300, Seattle, WA 98124-1069. (604) 925-0266. Fax: (604) 925-0566. E-mail iasl@rockland.com. Web site http://www.rhi.hi.is/~anne/iasl.html. Dr. Ken Haycock, Executive Dir. Seeks to encourage development of school libraries and library programs throughout the world, to promote professional preparation and continuing education of school librarians, to achieve collaboration among school libraries of the world, to foster relationships between school librarians and other professionals connected with children and youth and to coordinate activities, conferences and other projects in the field of school librarianship. *Membership:* 900 plus. *Dues:* $50, personal and institution for North America, Western Europe, Japan and Australia; $15 for all other countries. *Meetings:* 1998, Ramat-Gan, Israel, July. *Publications: IASL Newsletter* (q.); *School Libraries Worldwide* (semi-annual); *Annual Proceedings; Connections: School Library Associations and Contact People Worldwide; Indicators of Quality for School Library Media Programs; Books and Borrowers; Conference Proceedings Index 1972-1996; Sustaining the Vision: A collection of articles and papers on research in school librarianship.*

International Center of Photography (ICP). 1130 Fifth Ave., New York, NY 10128. (212) 860-1777. Fax (212) 360-6490. ICP Midtown, 1133 Avenue of the Americas, New York, NY 10036. (212) 768-4680. Fax (212) 768-4688. Willis Hartshorn, Dir.; Phyllis Levine, Dir. of Public Information. A comprehensive photographic institution whose exhibitions, publications, collections, and educational programs embrace all aspects of photography from aesthetics to technique; from the 19th century to the present; from master photographers to newly emerging talents; from photojournalism to the avant garde. Changing exhibitions, lectures, seminars, workshops, museum shops, and screening rooms make ICP a complete photographic resource. ICP offers a two-year NYU-ICP Master of Arts Degree in Studio Art with Studies in Photography and one-year certificate programs in Documentary Photography and Photojournalism and General Studies in Photography. *Membership:* 5,800. *Dues:* $50, Individual; $60, Double; $125, Supporting Patron; $250, Photography Circle; $500, Silver Card Patron; $1,000, Gold Card Patron; corporate memberships available. *Meetings:* ICP Infinity Awards. *Publications: Library of Photography; A Singular Elegance: The Photographs of Baron Adolph de Meyer; Talking Pictures: People Speak About the Photographs That Speak to Them; Encyclopedia of Photography: Master Photographs from PFA Collection; Man Ray in Fashion; Quarterly Program Guide; Quarterly Exhibition Schedule.*

International Copyright Information Center (INCINC). c/o Association of American Publishers, 1718 Connecticut Ave. NW, 7th Floor, Washington, DC 20009-1148. (202) 232-3335. Fax (202) 745-0694. E-mail CRISHER@publishers.org.//. Carol A. Risher, Dir. Assists developing nations in their efforts to secure permission to translate and/or reprint copyrighted works published in the United States.

International Council for Educational Media (ICEM). ICEM, Robert LeFranc, ICEM Secretariat, 29 rue d'Ulm, 25230 Oaris, Cedex 05, France. 33-1-46. Fax 33-1-46-35-78-89. Asgeir Godmundsmon, Pres. Richard Cornell, US member, University of Central Florida,

Education Room 310, Orlando, FL 32816-0992. (407) 823-2053. Fax (407) 823-5135. E-mail cornell@pogasus.cc.ucf.edu. The objective of ICEM is to provide a channel for the international exchange of information and experience in the field of educational technology, with particular reference to preschool, primary, and secondary education, technical and vocational training, and teacher and continuing education; to encourage organizations with a professional responsibility for the design, production, promotion, distribution, and use of educational media in member countries; to promote an understanding of the concept of educational technology on the part of both educators and those involved in their training; to contribute to the pool of countries by the sponsorship of practical projects involving international cooperation and co-production; to advise manufacturers of hardware and software on the needs of an information service on developments in educational technology; to provide consultancy for the benefit of member countries; and to cooperate with other international organizations in promoting the concept of educational technology. ICEM is a Class B Affiliate of UNESCO.

International Graphics Arts Education Association (IGAEA). 200 Deer Run Road, Sewickley, PA 15143-2328. (412) 741-6860. Fax (412) 741-2311. Web site http://www.igaea.org. 1996-97 Pres. Lee Weir (leeweir@clemson.edu), (864) 656-3647, Fax (864) 656-4808. 1997-98 Pres. Janet Robison (robison@al.western.tec.wi.us) (608) 789-6262. Fax (608) 785-9407. IGAEA is an association of educators in partnership with industry, dedicated to sharing theories, principles, techniques, and processes relating to graphic communications and imaging technology. Teachers network to share and improve teaching and learning opportunities in fields related to graphic arts, imaging technology, graphic design, graphic communications, journalism, photography, and other areas related to the large and rapidly changing fields in the printing, publishing, packaging, and allied industries. *Membership:* approx. 600. *Dues:* $20, regular; $12, associate (retired); $5, student; $10, library; $50-$200, sustaining membership based on number of employees. *Meetings:* 1998, California Poly State University, San Luis Obispo, Aug 2-7; 1999, Ferris State University, Big Rapids, MI, Aug 1-6. *Publications: The Communicator; Visual Communications Journal* (annual); *Research and Resources Reports.*

International Information Management Congress (IMC). 1650 38th St., 205W, Boulder, CO 80301. (303) 440-7085. Fax (303) 440-7234. Web site http://www.iimc.org. John A. Lacy, CEO. IMC's mission is to facilitate the successful adoption of imaging, document management, and workflow technologies. IMC's primary activities include conferences, exhibitions, publications, and membership functions. *Dues:* $85, affiliate (any individual with an interest in the document-based information systems field); $200, associate (any association or society with common goals within the industry); $350-$5,100, sustaining (any corporate organization with a common interest in the industry). *Meeting:* Future exhibitions planned for Dubai, UAE, and Singapore (please contact IMC for more information). *Publication: Document World Magazine* (bi-monthly).

International Society for Technology in Education (ISTE) (formerly International Council for Computers in Education [ICCE]). 1787 Agate St., Eugene, OR 97403-1923. (541) 346-4414. Fax (541) 346-5890. E-mail iste@oregon.uoregon.edu. David Moursund, CEO; Maia S. Howes, Exec. Secy. ISTE is the largest nonprofit professional organization dedicated to the improvement of all levels of education through the use of computer-based technology. Technology-using educators from all over the world rely on ISTE for information, inspiration, ideas, and updates on the latest electronic information systems available to the educational community. ISTE is a prominent information center and source of leadership to communicate and collaborate with educational professionals, policy makers, and other organizations worldwide. *Membership:* 12,000 individuals, 75 organizational affiliates, 25 Private Sector Council members. *Dues:* $55, individual; $215, all-inclusive (US); $420, institution; $1,500 - $5,000, Private Sector Council. *Meetings:* 1998: Tel-Ed, New Orleans.*Publications: The Update Newsletter* (7/yr.); *Learning and Leading with Technology: The ISTE Journal of Educational Technology Practice and Policy* (formerly *The Computing Teacher*) (8/yr.); *The Journal of Research on Computing in Education* (q.); guides to instructional uses of computers at the precollege level and in teacher training, about 80 books, and a range of distance education courses that carry graduate-level credit.

International Society for Performance Improvement (ISPI). 1300 L St. NW, Suite 1250, Washington, DC 20005. (202) 408-7969. Fax (202) 408-7972. E-mail info@ispi.org. Web site http://www.ispi.org. Richard D. Battaglia, Exec. Dir. ISPI is an international association dedicated to increasing productivity in the workplace through the application of performance and instructional technologies. Founded in 1962, its members are located throughout the US, Canada, and 45 other countries. The society offers an awards program recognizing excellence in the field. *Membership:* 5,500. *Dues:* $125, active members; $40, students and retirees. *Meetings:* Annual Conference and Expo, spring; Human Performance Technology Institute (HPTI), late spring and fall. HPTI is an educational institute providing knowledge, skills and resources necessary to make a successful transition from a training department to a human performance improvement organization. Joint conference with International Federation of Training and Development Organizations, Chicago, Mar 23-28,1998; Long Beach, CA, Mar 24-26,1999. *Publications: Performance & Instruction Journal* (10.); *Performance Improvement Quarterly; News & Notes* (newsletter, 10/yr.); *Annual Membership Directory; ISPI Book Program and Catalog.*

International Telecommunications Satellite Organization (INTELSAT). 3400 International Dr. NW, Washington, DC 20008. (202) 944-7500. Fax (202) 944-7890. Web site http://www.intelsat.int. Irving Goldstein, Dir. Gen. and CEO; Tony A. Trujillo, Dir., Corporate Communications. INTELSAT owns and operates the world's most extensive global communications satellite system. With 1996 revenues of over US $910 million, the INTELSAT system provides voice/data and video services to more than 200 countries via satellite.

International Teleconferencing Association (ITCA). 1650 Tysons Blvd., Suite 200, McLean, VA 22102. (703) 506-3280. Fax (703) 506-3266. Fax on demand (800) 891-8633. E-mail dasitca@aol.com. Web site http://www.itca.org. Jim Herbert, Exec. Dir.; Christie Scott, Mgr., Publications and Programming. ITCA, an international nonprofit association, is dedicated to the growth and development of teleconferencing as a profession and an industry. ITCA provides programs and services which foster the professional development of its members, champions teleconferencing and related technologies as primary communications tools, recognizes and promotes broader applications and the development of teleconferencing and related technologies, and serves as the authoritative resource for information and research on teleconferencing and related technologies. *Membership:* ITCA represents over 1,900 teleconferencing professionals throughout the world. ITCA members use teleconferencing, manage business television and teleconferencing networks, design the technology, sell products and services, advise customers and vendors, conduct research, teach courses via teleconference, and teach about teleconferencing. They represent such diverse industry segments as health care, aerospace, government, pharmaceutical, education, insurance, finance and banking, telecommunications, and manufacturing. *Dues:* $2,000, Gold Sustaining; $1,000, Sustaining; $500, Organizational; $250, Small Business; $100, Individual; and $30, Student. *Meetings:* annual trade show and convention. For more information, call (703) 506-3283. *Publications: ITCA Connections Newsletter* (mo.); *Videoconferencing Room Directory; Member Directory; Yearbook; Classroom of the Future; Teleconferencing in State Government Guide; Teleconferencing Success Stories.*

ITVA (International Television Association). 6311 N. O'Connor Rd., Suite 230, Irving, TX 75039. (972) 869-1112. Fax (972) 869-2980. E-Mail itvahq@worldnet.att.net. Web site http://www.itva.org. Fred M. Wehrli, Exec. Dir. Founded in 1968, ITVA's mission is to advance the video profession, to serve the needs and interests of its members, and to promote the growth and quality of video and related media. Association members are video professionals working in or serving the corporate, governmental, institutional, or educational markets. ITVA provides professional development opportunities through local, regional, and national workshops, video festivals, networking, and publications. ITVA welcomes anyone who is interested in professional video and who is seeking to widen horizons either through career development or networking. ITVA offers its members discounts on major medical, production, and liability insurance; hotel, car rental, and long distance telephone discounts; and a Master-Card program. The association is also a member of the Small Business Legislative Council. *Membership:* 9,000; 77 commercial member companies. *Dues:* $150, Individual; $425, Organizational; $1,750, Commercial Silver; $750, Commercial Bronze. *Meetings:* Annual International Conference, early summer. *Publications: ITVA News* (6/yr.); *Membership Directory* (annual); *Handbook of Treatments; It's a Business First . . . and a Creative Outlet Second; Handbook of Forms; How to Survive Being Laid Off; The Effectiveness of Video in Organizations: An Annotated Bibliography; Management Matters; A Report on the IRS Guidelines Classifying Workers in the Video Industry.*

International Visual Literacy Association, Inc. (IVLA). Gonzaga University, E. 502 Boone AD 25, Spokane, WA 99258-0001. (509) 328-4220 ext. 3478. Fax (509) 324-5812. E-mail bclark@soe.gonzaga.edu. Richard Couch, Pres. Dr. Barbara I. Clark, Exec. Treas. Provides a multidisciplinary forum for the exploration, presentation, and discussion of all aspects of visual learning, thinking, communication, and expression. IVLA was founded in 1968 to promote the concept of visual literacy and is an affiliate of AECT. *Dues:* $40, regular; $20, student and retired; $45 outside US. *Meeting:* 1998, Oct 21-25, Athens, GA. Also meets in conjunction with annual AECT Convention. *Publications: Journal of Visual Literacy; Readings from Annual Conferences.*

ITA (formerly International Tape/Disc Association). 182 Nassau St., Princeton, NJ 08542. (609) 279-1700. Fax (609) 279-1999. E-mail ita@bccom.com. Web site http://www.itaorg. com. Charles Van Horn, Exec. V.P.; Charles Riotto, Exec. Dir. An international association providing a forum for the exchange of management information on global trends and innovations which drive magnetic and optical recording media. Members include magnetic and optical recording media manufacturers, rights holders to video programs, recording and playback equipment manufacturers, and audio and video replicators. For more than 26 years, ITA has provided vital information and educational services throughout the magnetic and optical recording media industries. By promoting a greater awareness of marketing, merchandising, and technical developments, the association serves all areas of the entertainment, information, and delivery systems industries. *Membership:* 450 corporations. *Dues:* Corporate membership dues based on sales volume. *Meetings:* 28th Annual Seminar, Mar 18-22, 1998, Laguna Niguel, CA. REPLItech International (REPLItech is a seminar and trade show aimed at duplicators and replicators of magnetic and optical media.) *Publications: ITA Membership Newsletter; Seminar Proceedings; 1997 International Source Directory.*

Library Administration and Management Association (LAMA). 50 E. Huron St., Chicago, IL 60611. (312) 280-5038. Fax (312) 280-3257. E-mail lama@ala.org. Karen Muller, Exec. Dir.; William Sannwald, Pres., July 1996-July 1997. An affiliate of the American Library Association, LAMA provides an organizational framework for encouraging the study of administrative theory, improving the practice of administration in libraries, and identifying and fostering administrative skills. Toward these ends, the association is responsible for all elements of general administration that are common to more than one type of library. Sections include: Buildings and Equipment Section (BES); Fundraising & Financial Development Section (FRFDS); Library Organization & Management Section (LOMS); Personnel Administration Section (PAS); Public Relation Section (PRS); Systems & Services Section (SASS); and Statistics Section (SS). *Membership:* 5,064. *Dues:* $35 (in addition to ALA membership); $15, library school students. *Meetings:* 1998 ALA Annual Conference, Washington, DC, Jun 25-Jul 2. 1998 ALA Midwinter Meeting, Jan 9-15, New Orleans. *Publications: Library Administration & Management* (q); *LEADS from LAMA* (electronic newsletter, irregular).

Library and Information Technology Association (LITA). 50 E. Huron St., Chicago, IL 60611. (312) 280-4270, (800) 545-2433, ext. 4270. Fax (312) 280-3257. E-mail lita@ala.org. Jacqueline Mundell, Exec. Dir. An affiliate of the American Library Association, LITA is concerned with library automation, the information sciences, and the design, development, and implementation of automated systems in those fields, including systems development, electronic data processing, mechanized information retrieval, operations research, standards development, telecommunications, video communications, networks and collaborative efforts, management techniques, information technology, optical technology, artificial intelligence and expert systems, and other related aspects of audiovisual activities and hardware applications. *Membership:* 5,400. *Dues:* $45 plus membership in ALA; $25, library school students; $35, first year. *Publications: Information Technology and Libraries; LITA Newsletter.*

Library of Congress. James Madison Bldg., 101 Independence Ave. SE, Washington, DC 20540. (202) 707-5000. Fax (202) 707-1389. National Reference Service, (202) 707-5522. Web site http://www.loc.gov. The Library of Congress is the major source of research and information for the Congress. In its role as the national library, it catalogs and classifies library materials in some 460 languages, distributes the data in both printed and electronic form, and makes its vast collections available through interlibrary loan and on-site to anyone over high school age. The Library is the largest library in the world, with more than 111 million items on 532 miles of bookshelves. The collections include more than 17 million books, 2 million recordings, 12 million photographs, 4 million maps, and 47 million manuscripts. It contains the world's largest television and film archive, acquiring materials through gift, purchase, and copyright deposit. In 1996, the materials produced by the Library in braille and recorded formats for persons who are blind or physically handicapped were circulated to a readership of 780,000. The collections of the Motion Picture, Broadcasting, and Recorded Sound Division include 742,699 moving images. The Library of Congress computer system holds a total of more than 40 million records in its databases. Its 27 million catalog records, as well as other files containing copyright and legislative information, are available over the Internet. The telnet address to LOCIS is locis.loc.gov. *Publications:* listed in *Library of Congress Publications in Print* (free from Office Systems Services).

Lister Hill National Center for Biomedical Communications. National Library of Medicine, 8600 Rockville Pike, Bethesda, MD 20894. (301) 496-4441. Fax (301) 402-0118. Web site http://www.ncm.nih.gov. Harold M. Schoolman, M.D., Acting Dir. The center conducts research and development programs in three major categories: Computer and Information Science; Biomedical Image and Communications Engineering; and Educational Technology Development. Major efforts of the center include its involvement with the Unified Medical Language System (UMLS) project; research and development in the use of expert systems to embody the factual and procedural knowledge of human experts; research in the use of electronic technologies to distribute biomedical information not represented in text and in the storage and transmission of x-ray images over the Internet; and the development and demonstration of new educational technologies, including the use of microcomputer technology with videodisc-based images, for training health care professionals. A Learning Center for Interactive Technology serves as a focus for displaying new and effective applications of educational technologies to faculties and staff of health sciences, educational institutions and other visitors, and health professions educators are assisted in the use of such technologies through training, demonstrations, and consultations.

Magazine Publishers of America (MPA). 919 Third Ave., 22nd Floor, New York, NY 10022. (212) 872-3700. Fax (212) 888-4217. E-mail infocenter@magazine.org. Donald D. Kummerfeld, Pres. MPA is the trade association of the consumer magazine industry. MPA promotes the greater and more effective use of magazine advertising, with ad campaigns in the trade press and in MPA member magazines, presentations to advertisers and their ad agencies, and magazine days in cities around the US. MPA runs educational seminars, conducts surveys of its members on a variety of topics, represents the magazine industry in Washington, DC, and maintains an extensive library on magazine publishing. *Membership:* 230 publishers representing more than 1,200 magazines. *Meetings:* 1998 American Magazine Conference, Disney's Yacht & Beach Club, Orlando, FL, Oct 18-21. *Publications: Newsletter of Consumer Marketing; Newsletter of Research; Newsletter of International Publishing; Magazine; Washington Newsletter.*

Medical Library Association (MLA). 6 N. Michigan Ave., Suite 300, Chicago, IL 60602-4805. (312) 419-9094. Fax (312) 419-9094. Web site http://www.kumc.edu/mla. Naomi C. Broering, Pres.; Carla J. Funk, Exec. Dir., Kimberly Pierceall, Dir. of Communications. MLA is a professional organization of 5,000 individuals and institutions in the health sciences information field, dedicated to fostering medical and allied scientific libraries, promoting professional excellence and leadership of its members, and exchanging medical literature among its members. *Membership:* 5,000 individual and institutional. *Dues:* $110, regular; $25, students; $75, introductory; $65, affiliate; $2100, life. Institutional dues depend on number of periodical subscriptions. *Meeting:* Annual Meeting, spring. *Publications: MLA News* (newsletter, 10/yr.); *Bulletin of the Medical Library Association* (q.); *Dockit* series; monographs.

Mid-Continental Regional Educational Laboratory (McREL). 2550 S. Parker Rd., Suite 500, Aurora, CO 80014. (303) 337-0990. Fax (303) 337-3005. E-mail info@mcrel.org. Web site http://www.mcrel.org. J. Timothy Waters, Exec. Dir. One of 10 Office of Educational Research and Improvement (OERI) regional educational laboratories designed to help educators and policymakers work toward excellence in education for all students. Using the best available information and the experience and expertise of professionals, McREL seeks to identify solutions to education problems, tries new approaches, furnishes research results, conducts evaluation and policy studies, and provides training to teachers and administrators. McREL serves Colorado, Kansas, Missouri, Nebraska, North Dakota, South Dakota and Wyoming. Its specialty areas are curriculum, learning, and instruction. *Publications: Changing Schools* (q. newsletter). Check web site for catalog listing many other publications.

Minorities in Media (MIM). Wayne State University, College of Education, Instructional Technology, Detroit, Michigan 48202. (313) 577-5139. Fax (313) 577-1693. E-mail GPOWELL@CMS.CC.WAYNE.EDU. MIM is a special interest group of AECT that responds to the challenge of preparing students-of-color for an ever-changing international marketplace and recognizes the unique educational needs of today's diverse learners. It supports the creative development of curricula, instructional strategies, and computer-based instructional materials which promote an acceptance and appreciation of racial and cultural diversity. It promotes the effective use of educational communications and technology in the learning process. MIM seeks to facilitate changes in instructional design and development, traditional pedagogy, and instructional delivery systems by responding to and meeting the significant challenge of educating diverse individuals to take their place in an ever-changing international marketplace. MIM encourages all of AECT's body of members to creatively develop curricula, instructional treatments, instructional strategies, and instructional materials which promote an acceptance and appreciation of racial and cultural diversity. Doing so will make learning for all more effective, relevant, meaningful, motivating, and enjoyable. MIM actively supports the Wes McJulien Minority Scholarship, and selects the winner. *Membership:* contact MIM president. *Dues:* $20, student; $30, non-student. *Publications:* newsletter is forthcoming online. The MIM listserv is a membership benefit.

Museum Computer Network (MCN). 8720 Georgia Ave., Suite 501, Silver Spring, MD 20910. (301) 585-4413. Fax (301) 495-0810. E-mail mcn@athena.mit.edu; membership office: mdevine@asis.org. Web site http://world.std.com/nmcn/index.html. Michele Devine, Admin. Guy Herman, Pres. As a nonprofit professional association, membership in MCN provides access to professionals committed to using computer technology to achieve the cultural aims of museums. Members include novices and experts, museum professionals, and vendors and consultants, working in application areas from collections management to administrative computing. Activities include advisory services and special projects. *Dues:* $250, sponsor; $150, vendor; $100, institution; $50, individual. *Meeting:* Annual Conference, held in the fall; educational workshops. *Publications: Spectra* (newsletter); *CMI*. Subscription to *Spectra* is available to libraries only for $60 plus $10 surcharge for delivery.

Museum of Modern Art, Circulating Film and Video Library. 11 W. 53rd St., New York, NY 10019. (212) 708-9530. Fax (212) 708-9531. William Sloan, Libr. Provides film and video rentals and sales of over 1300 titles covering the history of film from the 1890's to the present.

It also incorporates the Circulating Video Library, an important collection of work by leading video artists. The Circulating Library continues to add to its holdings of early silents, contemporary documentaries, animation, avant-garde and independents and to make these available to viewers who otherwise would not have the opportunity to see them. The Circulating Film Library has 16mm prints available for rental, sale, and lease. A few of the 16mm titles are available on videocassette. The classic film collection is not. The video collection is available in all formats for rental and sale. *Publications:* Information on titles may be found in the free *Price List,* available from the Library. *Circulating Film and Video Catalog Vols. 1 and 2,* a major source book on film and history, is available from the Museum's Publications, Sales, and Service Dept. (For mail order, a form is included in the *Price List.*)

National Aeronautics and Space Administration (NASA). NASA Headquarters, Code FE, Washington, DC 20546. (202) 358-1110. Fax (202) 358-3048. E-mail mphelps@hr.hq. nasa.gov. Web site http://www.nasa.gov. Dr. Malcom V. Phelps, Asst. Dir.; Frank C. Owens, Dir., Education Division. From elementary through postgraduate school, NASA's educational programs are designed to capture students' interests in science, mathematics, and technology at an early age; to channel more students into science, engineering, and technology career paths; and to enhance the knowledge, skills, and experiences of teachers and university faculty. NASA's educational programs include NASA Spacelink (an electronic information system); videoconferences (60-minute interactive staff development videoconferences to be delivered to schools via satellite); and NASA Television (informational and educational television programming). Additional information is available from the Education Division at NASA Headquarters and counterpart offices at the nine NASA field centers. Over 200,000 educators make copies of Teacher Resource Center Network materials each year, and thousands of teachers participate in interactive video teleconferencing, use Spacelink, and watch NASA Television. Additional information may be obtained from Spacelink (spacelink.msfc.nasa.gov or http://spacelink.msfc.nasa.gov).

*National Alliance for Media Arts and Culture (NAMAC). 655 13th St., Suite 201, Oakland, CA 94612. (510) 451-2717. Fax (510) 451-2715. E-mail namac@aol.com. Julian Low, Dir. NAMAC is a nonprofit organization dedicated to increasing public understanding of and support for the field of media arts in the US. Members include media centers, cable access centers, universities, and media artists, as well as other individuals and organizations providing services for production, education, exhibition, distribution, and preservation of video, film, audio, and intermedia. NAMAC's information services are available to the general public, arts and non-arts organizations, businesses, corporations, foundations, government agencies, schools, and universities. *Membership:* 200 organizations, 150 individuals. *Dues:* \$50 - \$250, institutional (depending on annual budget); \$30, individual. *Publications: Media Arts Information Network*; *NAMAC Directory* (published biennially, available for \$25 to nonmembers).

National Association for the Education of Young Children (NAEYC). 1509 16th St. NW, Washington, DC 20036-1426. (202) 232-8777, (800) 424-2460. Fax (202) 328-1846. E-mail naeyc@naeyc.org. Web site http://www.naeyc.org/naeyc. Marilyn M. Smith, Exec. Dir.; Pat Spahr, contact person. Dedicated to improving the quality of care and education provided to young children (birth-8 years). *Membership:* Nearly 95,000. *Dues:* \$25. *Meeting:* Annual Conference held in the fall. *Publications: Young Children* (journal); more than 60 books, posters, videos, and brochures.

National Association for Visually Handicapped (NAVH). 22 W. 21st St., 6th Floor, New York, NY 10010. (212) 889-3141. Fax (212) 727-2931. E-mail staff@navh.org. Lorraine H. Marchi, Founder/Exec. Dir.; Eva Cohen, Asst. to Exec. Dir., 3201 Balboa St., San Francisco, CA 94121. (415) 221-3201. Serves the partially sighted (not totally blind). Offers informational literature for the layperson and the professional, most in large print. Maintains a loan library of large-print books. Provides counseling and guidance for the visually impaired and their families and the professionals and paraprofessionals who work with them. *Membership:* 12,000. *Dues:* Full membership \$40 for individuals. *Publications:* Newsletters for adults

(Seeing Clearly) and for children *(In Focus)* are published at irregular intervals and distributed free throughout the English-speaking world. *Visual Aids and Informational Material Catalog*; *Large Print Loan Library*; informational pamphlets on topics ranging from *Diseases of the Macula* to knitting and crochet instructions.

National Association of Regional Media Centers (NARMC). NARMC, Education Service Center, Region 20, 1314 Hines Ave., San Antonio, TX 78208. (210) 270-9256. Fax (210) 224-3130. E-mail jtaylor@tenet.edu. Web site http://esu3.k12.ne.us/prof/narmc. Larry Vice, Pres.; James H. Taylor, Treasurer. An affiliate of AECT, NARMC seeks to foster the exchange of ideas and information among educational communications professionals providing media and technology services to multiple sites and districts. Member institutions provide training in such areas as media utilization, Internet, and multimedia. Most centers maintain and manage media collections for distribution to educators for use in the classroom. In addition, NARMC initiates and disseminates research activities and feasibility studies to promote effective and efficient delivery of services and successful practices and procedures. Member institutions serve more than 20 million students. *Membership:* 285 regional centers (institutions), 70 corporations. *Dues:* $55, institutions; $250, corporations. *Meetings:* 1998 National Conference, affiliated with AECT Incite, Feb 18-22, St. Louis. Regional meetings are held throughout the US annually. *Publications:* Membership newsletter is *'ETIN*. NARMC Press was established in 1996 to provide members with publications related to the field of media and technology. These publications are available for purchase through this publication outlet. Publications are solicited and submitted from the NARMC membership. Current publications include *An Anthology of Internet Acceptable Use Policies* and *Basic MAC/Windows Internet*. In addition, there is the *Annual Membership Report* and the *Biannual Survey Report of Regional Media Centers*.

National Association of State Boards of Education (NASBE). 1012 Cameron St., Alexandria, VA 22314. (703) 684-4000. Fax (703) 836-2313. E-mail boards@nasbe.org. Web site http://www.nasbe.org. Brenda Lilienthal Welburn, Exec. Dir.; David Kysilko, contact person. Studies problems and improves communication among members, exchanges information, provides educational programs and activities, and serves as a liaison with other educators' groups. *Membership:* 650. *Publications: The State Board Connection* (member newsletter, 4/yr.); *Issues in Brief* (4/yr.); guides for policymakers and practitioners; task force reports.

National Association of State Textbook Administrators (NASTA). Instructional Materials, West Virginia Department of Education, 1900 Kanawha Boulevard East, Capitol Complex, Charleston, WV 25305, (304) 558-2691. Jim Snyder, Pres. NASTA's purposes are (1) to foster a spirit of mutual helpfulness in adoption, purchase, and distribution of instructional materials; (2) to arrange for study and review of textbook specifications; (3) to authorize special surveys, tests, and studies; and (4) to initiate action leading to better quality instructional materials. Services provided include a working knowledge of text construction, monitoring lowest prices, sharing adoption information, identifying trouble spots, and discussions in the industry. The members of NASTA meet to discuss the textbook adoption process and to improve the quality of the instructional materials used in the elementary, middle, and high schools. NASTA is not affiliated with any parent organization and has no permanent address. *Membership:* textbook administrators from each of the 23 states that adopt textbooks at the state level. *Dues:* $25, individual. *Meetings:* conducted with the American Association of Publishers and the Book Manufacturers' Institute.

*National Audiovisual Center (NAC). National Archives and Records Administration, 8700 Edgeworth Dr., Capitol Heights, MD 20743. (301) 763-1896, (800) 788-6282. Fax (301) 763-6025. George Ziener, Dir. Central information and distribution source for more than 8,000 audiovisual programs produced by or for the US government. Materials are made available for sale or rent on a self-sustaining basis, at the lowest price possible. *Publications: Media Resource Catalog* (1991), free listing of 600 of the latest and most popular programs. Also available free are specific subject listings such as science, history, medicine, and safety and health. A free quarterly update lists significant additions to the collection. A computer bulletin board has been available for information searches and production orders since late 1993.

The National Cable Television Institute (NCTI). 801 W. Mineral Ave., Littleton CO 80120. (303) 797-9393. Fax (303) 797-9394. E-mail info@ncti.com. Web site http://www.ncti.com. Roland Hieb, President; Don Oden, Dean of the Institute. The National Cable Television Institute is the largest independent provider of broadband technology training in the world. More than 100,000 students have enrolled since 1968. NCTI partners with companies by providing self-paced study manuals to be complemented by company hands-on experiences. NCTI administers lessons and final examinations and issues the Certificate of Graduation, which is recognized throughout the industry as a symbol of competence and technical achievement.

The National Center for Improving Science Education. 2000 L St. NW, Suite 603, Washington, DC 20036. (202) 467-0652. Fax (202) 467-0659. E-mail info@ncise.org. Senta A. Raizen, Dir. 300 Brickstone Square, Suite 900, Andover, MA 01810. (508) 470-1080, (508) 475-9220. A division of The NETWORK, Inc. (see separate listing) that works to promote changes in state and local policies and practices in science curriculum, teaching, and assessment through research and development, evaluation, technical assistance, and dissemination. *Publications: Science and Technology Education for the Elementary Years: Frameworks for Curriculum and Instruction; Developing and Supporting Teachers for Elementary School Science Education; Assessment in Elementary School Science Education; Getting Started in Science: A Blueprint for Elementary School Science Education; Elementary School Science for the 90s; Building Scientific Literacy: Blueprint for the Middle Years; Science and Technology Education for the Middle Years: Frameworks for Curriculum and Instruction; Assessment in Science Education: The Middle Years; Developing and Supporting Teachers for Science Education in the Middle Years; The High Stakes of High School Science; Future of Science in Elementary Schools: Educating Prospective Teachers; Technology Education in the Classroom: Understanding the Designed World; What College-Bound Students Abroad Are Expected to Know About Biology* (with AFT); *Examining the Examinations: A Comparison of Science and Mathematics Examinations for College-Bound Students in Seven Countries.* Bold Ventures series: *Vol. 1: Patterns of US Innovations in Science and Mathematics Education; Vol. 2: Case Studies of US Innovations in Science Education; Vol. 3: Case Studies of US Innovations in Mathematics.* A publications catalog and project summaries are available on request.

National Center to Improve Practice (NCIP). Education Development Center, Inc., 55 Chapel St., Newton, MA 02158-1060. (617) 969-7100 ext. 2387. TTY (617) 969-4529. Fax (617) 969-3440. E-mail ncip@edc.org. Web site http://www.edc.org/FSC/NCIP. Judith Zorfass, Project Dir.; Bonnie Johnson, information. NCIP is a five-year project funded by the US Department of Education's Office for Special Education Programs (OSEP). NCIP promotes the effective use of technology to enhance educational outcomes for students (preschool to grade 12) with sensory, cognitive, physical, social, and emotional disabilities. NCIP's award-winning Web site integrates online discussions about technology and students with disabilities, an expansive library of resources (text, pictures, and video clips), online workshops, "guided tours" of exemplary classrooms, online discussions with authors of articles published in CEC's journal *TEACHING Exceptional Children,* "spotlights" on new technology, and links to more than 100 sites dealing with technology and/or students with disabilities. NCIP also produces a series of videos, illustrating how students with disabilities use a range of assistive and instructional technologies to improve their learning. Excellent for use in trainings, workshops, and courses, videos may be purchased individually or as a set of five by calling (800) 793-5076. Membership and dues are not required. *Meetings:* NCIP presents sessions at various educational conferences around the country. *Publications:* Video Profile Series: *Multimedia and More: Help for Students with Learning Disabilities; Jeff with Expression: Writing in the Word Prediction Software; "Write" Tools for Angie: Technology for Students Who Are Visually Impaired; Telling Tales in ASL and English: Reading, Writing and Videotapes; Welcome to My Preschool: Communicating with Technology.*

National Clearinghouse for Bilingual Education (NCBE). The George Washington University, 1118 22nd St. NW, Washington, DC 20037. (202) 467-0867. Fax (800) 531-9347; (202) 467-4283. E-mail askncbe@ncbe.gwu.edu. Web site http://www.ncbe.gwu.edu. Joel Gomez, Dir. NCBE is funded by the US Department of Education's Office of Bilingual Education and Minority Languages Affairs (OBEMLA) to collect, analyze, synthesize, and disseminate information relating to the education of linguistically and culturally diverse students in the US. NCBE is operated by The George Washington University Graduate School of Education and Human Development, Center for the Study of Language and Education in Washington, DC. Online services include the NCBE web site containing an online library of over 300 cover-to-cover documents, resources for teachers and administrators, and library of links to related Internet sites; an e-mail-based, weekly news bulletin, *Newsline;* an electronic discussion group, *NCBE Roundtable;* and an e-mail-based question answering service, *AskNCBE. Publications:* short monographs, syntheses, and a quarterly newsletter (*CrossCurrents).* Request a publications catalog for prices. The catalog and some publications are available at no cost from the NCBE web site.

National Commission on Libraries and Information Science (NCLIS). 1110 Vermont Ave. NW, Suite 820, Washington, DC 20005-3522. (202) 606-9200. Fax (202) 606-9203. E-mail py_nclis@inet.ed.gov. Peter R. Young, Exec. Dir. A permanent independent agency of the US government charged with advising the executive and legislative branches on national library and information policies and plans. The commission reports directly to the White House and the Congress on the implementation of national policy; conducts studies, surveys, and analyses of the nation's library and information needs; appraises the inadequacies of current resources and services; promotes research and development activities; conducts hearings and issues publications as appropriate; and develops overall plans for meeting national library and information needs and for the coordination of activities at the federal, state, and local levels. The Commission provides general policy advice to the Institute of Museum and Library Services (IMLS) (established October 1, 1996) director relating to library services included in the Library Services and Technology Act (LSTA). *Membership:* 16 commissioners:14 appointed by the president and confirmed by the Senate, the Librarian of Congress, and the Director of the IMLS. *Publication: Annual Report.*

National Council for Accreditation of Teacher Education (NCATE). 2010 Massachusetts Ave. NW, Suite 500, Washington, DC 20036. (202) 466-7496. Fax (202) 296-6620. E-mail ncate@ncate.org. Arthur E. Wise, Pres. NCATE is a consortium of professional organizations that establishes standards of quality and accredits professional education units in schools, colleges, and departments of education, and is interested in the self-regulation and improvement of standards in the field of teacher education. *Membership:* 500 colleges and universities, 30 educational organizations. *Publications: Standards, Procedures and Policies for the Accreditation of Professional Education Units*; *Teacher Education: A Guide to NCATE-Accredited Colleges and Universities*; *Quality Teaching* (newsletter, 2/yr.).

National Council of Teachers of English (NCTE), Commission on Media. 1111 W. Kenyon Rd., Urbana, IL 61801-1096. (217) 328-3870. Fax (217) 328-9645. Miles Myers, Exec. Dir.; Lawrence B. Fuller, Commission Dir. The functions of NCTE are to study emerging technologies and their integration into English and language arts curricula and teacher education programs; to identify the effects of such technologies on teachers, students, and educational settings, with attention to people of color, handicapped, and other students who are not well served in current programs; to explore means of disseminating information about such technologies to the NCTE membership; to serve as liaison between NCTE and other groups interested in computer-based education in English and language arts; and to maintain liaison with the NCTE Commission on Media and other Council groups concerned with instructional technology. *Membership:* 68,000 individuals and 110,000 subscribers. *Dues:* $40 individual. *Publications: English Journal* (8/yr.); *College English* (8/yr.); *Language Arts* (8/yr.); *English Education* (q.); *Research in the Teaching of English* (q.); *Teaching English in the Two-Year*

College (q.); *College Composition and Communication* (q.); *English Leadership Quarterly*; *Quarterly Review of Doublespeak*; *Primary Voices* (q.); *Voices from the Middle* (q.).

National Council of the Churches of Christ in the USA. Communication Commission, 475 Riverside Dr., New York, NY 10115. (212) 870-2574. Fax (212) 870-2030. Randy Naylor, Dir. Ecumenical arena for cooperative work of Protestant and Orthodox denominations and agencies in broadcasting, film, cable, and print media. Offers advocacy to government and industry structures on media services. Services provided include liaison to network television and radio programming; film sales and rentals; distribution of information about syndicated religious programming; syndication of some programming; cable television and emerging technologies information services; news and information regarding work of the National Council of Churches, related denominations, and agencies. Works closely with other faith groups in Interfaith Broadcasting Commission. Online communication via Ecunet/NCCLink. *Membership:* 32 denominations. *Publication: EcuLink.*

National Education Telecommunications Organization & EDSAT Institute (NETO/EDSAT). 1899 "L" Street NW, Suite 600, Washington, DC 20036. (202) 293-4211. Fax (202) 293-4210. Shelly Weinstein, Pres. and CEO. NETO/EDSAT is a nonprofit organization bringing together US and non-US users and providers of telecommunications to deliver education, instruction, health care, and training in classrooms, colleges, workplaces, health centers, and other distance education centers. NETO/EDSAT facilitates and collaborates with key stakeholders in the education and telecommunications fields. Programs and services include research and education, outreach, seminars and conferences, and newsletters. The NETO/EDSAT mission is to help create an integrated multitechnology infrastructure, a dedicated satellite that links space and existing secondary access roads (telephone and cable) over which teaching and education resources are delivered and shared in a user friendly format with students, teachers, workers, and individuals. NETO/EDSAT seeks to create a modern-day "learning place" for rural, urban, migrant, suburban, disadvantaged, and at-risk students which provides equal and affordable access to and utilization of educational resources. *Membership:* Members include U.S. and non-U.S. school districts, colleges, universities, state agencies, public and private educational consortia, libraries, and other distance education providers. *Publications: NETO/EDSAT "UPDATE"* (newsletter, q.); *Analysis of a Proposal for an Education Satellite, EDSAT Institute,* 1991; and *Global Summit on Distance Education Final Report,* Oct. 1996.

National Endowment for the Humanities (NEH). Division of Public Programs, Media Program, 1100 Pennsylvania Ave., NW, Room 426, Washington, DC 20506. (202) 606-8267. E-mail info@neh.fed.us. Web site http://www.neh.fed.us. Jim Vore, Manager of Media/Special Projects. The NEH is an independent federal grant-making agency that supports research, educational, and public programs grounded in the disciplines of the humanities. The Media Program supports film and radio programs in the humanities for public audiences, including children and adults. *Publications: Overview of Endowment Programs*; *Humanities Projects in Media* (for application forms and guidelines).

National Federation of Community Broadcasters (NFCB). Ft. Mason Center, Bldg. D, San Francisco, CA 94123. (415) 771-1160. E-mail nfcb@aol.com. Lynn Chadwick, Pres. NFCB represents non-commercial, community-based radio stations in public policy development at the national level and provides a wide range of practical services, including technical assistance. *Membership:* 200. *Dues:* range from $150 to $2500 for participant and associate members. *Publications: Legal Handbook*; *Audio Craft*; *Community Radio News.*

National Film Board of Canada (NFBC). 1251 Avenue of the Americas, 6th Floor, New York, NY 10020. (212) 596-1770. Fax (212) 595-1779. E-mail gsem78a@prodigy.com. John Sirabella, US Marketing Mgr./Nontheatrical Rep. Established in 1939, the NFBC's main objective is to produce and distribute high-quality audiovisual materials for educational, cultural, and social purposes.

National Film Information Service (offered by the Margaret Herrick Library of the Academy of Motion Picture Arts and Sciences). Center for Motion Picture Study, 333 So. La Cienega Blvd., Beverly Hills, CA 90211. (310) 247-3000. The purpose of this organization is to provide information on film. The service is fee-based and all inquiries must be accompanied by a #10 self-addressed stamped envelope.

National Gallery of Art (NGA). Department of Education Resources: Art Information and Extension Programs, Washington, DC 20565. (202) 842-6273. Ruth R. Perlin, Head. This department of NGA is responsible for the production and distribution of educational audiovisual programs, including interactive technologies. Materials available (all loaned free to schools, community organizations, and individuals) range from films, videocassettes, and color slide programs to videodiscs. A free catalog of programs is available upon request. Two videodiscs on the gallery's collection are available for long-term loan. *Publication: Extension Programs Catalogue.*

National Information Center for Educational Media (NICEM). P.O. Box 8640, Albuquerque, NM 87198-8640. (505) 265-3591, (800) 926-8328. Fax (505) 256-1080. E-mail nicem@nicem.com. Web page http://www.nicem.com. Roy Morgan, Exec. Dir.; Marjorie M. K. Hlava, Pres., Access Innovations, Inc. The National Information Center for Educational Media maintains an international database of information about educational non-print materials for all age levels and subject areas in all media types. NICEM editors collect, catalog, and index information about media which is provided by producers and distributors. This information is entered into an electronic masterfile. Anyone who is looking for information about educational media materials can search the database by a wide variety of criteria to locate existing and archival materials. Producer and distributor information in each record then leads the searcher to the source of the educational media materials needed. NICEM makes the information from the database available in several forms and through several vendors. CD-ROM editions are available from NICEM, SilverPlatter, and BiblioFile. Online access to the database is available through NICEM, EBSCO, NlightN, Human Resources Information Network, and Dialog. Print versions are available from Plexus Publishing. NICEM will also conduct custom searches and prepare custom catalogs. NICEM is used by college and university media centers, public school libraries and media centers, public libraries, corporate training centers, students, media producers and distributors, and researchers. *Membership:* NICEM is a nonmembership organization. There is no charge for submitting information to be entered into the database. Corporate member of AECT, AIME, NARMC, CCUMC. *Publications: International Directory of Educational Audiovisuals; A-V Online on SilverPlatter; NICEM A-V MARC by BiblioFile; Film & Video Finder; Index to A-V Producers & Distributors.*

National ITFS Association (NIA). National ITFS Association, Box #1130, 3421 M Street, NW, Washington, DC 20007. Theodore Steinke, Chair, Bd. of Dirs. Established in 1978, NIA/ITFS is a nonprofit, professional organization of Instructional Television Fixed Service (ITFS) licensees, applicants, and others interested in ITFS broadcasting. The goals of the association are to gather and exchange information about ITFS, to gather data on utilization of ITFS, and to act as a conduit for those seeking ITFS information or assistance. The NIA represents ITFS interests to the FCC, technical consultants, and equipment manufacturers. The association provides its members with a quarterly newsletter and an FCC regulation update as well as information on excess capacity leasing and license and application data. *Meetings:* with AECT and InCITE. *Publications: National ITFS Association Newsletter* (q.); FCC regulation update.

National PTA. 330 N. Wabash, Suite 2100, Chicago, IL 60611. (312) 670-6782. Fax (312) 670-6783. Web site http://www.pta.com. Joan Dykstra, Pres.; Patty Yoxall, Public Relations Dir. Advocates for the education, health, safety, and well-being of children and teens. Provides parenting education and leadership training to PTA volunteers. The National PTA continues to be very active in presenting Family and Television Critical TV Viewing workshops across the country in cooperation with the National Cable Television Association. The workshops teach parents and educators how to evaluate programming so they can make informed decisions about what to allow their children to see. The National PTA has also been very active in trying to convince the television industry to create a content-based TV rating system, rather than one that is age based. *Membership:* 6.8 million. *Dues:* vary by local unit. *Meeting:* National convention, held annually in June in different regions of the country, is open to PTA members; convention information available on the web site. *Publications: Our Children* (magazine); *What's Happening in Washington* (legislative newsletters). In addition, information can be downloaded from the Web site. Catalog available.

National Press Photographers Association, Inc. (NPPA). 3200 Croasdaile Dr., Suite 306, Durham, NC 27705. (919) 383-7246. Fax (919) 383-7261. E-mail 72640.21@compuserve. com. Charles H. Cooper, Exec. Dir. An organization of professional news photographers who participate in and promote photojournalism in publications and through television and film. Sponsors workshops, seminars, and contests; maintains an audiovisual library of subjects of media interest. *Membership:* 11,000. *Dues:* $75, domestic; $105, international; $40, student. *Meetings:* Annual Convention and Education Days, July. An extensive array of other conferences, seminars, and workshops are held throughout the year. *Publications: News Photographer* magazine (mo.); *The Best of Photojournalism PJ022* (annual book).

National Public Broadcasting Archives (NPBA). Hornbake Library, University of Maryland at College Park, College Park, MD 20742. (301) 405-9255. Fax (301) 314-2634. Thomas Connors, Archivist. NPBA brings together the archival record of the major entities of noncommercial broadcasting in the US. NPBA's collections include the archives of the Corporation for Public Broadcasting (CPB), the Public Broadcasting Service (PBS), and National Public Radio (NPR). Other organizations represented include the Midwest Program for Airborne Television Instruction (MPATI), the Public Service Satellite Consortium (PSSC), America's Public Television Stations (APTS), and the Joint Council for Educational Telecommunications (JCET). NPBA also makes available the personal papers of many individuals who have made significant contributions to public broadcasting, and its reference library contains basic studies of the broadcasting industry, rare pamphlets, and journals on relevant topics, plus up-to-date clippings from the PBS press clipping service. NPBA also collects and maintains a selected audio and video program record of public broadcasting's national production and support centers and of local stations. Oral history tapes and transcripts from the NPR Oral History Project are also available at the archives. The archives are open to the public from 9 am to 5 pm, Monday through Friday. Research in NPBA collections should be arranged by prior appointment. For further information, call (301) 405-9988.

National Religious Broadcasters (NRB). 7839 Ashton Ave., Manassas, VA 22110. (703) 330-7000. Fax (703) 330-7100. E. Brandt Gustavson, Pres. NRB essentially has two goals: (1) to ensure that religious broadcasters have access to the radio and television airwaves, and (2) to encourage broadcasters to observe a high standard of excellence in their programming and station management for the clear presentation of the gospel. Holds national and regional conventions. *Membership:* 800 organizational stations, program producers, agencies, and individuals. *Dues:* based on income. *Meetings:* 55th Annual NRB Convention and Exhibition, Jan 31-Feb 3, 1998, Washington, DC. *Publications: Religious Broadcasting Magazine* (mo.); *Annual Directory of Religious Media; Religious Broadcasting Resources Library Brochure; Religious Broadcasting Cassette Catalog.*

National School Supply and Equipment Association (NSSEA). 8300 Colesville Rd., Suite 250, Silver Spring, MD 20910. (301) 495-0240. Fax (301) 495-3330. E-mail nssea@aol.com. Web site http://www.nssea.org. Tim Holt, Pres. A service organization of more than 1,600 manufacturers, distributors, retailers, and independent manufacturers' representatives of school supplies, equipment, and instructional materials. Seeks to maintain open communications between manufacturers and dealers in the school market, and to encourage the development of new ideas and products for educational progress. *Meetings:* 1998, The School Equipment Show, Feb 12-14, Charlotte, NC; Ed Expo '98, Mar 19-22, Charlotte, NC; 82nd Annual NSSEA Fall Show, Nov 19-22, New Orleans. *Publications: Tidings; Annual Membership Directory.*

National Science Foundation (NSF). 4201 Wilson Blvd., Arlington, VA 22230. (703) 306-1070. Mary Hanson, Chief, Media Relations and Public Affairs. NSF is an independent federal agency responsible for fundamental research in all fields of science and engineering, with an annual budget of about $3 billion. NSF funds reach all 50 states, through grants to more than 2,000 universities and institutions nationwide. NSF receives more than 50,000 requests for funding annually, including at least 30,000 new proposals. Applicants should refer to the NSF Guide to Programs. Scientific material and media reviews are available to help the public learn about NSF-supported programs. NSF news releases and tipsheets are available electronically via NSFnews. To subscribe, send an e-mail message to listmanager@nsf.gov; in the body of the message, type "subscribe nsfnews" and then type your name. Also see NSF news products at http://www.nsf.gov:80/od/lpa/start.htm, http://www.eurekalert.org/, and http://www.ari.net/newswise. In addition, NSF has developed a Web site that offers information about NSF directorates, offices, programs, and publications at http://nsf.gov.

National Science Teachers Association (NSTA). 1840 Wilson Blvd., Arlington, VA 22201. (703) 243-7100. Fax (703) 243-7177. E-mail chris.behrens@nsta.org. Web site http://www.nsta.org. Dr. Gerald Wheeler, Exec. Dir. A national nonprofit association of science teachers ranging from kindergarten through university level. NSTA conducts one national and three regional conventions and provides numerous programs and services, including awards and competitions, inservice teacher workshops, professional certification, and more. It has position statements on many issues, such as teacher preparation, laboratory science, and the use of animals in the classroom. It is involved in cooperative working relationships in a variety of projects with educational organizations, government agencies, and private industries. *Membership:* 53,000. *Dues:* $55 individual or institutional (includes one journal and other benefits). *Meetings:* 1998 National Convention, Apr 16-19, Las Vegas; 1999 National Convention, Mar 25-28, Boston. *Publications: Science and Children* (8/yr., journal for elementary teachers); *Science Scope* (8/yr., journal for middle-level teachers); *The Science Teacher* (9/yr., for high school teachers); *Journal of College Science Teaching* (6/yr., journal for college teachers); *NSTA Reports* (6/yr., newspaper for K-college teachers, free to all NSTA members); *Quantum* (magazine for physics and math high school students); *Dragonfly* (a new magazine for young investigators in grades 3-6); books (free catalog available).

National Telemedia Council Inc. (NTC). 120 E. Wilson St., Madison, WI 53703. (608) 257-7712. Fax (608) 257-7714. E-mail NTelemedia@aol.com. Web site http://danenet.wicip.org/NTC. Dr. Martin Rayala, Pres.; Marieli Rowe, Exec. Dir. The NTC is a national nonprofit professional organization dedicated to promoting media literacy, or critical television viewing skills. This is done primarily through work with teachers, parents, and caregivers. NTC activities include the development of the Media Literacy Clearinghouse and Center; the Teacher Idea Exchange (T.I.E.); national conferences and regional and local workshops; the Jessie McCanse Award for individual contribution to media literacy. *Dues:* $30, basic; $50, contributing; $100, patron. *Publications: Telemedium; The Journal of Media Literacy* (newsletter, q.).

Network for Continuing Medical Education (NCME). One Harmon Plaza, 7th Floor, Secaucus, NJ 07094. (201) 867-3550. Fax (201) 867-2491. Produces and distributes videocassettes to hospitals for physicians' continuing education. Programs are developed for physicians in the practice of General Medicine, Anesthesiology, Emergency Medicine, Gastroenterology, and Surgery. Physicians who view all the programs can earn up to 25 hours of Category 1 (AMA) credit and up to 10 hours of Prescribed (AAFP) credit each year. *Membership:* More than 1,000 hospitals provide NCME programs to their physicians. *Dues:* subscription fees: VHS-$2,160/yr. Sixty-minute videocassettes are distributed to hospital subscribers every eighteen days.

The NETWORK, Inc. 300 Brickstone Square, Suite 900, Andover, MA 01810. (508) 470-1080. Fax (508) 475-9220. E-mail davidcr@tiac.net. David Crandall, contact person. A research and service organization providing training, research and evaluation, technical assistance, and materials to schools, educational organizations, and private sector firms with educational interests. *Publications: Portrait of Our Mothers: Using Oral History in the Classroom; Juggling Lessons: A Curriculum for Women Who Go to School, Work, and Care for Their Families; An Action Guide for School Improvement; Making Change for School Improvement: A Simulation Game; Report on National Dissemination Efforts; The Effective Writing Teacher; Cumulative Writing Folder; Developing Writing and Thinking Skills Across the Curriculum: A Practical Program for Schools; Five Types of Writing Assignments; Systems Thinking/Systems Changing: A Simulation Game; People, Policies, and Practices: Examining the Chain of School Improvement.* Publications catalog is available upon request.

New England Educational Media Association (NEEMA). c/o Jean Keilly, 58 South Mammoth Road, Manchester, NH 03109. (603) 622-9626. Fax (603) 424-6229. Dorothy Crazler, Pres. An affiliate of AECT, NEEMA is a regional professional association dedicated to the improvement of instruction through the effective utilization of school library media services, media, and technology applications. For over 75 years, it has represented school library media professionals through activities and networking efforts to develop and polish the leadership skills, professional representation, and informational awareness of the membership. The Board of Directors consists of Departments of Education as well as professional leaders of the region. An annual conference program and Leadership Program are offered in conjunction with the various regional state association conferences.

The New York Festivals (formerly the International Film and TV Festival of New York). 780 King St., Chappaqua, NY 10514. (914) 238-4481. Fax (914) 236-5040. Web site http://www.nyfests.com. Bilha Goldberg, Vice Pres. The New York Festivals sponsors the International Non-Broadcast Awards, which are annual competitive festivals for industrial and educational film and video productions, filmstrips and slide programs, multi-image business theater and interactive multimedia presentations, and television programs. Entry fees begin at $125. First entry deadline is Aug 4 for U.S. entrants and Sept 16 for overseas entrants. The Non-Broadcast competition honors a wide variety of categories including Education Media. As one of the largest competitions in the world, achieving finalist status is a notable credit to any company's awards roster. Winners are announced each year at a gala awards show in New York City and published on the World Wide Web.

North Central Regional Educational Laboratory (NCREL). 1900 Spring Rd., Suite 300, Oak Brook, IL 60521-1480. (708) 571-4700, (800) 356-2735. Fax (708) 571-4716. E-mail info@ncrel.org. Web site http://www.ncrel.org/pathways. Jan Bakker, Resource Center Dir. NCREL's work is guided by a focus on comprehensive and systemic school restructuring that is research-based and learner-centered. One of 10 Office of Educational Research and Improvement (OERI) regional educational laboratories, NCREL disseminates information about effective programs, develops educational products, holds conferences, provides technical assistance, and conducts research and evaluation. A special focus is on technology and learning. In addition to conventional print publications, NCREL uses computer networks, videoconferencing via satellite, and video and audio formats to reach its diverse audiences. NCREL's Web site includes the acclaimed "Pathways to School Improvement." NCREL operates the Midwest Consortium for Mathematics and Science Education which works to advance systemic change in mathematics and science education. Persons living in Illinois, Indiana, Iowa, Michigan, Minnesota, Ohio, and Wisconsin are encouraged to call NCREL Resource Center with any education-related questions. *Meetings:* The annual Leadership Academy, a leadership development program for practicing and aspiring school leaders, supports leaders in undertaking and implementing effective schoolwide improvement and reform. NCREL also hosts the North Central Regional Technology in Education Consortium which helps states and local educational agencies successfully integrate advanced technologies into K-12 classrooms, library media centers, and other educational settings. *Publications: R&D Watch* (q.). A catalog of print, video, and other media products is available by calling the main number.

Northwest College and University Council for the Management of Educational Technology (NW/MET). c/o Learning Resources Center, Willamette University, 900 State St., Salem, OR 97301. (503) 370-6054. Fax (503) 370-6148. E-mail mmorandi@willamette.edu. Listserv NW-MET@willamette.edu. John Root, Pres.; Marti Morandi, Membership Chair. NW/MET is the first regional group representing institutions of higher education in Alberta, Alaska, British Columbia, Idaho, Montana, Oregon, Saskatchewan, and Washington to receive affiliate status in AECT. Membership is restricted to media managers with campus-wide responsibilities for educational technical services in the membership region. Corresponding membership is available to those who work outside the membership region. An annual conference and business meeting are held the last weekend of October each year, rotating throughout the region. Current issues under consideration include managing emerging telecommunication technologies, copyright, accreditation, and certification. Organizational goals include identifying the unique status problems of media managers in higher education and improving the quality of the major publication. *Membership:* approx. 85. *Dues:* $35. *Meetings:* 1998, Idaho, April. *Publications:* two annual newsletters and *NW/MET Journal.*

Northwest Regional Educational Laboratory (NWREL). 101 SW Main St., Suite 500, Portland, OR 97204. (503) 275-9500. Fax (503) 275-0448. Dr. Ethel Simon-McWilliams, Exec. Dir. One of 10 Office of Educational Research and Improvement (OERI) regional educational laboratories, NWREL works with schools and communities to improve educational outcomes for children, youth, and adults. NWREL provides leadership, expertise, and services based on the results of research and development. The specialty area of NWREL is school change processes. It serves Alaska, Idaho, Oregon, Montana, and Washington. *Membership:* 817. *Dues:* None. *Publication: Northwest Report* (newsletter).

On-line Audiovisual Catalogers (OLAC). c/o Columbia University Health Sciences Library, 701 West 168th St., New York, NY 10032. (212) 305-1406. Fax (212) 234-0595. Johanne LaGrange, Treas. Formed as an outgrowth of the ALA conference, OLAC seeks to permit members to exchange ideas and information, and to interact with other agencies that influence audiovisual cataloging practices. *Membership:* 725. *Dues:* available for single or multiple years; $10-$27, individual; $16-$45, institution. *Publication: OLAC Newsletter.*

Online Computer Library Center, Inc. (OCLC). 6565 Frantz Rd., Dublin, OH 43017-3395. (614) 764-6000. Fax (614) 764-6096. E-mail oclc@oclc.org. K. Wayne Smith, Pres. and CEO. Nita Dean, Mgr., Public Relations. A nonprofit membership organization that engages in computer library service and research and makes available computer-based processes, products, and services for libraries, other educational organizations, and library users. From its facility in Dublin, Ohio, OCLC operates an international computer network that libraries use to catalog books, order custom-printed catalog cards and machine-readable records for local catalogs, arrange interlibrary loans, and maintain location information on library materials. OCLC also provides online and offline reference products and services for the electronic delivery of information. More than 23,000 libraries contribute to and/or use information in the OCLC Online Union Catalog. *Publications: OCLC Newsletter* (6/yr.); *OCLC Reference News* (4/yr.); *Annual Report*; *Annual Review of Research.*

Pacific Film Archive (PFA). University of California, Berkeley Art Museum, 2625 Durant Ave., Berkeley, CA 94720-2250. (510) 642-1437 (library); (510) 642-1412 (general). Fax (510) 642-4889. Edith Kramer, Dir. and Curator of Film; Nancy Goldman, Head, PFA Library and Film Study Center. Sponsors the exhibition, study, and preservation of classic, international, documentary, animated, and avant-garde films. Provides on-site research screenings of films in its collection of over 7,000 titles. Provides access to its collections of books, periodicals, stills, and posters (all materials are noncirculating). Offers BAM/PFA members and University of California, Berkeley affiliates reference and research services to locate film and video distributors, credits, stock footage, etc. Library hours are 1pm-5pm weekdays. *Membership:* through parent organization, the Berkeley Art Museum. *Dues:* $40 individual and nonprofit departments of institutions. *Publication: BAM/PFA Calendar* (6/yr.).

Pacific Resources for Education and Learning (PREL) (formerly Pacific Region Educational Laboratory). 828 Fort Street Mall Suite 500, Honolulu, HI 96813-4321. (808) 533-6000. Fax (808) 533-7599. Web site http://prel.hawaii.edu. John W. Kofel, Exec. Dir. One of 10 Office of Educational Research and Improvement (OERI) regional educational laboratories designed to help educators and policymakers solve educational problems in their schools. Using the best available information and the experience and expertise of professionals, PREL seeks to identify solutions to education problems, tries new approaches, furnishes research results, and provides training to teachers and administrators. The specialty area of PREL is language and cultural diversity. It serves American Samoa, Commonwealth of the Northern Mariana Islands, Federated States of Micronesia, Guam, Hawaii, Republic of the Marshall Islands, and Republic of Palau.

PCR: Films and Video in the Behavioral Sciences. Penn State Media Sales, 118 Wagner Building, University Park, PA 16802. Purchasing info (800) 770-2111, (814) 863-3102. Fax (814) 865-3172. Rental information (800) 826-0132. Fax (814) 863-2574. Special Services Building, Penn State University, University Park, PA 16802. E-mail mediasales@cde.psu.edu. Web site http://www.cde.psu.edu/MediaSales. Sue Oram, Media Sales Coordinator. Makes available to professionals video in the behavioral sciences judged to be useful for university teaching and research. A free catalog of the films in PCR is available. The PCR catalog now contains some 1,400 films in the behavioral sciences (psychology, psychiatry, anthropology, animal behavior, sociology, teaching and learning, and folklife). Some 7,000 professionals now use PCR services. Films and tapes are available on loan for a rental charge. Many films may also be purchased. Films may be submitted for international distribution.

Photographic Society of America (PSA). 3000 United Founders Blvd., Suite 103, Oklahoma City, OK 73112. (405) 843-1437. Fax (405) 843-1438. E-mail 74521,2414@compuserve.com. Jacque Noel, Operations Mgr. A nonprofit organization for the development of the arts and sciences of photography and for the furtherance of public appreciation of photographic skills. Its members, largely advanced amateurs, consist of individuals, camera clubs, and other photographic organizations. Divisions include color slide, video motion picture, nature, photojournalism, travel, pictorial print, stereo, and techniques. Sponsors national, regional, and local meetings, clinics, and contests. Request dues information from preceding address. *Meetings:* 1998 International Conference Aug 31-Sep 5, Orlando, FL. *Publication: PSA Journal.*

Professors of Instructional Design and Technology (PIDT). Instructional Technology Dept., 220 War Memorial Hall, Virginia Tech, Blacksburg, VA 24061-0341. (540) 231-5587. Fax (540) 231-3717. E-mail moorem@VT.EDU. Web site http://www.conted.VT.edu/pidt_97. html. Dr. Mike Moore, contact person. An organization designed to encourage and facilitate the exchange of information among members of the instructional design and technology academic and corporate communities. Also serves to promote excellence in academic programs in instructional design and technology and to encourage research and inquiry that will benefit the field while providing leadership in the public and private sectors in its application and practice. *Membership:* 300 faculty employed in higher education institutions whose primary responsibilities are teaching and research in this area, their corporate counterparts, and other persons interested in the goals and activities of the PIDT. *Dues:* none.

*Public Broadcasting Service (PBS). 1320 Braddock Pl., Alexandria, VA 22314-1698. (703) 739-5000. Ervin S. Duggan, CEO and Pres. National distributor of public television programming, obtaining all programs from member stations, American independent producers, or foreign sources. PBS also offers educational services for teachers, students, and parents including: PTV, The Ready to Learn Service on PBS; Going the Distance; PBS MATHLINE; and PBS ONLINE. PBS services include program acquisition, distribution, and scheduling; development and fundraising support; and engineering and technical development. Subsidiaries of PBS include PBS Adult Learning Service, and PBS Video, which are described below. PBS is owned and operated by local public television organizations through annual membership fees, and governed by a board of directors elected by PBS members for three-year terms. *Membership:* 198 organizations operating 346 stations.

PBS Adult Learning Service (ALS). 1320 Braddock Pl., Alexandria, VA 22314-1698. (800) 257-2578. Fax (703) 739-8471. E-mail als@pbs.org. Web site http://www.pbs. org/als/college. Will Philipp, Dir. The mission of ALS is to help colleges, universities, and public television stations increase learning opportunities for distance learners; enrich classroom instruction; update faculty; train administrators, management, and staff; and provide other educational services for local communities. A pioneer in the widespread use of video and print packages incorporated into curricula and offered for credit by local colleges, ALS began broadcasting telecourses in 1981. Since that time, over 2 million students have earned college credit through telecourses offered in partnership with more than two-thirds of the nation's colleges and universities. In 1988, ALS established the Adult Learning Satellite Service (ALSS) to provide colleges, universities, businesses, hospitals, and other organizations with a broad range of educational programming via direct satellite. *Membership:* 650-plus colleges, universities, hospitals, government agencies, and Fortune 500 businesses are now ALSS Associates. Organizations that are not Associates can still acquire ALS programming, but at higher fees. *Dues:* $1,500; multisite and consortia rates are available. *Publications: ALSS Programming Line-Up* (catalog of available programming, 3/yr.); *The Agenda* (news magazine about issues of interest to distance learning and adult learning administrators); *Changing the Face of Higher Education* (an overview of ALS services); *Teaching Telecourses: Opportunities and Options*; *Ideas for Increasing Telecourse Enrollment*.

*PBS VIDEO. 1320 Braddock Pl., Alexandria, VA 22314. (703) 739-5380; (800) 344-3337. Fax (703) 739-5269. Jon Cecil, Dir., PBS VIDEO Marketing. Markets and distributes PBS television programs for sale on videocassette or videodisc to colleges, public libraries, schools, governments, and other organizations and institutions. *Publications: PBS VIDEO Resource Catalog*; *PBS VIDEO Catalogs of New and Popular Videos* (6/yr.); and the *PBS VIDEO Elementary Catalog*.

Public Library Association (PLA). 50 E. Huron St., Chicago, IL 60611. (312) 280-5PLA. Fax (312) 280-5029. E-mail George.Needham@ala.org. Greta Southard, Acting Exec. Dir. An affiliate of the American Library Association, PLA is concerned with the development, effectiveness, and financial support of public libraries. It speaks for the profession and seeks to enrich the professional competence and opportunities of public libraries. Sections include Adult Lifelong Learning, Community Information, Metropolitan Libraries, Public Library Systems, Small and Medium-sized Libraries, Public Policy for Public Libraries, Planning, Measurement and Evaluation, and Marketing of Public Library Services. *Membership:* 8,500. *Dues:* $50, open to all ALA members. *Meetings:* 1998 PLA National Conference, Mar 10-14, "Public Libraries: Vital, Valuable, Virtual." *Publication: Public Libraries* (bi-mo.). Two PLA Committees of particular interest to the Educational Technology field are listed below.

Audiovisual Committee (of the Public Library Association). 50 E. Huron St., Chicago, IL 60611. (312)280-5752. James E. Massey; Chair. Promotes use of audiovisual materials in public libraries.

Technology in Public Libraries Committee (of the Public Library Association). 50 E. Huron St., Chicago, IL 60611. (312)280-5752. William Ptacek, Chair. Collects and disseminates information on technology applications in public libraries.

Puppeteers of America, Inc. (POA). #5 Cricklewood Path, Pasadena, CA 91107. (818) 797-5748. Gayle Schluter, Membership Officer. Formed in 1937, POA holds festivals for puppetry across the country, sponsors local guilds, presents awards, sponsors innovative puppetry works, provides consulting, and provides materials through the Audio-Visual Library. *Members:* over 2,000. *Dues:* $35, regular; $45, couple; $20, junior; $55, group or family; $30, journal subscription. *Publications: The Puppetry Journal* (q); *Playboard*; bimonthly newsletter.

Recording for the Blind and Dyslexic (RFB&D). 20 Roszel Road, Princeton, NJ 08540. Main phone (609) 452-0606. Customer Service (800) 221-4792. Fax (609) 987-8116. Web site http://www.rfbd.org. Ritchie Geisel, President. RFB&D is a national nonprofit organization that provides educational and professional books in accessible format to people with visual impairments, learning disabilities, or other physical disabilities that prevent them from reading normal printed material. This includes students from kindergarten to graduate school and people who no longer attend school but who use educational books to pursue careers or personal interests. RFB&D's 75,000-volume collection of audio titles is the largest educational resource of its kind in the world. RFB&D provides a wide range of library services as well as "E-Text" books on computer disk, including dictionaries, computer manuals, and other reference books. Potential individual members must complete an application form, which contains a "disability verification" section. *Membership:* 39,139 individuals, 275 institutions. *Dues:* for qualified individuals, $50 registration, $25 annual. Institutional Memberships also available (contact Customer Service).

Reference and User Services Association (RUSA). 50 E. Huron St., Chicago, IL 60611. (800) 545-2433, ext. 4398. Fax (312) 944-8085. Cathleen Bourdon, Exec. Dir. An affiliate of the American Library Association, RUSA is responsible for stimulating and supporting in every type of library the delivery of reference information services to all groups and of general library services and materials to adults. *Membership:* 5,500. *Dues:* $45 plus membership in ALA. *Publications: RQ* (q.); *RUSA Update.*

Research for Better Schools, Inc. (RBS). 444 North Third St., Philadelphia, PA 19123-4107. (215) 574-9300. Fax (215) 574-0133. E-mail webmaster@www.rbs.org. Web site http://www.rbs.org/. John Connolly, Exec. Dir. RBS is a private, nonprofit corporation which currently operates the Mid-Atlantic Eisenhower Consortium for Mathematics and Science Education, and the Mid-Atlantic Telecommunications Alliance. In its 30 years of service to the education community, RBS has also offered educational technology, development, evaluation, technical assistance, and training services with client funding. RBS also operates an educational publications division.

Smithsonian Institution. 1000 Jefferson Drive SW, Washington, DC 20560. (202) 357-2700. Fax (202) 786-2515. I. Michael Heyman, Secy. An independent trust instrumentality of the US that conducts scientific, cultural, and scholarly research; administers the national collections; and performs other educational public service functions, all supported by Congress, trusts, gifts, and grants. Includes 16 museums, including the National Museum of Natural History, the National Museum of American History, the National Air and Space Museum, and the National Zoological Park. Museums are free and open daily except December 25. The Smithsonian Institution Traveling Exhibition Service (SITES) organizes exhibitions on art, history, and science and circulates them across the country and abroad. *Membership:* Smithsonian Associates. *Dues:* vary. *Publications: Smithsonian; Air & Space/Smithsonian; The Torch* (staff newsletter, mo.); *Research Reports* (semitechnical, q.); Smithsonian Institution Press Publications, 470 L'Enfant Plaza, Suite 7100, Washington, DC 20560.

Society for Applied Learning Technology (SALT). 50 Culpeper St., Warrenton, VA 20186. (540) 347-0055. Fax (540) 349-3169. E-mail info@salt.org. Raymond G. Fox, Pres. The society is a nonprofit, professional membership organization that was founded in 1972. Membership in the society is oriented to professionals whose work requires knowledge and communication in the field of instructional technology. The society provides members a means to enhance their knowledge and job performance by participation in society-sponsored meetings, subscription to society-sponsored publications, association with other professionals at conferences sponsored by the society, and membership in special interest groups and special society-sponsored initiatives. In addition, the society offers member discounts on society-sponsored journals, conferences, and publications. *Membership:* 1,000. *Dues:* $45. *Meetings:*

Orlando Multimedia '98, Kissimmee, FL; Interactive Multimedia '98, Arlington, VA. *Publications: Journal of Educational Technology Systems*; *Journal of Instruction Delivery Systems*; *Journal of Interactive Instructional Development*; *Journal of Medical Education Technologies*. Send for list of books.

Society for Computer Simulation (SCS). P.O. Box 17900, San Diego, CA 92177-7900. (619) 277-3888. Fax (619) 277-3930. E-mail info@scs.org. Web site http://www.scs.org. Bill Gallagher, Exec. Dir. Founded in 1952, SCS is a professional-level technical society devoted to the art and science of modeling and simulation. Its purpose is to advance the understanding, appreciation, and use of all types of computer models for studying the behavior of actual or hypothesized systems of all kinds and to sponsor standards. Additional office in Ghent, Belgium. *Membership:* 1,900. *Dues:* $75 (includes journal subscription). *Meetings:* local, regional, and national technical meetings and conferences, such as the Western Simulation Multiconference Jan 11-14, 1998, San Diego; Summer and Winter Computer Simulation Conferences, Simulation Multiconference, Apr 5-9, 1998, Boston; and National Educational Computing Conference (NECC). *Publications: Simulation* (mo.); *Simulation* series (q.); *Transactions of SCS* (q.).

Society for Photographic Education (SPE). P.O. Box 222116, Dallas, TX 75222-2116. (817) 272-2845. Fax (817) 272-2846. M. Lee Hutchins, Exec. Dir. An association of college and university teachers of photography, museum photographic curators, writers, and publishers. Promotes discourse in photography education, culture, and art. *Membership:* 1,700. *Dues:* $55. *Meetings:* 1998, March, Philadelphia. *Publication: Exposure* (newsletter).

Society of Cable Television Engineers (SCTE). 140 Philips Rd., Exton, PA 19341-1319. (610) 363-6888. Fax (610) 363-5898. William W. Riker, Pres. SCTE is dedicated to the technical training and further education of members. A nonprofit membership organization for persons engaged in engineering, construction, installation, technical direction, management, or administration of cable television and broadband communications technologies. Also eligible for membership are students in communications, educators, government and regulatory agency employees, and affiliated trade associations. SCTE provides technical training and certification, and is an American National Standards Institute (ANSI)-approved Standards Development Organization for the cable telecommunications industry. *Membership:* 15,500 U.S. and International. *Dues:* $40. *Meetings:* Conference on Emerging Technologies, winter; Cable-Tec Expo, summer (hardware exhibits and engineering conference). *Publications: The Interval*; technical documents, training materials, and videotapes (some available in Spanish).

Society of Photo Technologists (SPT). 425 N. Federal Blvd., Denver, CO 80204. (888) 662-7678. An organization of photographic equipment repair technicians, which improves and maintains communications between manufacturers and independent repair technicians. *Membership:* 1,000. *Dues:* $60-$250. *Publications: SPT Journal*; *SPT Parts and Services Directory*; *SPT Newsletter*; *SPT Manuals—Training and Manufacturer's Tours*.

Southeastern Regional Media Leadership Council (SRMLC). University of Tennessee at Chattanooga, 615 McCallie Ave., Chattanooga, TN 37403. (423) 755-5376. Fax (423) 755-5381. E-mail dmcallis@cecasun.utc.edu. Deborah A. McAllister, Dir. An affiliate of AECT, the purpose of the SRMLC is to strengthen the role of the individual state AECT affiliates within the Southeastern region; to seek positive change in the nature and status of instructional technology as it exists within the Southeast; to provide opportunities for the training and development of leadership for both the region and the individual affiliates; and to provide opportunities for the exchange of information and experience among those who attend the annual conference.

SouthEastern Regional Vision for Education (SERVE). SERVE Tallahassee Office, 345 South Magnolia Dr., Suite D-23, Tallahassee, FL 32301. (800) 352-6001, (904) 671-6000. Fax (904) 671-6020. E-mail bfry@SERVE.org. Dr. Roy H. Forbes, Exec. Dir. Betty Fry, Contact Person. SERVE is a regional educational research and development laboratory funded by the

U.S. Department of Education to help educators, policymakers, and communities improve schools so that all students achieve their full potential. The laboratory offers the following services: field-based models and strategies for comprehensive school improvement; publications on hot topics in education, successful implementation efforts, applied research projects and policy issues; database searches and information search training; a regional bulletin board service that provides educators electronic communication and Internet access; information and assistance for state and local policy development; and services to support the coordination and improvement of assistance for young children and their families. The Eisenhower Mathematics and Science Consortium at SERVE promotes improvement of education in these targeted areas by coordinating regional resources, disseminating exemplary instructional materials, and offering technical assistance for implementation of effective teaching methods and assessment tools. *Meetings:* For dates and topics of conferences and workshops, contact Betty Fry, (800) 352-6001. *Publications: Reengineering High Schools for Student Success; Schools for the 21st Century: New Roles for Teachers and Principals* (rev. ed.); *Designing Teacher Evaluation Systems That Promote Professional Growth; Learning by Serving: 2,000 Ideas for Service-Learning Projects; Sharing Success: Promising Service-Learning Programs; Future Plans* (videotape, discussion guide, and pamphlet); *Future Plans Planning Guides.*

Southwest Educational Development Laboratory (SEDL). 211 East Seventh St., Austin, TX 78701. (512) 476-6861. Fax (512) 476-2286. E-mail jpollard@sedl.org. Web site http://www.sedl.org/. Dr. Wesley A. Hoover, President and CEO; Dr. Joyce Pollard, Dir., Institutional Communications & Policy Services. One of 10 Office of Educational Research and Improvement (OERI) regional educational laboratories designed to help educators and policymakers solve educational problems in their schools. Using the best available information and the experience and expertise of professionals, SEDL seeks to identify solutions to education problems, tries new approaches, furnishes research results, and provides training to teachers and administrators. SEDL serves Arkansas, Louisiana, New Mexico, Oklahoma, and Texas. *Publications: SEDLETTER* for free general distribution and a range of topic-specific publications related to educational change, education policy, mathematics, language arts, science, and disability research. It also maintains a presence on the World Wide Web.

Special Libraries Association. 1700 Eighteenth St., NW, Washington, DC, 20009-2514. (202) 234-4700. Fax (202) 265-9317. E-mail sla@sla.org. Web site http://www.sla.org. Dr. David R. Bender, Exec. Dir. The Special Libraries Association is an international association representing the interests of over 15,000 information professionals in 60 countries. Special Librarians are information and resource experts who collect, analyze, evaluate, package, and disseminate information to facilitate accurate decision-making in corporate, academic, and government settings. The association offers myriad programs and services designed to help its members serve their customers more effectively and succeed in an increasingly challenging environment of information management and technology. These services include career and employment services, and professional development opportunities. *Membership:* 16,000. *Dues:* $105, regular. Student and retired memberships available. *Meetings:* 1998 Jan 22-27, Washington DC; Jun 6-11, Indianapolis. *Publications: Information Outlook* (monthly glossy magazine which accepts advertising). Special Libraries Association also has an active book publishing program.

Speech Communication Association (SCA). 5105 Backlick Rd., Bldg. E, Annandale, VA 22003. (703) 750-0533. Fax (703) 914-9471. Web page http://www.scassn.org. James L. Gaudino, Exec. Dir. A voluntary society organized to promote study, criticism, research, teaching, and application of principles of communication, particularly of speech communication. *Membership:* 7,000. *Meetings:* 1998 Annual Meeting, Nov 21-24, New York. *Publications: Spectra Newsletter* (mo.); *Quarterly Journal of Speech; Communication Monographs; Communication Education; Critical Studies in Mass Communication; Journal of Applied Communication Research; Text and Performance Quarterly; Speech Communication Teacher; Index to Journals in Communication Studies through 1990; Speech Communication Directory* *of SCA and the Regional Speech Communication Organizations* (CSSA, ECA, SSCA, WSCA). For additional publications, request brochure.

Teachers and Writers Collaborative (T&W). 5 Union Square W., New York, NY 10003-3306. (212) 691-6590. Toll-free (888) 266-5789. Fax (212) 675-0171. E-mail info@twc.org. Web site http://www.twc.org. Nancy Larson Shapiro, Dir. Sends writers and other artists into New York public schools to work with teachers and students on writing and art projects. Hosts seminars for creative work from across the US and beyond. Recent projects include creative workshops with The School for the Physical City and the Ralph Bunche School in New York integrating computer technologies into the writing class. *Membership:* over 1,000; for people interested in the teaching of writing. *Dues:* $35, basic personal membership. *Publications: Teachers & Writers* (magazine, 5/yr); *The Story in History; The T&W Handbook of Poetic Forms; Personal Fiction Writing; Like It Was: A Complete Guide to Writing Oral History; Poetic Forms; The Nearness of You: Students and Teachers Writing On-Line.* Request free publications catalog for list of titles.

Theater Library Association (TLA). 149 W. 45th St., New York, NY 10036. (212) 944-3895. Fax (212) 944-4139. Maryann Chach, Exec. Secretary. Seeks to further the interests of collecting, preserving, and using theater, cinema, and performing arts materials in libraries, museums, and private collections. *Membership:* 500. *Dues:* $20, individual; $25, institutional. *Publications: Performing Arts Resources* (membership annual, Vol. 20, Denishawn Collections).

USA Toy Library Association (USA-TLA). 2530 Crawford Ave., Suite 111, Evanston, IL 60201. (847) 864-3330. Fax (847) 864-3331. E-mail foliog@aol.com. Judith Q. Iacuzzi, Exec. Dir. The mission of the USA-TLA is to provide a networking system answering to all those interested in play and play materials to provide a national resource to toy libraries, family centers, resource and referrals, public libraries, schools, institutions serving families of special need, and other groups and individuals involved with children; to support and expand the number of toy libraries; and to advocate for children and the importance of their play in healthy development. Individuals can find closest toy libraries by sending a written inquiry. *Membership:* 60 institutions, 150 individuals. *Dues:* $150, institutions; $50, individual; $15, student. *Meetings:* national meetings in the spring and fall. *Publications: Child's Play* (q. newsletter); *How to Start and Operate a Toy Library; Play Is a Child's Work* (videotapes), other books on quality toys and play.

University Continuing Education Association (UCEA). One Dupont Cir. NW, Suite 615, Washington, DC 20036. (202) 659-3130. Fax (202) 785-0374. Gordon Mueller, Pres. 1997-98; Kay J. Kohl, Exec. Dir.; Susan Goewey, Dir. of Pubs.; Edward Gehres, Dir. of Govt. Relations & Public Affairs. UCEA is an association of public and private higher education institutions concerned with making continuing education available to all population segments and to promoting excellence in continuing higher education. Many institutional members offer university and college courses via electronic instruction. *Membership:* 425 institutions, 2,000 professionals. *Dues:* vary according to membership category. *Meetings:* UCEA has an annual national conference and several professional development seminars throughout the year. *Publications:* monthly newsletter; quarterly; occasional papers; scholarly journal; *Independent Study Catalog.* With Peterson's, *The Guide to Distance Learning; Guide to Certificate Programs at American Colleges and Universities;* UCEA-ACE/Oryx Continuing Higher Education book series; *Lifelong Learning Trends* (a statistical factbook on continuing higher education); organizational issues series; membership directory.

WestEd. 730 Harrison St., San Francisco, CA 94107-1242. (415) 565-3000. Fax (415) 565-3012. E-mail tross@wested.org. Web site http://www.WestEd.org. Ed Myers, interim CEO. WestEd is a nonprofit research, development, and service agency dedicated to improving education and other opportunities for children, youth, and adults. Drawing on the best from research and practice, WestEd works with practitioners and policymakers to address critical issues in education and other related areas, including early childhood intervention; curriculum, instruction and assessment; the use of technology; career and technical preparation; teacher and administrator professional development; science and mathematics education; and safe schools and communities. WestEd was created in 1995 to unite and enhance the capacity of Far West Laboratory and Southwest Regional Laboratory, two of the nation's original education laboratories. In addition to its work across the nation, WestEd serves as the regional education laboratory for Arizona, California, Nevada, and Utah. A publications catalog is available.

Western Public Radio (WPR). Ft. Mason Center, Bldg. D, San Francisco, CA 94123. (415)771-1160. Lynn Chadwick, CEO. WPR provides public radio production training and studio facilities for rent. *Membership:* public radio producers.

World Future Society (WFS). 7910 Woodmont Ave., Suite 450, Bethesda, MD 20814. (301) 656-8274. Fax (301)951-0394. E-mail wfsinfo@wfs.org. Web site http://www.wfs.org/wfs. Edward Cornish, Pres. Organization of individuals interested in the study of future trends and possibilities. Its purpose is to provide information on trends and scenarios so that individuals and organizations can better plan their future. *Membership:* 30,000. *Dues:* $35, general; $95, professional; call Society for details on all membership levels and benefits. *Meeting:* 1998: Annual Conference, Jul 19-21, Chicago. *Publications: The Futurist: A Journal of Forecasts, Trends and Ideas About the Future; Futures Research Quarterly; Future Survey.* The society's bookstore offers audio- and videotapes, books, and other items.

Young Adult Library Services Association (YALSA). 50 E. Huron St., Chicago, IL 60611. (312) 280-4390. Fax (312) 664-7459. E-mail yalsa@ala.org. Linda Waddle, Deputy Exec. Dir.; Deborah Taylor, Pres. An affiliate of the American Library Association, YALSA seeks to advocate, promote, and strengthen service to young adults as part of the continuum of total library services, and assumes responsibility within the ALA to evaluate and select books and nonbook media, and to interpret and make recommendations regarding their use with young adults. Committees include Best Books for Young Adults, Popular Paperbacks, Recommended Books for the Reluctant Young Adult Reader, Media Selection and Usage, Publishers' Liaison, and Selected Films for Young Adults. *Membership:* 2,223. *Dues:* $40 (in addition to ALA membership); $15, students. *Publication: Journal of Youth Services in Libraries* (q.).

Canada

This section includes information on eight Canadian organizations whose principle interests lie in the general fields of educational media, instructional technology, and library and information science. Organizations listed in the 1997 *EMTY* were contacted for updated information and changes have been made accordingly.

ACCESS NETWORK. 3720 - 76 Ave., Edmonton, AB T6B 2N9, Canada. (403) 440-7777. Fax (403) 440-8899. E-mail promo@ccinet.ab.ca. Dr. Ronald Keast, Pres.; John Verburgt, Creative Services Manager. The ACCESS Network (Alberta Educational Communications Corporation) was purchased by Learning and Skills Television of Alberta in 1995. In acquiring ACCESS, LTA has taken over the responsibility for educational television in the province, and has moved to provide an enhanced schedule of formal curriculum-related programming for students at all levels and both formal and informal educational programming for adults. The newly privatized network will work with Alberta's educators to provide all Albertans with a progressive and diverse television-based educational and training resource to support their learning and skills development needs using cost-effective methods and innovative techniques, and to introduce a new private sector model for financing and efficient operation of educational television in the province.

Association for Media and Technology in Education in Canada (AMTEC). 3-1750 The Queensway, Suite 1318, Etobicoke, ON M9C 5H5, Canada. Web site http://www.canosun. bc.ca/~amtec/. Dr. Richard Schwier, Pres.; Dr. Katy Campbell, Pres. Elect; Mary Anne Epp, Secy./Treas. AMTEC is Canada's national association for educational media and technology professionals. The organization provides national leadership through annual conferences, publications, workshops, media festivals, and awards. It responds to media and technology issues at the international, national, provincial, and local levels, and maintains linkages with other organizations with similar interests. *Membership:* AMTEC members represent all sectors of the educational media and technology fields. *Dues:* $101.65, Canadian regular; $53.50, student and retiree. *Meeting:* Annual Conferences take place in late May or early June. *Publications: Canadian Journal of Educational Communication* (q.); *Media News* (q.); *Membership Directory* (with membership).

Canadian Broadcasting Corporation (CBC)/Société Radio-Canada (SRC). 1500 Bronson Ave., P.O. Box 8478, Ottawa, ON K1G 3J5, Canada. (613) 738-6784. Fax (613) 738-6742. Perrin Beatty, Pres. and CEO; Paula Sandes, Communications Officer. The CBC is a publicly owned corporation established in 1936 by an Act of the Canadian Parliament to provide a national broadcasting service in Canada in the two official languages. CBC services include English and French television networks; English and French AM Mono and FM Stereo radio networks virtually free of commercial advertising; CBC North, which serves Canada's North by providing radio and television programs in English, French, and eight native languages; Newsworld and its French counterpart, Le Réseau de l'information (RDI), 24-hour national satellites to cable English-language and French-language news and information service respectively, both funded entirely by cable subscription and commercial advertising revenues; and Radio Canada International, a shortwave radio service that broadcasts in seven languages and is managed by CBC and financed by External Affairs. The CBC is financed mainly by public funds voted annually by Parliament.

Canadian Education Association/Association canadienne d'éducation (CEA). 252 Bloor St. W., Suite 8-200, Toronto, ON M5S 1V5, Canada. (416) 924-7721. Fax (416) 924-3188. E-mail acea@hookup.net. Penny Milton, Exec. Dir.; Suzanne Tanguay, Communications Officer. The Canadian equivalent of the US National Education Association, CEA has one central objective: to promote the improvement of education. It is the only national, bilingual organization whose function is to inform, assist, and bring together all sectors of the educational community. *Membership:* 400 individuals, 100 organizations, 100 school boards. *Dues:* $90, individual; $280, organization; 10 cents per pupil, school boards. *Meetings:* Annual CEA Convention, September. *Publications: CEA Handbook; Education Canada* (q.); *CEA Newsletter* (9/yr.); *Disruptive Behaviour in Today's Classroom; Financing Canadian Education; The Entrepreneurial School; Secondary Schools in Canada: The National Report of the Exemplary Schools Project; Improving School Attendance; Evaluating Achievement of Senior High School Students in Canada; Making Sense of the Canadian Charter of Rights and Freedom: A Handbook for Administrators and Teachers; An Overview of Canadian Education; The School Calendar.*

Canadian Library Association. 200 Elgin St., Suite 602, Ottawa, ON K2P IL5, Canada. (613) 232-9625. Fax (613) 563-9895. E-mail ai281@freenet.carleton.ca. Karen Adams, Exec. Dir. The mission of the Canadian Library Association is to provide leadership in the promotion, development, and support of library and information services in Canada for the benefit of Association members, the profession, and Canadian society. In the spirit of this mission, CLA aims to engage the active, creative participation of library staff, trustees, and governing bodies in the development and management of high quality Canadian library service; to assert and support the right of all Canadians to the freedom to read and to free universal access to a wide variety of library materials and services; to promote librarianship and to enlighten all levels of government as to the significant role that libraries play in educating and socializing the Canadian people; and to link libraries, librarians, trustees, and others across the country for the purpose of providing a unified nationwide voice in matters of critical concern. *Membership:*

2,300 individuals, 700 institutions, 100 Associates and Trustees. *Dues:* $50-$1,600. *Meetings:* Annual Conference, summer. *Publication: Feliciter* (membership magazine, 10/yr.).

Canadian Museums Association/Association des musées canadiens (CMA/AMC). 280 Metcalfe St., Suite 400, Ottawa, ON K2P 1R7, Canada. (613) 567-0099. Fax (613) 233-5438. John G. McAvity, Exec. Dir. The Canadian Museums Association is a nonprofit corporation and registered charity dedicated to advancing public museums and museum works in Canada, promoting the welfare and better administration of museums, and fostering a continuing improvement in the qualifications and practices of museum professionals. *Membership:* 2,000. *Meeting:* CMA Annual Conference, summer. *Publications: Museogramme* (bi-mo. newsletter); *Muse* (q. journal, Canada's only national, bilingual, scholarly magazine devoted to museums, it contains museum-based photography, feature articles, commentary, and practical information); *The Official Directory of Canadian Museums and Related Institutions* (1997-99 edition) lists all museums in Canada plus information on government departments, agencies, and provincial and regional museum associations.

Canadian Publishers' Council (CPC). 250 Merton St., Suite 203, Toronto, ON M4S 1B1 Canada. (416) 322-6999. Fax (416) 322-6999. Web site http://www.pubcouncil.ca. Jacqueline Hushion, Exec. Dir. CPC members publish and distribute an extensive list of Canadian and imported learning materials in a complete range of formats from traditional textbook and ancillary materials to CDs and interactive video. The primary markets for CPC members are schools, universities and colleges, bookstores, and libraries. CPC also provides exhibits throughout the year and works through a number of subcommittees and groups within the organization to promote effective book publishing. CPC was founded in 1910. *Membership:* 30 companies, educational institutions, or government agencies that publish books as an important facet of their work.

National Film Board of Canada (NFBC). 1251 Avenue of the Americas, 16th Floor, New York, NY 10020. (212) 596-1770. Fax (212) 595-1779. E-mail johnnfbc@aol.com. Web site http://www.nfb.ca. John Sirabella, US Marketing Mgr./Nontheatrical Rep. Established in 1939, the NFBC's main objective is to produce and distribute high-quality audiovisual materials for educational, cultural, and social purposes.

Ontario Film Association, Inc. (also known as the Association for the Advancement of Visual Media/L'association pour l'avancement des médias visuels). 3-1750 The Queensway, Suite 1341, Etobicoke, ON M9C 5H5, Canada. (416) 761-6056. Fax (905) 820-7397. Margaret Nix, Exec. Dir. A volunteer organization of buyers and users of media whose objectives are to promote the sharing of ideas and information about media, to showcase media, to publish *Visual Média/Medias Visuels*, to do advocacy, and to present workshops. *Membership:* 122. *Dues:* $120, regular and commercial; $180, extended. *Meeting:* OFA Media Showcase, spring. *Publication: Visual Media/Médias Visuels* (5/yr.).

Part Six
Graduate Programs

Introduction

This directory describes 141 graduate programs in Instructional Technology, Educational Media and Communications, School Library Media, and closely allied programs in 40 states and the District of Columbia. This year's list includes one new program. Five institutions indicated that their programs had been discontinued, and have been deleted from the listings. Master's, Specialist, and doctoral degrees are combined into one unified list, a major change from the 1997 *Yearbook.*

Information in this section can be considered current as of early 1997 for 134 of the programs. In most cases, department chairs or their representatives responded to a questionnaire mailed to them during November of 1996. The seven programs for which we received no updated information are indicated by an asterisk (*). In addition, six listings were dropped for lack of replies for two consecutive years.

Entries provide as much of the following information as furnished by respondents: (1) name and address of the institution; (2) chairperson or other individual in charge of the program; (3) types of degrees offered and specializations, emphases, or tracks, including information on careers for which candidates are prepared; (4) special features of the degree program; (5) admission requirements; (6) degree requirements; (7) number of full-time and part-time faculty; (8) number of full-time and part-time students; (9) types of financial assistance available; and (10) the number of degrees awarded by type in 1996. All grade-point averages (GPAs), test scores, and degree requirements are minimums unless stated otherwise. The Graduate Record Examination, Miller Analogies Test, National Teacher's Examination, and other standardized tests are referred to by their acronyms. The Test of English as a Foreign Language (TOEFL) appears in many of the *Admission Requirements,* and in most cases this test is required only for non-native English speakers. Although some entries explicitly state application fees, most do not. Prospective students should assume that most institutions require a completed application, transcripts of all previous collegiate work, and a non-refundable application fee.

Directors of advanced professional programs for instructional technology or media specialists should find this degree program information useful as a means of comparing their own offerings and requirements with those of institutions offering comparable programs. This listing, along with the Classified List, should also assist individuals in locating institutions that best suit their interests and requirements.

Additional information on the programs listed, including admission procedure instructions, may be obtained by contacting individual program coordinators. General or graduate catalogs and specific program information usually are furnished for a minimal charge. In addition, many graduate programs now have e-mail contact addresses and Web sites which provide a wealth of descriptive information. Electronic access information is provided where available.

We are greatly indebted to those individuals who responded to our requests for information. Although the editors expended considerable effort to ensure currency and completeness of the listings, there may be institutions within the United States that now have programs of which we are unaware. Readers are encouraged to furnish new information to the publisher who, in turn, will investigate the program for the next edition of *EMTY.* Institutions in this section are listed alphabetically by state.

CLASSIFIED LIST

Computer Applications

California State University-San Bernardino [M.A.]

State University of New York at Stony Brook [Master's: Technological Systems Management/Educational Computing]

University of Iowa [M.A.]

Valdosta State University [M.Ed. in IT/ Technology Applications]

Computer Education

Appalachian State University [M.A.: Educational Media and Technology/Computers]

Arizona State University, Department of Educational Media and Computers [M.A., Ph.D.: Educational Media and Computers]

Arkansas Tech University [Master's]

Buffalo State College [M.S.: Education/ Educational Computing]

California State University-Dominguez Hills [M.A., Certificate: Computer-Based Education]

California State University-Los Angeles [M.A. in Education/Computer Education]

California State University-San Bernardino [Advanced Certificate Program: Educational Computing]

Central Connecticut State University [M.S.: Educational Technology/Computer Technologies]

Concordia University [M.A.: Computer Science Education]

East Carolina University [M.A.: Education/IT Computers]

Eastern Washington University [M.Ed.: Computer Education]

Fairfield University [M.A.: Media/Educational Technology with Computers in Education]

Florida Institute of Technology [Master's, Ph.D.: Computer Education]

Fontbonne College [M.S.]

George Mason University [M.Ed.: Special Education Technology, Computer Science Educator]

Iowa State University [M.S., M.Ed., Ph.D.: Curriculum and IT/Instructional Computing]

Jacksonville University [Master's: Computer Education]

Kansas State University [M.S. in Secondary Education/Educational Computing; Ed.D., Ph.D.: Curriculum and Instruction/ Educational Computing]

Kent State University [M.A., M.Ed.: Instructional Computing]

Minot State University [M.Ed., M.S.: Math and Computer Science]

New York Institute of Technology [Specialist Certificate: Computers in Education]

North Carolina State University [M.S., M.Ed.: IT-Computers]

Northern Illinois University [M.S.Ed., Ed.D.: IT/Educational Computing]

Northwest Missouri State University [M.S.: School Computer Studies; M.S.Ed.: Educational Uses of Computers]

Nova Southeastern University [M.S., Ed.S.: Computer Science Education]

The Ohio State University [M.A., Ph.D.: Art Education/Computer Graphics, Computer Art]

Ohio University [M.Ed.: Computer Education and Technology]

Pace University [M.S.E.: Curriculum and Instruction/Computers]

San Diego State University [Master's in Educational Technology/Computers in Education]

San Francisco State University [Master's: Instructional Computing]

State University of New York at Stony Brook [Master's: Technological Systems Management/Educational Computing]

State University College of Arts and Sciences at Potsdam [M.S.Ed.: IT and Media Management/Educational Computing]

Syracuse University [M.S., Ed.D., Ph.D., Advanced Certificate: Media Production]

Texas A&M University-Commerce [Master's: Learning Technology and Information Systems/Educational Micro Computing]

Texas Tech University [M.Ed.: IT/Educational Computing]

University of Georgia [M.Ed., Ed.S.: Computer-Based Education]

University of Illinois at Urbana-Champaign [M.A., M.S., Ed.M.: Educational Computing; Ph.D.: Education Psychology/ Educational Computing]

University of North Texas [M.S.: Computer Education and Instructional Systems]

The University of Oklahoma [Master's: Computer Applications]

University of Toledo [Master's, Ed.S., D.Ed.: Instructional Computing]

University of Washington [Master's, Ed.D., Ph.D.]

Virginia Polytechnic Institute and State University [M.A., Ed.D., Ph.D.: IT]

Wright State University [M.Ed.: Computer Education; M.A.: Computer Education]

Distance Education

Fairfield University [M.A.: Media/Educational Technology with Satellite Communications]

Iowa State University [M.S., M.Ed., Ph.D.: Curriculum and IT]

New York Institute of Technology [Specialist certificate]
Nova Southeastern University [M.S., Ed.D.: IT]
Texas A&M University [Ph.D.: EDCI]
Texas Tech University [M.Ed.: IT]
University of Northern Colorado [Ph.D.: Educational Technology]
Western Illinois University [Master's]

Educational Leadership
Auburn University [Ed.D.]
Barry University [Ph.D.: Educational Technology Leadership]
George Washington University [M.A.: Education and Human Development/Educational Technology Leadership]
United States International University [Master's, Ed.D.: Technology Leadership for Learning]
University of Colorado at Denver [Ph.D.: Educational Leadership and Innovation/Curriculum, Learning, and Technology]
Valdosta State University [M.Ed., Ed.S.: IT/Technology Leadership]

Human Performance
Boise State University [M.S.: IT and Performance Technology]
Governors State University [M.A.: Communication with Human Performance and Technology]
University of Southern California [Ed.D.: Human Performance Technology]
University of Toledo [Master's, Ed.S., Ed.D.: Human Resources Development]

Information Studies
Drexel University [M.S., M.S.I.S.]
Emporia State University [Ph.D.: Library and Information Management]
Rutgers [M.L.S.: Information Retrieval; Ph.D.: Communication (Information Systems)]
Simmons College [M.S.: Information Science/Systems]
Southern Connecticut State University [Sixth Year Professional Diploma: Library-Information Studies/IT]
St. Cloud State University [Master's, Ed.S.: Information Technologies]
Texas A&M-Commerce [Master's: Learning Technology and Information Systems/Library and Information Science]
University of Alabama [Ph.D.]
University of Arizona [M.A.: Information Resources and Library Science]
University of Central Arkansas [M.S.: Information Science/Media Information Studies]
University of Maryland [Doctorate: Library and Information Services]
University of Missouri-Columbia [Ph.D.: Information and Learning Technologies]

The University of Oklahoma [Dual Master's: Educational Technology and Library and Information Systems]
The University of Rhode Island [M.L.I.S.]
University of Washington [Master's, Ed.D., Ph.D.]
Western Oregon State College [MS: Information Technology]

Innovation
Pennsylvania State University [M.Ed., M.S., Ed.D., Ph.D.: Instructional Systems/Emerging Technologies]
University of Colorado at Denver [Ph.D: Educational Leadership and Innovation]
Walden University [M.S., Ph.D.: Educational Change and Technology Innovation]

Instructional Design and Development
Auburn University [M.Ed., M.S.]
Bloomsburg University [M.S.: IT]
Brigham Young University [M.S., Ph.D.]
Clarion University of Pennsylvania [M.S.: Communication/Training and Development]
Fairfield University [Certificate of Advanced Studies: Media/Educational Technology: Instructional Development]
George Mason University [M.Ed.: IT/Instructional Design and Development]
Governors State University [M.A.: Communication with Human Performance and Training/Instructional Design]
Indiana University [Ph.D., Ed.D.: Instructional Analysis, Design, and Development]
Iowa State University [M.S., M.Ed., Ph.D.: Curriculum and IT/Instruction Design]
Ithaca College [M.S.: Corporate Communications]
Lehigh University [Master's]
Michigan State University [M.A.: Educational Technology and Instructional Design]
North Carolina Central University [M.S.: Instructional Development/Design]
Northern Illinois University [M.S.Ed., Ed.D.: IT/Instructional Design]
Pennsylvania State University [M.Ed., M.S., D.Ed., Ph.D.: Instructional Systems/Systems Design]
Purdue University [Master's, Specialist, Ph.D.: Instructional Development]
San Francisco State University [Master's/Training and Designing Development]
Southern Illinois University at Carbondale [M.S.: Education/Instructional Design]
State University of New York at Albany [M.Ed., Ph.D.: Curriculum and Instruction/Instructional Design and Technology]
State University of New York at Stony Brook [Master's: Technological Systems Management/Educational Computing]

Syracuse University [M.S., Ed.D., Ph.D., Advanced Certificate: Instructional Design; Educational Evaluation; Instructional Development]

Towson State University [M.S.: Instructional Development]

University of Cincinnati [M.A., Ed.D.: Curriculum and Instruction/Instructional Design and Technology]

University of Colorado at Denver [Master's, Ph.D.: Instructional Design]

University of Illinois at Urbana-Champaign [M.A., M.S., Ed.M.; Ph.D. in Educational Psychology/Instructional Design]

University of Iowa [M.A., Ph.D.: Training and Human Resources Development]

University of Massachusetts-Boston [M.Ed.]

University of Northern Colorado [Ph.D. in Educational Technology/Instructional Development and Design]

The University of Oklahoma [Master's]

University of Toledo [Master's, Specialist, doctorate: Instructional Development]

University of Washington [Master's, Ed.D., Ph.D.]

Utah State University [M.S., Ed.S.: Instructional Development]

Virginia Polytechnic Institute and State University [Master's, Ed.D., Ph.D.: IT]

Instructional Technology [IT]

Appalachian State University [M.A.: Educational Media and Technology]

Arizona State University, Learning and IT Dept. [M.Ed., Ph.D.]

Barry University [M.S., Ed.S.: Educational Technology]

Bloomsburg University [M.S.: IT]

Boise State University [M.S.]

Boston University [Ed.M., Certificate of Advanced Graduate Study: Educational Media & Technology; Ed.D.: Curriculum and Teaching/Educational Media and Technology]

California State University-Los Angeles [M.A.: Education/IT]

California State University-San Bernardino [Advanced Certificate in Educational Technology]

Central Connecticut State University [M.S.: Educational Technology]

Dubuque Tri-College [M.A.: Technology and Education]

East Carolina University [M.A.: Education/IT Computers]

East Tennessee State [M.Ed.]

Eastern Michigan University [M.A.: Educational Psychology/Educational Technology]

Edgewood College [M.A.: Education/IT]

Fairfield University [M.A., Certificate of Advanced Study: Media/Educational Technology]

Fitchburg State College [M.S.: Communications Media/IT]

Florida Institute of Technology [Master's, Ph.D.]

George Mason University [M.Ed., Ph.D.]

George Washington University [M.A.: Education and Human Development/Educational Technology Leadership]

Georgia Southern University [M.Ed., Ed.S.: IT; Ed.D.: Curriculum Studies/IT]

Georgia State University [M.S., Ph.D.]

Harvard University [M.Ed.: Technology in Education]

Indiana State University [Master's, Ed.S.]

Indiana University [M.S., Ed.S., Ed.D., Ph.D.]

Iowa State University [M.S., M.Ed., Ph.D: Curriculum and IT]

Jacksonville University [Master's: Educational Technology and Integrated Learning]

Johns Hopkins University [M.S. in Educational Technology for Educators]

Kent State University [M.Ed., M.A; Ph.D.: Educational Psychology/IT]

Lehigh University [Master's; Ed.D.: Educational Technology]

Lesley College [M.Ed., Certificate of Advanced Graduate Study: Technology Education; Ph.D.: Education/Technology Education]

Mankato State University [M.S.: Educational Technology]

Michigan State University [M.A.: Educational Technology]

Montclair State College [certification]

New York Institute of Technology [Master's]

New York University [M.A., Certificate of Advanced Study in Education, Ed.D., Ph.D.]

North Carolina Central University [M.A.: Educational Technology]

North Carolina State University [M.Ed., M.S.: IT—Computers; Ph.D.: Curriculum and Instruction/IT]

Northern Illinois University [M.S.Ed., Ed.D.]

Nova Southeastern University [Ed.S., M.S.: Educational Technology; M.S., Ed.D.: IT]

Ohio University [M.Ed.: Computer Education and Technology]

Purdue University [Master's, Specialist, Ph.D.: Educational Technology]

Radford University [M.S.: Education/Educational Media/Technology]

Rosemont College [M.Ed.: Technology in Education; Certificate in Professional Study in Technology in Education]

San Diego State University [Master's: Educational Technology]

Southern Connecticut State University [M.S.]

Southern Illinois University at Carbondale [M.S.: Education; Ph.D.: Education/IT]

State University College of Arts and Sciences at Potsdam [M.S.: Education/IT]

State University of New York at Albany
[M.Ed., Ph.D.: Curriculum and Instruction/
Instructional Theory, Design, and
Technology]
State University of West Georgia [M.Ed., Ed.S.]
Texas A&M University [M.Ed.: Educational
Technology; Ph.D.: EDCI/Educational
Technology; Ph.D.: Educational Psychol-
ogy Foundations/Learning and Technology]
Texas A&M-Commerce [Master's: Learning
Technology and Information Systems/
Educational Media and Technology]
Texas Tech University [M.Ed.; Ed.D.]
United States International University [Ed.D.:
Technology and Learning]
University of Central Florida [M.A.: IT/
Instructional Systems, IT/Educational
Media; doctorate: Curriculum and
Instruction/IT]
University of Cincinnati [M.A., Ed.D.: Curricu-
lum and Instruction/Instructional Design
and Technology]
University of Colorado at Denver [Master's,
Ph.D.: Learning Technologies]
University of Connecticut [Master's, Ph.D.:
Educational Technology]
University of Georgia [M.Ed., Ed.S., Ph.D.]
University of Hawaii-Manoa [M.Ed.: Educational
Technology]
University of Louisville [M.Ed.: Occupational
Education/IT]
University of Maryland [Ph.D.: Library Science
and Educational Technology/Instructional
Communication]
University of Massachusetts-Lowell [M.Ed.,
Ed.D., Certificate of Advanced Graduate
Study: Educational Technology]
University of Michigan [Master's, Ph.D.: IT]
University of Missouri-Columbia [Master's,
Ed.S., Ph.D.]
University of Nebraska at Kearney [M.S.]
University of Nevada [M.S., Ph.D.]
University of Northern Colorado [M.A., Ph.D.:
Educational Technology]
University of Northern Iowa [M.A.: Educational
Technology]
The University of Oklahoma [Master's: Educa-
tional Technology Generalist; Educational
Technology; Teaching with Technology;
dual Master's: Educational Technology and
Library and Information Systems;
doctorate: Instructional Psychology and
Technology]
University of South Carolina [Master's]
University of Southern California [M.A., Ed.D.,
Ph.D.]
University of Tennessee-Knoxville [M.S.:
Education, Ed.S., Ed.D., Ph.D.]
The University of Texas [Master's, Ph.D.]
University of Toledo [Master's, Specialist,
doctorate]

University of Virginia [M.Ed., Ed.S., Ed.D.,
Ph.D.]
University of Washington [Master's, Ed.D.,
Ph.D.]
University of Wisconsin-Madison [M.S., Ph.D.]
Utah State University [M.S., Ed.S., Ph.D.]
Virginia Polytechnic Institute and State Univer-
sity [M.A., Ed.D., Ph.D.: IT]
Virginia State University [M.S., M.Ed.: Educa-
tional Media and Technology]
Wayne State University [Master's, Ed.D., Ph.D.,
Ed.S.]
Webster University [Master's]
Western Illinois University [Master's]
Western Washington University [M.Ed.: IT in
Adult Education; Elementary Education; IT
in Secondary Education]
Wright State University [Specialist: Curriculum
and Instruction/Educational Technology;
Higher Education/Educational Technology]

Integration

Bloomsburg University [M.S.: IT]
George Mason University [M.Ed.: IT/Integration
of Technology in Schools]
Jacksonville University [Master's: Educational
Technology and Integrated Learning]
University of Northern Colorado [Ph.D.: Educa-
tional Technology/Technology Integration]

Management

Bloomsburg University [M.S.: IT]
Central Connecticut State University [M.S.: Edu-
cational Technology/Media Management]
Drexel University [M.S., M.S.I.S.]
Emporia State University [Ph.D.: Library and
Information Management]
Fairfield University [Certificate of Advanced
Studies: Media/Educational Technology
with Media Management]
Fitchburg State College [M.S.: Communications
Media/Management]
Indiana University [Ed.D., Ph.D.: Implementa-
tion and Management]
Minot State University [M.S.: Management]
Northern Illinois University [M.S.Ed., Ed.D.:
IT/Media Administration]
Rutgers [M.L.S.: Management and Policy Issues]
Simmons College [M.L.S.: History (Archives
Management); Doctor of Arts: Administra-
tion; Media Management]
State University College of Arts and Science
[M.S.: Education/IT and Media
Management]
State University of New York at Stony Brook
[Master's: Technological Systems
Management]
Syracuse University [M.S., Ed.D., Ph.D.,
Advanced Certificate]
University of Tennessee-Knoxville [Certifica-
tion: Instructional Media Supervisor]

Virginia Polytechnic Institute and State
University [M.A., Ed.D., Ph.D.: IT]
Wright State University [M.Ed.: Media
Supervisor; Computer Coordinator]

Media

Appalachian State University [M.A.: Educational
Media and Technology/Media
Management]
Arizona State University, Department of Educa-
tional Media and Computers [M.A., Ph.D.:
Educational Media and Computers]
Boston University [Ed.M., Certificate of
Advanced Graduate Study: Educational
Media and Technology; Ed.D.: Curriculum
and Teaching/Educational Media and
Technology]
Central Connecticut State University [M.S.: Edu-
cational Technology/Materials Production]
Fitchburg State College [M.S.: Communications
Media]
Indiana State University [Ph.D.: Curriculum and
Instruction/Media Technology]
Indiana University [Ed.D., Ph.D.: Instructional
Development and Production]
Jacksonville State University [M.S.:
Education/Instructional Media]
Montclair State College [certification]
Radford University [M.S.: Education/Educa-
tional Media/Technology]
Shippensburg University [Master's: Radio/TV]
Simmons College [Master's: Media Management]
St. Cloud State University [Master's, Ed.S.:
Educational Media]
State University College of Arts and Science at
Potsdam [M.S.: Education/IT and Media
Management]
Syracuse University [M.S., Ed.D., Ph.D.,
Advanced Certificate: Media Production]
Texas A&M-Commerce [Master's: Learning
Technology and Information Systems/
Educational Media and Technology]
University of Central Florida [M.Ed.: IT/
Educational Media]
University of Iowa [M.A.: Media Design and
Production]
University of Nebraska at Kearney [M.S., Ed.S.:
Educational Media]
University of Nebraska-Omaha [M.S.: Education/
Educational Media; M.A.: Education/
Educational Media]
University of Tennessee-Knoxville [Ph.D.: In-
structional Media and Technology; Ed.D.:
Curriculum and Instruction/Instructional
Media and Technology]
University of Virginia [M.Ed., Ed.S., Ed.D.,
Ph.D.: Media Production]
Virginia Polytechnic Institute and State
University [M.A., Ed.D., Ph.D.: IT]
Virginia State University [M.Ed., M.S.:
Educational Media and Technology]

Wright State University [M.Ed.: Educational
Media; Media Supervision; M.A.:
Educational Media]

Multimedia

Bloomsburg University [M.S.: IT]
Brigham Young University [M.S.: Multimedia
Production]
Fairfield University [M.A.: Media/Educational
Technology with Multimedia]
Ithaca College [M.S.: Corporate
Communications]
Jacksonville University [Master's: Educational
Technology and Integration Learning]
Lehigh University [Master's]
New York Institute of Technology [Specialist
Certificate]
The Ohio State University [M.A., Ph.D.: Art
Education/Multimedia Production]
San Francisco State University [Master's:
Instructional Multimedia Design]
State University of New York at Stony Brook
[Master's: Technological Systems
Management/Educational Computing]
Syracuse University [M.S., Ed.D., Ph.D.,
Advanced Certificate: Media Production]
Texas A&M University [M.Ed.: Educational
Technology]
University of Northern Colorado [Ph.D.: Educa-
tional Technology/Interactive Technology]
University of Virginia [M.Ed., Ed.S., Ed.D.,
Ph.D.: Interactive Multimedia]
University of Washington [Master's, Ed.D.,
Ph.D.]
Utah State University [M.S., Ed.S.]
Wayne State University [Master's: Interactive
Technologies]
Western Illinois University [Master's: Interactive
Technologies]

Research

Brigham Young University [M.S., Ph.D.:
Research and Evaluation]
Drexel University [M.S., M.S.I.S.]
Iowa State University [Ph.D.: Educational/
Technology Research]
Syracuse University [M.S., Ed.D., Ph.D.,
Advanced Certificate: Educational
Research and Theory]
University of Washington [Master's, Ed.D.,
Ph.D.]

School Library Media

Alabama State University [Master's, Ed.S.,
Ph.D.]
Arkansas Tech University [Master's]
Auburn University [M.ED., Ed.S.]
Bloomsburg University [M.S.]
Boston University [Massachusetts certification]
Central Connecticut State University [M.S.:
Educational Technology/Librarianship]

Chicago State University [Master's]
East Carolina University [M.L.S., Certificate of Advanced Study]
East Tennessee State [M.Ed.: Instructional Media]
Emporia State University [Ph.D.: Library and Information Management; M.L.S.; School Library certification]
Kent State University
Louisiana State University [M.L.I.S., C.L.I.S. (post-Master's certificate), Louisiana School Library certification]
Mankato State University [M.S.]
Northern Illinois University [M.S.Ed.: Instructional Technology with Illinois state certification]
Nova Southeastern University [Ed.S, M.S.: Educational Media]
Radford University [M.S.: Education/ Educational Media; licensure]
Rutgers [M.L.S., Ed.S.]
Simmons College [M.L.S.: Education]
Southern Illinois University at Edwardsville [M.S. in Education: Library/Media]
Southwestern Oklahoma State University [M.Ed.: Library/Media Education]
St. Cloud State University [Master's, Ed.S.]
St. John's University [M.L.S.]
State University of West Georgia [M.Ed., Ed.S.: Media]
Towson State University [M.S.]
University of Alabama [Master's, Ed.S.]
University of Central Arkansas [M.S.]
University of Georgia [M.Ed., Ed.S]
University of Maryland [M.L.S.]
University of Montana [Master's, Ed.S.]
University of North Carolina [M.S.]
University of Northern Colorado [M.A.: Educational Media]
University of South Florida [Master's]
University of Toledo
University of Wisconsin-La Crosse [M.S.: Professional Development/Initial Instructional Library Specialist; Instructional Library Media Specialist]
Utah State University [M.S., Ed.S.]
Valdosta State University [M.Ed., Ed.S.: Instructional Technology/Library/Media]
Webster University
Western Maryland College [M.S.]
William Paterson College [M.Ed., Ed.S., Associate]
Winthrop University [M.Ed.]

Special Education
George Mason University [M.Ed.: IT/ Assistive/Special Education Technology; M.Ed.: Special Education Technology; Ph.D.: Special Education Technology]
Johns Hopkins University [M.S. in Special Education/Technology in Special Education]
Minot State University [M.S.: Early Childhood Special Education; Severe Multiple Handicaps; Communication Disorders]
Western Washington University [M.Ed.: IT in Special Education]

Systems
Bloomsburg University [M.S.: IT]
Drexel University [M.S., M.S.I.S.]
Florida State University [M.S., Ed.S., Ph.D.: Instructional Systems]
Pennsylvania State University [M.Ed., M.S., D.Ed., Ph.D.: Instructional Systems]
Simmons College [Master's: Information Science/Systems]
Southern Illinois University at Edwardsville [M.S.: Education/Instructional Systems Design]
State University of New York at Stony Brook [Master's: Technological Systems Management]
Texas A&M University-Commerce [Master's: Learning Technology and Information Systems]
University of Central Florida [M.A.: IT/ Instructional Systems]
University of Maryland, Baltimore County [Master's: School Instructional Systems]
University of North Texas [M.S.: Computer Education and Instructional Systems]
The University of Oklahoma [Dual Master's: Educational Technology and Library and Information Systems]

Technology Design
Governors State University [M.A.: Design Logistics]
Kansas State University [Ed.D., Ph.D.: Curriculum and Instruction/Educational Computing, Design, and Telecommunications]
United States International University [Master's, Ed.D.: Designing Technology for Learning]
University of Colorado at Denver [Master's, Ph.D.: Design of Learning Technologies]

Telecommunications
Appalachian State University [M.A.: Educational Media and Technology/ Telecommunications]
Kansas State University [Ed.D., Ph.D.: Curriculum and Instruction/Educational Computing, Design, and Telecommunications]
The Ohio State University [M.A., Ph.D.: Art Education/Telecommunications in the Arts]
Western Illinois University [Masters: Telecommunications]

Training
Clarion University of Pennsylvania [M.S.: Communication/Training and Development]

Pennsylvania State University [M.Ed., M.S., D.Ed., Ph.D.: Instructional Systems/ Corporate Training]

St. Cloud State University [Master's, Ed.S.: Human Resources Development/Training]

Syracuse University [M.S., Ed.D., Ph.D., Advanced Certificate]

University of Maryland, Baltimore County [Master's: Training in Business and Industry]

University of Northern Iowa [M.A.: Communications and Training Technology]

Wayne State University [Master's: Business and Human Services Training]

Video Production

California State University-San Bernardino [M.A.]

Fairfield University [Certificate of Advanced Study: Media/Educational Technology with TV Production]

San Francisco State University [Master's: Instructional Video Production]

ALPHABETICAL LIST

ALABAMA

Alabama State University. P.O. Box 271, Montgomery, AL 36101-0271. (334) 229-4107. Fax (334) 229-4961. Dr. Katie R. Bell, Chair. *Specializations:* School media specialist preparation (K-12) only; Master's and Specialist degrees. *Admission Requirements:* Master's: undergraduate degree with teacher certification. Specialist: Master's degree in library/media education. *Degree Requirements:* Master's: 33 semester hours with 300 clock-hour internship. Specialist: 33 semester hours in 600-level courses. *Faculty:* 3 full-time, 2 part-time. *Students:* Master's, 45 part-time; Specialist, 10 part-time. *Financial Assistance:* assistantships, student loans, scholarships. *Degrees Awarded 1996:* Master's, 10; Specialist, 3.

Auburn University. Educational Foundations, Leadership, and Technology, 4036 Haley Center, Auburn, AL 36849-5221. (334) 844-4291. Fax (334) 844-5785. E-mail bannosh@mail. auburn.edu. Susan H. Bannon, Coord., Educational Media and Technology. *Specializations:* M.Ed. (non-thesis) and Ed.S. for Library Media certification; M.Ed. (non-thesis) or M.S. (with thesis) for instructional design specialists who want to work in business, industry, and the military. Ed.D. in Educational Leadership with emphasis on curriculum and new instructional technologies. *Features:* All programs emphasize interactive technologies and computers. *Admission Requirements:* all programs: recent GRE test scores, 3 letters of recommendation, Bachelor's degree from accredited institution, teacher certification (for library media program only). *Degree Requirements:* Library Media Master's: 52 qtr. hours. Instructional Design: 48 qtr. hours. Specialist: 48 qtr. hours. Ed.D.: 120 qtr. hours beyond B.S. degree. *Faculty:* 5 full-time, 3 part-time. *Students:* 3 full-time, 18 part-time. *Financial Assistance:* graduate assistantships. *Degrees Awarded 1996:* Master's, 8.

Jacksonville State University. Instructional Media Division, Jacksonville, AL 36265. (205) 782-5011. E-mail mmerrill@jsucc.jsu.edu. Martha Merrill, Coord., Dept. of Educational Resources. *Specializations:* M.S. in Education with emphasis on Instructional Media. *Admission Requirements:* Bachelor's degree in Education. *Degree Requirements:* 36 semester hours including 24 in library media. *Faculty:* 2 full-time. *Students:* 30 full- and part-time. *Degrees Awarded 1996:* approx. 20.

University of Alabama. School of Library and Information Studies, Box 870252, Tuscaloosa, AL 35487-0252. (205) 348-4610. Fax (205) 348-3746. E-mail GCOLEMAN@UA1VM. UA.EDU. J. Gordon Coleman, Jr., Chair. *Specializations:* Master's, Specialist, and Ph.D. degrees in a varied program including school, public, academic, and special libraries. Ph.D. specializations in Historical Studies, Information Studies, Management, and Youth Studies; considerable flexibility in creating individual programs of study. *Admission Requirements:* Master's and Specialist: 3.0 GPA; 50 MAT or 1500 GRE. Doctoral: 3.0 GPA; 60 MAT or 1650 GRE. *Degree Requirements:* Master's: 36 semester hours. Specialist: 33 semester hours. Doctoral: 48 semester hours plus 24 hours dissertation research. *Faculty:* 10 full-time. *Students:* Master's, 75 full-time; Specialist, 2 full-time; doctoral, 12 full-time. *Financial Assistance:* assistantships, grants, student loans, scholarships, work assistance, campus work. *Degrees Awarded 1996:* Master's, 65; Specialist, 1; Ph.D., 2.

ARIZONA

Arizona State University, Dept. of Learning and Instructional Technology. Box 870611, Tempe, AZ 85287-0611. (602) 965-3384. Fax (602) 965-0300. Web site http://seamonkey.ed.asu. edu/~gail/programs/lnt.htm. James D. Klein, Program Coord. (atjdk@asuvm.inre.asu.edu). Nancy Archer, Admissions Secretary (icnla@asuvm.inre.asu.edu). *Specializations*: M.Ed. and

Ph.D. with focus on the design, development, and evaluation of effective instruction. *Features*: research and publication prior to candidacy. *Admission Requirements*: M.Ed.: 3.0 undergraduate GPA, 500 GRE (verbal) or 46 MAT. Ph.D.: 3.0 undergraduate GPA, 1200 GRE (verbal + quantitative). *Degree Requirements*: M.Ed.: 30 semester hours, comprehensive exam. Ph.D.: 84 semester hours beyond Bachelor's degree, comprehensive exam, research/publication, dissertation. *Faculty*: 5 full-time. *Students*: M.Ed., 15 full-time, 20 part-time; Ph.D., 12 full-time, 10 part-time. *Financial Assistance*: assistantships, tuition waivers, and student loans for qualified applicants. *Degrees Awarded 1996:* M.Ed., 8; Ph.D., 4.

Arizona State University, Dept. of Educational Media and Computers. Box 870111, Tempe, AZ 85287-0111. (602) 965-7192. Fax (602) 965-7193. E-mail bitter@asu.edu. Dr. Gary G. Bitter, Coord. *Specializations:* M.A. and Ph.D. in Educational Media and Computers. *Features:* A three semester-hour course in Instructional Media Design is offered via CD-ROM or World Wide Web. *Admission Requirements:* M.A.: Bachelor's degree, 550 TOEFL, 500 GRE, 45 MAT. *Degree Requirements:* M.A.: 36 semester hours (24 hours in educational media and computers, 9 hours education, 3 hours outside education); internship; comprehensive exam; practicum; thesis not required. Ph.D.: 93 semester hours (24 hours in educational media and computers, 57 hours in education, 12 hours outside education); thesis; internship; practicum. *Faculty:* 5 full-time, 1 part-time. *Financial Assistance:* assistantships, grants, student loans, scholarships.

University of Arizona. School of Information Resources and Library Science, 1515 E. First St., Tucson, AZ 85719. (520) 621-3565. Fax (520) 621-3279. E-mail wilka@u.arizona.edu. Web site http://www.sir.arizona.edu. C.D. Hurt, Professor and Dir. *Specializations:* M.A. and Ph.D. in Library Science. The School of Information Resources and Library Science offers courses focusing on the study of information and its impact as a social phenomenon. The School offers a M.A. degree with a major in Information Resources and Library Science, which is heavily weighted in technology and emphasizes theoretical constructs. Competence and adaptability in managing information and in utilizing advancing technologies are key aims of the curriculum. The program is fully accredited by the American Library Association. The School offers course work that leads toward the Ph.D. degree with a major in Library Science. *Features:* The School offers a virtual education program via the Internet. Between two and three courses are offered per semester. *Admission Requirements:* Please see the School's Web site. *Degree Requirements:* M.A.: a minimum of 36 units of graduate credit. Students may elect the thesis option replacing 6 units of course work. Ph.D.: at least 48 hours of course work in the major, a substantial number of hours in a minor subject supporting the major, dissertation. The University has a 12-unit residency requirement which may be completed in the summer or in a regular semester. More detailed descriptions of the program are available on the School's Web site. *Faculty*: 7. *Degrees Awarded 1996:* Master's, 108.

ARKANSAS

Arkansas Tech University. Russellville, AR 72801-2222. (501) 968-0434. Fax (501) 964-0811. E-mail SECZ@ATUVM.ATU.EDU. Connie Zimmer, Coord. *Specializations:* Master's degrees in Library Media Education and Computer Education (Training Program and General Program); NCATE accredited institution. *Admission Requirements:* GRE, 2.5 undergraduate GPA, Bachelor's degree. *Degree Requirements:* 36 semester hours, B average in major hours, comprehensive exam, thesis or action research project. *Faculty:* 1 full-time, 9 part-time. *Students:* 57 full-time, 30 part-time. *Financial Assistance:* assistantships, grants, student loans. *Degrees Awarded 1996:* 26.

University of Central Arkansas. Educational Media/Library Science, Campus Box 4918, Conway, AR 72035. (501) 450-5463. Fax (501) 450-5680. E-mail selvinr@cc1.uca.edu. Selvin W. Royal, Prof., Chair, Applied Academic Technologies. *Specializations:* M.S. in Educational Media/Library Science and Information Science. Tracks: School Library Media, Public Information Agencies, Media Information Studies. *Admission Requirements:* transcripts, GRE scores, 2 letters of recommendation, personal interview, written rationale for entering the profession. *Degree Requirements:* 36 semester hours, optional thesis, practicum (for School Library Media), professional research paper. *Faculty:* 5 full-time, 2 part-time. *Students:* 6 full-time, 42 part-time. *Financial Assistance:* 3 to 4 graduate assistantships each year, 7 grants, Federal Grant. *Degrees Awarded 1996:* 25.

CALIFORNIA

California State University-Dominguez Hills. 1000 E. Victoria St., Carson, CA 90747. (310) 243-3524. Fax (310) 243-3518. E-mail pdesberg@dhvx20.csudh.edu. Web site http://www. csudh.soe.edu. Peter Desberg, Prof., Coord., Computer-Based Education Program. *Specializations*: M.A. and Certificate in Computer-Based Education. *Admission Requirements*: 2.75 GPA. *Degree Requirements*: M.A.: 30 semester hours including project. Certificate: 15 hours. *Faculty*: 2 full-time, 2 part-time. *Students*: 50 full-time, 40 part-time. *Degrees Awarded 1996*: M.A., 24.

California State University-Los Angeles. Division of Educational Foundations and Interdivisional Studies, Charter School of Education, 5151 State University Drive, Los Angeles, CA 90032. (213) 343-4330. Fax (213) 343-5336. Web site http://web.calstatela.edu/academic/found/efis/index.html. Dr. Simeon P. Slovacek, Division Chairperson. *Specializations:* M.A. degree in Education, option in Instructional Technology or Computer Education. *Degree Requirements:* 2.75 GPA in last 90 qtr. units, 45 qtr. units, comprehensive written exam or thesis or project. Must also pass Writing Proficiency Examination (WPE), a California State University-Los Angeles requirement. *Faculty:* 7 full-time. *Degrees Awarded 1996:* approx. 15.

California State University-San Bernardino. 5500 University Parkway, San Bernardino, CA 92407. (909) 880-5600, (909) 880-5610. Fax (909) 880-7010. E-mail monaghan@wiley. csusb.edu. Web site http://soe.csusb.edu/soe/programs/eyec/. Dr. Jim Monaghan, Program Coord. *Specializations:* M.A. with two emphases: Video Production and Computer Applications. These emphases allow students to choose courses related to the design and creation of video products or courses involving lab and network operation of advanced microcomputer applications. The program does not require teaching credential certification. Advanced certificate programs in Educational Computing and Educational Technology are available. *Admission Requirements:* Bachelor's degree, appropriate work experience, 3.0 GPA, completion of introductory computer course and expository writing course. *Degree Requirements:* 48 units including a Master's project (33 units completed in residence); 3.0 GPA; grades of "C" or better in all courses. *Faculty:* 5 full-time, 1 part-time. *Students:* 106. *Financial Assistance:* Contact Office of Graduate Studies. *Degrees Awarded 1996:* 12.

San Diego State University. Educational Technology, San Diego, CA 92182-1182. (619) 594-6718. Fax (619) 594-6376. E-mail patrick.harrison@sdsu.edu. Web site http://edweb. sdsu.edu. Dr. Patrick Harrison, Prof., Chair. *Specialization:* Master's degree in Educational Technology with specializations in Computers in Education, Workforce Education, and Lifelong Learning. The Educational Technology Department participates in a College of Education joint doctoral program with The Claremont Graduate School. *Degree Requirements:* 36 semester hours (including 6 prerequisite hours), 950 GRE (verbal + quantitative). *Faculty:* 8 full-time, 5 part-time. *Students:* 120. *Financial Assistance:* graduate assistantships. *Degrees Awarded 1996:* Master's, 40.

*San Francisco State University. College of Education, Department of Instructional Technology, 1600 Holloway Ave., San Francisco, CA 94132. (415) 338-1509. Fax (415) 338-0510. E-mail michaels@sfsu.edu. Dr. Eugene Michaels, Chair; Mimi Kasner, Office Coord. *Specializations:* Master's degree with emphasis on Instructional Multimedia Design, Training and Designing Development, Instructional Computing, and Instructional Video Production. The school also offers an 18-unit Graduate Certificate in Training Systems Development, which can be incorporated into the Master's degree. *Features:* This program emphasizes the instructional systems approach, cognitivist principles of learning design, practical design experience, and project-based courses. *Admission Requirements:* Bachelor's degree, appropriate work experience, 2.5 GPA, interview with the department chair. *Degree Requirements:* 30 semester hours, field study thesis or project. *Faculty:* 3 full-time, 11 part-time. *Students:* 250-300. *Financial Assistance:* Contact Office of Financial Aid. *Degrees Awarded 1995:* 50.

United States International University. School of Education, 10455 Pomerado Rd., San Diego, CA 92131-1799. (619) 635-4715. Fax (619) 635-4714. E-mail feifer@sanac.usiu.edu. Richard Feifer, contact person. *Specializations:* Master's in Designing Technology for Learning, Planning Technology for Learning, and Technology Leadership for Learning. Ed.D. in Technology and Learning offers three specializations: Designing Technology for Learning, Planning Technology for Learning, and Technology Leadership for Learning. *Features:* interactive multimedia, cognitive approach to integrating technology and learning. *Admission Requirements:* Master's: English proficiency, interview, 3.0 GPA with 1900 GRE or 2.0 GPA with satisfactory MAT score. *Degree Requirements:* Ed.D.: 88 graduate qtr. units, dissertation. *Faculty:* 2 full-time, 4 part-time. *Students:* Master's, 32 full-time, 12 part-time; doctoral, 6 full-time, 1 part-time. *Financial Assistance:* internships, graduate assistantships, grants, student loans, scholarships. *Degrees Awarded 1996:* Master's, 40; Ed.D., 2.

University of Southern California. 702C W.P.H., School of Education, Los Angeles, CA 90089-0031. (213) 740-3288. Fax (213) 740-3889. Instructional Technology, Dept. of Educational Psychology and Technology. E-mail kazlausk@mizar.usc.edu. Dr. Richard Clark, Prof., Doctoral programs; Dr. Edward J. Kazlauskas, Prof., Program Chair, Master's programs in Instructional Technology. *Specializations:* M.A., Ed.D., Ph.D. to prepare individuals to teach instructional technology; manage educational media and training programs in business, industry, research and development organizations, schools, and higher educational institutions; perform research in instructional technology and media; and deal with computer-driven technology. Satellite Ed.D. program in Silicon Valley in northern California. A new Ed.D. program in Human Performance Technology was implemented in 1996. *Features:* special emphasis upon instructional design, systems analysis, and computer-based training. *Admission Requirements:* Bachelor's degree, 1000 GRE. *Degree Requirements:* M.A.: 28 semester hours, thesis optional. Doctoral: 67 units, 20 of which can be transferred from a previous Master's degree. Requirements for degree completion vary according to type of degree and individual interest. Ph.D. requires an outside field in addition to course work in instructional technology and education. *Faculty:* 5 full-time, 1 part-time. *Students:* M.A., 5 full-time, 15 part-time; doctoral, 3 full-time, 65 part-time. *Financial Assistance:* part-time, instructional technology-related work available in the Los Angeles area and on campus.

COLORADO

University of Colorado at Denver. School of Education, Campus Box 106, P.O. Box 173364, Denver, CO 80217-3364. (303) 556-8451. Fax (303) 556-4479. E-mail bwilson@carbon. cudenver.edu. Web site http://www.cudenver.edu/public/education/. Dian Walster, Program Chair, Formation and Learning Technologies, Division of Technology and Special Services. *Specializations:* Master's degree; Ph.D. in Educational Leadership and Innovation with emphasis in Curriculum, Learning, and Technology. *Features:* design and use of learning technologies; instructional design. Ph.D. students complete 10 semester hours of doctoral labs (small groups collaborating with faculty on difficult problems of practice). Throughout the program, students complete a product portfolio of research, design, teaching, and applied projects. The program is cross-disciplinary, drawing on expertise in technology, adult learning, systemic change, research methods, reflective practice, and cultural studies. *Admission Requirements:* Ph.D.: satisfactory GPA, GRE, writing sample, letters of recommendation, transcripts. *Degree Requirements:* Master's: 36 semester hours including 19 hours of core course work, comprehensive project, and portfolio; practicum and additional requirements for state certification in library media; internship required for careers in corporate settings. *Faculty:* 5 full-time, 3 part-time. *Students:* Master's, 4 full-time, 200 part-time; Ph.D., 12 full-time, 29 part-time. *Financial Assistance:* assistantships, internships. *Degrees Awarded 1996:* Master's, 32; Ph.D., 5.

University of Northern Colorado. Division of Educational Psychology, Statistics, and Technology, College of Education, Greeley, CO 80639. (970) 351-2687. Fax (970) 351-1622. E-mail caffarel@edtech.univnorthco.edu. Edward Caffarella, Prof., Chair, Educational Technology. *Specializations:* M.A. in Educational Technology; M.A. in Educational Media; Ph.D. in Educational Technology with emphases in Distance Education, Instructional Development/Design, Interactive Technology, and Technology Integration. *Features:* Graduates are prepared for careers as instructional technologists, course designers, trainers, instructional developers, media specialists, and human resource managers. *Admission Requirements:* M.A.: Bachelor's degree, 3.0 undergraduate GPA, 1500 GRE. Ph.D.: 3.2 GPA, three letters of recommendation, congruency between applicant's statement of career goals and program goals, 1650 GRE, interview with faculty. *Faculty:* 5 full-time, 2 part-time. *Students:* M.A., 6 full-time, 32 part-time; Ph.D., 14 full-time, 12 part-time. *Financial Assistance:* assistantships, grants, student loans, scholarships. *Degrees Awarded 1996:* M.A., 16; Ph.D., 4.

CONNECTICUT

Central Connecticut State University. 1615 Stanley St., New Britain, CT 06050. (860) 832-2130. Fax (860) 832-2109. E-mail abedf@ccsu.ctstateu.edu. Farough Abed, Coord., Educational Technology Program. *Specializations:* M.S. in Educational Technology. Curriculum emphases include Media Management, Materials Production, Librarianship, and Computer Technologies. *Features:* The program supports the Center for Innovation in Teaching and Technology to link students with client-based projects. *Admission Requirements:* Bachelor's degree, 2.7 undergraduate GPA. *Degree Requirements:* 33 semester hours, optional thesis or Master's final project (3 credits). *Faculty:* 2 full-time, 4 part-time. *Students:* 38. *Financial Assistance:* graduate assistant position. *Degrees Awarded 1996:* 12.

Fairfield University. N. Benson Road, Fairfield, CT 06430. (203) 254-4000. Fax (203) 254-4087. E-mail imhefzallah@fair1.fairfield.edu. Dr. Ibrahim M. Hefzallah, Prof., Dir., Media/Educational Technology Program; Dr. John Schurdak, Assoc. Prof., Dir., Computers in Education Program. *Specializations:* M.A. in Media/Educational Technology. A Certificate of Advanced Studies in Media/Educational Technology is available, which includes instructional development, television production, and media management; customized course of study also available. *Features:* emphasis on theory, practice, and new instructional developments in computers in education, multimedia, and satellite communications. *Admission Requirements:* Bachelor's degree from accredited institution with 2.67 GPA. *Degree Requirements:* 33 credits. *Faculty:* 2 full-time, 6 part-time. *Students:* 6 full-time, 54 part-time. *Financial Assistance:* assistantships, student loans. *Degrees Awarded 1996:* 12.

Southern Connecticut State University. Department of Library Science and Instructional Technology, 501 Crescent St., New Haven, CT 06515. (203) 392-5781. Fax (203) 392-5780. E-mail libscienceit@scsu.ctstateu.edu. Nancy Disbrow, Chair. *Specializations:* M.S. in Instructional Technology; Sixth-Year Professional Diploma Library-Information Studies (student may select area of specialization in Instructional Technology). *Degree Requirements:* for Instructional Technology only, 30 semester hours including 21 in media with comprehensive exam; 36 hours without exam. For sixth-year degree: 30 credit hours with 6 credit hours of core requirements, 9-15 credit hours in specialization. *Faculty:* 1 full-time. *Students:* 42 in M.S./IT program. *Financial Assistance:* graduate assistantship (salary $1,800 per semester; assistants pay tuition and a general university fee sufficient to defray cost of student accident insurance). *Degrees Awarded 1996:* M.S., 6.

University of Connecticut. U-64, Storrs, CT 06269-2064. (203) 486-0181. Fax (203) 486-0210. E-mail sbrown@UConnvm.UConn.edu, or myoung@UConnvm.UConn.edu. Web site http://www.ucc.uconn.edu/~wwwepsy/. Scott W. Brown, Chair; Michael Young, contact person. *Specializations:* Master's and Ph.D. degrees with an emphasis in Educational Technology as a specialization within the Program of Cognition and Instruction, in the Department of Educational Psychology. *Features:* The emphasis in Educational Technology is a unique program at UConn. It is co-sponsored by the Department of Educational Psychology in the School of Education and the Psychology Department in the College of Liberal Arts and Sciences. The emphasis in Educational Technology within the Cognition and Instruction Program seeks to provide students with knowledge of theory and applications regarding the use of advanced technology to enhance learning and thinking. This program provides suggested courses and opportunities for internships and independent study experiences that are directed toward an understanding of both the effects of technology on cognition and instruction, and the enhancement of thinking and learning with technology. Facilities include the UCEML computer lab featuring Mac and IBM networks upgraded for 1997 and a multimedia development center. The School of Education also features a multimedia classroom and auditorium. Faculty research interests include interactive videodisc for anchored instruction and situated learning, telecommunications for cognitive apprenticeship, technology-mediated interactivity for generative learning, and in cooperation with the National Research Center for Gifted and Talented, research on the use of technology to enhance cooperative learning and the development of gifted performance in all students. *Admission Requirements:* admission to the graduate school at Uconn, GRE scores (or other evidence of success at the graduate level). Previous experience in a related area of technology, education, or training is a plus. *Faculty:* The program in Cognition and Instruction has 7 full-time faculty; 2 full-time faculty administer the emphasis in Educational Technology. *Students:* Ph.D., 13. *Financial Assistance:* graduate assistantships, research fellowships, teaching assistantships, and federal and minority scholarships are available competitively. *Degrees Awarded 1996:* Ph.D., 2.

DISTRICT OF COLUMBIA

George Washington University. School of Education and Human Development, Washington, DC 20052. (202) 994-1701. Fax (202) 994-2145. Web site http://www.gwu.edu/~etl. Dr. William Lynch, Educational Technology Leadership Program. Program is offered through Jones Education Company (JEC). Contact student advisors at (800) 777-MIND. *Specialization:* M.A. in Education and Human Development with a major in Educational Technology Leadership. *Features:* 36-hour degree program available via cable television, satellite, Internet, and/or videotape to students across North America and in other locations. The degree is awarded by George Washington University (GWU). Students may work directly with JEC or GWU to enroll. Student advisors at JEC handle inquiries about the program, send out enrollment forms and applications, process book orders, and set up students on an electronic listserv or Web forum. *Admission Requirements:* application fee, transcripts, GRE or MAT scores (50th percentile), two letters of recommendation from academic professionals, computer access, undergraduate degree with 2.75 GPA. *Degree Requirements:* 36 credit hours (including 24 required hours). Required courses include computer application management, media and technology application, software implementation and design, public education policy, and quantitative research methods. *Faculty:* Courses are taught by GWU faculty. *Financial Assistance:* For information, contact the Office of Student Financial Assistance, GWU. Some cable systems that carry JEC offer local scholarships.

FLORIDA

Barry University. School of Education, 11300 N.E. Second Ave., Miami Shores, FL 33161. (305) 899-3608. Fax (305) 899-3718. E-mail jlevine@bu4090.barry.edu. Joel S. Levine, Dir. of Educational Computing and Technology Dept. *Specializations:* M.S. and Ed.S. in Educational Technology, Ph.D. degree in Educational Technology Leadership. *Features:* Majority of the courses (30/36) in M.S. and Ed.S. programs are in the field of Educational Technology. *Admission Requirements:* GRE scores, letters of recommendation, GPA, interview, achievements. *Degree Requirements:* M.S. or Ed. S.: 36 semester credit hours. Ph.D.: 54 credits beyond the Master's including dissertation credits. *Faculty:* 7 full-time, 10 part-time. *Students:* M.S., 8 full-time, 181 part-time; Ed.S., 5 full-time, 44 part-time; Ph.D., 3 full-time, 15 part-time. *Financial Assistance:* assistantships, student loans. *Degrees Awarded 1996:* M.S., 42; Ed.S., 8; Ph.D., 2.

Florida Institute of Technology. Science Education Department, 150 University Blvd., Melbourne, FL 32901-6988. (407) 768-8000, ext. 8126. Fax (407) 768-8000, ext. 7598. E-mail fronk@fit.edu. Dr. Robert Fronk, Dept. Head. Web site http://www.fit.edu/AcadRes/sci-ed/degree.html#comp-tech-ed. *Specializations*: Master's degree options in Computer Education and Instructional Technology; Ph.D. degree options in Computer Education and Instructional Technology. *Admission Requirements:* 3.0 GPA for regular admission; 2.75 for provisional admission. *Degree Requirements:* Master's: 33 semester hours (15 in computer or and technology education, 9 in education, 9 electives); practicum; no thesis or internship required. Ph.D.: 48 semester hours (12 in computer and technology education, 12 in education, 24 dissertation and research). *Faculty:* 5 full-time. *Students:* 10 full-time, 9 part-time. *Financial Assistance:* graduate student assistantships (full tuition plus stipend) available. *Degrees Awarded 1996:* Master's, 8; Ph.D., 4.

*Florida State University. Instructional Systems Program, Department of Educational Research, College of Education, 305 Stone Bldg., Tallahassee, FL 32306. (904) 644-4592. Fax (904) 644-8776. *Specializations:* M.S., Ed.S, Ph.D. in Instructional Systems with specializations for persons planning to work in academia, business, industry, government, or military. *Features:* Core courses include systems and materials development, analysis of media, project management, psychological foundations, current trends in instructional design, and research and statistics. Internships are recommended. *Admission Requirements:* M.S.: 3.0 GPA in last two years of undergraduate program, 550 TOEFL (for international applicants). Ph.D.: 1000 GRE (verbal + quantitative) or 3.3 GPA; international students, 550 TOEFL. *Degree Requirements:* M.S.: 36 semester hours, 2-4 hour internship, written comprehensive exam. *Faculty:* 5 full-time, 5 part-time. *Students:* M.S., 51; Ph.D., 45. *Financial Assistance:* some graduate research assistantships on faculty grants and contracts, university fellowships. *Degrees Awarded 1995:* M.S., 29; Ph.D., 15.

Jacksonville University. Division of Education, 2800 University Boulevard North, Jacksonville, FL 32211. (904) 745-7132. Fax (904) 745-7159. E-mail tvicker@junix.ju.edu. Dr. Tom Russ Vickery, Dir., MAT and Teacher Education Programs. *Specializations:* Master's degrees in Computer Education and in Educational Technology and Integrated Learning. *Features:* The Master's in Educational Technology and Integrated Learning is a program for certified teachers who wish to learn to use multimedia in their own instruction and to advance the incorporation of emerging technologies throughout the school. *Degree Requirements:* Computer Education: 36 hours, including 21 in computer science and 15 in education; comprehensive exam required. Educational Technology and Integrated Learning: 36 hours, including 6 in computer science and 30 in education; comprehensive exam to be done as a multimedia project. *Financial Assistance:* student loans and discounts to area teachers as well as to evening students.

Nova Southeastern University. Fischler Center for the Advancement of Education, 3301 College Ave., Fort Lauderdale, FL 33314. (954) 475-7440. (800) 986-3223, ext. 7440. Fax (954) 476-4764. E-mail gtep@fcae.nova.edu; pet@fcae.nova.edu. Web site http://www.fcae.nova.edu/. Dr. Abbey Manburg, Dir., programs in Instructional Technology and Distance Education (ITDE); Deo Nellis, Dir., Graduate Teacher Education Program. *Specializations:* Ed.S. and M.S. programs for teachers in Educational Technology, Educational Media, and Computer Science Education; M.S. and Ed.D. program in Instructional Technology and Distance Education (ITDE). *Features:* ITDE is delivered online via Internet to students worldwide, who also spend a few extended weekends on campus. *Admission Requirements:* B.A. or B.S. for M.S. and Ed.S. programs plus field experience. *Degree Requirements:* M.S.: 36 semester hours including practicum (1 to 1.5 years). Ed.S.: 62 semester hours including practicum (2 years). *Faculty:* 9 full-time, 40 part-time. *Students:* 100. *Financial Assistance:* student loans.

University of Central Florida. College of Education, ED Room 318, UCF, Orlando, FL 32816-1250. (407) 823-2153. Fax (407) 823-5622. Richard Cornell and Gary Orwig, Instructional Systems; Judy Lee, Educational Media; Glenda Gunter, Educational Technology. *Specializations:* M.A. in Instructional Technology/Instructional Systems; M.Ed. in Instructional Technology/Educational Media; M.A. in Instructional Technology/Educational Technology. A doctorate in Curriculum and Instruction with an emphasis on Instructional Technology is offered. *Admission Requirements:* interviews for Educational Media and Educational Technology programs. *Degree Requirements:* M.A. in Instructional Technology/ Instructional Systems, 39-42 semester hours; M.Ed. in Instructional Technology/Educational Media, 39-45 semester hours; M.A. in Instructional Technology/Educational Technology, 36-45 semester hours. Practicum required in all three programs; thesis, research project, or substitute additional course work. *Students:* Instructional Systems, 70; Educational Media, 35; Educational Technology, 50. Full-time, 120; part-time, 35. *Faculty:* 4 full-time, 6 part-time. *Financial Assistance:* competitive graduate assistantships in department and college, numerous paid internships, limited number of doctoral fellowships. *Degrees Awarded 1996:* 40.

*University of South Florida. School of Library and Information Science, Tampa, FL 33620. (813) 974-3520. Fax (813) 974-6840. Kathleen de la Peña McCook, Prof., Dir., School of Library and Information Science. *Specialization:* Master's degree. *Degree Requirements:* 36 semester hours; thesis optional. *Faculty:* 7 full-time, 5 part-time. *Degrees Awarded 1994-95:* 120.

GEORGIA

Georgia Southern University. College of Education, Statesboro, GA 30460-8131. (912) 681-5307. Fax (912) 681-5093. Kenneth F. Clark, Assoc. Prof., Dept. of Leadership, Technology, and Human Development. *Specialization:* M.Ed. The school also offers a six-year specialist degree program, and an Instructional Technology strand is available in the Ed.D. program in Curriculum Studies. *Features:* strong emphasis on technology. *Degree Requirements:* 60 qtr. credit hours, including a varying number of hours of media for individual students. *Faculty:* 4 full-time. *Financial Assistance:* See graduate catalog for general financial aid information.

Georgia State University. Middle-Secondary Education and Instructional Technology, University Plaza, Atlanta, GA 30303. (404) 651-2510. Fax (404) 651-2546. E-mail swharmon@gsu.edu. Dr. Stephen W. Harmon, contact person. *Specializations:* M.S. and Ph.D. in Instructional Technology. *Features:* focus on research and practical application of instructional technology. *Admission Requirements:* Bachelor's degree, 2.5 undergraduate GPA, 44 MAT or 800 GRE, 550 TOEFL. *Degree Requirements:* M.S.: 60 qtr. hours, internship. Ph.D: 110 hours, internship, dissertation. *Faculty:* 4 full-time, 3 part-time. *Students:* 30 full-time, 70 part-time. *Financial Assistance:* assistantships, grants, student loans.

State University of West Georgia (formerly West Georgia College). Department of Research, Media, and Technology, 137 Education Annex, Carrollton, GA 30118. (770) 836-6558. Fax (770) 836-6729. E-mail bmckenzi@westga.edu. Dr. Barbara K. McKenzie, Assoc. Prof., Chair. *Specializations:* M.Ed. with specializations in Media and Instructional Technology and add-on certification for students with Master's degrees in other disciplines. The school also offers an Ed.S. program in Media with two options, Media Specialist or Instructional Technology. The program strongly emphasizes technology in the schools. *Admission Requirements:* M.Ed.: 800 GRE, 44 MAT, 550 NTE Core, 2.5 undergraduate GPA. Ed.S.: 900 GRE, 48 MAT, or 575 NTE and 3.25 graduate GPA. *Degree Requirements:* 60 qtr. hours. *Faculty:* 4 full-time in Media/Technology and 2 in Research; 1 part-time in Media/Technology. *Students:* 8 full-time, 90 part-time. *Financial Assistance:* three graduate assistantships and three graduate research assistantships for the department. *Degrees Awarded 1996:* M.Ed., 20.

University of Georgia. Department of Instructional Technology, College of Education, 607 Aderhold Hall, Athens, GA 30602-7144. (706) 542-3810. Fax (706) 542-4032. E-mail kgustafs@ coe.uga.edu. Web site http://itech1.coe.uga.edu. Kent L. Gustafson, Prof. and Chair. *Specializations:* M.Ed. and Ed.S. in Instructional Technology or Computer-Based Education; Ph.D. for leadership positions as specialists in instructional design and development. The program offers advanced study for individuals with previous preparation in instructional media and technology, as well as a preparation for personnel in other professional fields requiring a specialty in instructional systems or instructional technology. Representative career fields for graduates include designing new courses, tutorial programs, and instructional materials in the military, industry, medical professional schools, allied health agencies, teacher education, staff development, state and local school systems, higher education, research, and in instructional products development. *Features:* minor areas of study available in a variety of other departments. Personalized programs are planned around a common core of courses and include practica, internships, or clinical experiences. Research activities include special assignments, applied projects, and task forces, as well as thesis and dissertation studies. *Admission Requirements:* Ph.D.: application to graduate school, satisfactory GRE score, other criteria as outlined in Graduate School Bulletin. *Degree Requirements:* Master's: 60 qtr. hours with 3.0 GPA, portfolio with oral exam. Ph.D.: three full years of study beyond Bachelor's degree, three consecutive quarters full-time residency, comprehensive exam with oral defense, dissertation with oral defense. *Faculty:* 10 full-time, 3 part-time. *Students:* M.Ed and Ed.S., 28 full-time, 47 part-time; Ph.D., 25 full-time, 10 part-time. *Financial Assistance:* graduate assistantships available. *Degrees Awarded 1996:* M.Ed. and Ed.S., 24; Ph.D., 2.

Valdosta State University. College of Education, 1500 N. Patterson St., Valdosta, GA 31698. (912) 333-5927. Fax (912) 333-7167. E-mail cprice@grits.valdosta.peachnet.edu. Catherine B. Price, Prof., Head, Dept. of Instructional Technology. *Specializations:* M.Ed. in Instructional Technology with three tracks: Library/Media, Technology Leadership, or Technology Applications. Ed.S. in Instructional Technology with two tracks: Library/Media, Technology Leadership. *Features:* The program has a strong emphasis on technology in M.Ed. and Ed.S.; strong emphasis on applied research in Ed.S. *Admission Requirements:* M.Ed.: 2.5 GPA, 750 GRE. Ed.S.: Master's in Instructional Technology or related area, 3.0 GPA, 850 GRE. *Degree Requirements:* M.Ed.: 36 semester hours. Ed.S.: 30 semester hours. *Faculty:* 6 full-time, 3 part-time. *Students:* 15 full-time, 90 part-time. *Financial Assistance:* graduate assistantships, student loans, scholarships. *Degrees Awarded 1996:* M.Ed., 12; Ed.S., 0 (new program).

HAWAII

University of Hawaii-Manoa. Educational Technology Department, 1776 University Ave., Honolulu, HI 96822. (808) 956-7671. Fax (808) 956-3905. E-mail ETDEPT-L@uhunixuhcc hawaii.edu. Web site http://pegasus.ed/hawaii.edu/edtech. Geoffrey Z. Kucera, Prof., Chair, Educational Technology Dept. *Specialization:* M.Ed. in Educational Technology. *Degree Requirements:* 39 semester hours (all in educational technology, including 3 in practicum, 3 in internship), thesis and non-thesis available. *Faculty:* 3 full-time, 3 part-time. *Students:* 4 full-time, 32 part-time. *Financial Assistance:* Consideration given to meritorious second-year students for tuition waivers and scholarship applications. *Degrees Awarded July 1995 through June 1996:* 3.

IDAHO

Boise State University. Division of Continuing Education-IPT, 1910 University Drive, Boise, ID 83725. (208) 385-4457, (800) 824-7017 ext. 4457. Fax (208) 385-3467. E-mail bsu-ipt@ micron.net. Dr. David Cox, IPT Program Dir.; Jo Ann Fenner, IPT Program Developer and distance program contact person. *Specialization:* M.S. in Instructional & Performance Technology available in a traditional campus setting or via computer conferencing to students located anywhere on the North American continent. The program is fully accredited by the Northwest Association of Schools and Colleges and is the recipient of an NUCEA award for

Outstanding Credit Program offered by distance education methods. *Features:* Leading experts in learning styles, evaluation, and leadership principles serve as adjunct faculty in the program via computer and modem from their various remote locations. *Admission Requirements:* undergraduate degree with 3.0 GPA, one-to-two page essay describing why you want to pursue this program and how it will contribute to your personal and professional development, and a resume of personal qualifications and work experience. *Degree Requirements:* 36 semester hours in instructional and performance technology and related course work; project or thesis available for on-campus program and an oral comprehensive exam required for distance program (included in 36 credit hours). *Faculty:* 3 full-time, 7 part-time. *Students:* 140 part-time. *Financial Assistance:* DANTES funding for some military personnel, low-interest loans to eligible students, graduate assistantships for on-campus enrollees. *Degrees Awarded 1996:* 12. (A total of 73 degrees have been awarded since the program's first graduates in 1989.)

ILLINOIS

Chicago State University. Department of Library Science and Communications Media, Chicago, IL 60628. (312) 995-2278, (312) 995-2503. Fax (312) 995-2473. Janice Bolt, Prof., Chair, Dept. of Library Science and Communications Media. *Specialization:* Master's degree in School Media. Program has been approved by NCATE: AECT/AASL through accreditation of University College of Education; State of Illinois Entitlement Program. *Admission Requirements:* teacher's certification or Bachelor's in Education; any B.A. or B.S. *Degree Requirements:* 36 semester hours; thesis optional. *Faculty:* 2 full-time, 5 part-time. *Students:* 88 part-time. *Financial Assistance:* assistantships, grants, student loans. *Degrees Awarded 1996:* 15.

Concordia University. 7400 Augusta St., River Forest, IL 60305-1499. (708) 209-3088. Fax (708) 209-3176. E-mail boosmb@crf.cuis.edu. Web site http://www.curf.edu. Dr. Manfred Boos, Chair, Mathematics/Computer Science Education Dept. *Specialization:* M.A. in Computer Science Education. *Admission Requirements:* 2.85 GPA (2.25 to 2.85 for provisional status); Bachelor's degree from regionally accredited institution; two letters of recommendation. *Degree Requirements:* 33 semester hours of course work. *Faculty:* 7 full-time, 5 part-time. *Students:* 16 part-time. *Financial Assistance:* a number of graduate assistantships, Stafford student loans, Supplement Loan for Students. *Degrees Awarded 1996:* 4.

Governors State University. College of Arts and Sciences, University Park, IL 60466. (708) 534-4082. Fax (708) 534-7895. Michael Stelnicki, Prof., Human Performance and Training. *Specializations:* M.A. in Communication with HP&T major. *Features:* emphasizes 3 professional areas: Instructional Design, Performance Analysis, and Design Logistics. *Degree Requirements:* 36 credit hours (trimester), all in instructional and performance technology; internship or advanced field project required. Metropolitan Chicago area based. *Faculty:* 2 full-time. *Students:* 38 part-time. *Degrees Awarded 1996:* 8.

Northern Illinois University. LEPS Department, College of Education, DeKalb, IL 60115-2896. (815) 753-0464. Fax (815) 753-9371. E-mail LSTOTT@NIU.EDU. Dr. James Lockard, Chair, Instructional Technology. *Specializations:* M.S.Ed. in Instructional Technology with concentrations in Instructional Design, Educational Computing, and Media Administration; Ed.D. in Instructional Technology, emphasizing instructional design and development, computer education, media administration, and preparation for careers in business, industry, and higher education. In addition, Illinois state certification in school library media is offered in conjunction with either degree or alone. *Features:* considerable flexibility in course selection, including advanced seminars, numerous practicum and internship opportunities, individual study, and research. Program is highly individualized. More than 60 courses offered by several departments or faculties, including communications, radio/television/film, art, journalism, educational psychology, computer science, and research and evaluation. Facilities include well-equipped computer labs. Students are encouraged to create individualized Web pages. Master's program started in 1968, doctorate in 1970. *Admission Requirements:* M.S.: 2.75

undergraduate GPA, GRE verbal and quantitative scores, two references. Ed.D.: 3.5 M.S. GPA, GRE verbal and quantitative scores (waiver possible), writing sample, three references. *Degree Requirements:* M.S.: 39 hours, including 30 in instructional technology; no thesis. Ed.D.: 63 hours beyond Master's, including 15 hours for dissertation. *Faculty:* 8 full-time, 8 part-time. *Students:* M.S., 135 part-time; Ed.D., 115 part-time. *Financial Assistance:* assistantships available at times in various departments, scholarships, minority assistance. *Degrees Awarded 1996:* M.S., 20; Ed.D., 5.

Southern Illinois University at Carbondale. Department of Curriculum and Instruction, Carbondale, IL 62901-4610. (618) 536-2441. Fax (618) 453-4244. E-mail sashrock@siu.edu. Sharon Shrock, Coord., Instructional Technology/Development. *Specializations:* M.S. in Education with specializations in Instructional Development and Instructional Technology; Ph.D. in Education including specialization in Instructional Technology. *Features:* All specializations are oriented to multiple education settings. The ID program emphasizes nonschool (primarily corporate) learning environments. *Admission Requirements:* M.S.: Bachelor's degree, 2.7 undergraduate GPA, transcripts. Ph.D.: Master's degree, 3.25 GPA, MAT or GRE scores, letters of recommendation, transcripts, writing sample. *Faculty:* 5 full-time, 2 part-time. *Students:* 80 Master's, 27 Ph.D. *Financial Assistance:* some graduate assistantships and scholarships available to qualified students. *Degrees Awarded 1996:* Master's, 15; Ph.D., 3.

Southern Illinois University at Edwardsville. Instructional Technology Program, School of Education, Edwardsville, IL 62026-1125. (618) 692-3277. Fax (618) 692-3359. E-mail cnelson@siue.edu. Dr. Charles E. Nelson, Dir., Dept. of Educational Leadership. *Specialization:* M.S. in Education with concentrations in Library/Media Specialist or Instructional Systems Design Specialist. *Features:* evening classes only. *Degree Requirements:* 36 semester hours; thesis optional. *Faculty:* 6 part-time. *Students:* 125. *Degrees Awarded 1996:* 18.

University of Illinois at Urbana-Champaign. Department of Educational Psychology, 210 Education Bldg., 1310 S. 6th St., Champaign, IL 61820. (217) 333-2245. Fax (217) 244-7620. E-mail c-west@uiuc.edu. Charles K. West, Prof., Div. of Learning and Instruction, Dept. of Educational Psychology. *Specializations:* M.A., M.S., and Ed.M. with emphasis in Instructional Design and Educational Computing. Ph.D. in Educational Psychology with emphasis in Instructional Design and Educational Computing. *Features:* Ph.D. program is individually tailored and strongly research-oriented with emphasis on applications of cognitive science to instruction. *Admission Requirements:* Ph.D.: excellent academic record, high GRE scores, and strong letters of recommendation. *Degree Requirements:* 8 units for Ed.M., 6 units and thesis for M.A. or M.S. *Faculty:* 13. *Students:* 38. *Financial Assistance:* scholarships, research assistantships, and teaching assistantships available; fellowships for very highly academically talented; some tuition waivers. *Degrees Awarded 1996:* Ph.D., 4.

Western Illinois University. Instructional Technology and Telecommunications, 37 Harrabin Hall, Macomb, IL 61455. (309) 298-1952. Fax (309) 298-2978. E-mail bo-barker@wiu.edu. Bruce O. Barker, Chair. *Specialization:* Master's degree. *Features:* new program approved by Illinois Board of Higher Education in January 1996 with emphases in Instructional Technology, Telecommunications, Interactive Technologies, and Distance Education. Selected courses delivered via satellite TV and compressed video. *Admission Requirements:* Bachelor's degree. *Degree Requirements:* 32 semester hours, thesis or practicum. *Faculty:* 7 full-time. *Students:* 15 full-time, 105 part-time. *Financial Assistance:* graduate and research assistantships, internships, residence hall assistants, veterans' benefits, loans, and part-time employment. *Degrees Awarded 1996:* 8 (program is now in its first full year of operation.)

INDIANA

Indiana State University. Dept. of Curriculum, Instruction, and Media Technology, Terre Haute, IN 47809. (812) 237-2937. Fax (812) 237-4348. E-mail efthomp@befac.indstate.edu. Dr. James E. Thompson, Program Coord. *Specializations:* Master's degree; Specialist Degree program in Instructional Technology; Ph.D. in Curriculum, Instruction with specialization in

Media Technology. *Degree Requirements:* Master's: 32 semester hours, including 18 in media; thesis optional. *Faculty:* 5 full-time. *Students:* 17 full-time, 13 part-time. *Financial Assistance:* 7 assistantships. *Degrees Awarded 1996:* Master's, 7; Specialist, 1.

Indiana University. School of Education, W. W. Wright Education Bldg., Rm 2276, 201 N. Rose Ave., Bloomington, IN 47405-1006. (812) 856-8451 (information), (812) 856-8239 (admissions). Fax (812) 856-8239. Thomas Schwen, Chair, Dept. of Instructional Systems Technology. *Specializations:* M.S. and Ed.S. degrees designed for individuals seeking to be practitioners in the field of Instructional Technology. Offers Ph.D. and Ed.D. degrees with four program focus areas: Foundations; Instructional Analysis, Design, and Development; Instructional Development and Production; and Implementation and Management. *Features:* requires computer skills as a prerequisite and makes technology utilization an integral part of the curriculum; eliminates separation of various media formats; and establishes a series of courses of increasing complexity integrating production and development. The latest in technical capabilities have been incorporated in the new Center for Excellence in Education, including teaching, photographic, computer, and science laboratories, a 14-station multimedia laboratory, and television studios. *Admission Requirements:* M.S.: Bachelor's degree from an accredited institution, 1350 GRE (3 tests required), 2.65 undergraduate GPA. Ed.D and Ph.D: 1550 GRE (3 tests required), 3.5 graduate GPA. *Degree Requirements:* M.S.: 40 credit hours (including 16 credits in required courses); colloquia; an instructional product or Master's thesis; and 12 credits in outside electives. Ed.D.: 60 hours in addition to previous Master's degree, thesis. Ph.D.: 90 hours, thesis. *Faculty:* 6 full-time, 5 part-time. *Financial Assistance:* assistantships, scholarships. *Degrees Awarded 1996:* M.S., 59; Ed.S., 1; Ed.D., 1; Ph.D.: 5.

Purdue University. School of Education, Department of Curriculum and Instruction, W. Lafayette, IN 47907-1442. (317) 494-5673. Fax (317) 494-1622. Dr. James D. Russell, Prof. of Educational Technology. *Specializations:* Master's degree, Educational Specialist, and Ph.D. in Educational Technology and Instructional Development. Master's program started in 1982, Specialist and Ph.D. in 1985. *Admission Requirements:* Master's and Ed.S.: 3.0 GPA, three letters of recommendation, statement of personal goals. Ph.D.: 3.0 GPA, three letters of recommendation, statement of personal goals, 1000 GRE. *Degree Requirements:* Master's: 36 semester hours (15 in educational technology, 9 in education, 12 unspecified); thesis optional. Specialist: 60-65 semester hours (15-18 in educational technology, 30-35 in education); thesis, internship, practicum. Ph.D.: 90 semester hours (15-18 in educational technology, 42-45 in education); thesis, internship, practicum. *Faculty:* 6 full-time. *Students:* M.S. and Ed.S, 12 full-time, 20 part-time; Ph.D., 12 full-time, 24 part-time. *Financial Assistance:* assistantships and fellowships. *Degrees Awarded 1996:* Master's, 15; Ph.D., 8.

IOWA

Dubuque Tri-College Department of Education (a consortium of Clarke College, The University of Dubuque, and Loras College). Graduate Studies, 1550 Clarke Drive, Dubuque, IA 52001. (319) 588-6331. Fax (319) 588-6789. E-mail RADAMS@KELLER.CLARKE. EDU. Robert Adams, Clarke College, (319) 588-6416. *Specializations:* M.A. in Technology and Education. *Admission Requirements:* 2.5 GPA, GRE (verbal + quantitative) or MAT, $25 application fee, two letters of recommendation. *Degree Requirements:* 25 semester hours in computer courses, 12 hours in education. *Faculty:* 1 full-time, 1-2 part-time. *Students:* 20 part-time. *Financial Assistance:* scholarships, student loans. *Degrees Awarded 1996:* 0 (first graduates due in 1997).

Iowa State University. College of Education, Ames, IA 50011. (515) 294-6840. Fax (515) 294-9284. E-mail mrs@iastate.edu. Michael Simonson, Prof. and Coord., Curriculum and Instruction Technology (including Media and Computers). *Specializations:* M.S., M.Ed., and Ph.D. in Curriculum and Instructional Technology with specializations in Instructional Computing, Instructional Design, and Distance Education; Ph.D. in Education with emphasis in Instructional Computing, Instructional Design, and Technology Research. Participates in Iowa

Distance Education Alliance, Iowa Star Schools Project. *Features:* practicum experiences related to professional objectives, supervised study and research projects tied to long-term studies within the program, development and implementation of new techniques, teaching strategies, and operational procedures in instructional resources centers and computer labs. *Admission Requirements:* M.S. and M.Ed.: three letters, top half of undergraduate class, autobiography. Ph.D.: the same plus GRE scores. *Degree Requirements:* Master's: 30 semester hours, thesis, no internship or practicum. Ph.D.: 78 semester hours, thesis, no internship or practicum. *Faculty:* 4 full-time, 6 part-time. *Students:* Master's, 40 full-time, 40 part-time; Ph.D., 30 full-time, 20 part-time. *Financial Assistance:* 10 assistantships. *Degrees Awarded 1996:* Master's, 12; Ph.D., 6.

University of Iowa. Division of Psychological and Quantitative Foundations, College of Education, Iowa City, IA 52242. (319) 335-5519. Fax (319) 335-5386. Web site http://www. uiowa.edu/~coe2/facstaff/salessi.htm. Stephen Alessi, 361 Lindquist Center, Iowa City, IA 52242. *Specializations:* M.A. and Ph.D. with specializations in Training and Human Resources Development, Computer Applications, and Media Design and Production (MA only). *Features:* flexibility in planning to fit individual needs, backgrounds, and career goals. The program is interdisciplinary, involving courses within divisions of the College of Education, as well as in the schools of Business, Library Science, Radio and Television, Linguistics, and Psychology. *Admission Requirements:* MA: 2.8 undergraduate GPA, 500 GRE (quantitative + verbal), personal letter of interest. Ph.D.: Master's degree, 1000 GRE (verbal + quantitative), 3.2 GPA on all previous graduate work for regular admission. (Conditional admission may be granted.) Teaching or relevant experience may be helpful. *Degree Requirements:* MA: 35 semester hours, 3.0 GPA, final project or thesis, comprehensive exam. Ph.D.: 90 semester hours, comprehensive exams, dissertation. *Faculty:* 4 full-time, 3 part-time. *Financial Assistance:* assistantships, grants, student loans, and scholarships.

University of Northern Iowa. Educational Technology Program, Cedar Falls, IA 50614-0606. (319) 273-3250. Fax (319) 273-5886. E-mail Smaldinos@uni.edu. Sharon E. Smaldino, contact person. *Specialization:* M.A. in Educational Technology, M.A. in Communications and Training Technology. *Admission Requirements:* Bachelor's degree, 3.0 undergraduate GPA, 500 TOEFL. *Degree Requirements:* 38 semester credits, optional thesis worth 6 credits or alternative research paper of project, comprehensive exam. *Faculty:* 2 full-time, 6 part-time. *Students:* 120. *Financial Assistance:* assistantships, grants, student loans, scholarships, student employment. *Degrees Awarded 1996:* 25.

KANSAS

Emporia State University. School of Library and Information Management, 1200 Commercial, P.O. Box 4025, Emporia, KS 66801. (316) 341-5203. Fax (316) 341-5233. E-mail vowellfa@esumail.emporia.edu. Faye N. Vowell, Dean. *Specializations:* Master's of Library Science (ALA accredited program); School Library Certification program, which includes 27 hours of the M.L.S. program; Ph.D. in Library and Information Management. *Features:* The M.L.S. program is also available in Colorado, Oregon, Utah, and Nebraska. Internet courses are under development. *Admission Requirements:* selective admissions process for M.L.S. and Ph.D. based on a combination of admission criteria, including (but not limited to) GRE or TOEFL score, personal interview, GPA, statement of goals and references. Request admission packet for specific criteria. *Degree Requirements:* M.L.S.: 42 semester hours, comprehensive exam. Ph.D.: total of 83-97 semester hours depending on the number of hours received for an M.L.S. *Faculty:* 12 full-time, 35 part-time. *Students:* 100 full-time, 500 part-time in all sites. *Financial Assistance:* assistantships, grants, student loans, scholarships.

Kansas State University. Educational Computing, Design, and Telecommunications, 363 Bluemont Hall, Manhattan, KS 66506. (913) 532-7686. Fax (913) 532-7304. E-mail dmcgrath@coe.educ.ksu.edu. Dr. Diane McGrath, contact person. *Specializations:* M.S. in Secondary Education with an emphasis in Educational Computing; Ph.D. and Ed.D. in

Curriculum & Instruction with an emphasis in Educational Computing, Design, and Telecommunications. Master's program started in 1982; doctoral in 1987. *Admissions Requirements:* M.S.: B average in undergraduate work, one programming language, 590 TOEFL. Ed.D. and Ph.D.: B average in undergraduate and graduate work, one programming language, GRE or MAT, three letters of recommendation, experience or course in educational computing. *Degree Requirements:* M.S.: 30 semester hours (minimum of 12 in Educational Computing); thesis, internship, or practicum not required, but all three are possible. Ed.D.: 94 semester hours (minimum of 18 hours in Educational Computing or related area approved by committee, 16 hours dissertation research, 12 hours internship); thesis. Ph.D.: 90 semester hours (minimum of 21 hours in Educational Computing, Design, and Telecommunications or related area approved by committee, 30 hours for dissertation research); thesis; internship or practicum not required but available. *Faculty:* 2 full-time, 1 part-time. *Students:* M.S., 3 full-time, 36 part-time; doctoral, 9 full-time, 19 part-time. *Financial Assistance:* two assistantships; other assistantships sometimes available in other departments depending on skills and funds available. *Degrees Awarded 1996:* M.S., 15; Ph.D., 2.

KENTUCKY

University of Louisville. School of Education, Louisville, KY 40292. (502) 852-0609. Fax (502) 852-1417. E-mail crrude01@ulkyvm.louisville.edu. Carolyn Rude-Parkins, Dir., Education Resource & Technology Center. *Specialization:* M.Ed. in Occupational Education with Instructional Technology focus. *Features:* technology courses appropriate for business or school audiences. Program has newly undergone revision, offering more classes and sections. *Admission Requirements:* 2.75 GPA, 800 GRE, 2 letters of recommendation, application fee. *Degree Requirements:* 30 semester hours, thesis optional. *Faculty:* 2 full-time, 1 part-time. *Students:* 3 full-time, 17 part-time. *Financial Assistance:* graduate assistantships. *Degrees Awarded 1996:* 4.

LOUISIANA

Louisiana State University. School of Library and Information Science, Baton Rouge, LA 70803. (504) 388-3158. Fax (504) 388-4581. Bert R. Boyce, Dean, Prof., School of Library and Information Science. *Specializations:* M.L.I.S., C.L.I.S. (post-Master's certificate), Louisiana School Library Certification. An advanced certificate program is available. *Degree Requirements:* M.L.I.S.: 37 hours, comprehensive exam, one semester full-time residence, completion of degree program in five years. *Faculty:* 10 full-time. *Students:* 72 full-time, 74 part-time. *Financial Assistance:* A large number of graduate assistantships are available to qualified students.

MARYLAND

The Johns Hopkins University. School of Continuing Studies, Division of Education, Center for Technology in Education, 2500 E. Northern Parkway, Baltimore, MD 21214-1113. (410) 254-8466. Fax (410) 254-8266. E-mail jnunn@jhunix.hcf.jhu.edu. Dr. Jacqueline A. Nunn, Dir., Center for Technology in Education. *Specialization:* M.S. in Education with major in Technology for Educators; M.S. in Special Education with major in Technology in Special Education. *Features:* focuses on training educators to become decision makers and leaders in the use of technology, with competencies in the design, development, and application of emerging technologies for teaching and learning. Incorporates basic elements that take into account the needs of adult learners, the constantly changing nature of technology, and the need for schools and universities to work together for schoolwide change. *Admission Requirements:* Bachelor's degree with strong background in teaching, curriculum and instruction, special education, or a related service field. *Degree Requirements:* M.S. in Education, Technology for Educators: 36 semester hours (including 9 credits technical courses, 18 credits instructional courses, 9 credits research and school improvement courses). M.S. in Special Education, Technology in Special Education: 36 semester hours (including 9 credits technical courses, 15 credits instructional courses, 12 credits research and school improvement courses). *Faculty:* 2 full-time, 30 part-time. *Students:* 161 part-time. *Financial Assistance:* grants, student loans, scholarships. *Degrees Awarded 1996:* 38.

Towson State University. College of Education, Hawkins Hall, Rm. 206, Towson, MD 21204. (410) 830-2194. Fax (410) 830-2733. E-mail rosecransg@toe.towson.edu. Web site http://www.towson.edu/~coe/istc.html. Dr. Gary W. Rosecrans, Assoc. Prof., General Education Dept. *Specializations:* M.S. degrees in Instructional Development and School Library Media. *Admission Requirements:* Bachelor's degree from accredited institution with 3.0 GPA. (Conditional admission required 2.5 GPA.) Instructional Development program requires media utilization course as prerequisite. School Media program requires teacher certification or completion of specified course work in education. *Degree Requirements:* 36 graduate semester hours without thesis; 33 hours with thesis. *Faculty:* 7 full-time, 4 adjunct. *Students:* 150. *Financial Assistance:* graduate assistantships, work assistance, scholarships. *Degrees Awarded 1996:* 7.

University of Maryland. College of Library and Information Services, 4105 Hornbake Library Bldg., South Wing, College Park, MD 20742-4345. (301) 405-2038. Fax (301) 314-9145. Ann Prentice, Dean and Program Chair. *Specializations:* Master's of Library Science, including specialization in School Library Media; doctorate in Library and Information Services; Ph.D. in Library Science and Educational Technology/Instructional Communication. *Features:* Program is broadly conceived and interdisciplinary in nature, using the resources of the entire campus. The student and the advisor design a program of study and research to fit the student's background, interests, and professional objectives. Students prepare for careers in teaching and research in information science and librarianship and elect concentrations including Educational Technology and Instructional Communication. *Admission Requirements:* doctoral: Bachelor's degree (the majority enter with Master's degrees in Library Science, Educational Technology, or other relevant disciplines), GRE general tests, three letters of recommendation, statement of purpose. Interviews required when feasible. *Degree Requirements:* MLS: 36 semester hours; thesis optional. *Faculty:* 15 full-time, 8 part-time. *Students:* Master's, 106 full-time, 149 part-time; doctoral, 5 full-time, 11 part-time. *Financial Assistance:* assistantships, grants, student loans, scholarships. *Degrees Awarded 1996:* Master's, 109.

University of Maryland, Baltimore County (UMBC). Department of Education, 1000 Hilltop Circle, Baltimore, MD 21250. (410) 455-2310. Fax (410) 455-3986. Dr. William R. Johnson, Dir., Graduate Programs in Education. *Specializations:* Master's degrees in School Instructional Systems, Post-Baccalaureate Teacher Certification, Training in Business and Industry. *Admissions Requirements:* 3.0 undergraduate GPA, GRE scores. *Degree Requirements:* 36 semester hours (including 18 in systems development for each program); internship. *Faculty:* 15 full-time, 25 part-time. *Students:* 63 full-time, 274 part-time. *Financial Assistance:* assistantships, scholarships. *Degrees Awarded 1996:* 67.

Western Maryland College. Department of Education, Main St., Westminster, MD 21157. (410) 857-2507. Fax (410) 857-2515. E-mail rkerby@ns1.wmc.car.md.us. Dr. Ramona N. Kerby, Coord., School Library Media Program, Dept. of Education. *Specializations:* M.S. in School Library Media. *Degree Requirements:* 33 credit hours (including 19 in media and 6 in education), comprehensive exam. *Faculty:* 1 full-time, 7 part-time. *Students:* 120.

MASSACHUSETTS

Boston University. School of Education, 605 Commonwealth Ave., Boston, MA 02215-1605. (617) 353-3181. Fax (617) 353-3924. E-mail whittier@bu.edu. Web site http://web.bu.edu/EDUCATION. David B. Whittier, Asst. Professor and Coord., Program in Educational Media and Technology. *Specializations:* Ed.M., CAGS in Educational Media and Technology; Ed.D. in Curriculum and Teaching, Specializing in Educational Media and Technology; preparation for Massachusetts public school certificates as Library Media Specialist and

Instructional Technologist. The Master's Program prepares graduates for professional careers as educators, instructional designers, developers of educational materials, and managers of the human and technology-based resources necessary to support education and training with technology. Graduates are employed in settings such as K-12 schools, higher education, industry, medicine, government, and publishing. Students come to the program from many different backgrounds and with a wide range of professional goals. The doctoral program sets the study of Educational Media & Technology within the context of education and educational research in general, and curriculum and teaching in particular. In addition to advanced work in the field of Educational Media and Technology, students examine and conduct research and study the history of educational thought and practice relating to teaching and learning. Graduates make careers in education as professors and researchers, technology directors and managers, and as developers of technology-based materials and systems. Graduates also make careers in medicine, government, business, and industry as instructional designers, program developers, project managers, and training directors. Graduates who work in both educational and non-educational organizations are often responsible for managing the human and techno-logical resources required to create learning experiences that include the development and delivery of technology-based materials and distance education. *Features:* Ed.M.: 36 credit hours (including 22 hours from required core curriculum, 14 from electives). The core curriculum sets the study of Educational Media & Technology within the context of general education and gives all students a foundation of knowledge of instructional design, learning theory, historical and contemporary. *Admission Requirements:* Ed.D.: 3 letters of recommen-dation, 50 MAT or GRE scores, transcripts, writing samples, statement of goals and qualifica-tions, analytical essay, 2.7 GPA. *Degree Requirements:* Ed.D.: 60 credit hours of courses in Educational Media and Technology, curriculum and teaching, and educational thought and practice with comprehensive exams; course work and apprenticeship in research; 60 credit hours; dissertation. *Faculty:* 1 full-time, 1 half-time, 10 part-time. *Students:* 2 full-time, 12 part-time. *Financial Assistance:* assistantships, grants, student loans, scholarships. *Degrees Awarded 1996:* Ed.M., 7; Ed.D., 3.

Fitchburg State College. Division of Graduate and Continuing Education, 160 Pearl St., Fitchburg, MA 01420. (508) 665-3181. Fax (508) 665-3658. E-mail dgce@fsc.edu. Dr. Elena Kyle, Chair. *Specialization:* M.S. in Communications Media with specializations in Manage-ment and Instructional Technology. *Features:* Collaborating with professionals working in the field both for organizations and as independent producers, Fitchburg offers a unique M.S. program. Building on communications experience, this program enables students to layer on the knowledge and skills for effectively developing and managing communications and media operations. *Admission Requirements:* MAT or GRE scores, two or more years of experience in communications or media, department interview and portfolio presentation, three letters of recommendation. *Degree Requirements:* 36 semester credit hours. *Faculty:* 1 full-time, 5 part-time. *Students:* 25 part-time. *Financial assistance:* assistantships, student loans, scholar-ships. *Degrees Awarded 1996:* 18.

Harvard University. Appian Way, Cambridge, MA 02138. (617) 495-3541. Fax (617) 495-3626. E-mail Admit@hugse2.harvard.edu. Web site http://GSEWeb.harvard.edu/TIEHome.html. George Brackett, Interim Dir. of Technology in Education Program. *Speciali-zation:* M.Ed. in Technology in Education; an advanced certificate program is available. *Admission Requirements:* Bachelor's degree, MAT or GRE scores, 600 TOEFL, 3 recommen-dations. Students interested in print information about the TIE Program should E-mail a request to the address above. *Degree Requirements:* 32 semester credits. *Faculty:* 1 full-time, 10 part-time. *Students:* approx. 45. *Financial Assistance:* within the school's policy. *Degrees Awarded 1996:* 38.

Lesley College. 29 Everett St., Cambridge, MA 02138-2790. (617) 349-8419. Fax (617) 349-8169. E-mail nroberts@mail.lesley.edu. Dr. Nancy Roberts, Prof. of Education. *Speciali-zations:* M.Ed. in Technology Education; C.A.G.S. in Technology Education; Ph.D in Educa-tion with a Technology Education major. *Features:* M.Ed. program is offered off-campus at

45 sites in 16 states; contact Professional Outreach Associates [(800) 843-4808] for information. *Degree Requirements:* M.Ed.: 33 semester hours in technology, integrative final project in lieu of thesis, no internship or practicum. Specialist: 36 semester hours. Ph.D. requirements available on request. *Faculty:* 7 full-time, 122 part-time on the Master's and specialist levels. *Students:* 968 part-time. *Degrees Awarded 1996:* 450.

Simmons College. Graduate School of Library and Information Science, 300 The Fenway, Boston, MA 02115-5898. (617) 521-2800. Fax (617) 521-3192. E-mail jmatarazzo@vmsvaxsimmons.edu. Dr. James M. Matarazzo, Dean. *Specializations:* M.S. Dual degrees: D.H./M.L.S.; M.L.S./H.S. in Education (for School Library Media Specialists); M.L.S./M.A. in History (Archives Management Program). A Doctor of Arts in Administration is also offered. *Features:* The program prepares individuals for a variety of careers, media technology emphasis being only one. There are special programs for Unified Media Specialist and Archives Management with strengths in Information Science/Systems, Media Management. *Admission Requirements:* B.A. or B.S. degree with 3.0 GPA, statement, three letters of reference. *Degree Requirements:* 36 semester hours. *Faculty:* 14 full-time. *Students:* 75 full-time, 393 part-time. *Financial Assistance:* assistantships, grants, student loans, scholarships. *Degrees Awarded 1996:* Master's, 208.

University of Massachusetts-Boston. Graduate College of Education, 100 Morrissey Blvd., Boston, MA 02125. (617) 287-5980. Fax (617) 265-7173. E-mail mcgarry@umbsky.cc.umb.edu. Canice H. McGarry, Graduate Program Dir. *Specialization:* M.Ed. in Instructional Design. *Admission Requirements:* MAT or previous Master's degree, goal statement, three letters of recommendation, resume, interview. *Degree Requirements:* 36 semester hours, thesis or project. *Faculty:* 1 full-time, 8 part-time. *Students:* 10 full-time, 95 part-time. *Financial Assistance:* graduate assistantships providing tuition plus stipend. *Degrees Awarded 1996:* 22.

University of Massachusetts-Lowell. College of Education, One University Ave., Lowell, MA 01854-2881. (508) 934-4621. Fax (508) 934-3005. E-mail lebaronj@woods.uml.edu. John LeBaron, Faculty Chair. *Specializations:* M.Ed and Ed.D. Educational Technology may be pursued in the context of any degree program area. The Certificate of Advanced Graduate Study (CAGS), equivalent to 30 credits beyond a M.Ed., is also offered. *Admission Requirements:* Bachelor's degree in cognate area, GRE or MAT, statement of purpose, three recommendations. *Degree Requirements:* M.Ed.: 30 credits beyond Bachelor's. Ed.D.: 60 credits beyond Master's. *Faculty:* 2 full-time for technology courses. *Students:* 375. *Financial Assistance:* assistantships, student loans, limited scholarships. *Degrees Awarded 1996:* M.Ed., 92; Ed.D., 19; CAGS, 4.

MICHIGAN

Eastern Michigan University. 234 Boone Hall, Ypsilanti, MI 48197. (313) 487-3260. Fax (313) 484-6471. Anne Bednar, Prof., Coord., Dept. of Teacher Education. *Specialization:* M.A. in Educational Psychology with concentration in Educational Technology. *Admission Requirements:* Bachelor's degree, 2.75 undergraduate GPA or MAT score, 500 TOEFL. *Degree Requirements:* 30 semester hours, optional thesis worth 6 credits. *Faculty:* 4 full-time. *Students:* 15. *Financial Assistance:* graduate assistantship. *Degrees Awarded 1996:* 10.

Michigan State University. College of Education, 431 Erickson, East Lansing, MI 48824. (517) 355-6684. Fax (517) 353-6393. E-mail yelons@msu.edu. Dr. Stephen Yelon. *Specialization:* M.A. in Educational Technology and Instructional Design. *Admission Requirements:* Bachelor's degree, 800 TOEFL, recommendations, goal statement. *Degree requirements:* 30 semester hours, comprehensive exam, field experience. *Faculty:* 5 full-time. *Students:* approx. 45. *Financial Assistance:* some assistantships for highly qualified students.

University of Michigan. Department of Educational Studies, Suite 1600, 610 East University, Ann Arbor MI 48109-1259. (313) 763-4668. Fax (313) 763-4663. E-mail carl.berger@umich.edu. Carl F. Berger, Chair. *Specializations:* Master's; Ph.D. in Instructional Technology with concentrations in Science, Math, or Literacy. *Features:* Programs are individually designed. *Admission Requirements:* GRE, B.A. for Master's, Master's for Ph.D. *Degree Requirements:* Master's: 30 hours beyond B.A. Ph.D.: 60 hours beyond B.A. or 30 hours beyond M.A. plus comprehensive exams and dissertation. *Faculty:* 1 full-time, 6 part-time. *Students:* 22 full-time, 10 part-time. *Financial Assistance:* assistantships, grants, student loans, scholarships, internships. *Degrees Awarded 1996:* Master's, 16; Ph.D., 6.

Wayne State University. 381 Education, Detroit, MI 48202. (313) 577-1728. Fax (313) 577-1693. E-mail rrichey@cms.cc.wayne.edu. Rita C. Richey, Prof., Program Coord., Instructional Technology Programs, Div. of Administrative and Organizational Studies, College of Education. *Specializations:* Master's degrees in Business and Human Services Training, K-12 Educational Technology, Interactive Technologies, and Adult and Continuing Education. Ed.D. and Ph.D. programs to prepare individuals for leadership in business, industry, health care, and the K-12 school setting as instructional design and development specialists; media or learning resources managers or consultants; specialists in instructional video; and computer-assisted instruction and multimedia specialists. The school also offers a six-year specialist degree program in Instructional Technology. *Features:* Guided experiences in instructional design and development activities in business and industry are available. *Admission Requirements:* Ph.D.: Master's degree, 3.5 GPA, GRE, MAT, strong professional recommendations, interview. *Degree Requirements:* Master's: 36 semester hours, including required project; internship recommended. *Faculty:* 4.5 full-time, 5 part-time. *Students:* Master's, 400; doctoral, 125, most part-time. *Financial Assistance:* student loans, scholarships, and paid internships. *Degrees Awarded 1996:* Master's, 36; doctoral, 8.

MINNESOTA

Mankato State University. MSU Box 20, P.O. Box 8400, Mankato, MN 56001-8400. (507) 389-1965. Fax (507) 389-5751. E-mail pengelly@vax1.mankato.msus.edu. Kenneth C. Pengelly, Assoc. Prof., Dept. of Library Media Education. *Specialization:* M.S. in Educational Technology. *Admission Requirements:* Bachelor's degree, 3.0 undergraduate GPA. *Degree Requirements:* 51 qtr. credits, comprehensive exam. *Faculty:* 4 full-time. *Degrees Awarded 1996:* 5.

St. Cloud State University. College of Education, St. Cloud, MN 56301-4498. (612) 255-2022. Fax (612) 255-4778. E-mail jberling@tigger.stcloud.msus.edu. John G. Berling, Prof., Dir., Center for Information Media. *Specializations:* Master's degrees in Information Technologies, Educational Media, and Human Resources Development/Training. A Specialist degree is also offered. *Degree Requirements:* Master's: 51 qtr. hours with thesis; 54 qtr. hours, Plan B; 57 qtr. hours, portfolio; 200-hour practicum is required for media generalist licensure; course work applies to Educational Media Master's program. *Faculty:* 7 full-time. *Students:* 15 full-time, 150 part-time. *Financial Assistance:* assistantships, scholarships. *Degrees Awarded 1996:* Master's, 14; Specialist, 1.

Walden University. 155 5th Avenue South, Minneapolis, MN 55401. (800) 444-6795. E-mail www@waldenu.edu or info@waldenu.edu. Dr. Gwen Hillesheim, Chair. *Specializations:* M.S. in Educational Change and Technology Innovation. Ph.D-level programming also available. *Features:* delivered primarily on-line. *Admission Requirements:* accredited Bachelor's. *Degree Requirements:* 48 credit curriculum, 2 brief residencies, Master's project. *Faculty:* 14 part-time. *Students:* 50 full-time, 26 part-time. *Financial Assistance:* student loans, 3 fellowships with annual review. *Degrees Awarded 1996:* 0 (program instituted in 1996; first graduates expected early 1998).

MISSOURI

Fontbonne College. 6800 Wydown Blvd., St. Louis, MO 63105. (314) 889-1497. Fax (314) 889-1451. E-mail mabkemei@fontbonne.edu. Dr. Mary K. Abkemeier, Chair. *Specialization:* M.S. in Computer Education. *Features:* small classes and course work immediately applicable to the classroom. *Admission Requirements:* 2.5 undergraduate GPA, 3 letters of recommendation. *Degree Requirements:* 33 semester hours, 3.0 GPA. *Faculty:* 2 full-time, 12 part-time. *Students:* 1 full-time, 110 part-time. *Financial Assistance:* grants. *Degrees Awarded 1996:* 22.

Northwest Missouri State University. Department of Computer Science/Information Systems, 800 University Ave., Maryville MO 64468. (816) 562-1600. E-mail pheeler@acad. nwmissouri.edu. Dr. Phillip Heeler, Chairperson. *Specializations:* M.S. in School Computer Studies; M.S.Ed. in Educational Uses of Computers. *Features:* These degrees are designed for computer educators at the elementary, middle school, high school, and junior college level. *Admission Requirements:* 3.0 undergraduate GPA, 700 GRE (verbal + quantitative). *Degree Requirements:* 32 semester hours of graduate courses in computer science and/or educational computing courses. *Faculty:* 12 full-time, 4 part-time. *Students:* 5 full-time, 20 part-time. *Financial Assistance:* assistantships, grants, student loans, and scholarships. *Degrees Awarded 1996:* 10.

University of Missouri-Columbia. College of Education, 110 Townsend Hall, Columbia, MO 65211. (573) 882-4546. Fax (573) 884-4944. Jim Laffey, Assoc. Prof. (cilaffey@showme. missouri.edu). Gail Fitzgerald, Assoc. Prof. (spedfitz@showme.missouri.edu), Information and Learning Technologies Program, School of Information & Learning Technologies. *Specializations:* Master's degree program prepares professionals to design, develop, and implement technology in educational settings. Ph.D. in Instructional & Learning Technologies prepares professionals to understand and influence learning, information organization and retrieval, and performance in diverse learning environments, especially through the design, development, and use of interactive technologies. An Education Specialist degree program is also available. *Features:* Master's program is competency-based. Graduates leave with the ability to plan, implement, and evaluate educational technology innovations, and to design, develop, and evaluate technology-based learning and performance support products. Ph.D. program includes a major in Information and Learning Technologies with two support areas (e.g., Educational Psychology and Computer Science), research tools, and R&D apprenticeship experiences. In addition to the competency-based objectives of the Master's program, doctoral graduates will be able to conduct systematic research which contributes to the knowledge base of learning, information organization and retrieval, performance, and technology. *Admission Requirements:* Master's: Bachelor's degree, MAT score. Ph.D.: 3.2 graduate GPA, 1500 GRE, letters of recommendation, statement of purpose. *Faculty:* Master's, 8 full-time, 10 part-time; Ph.D., 13 full-time, 20 part-time, plus selected faculty in related fields. *Students:* Master's, 20 full-time, 10 part-time; Ph.D., 20 full-time, 12 part-time. *Financial Assistance:* Master's: assistantships, grants, student loans, scholarships. Ph.D.: graduate assistantships with tuition waivers; numerous academic scholarships ranging from $200 to $18,000. *Degrees Awarded 1996:* Master's, 10; Ph.D., 3.

Webster University. Instructional Technology, St. Louis, MO 63119. (314) 968-7490. Fax (314) 968-7118. E-mail steinmpe@websteruniv.edu. Web site http://www.websteruniv.edu. Paul Steinmann, Assoc. Dean and Dir., Graduate Studies and Instructional Technology. *Specialization:* Master's degree. State Certification in Media Technology is a program option. *Admission Requirements:* Bachelor's degree with 2.5 GPA. *Degree Requirements:* 33 semester hours (including 24 in media); internship required. *Faculty:* 5. *Students:* 4 full-time, 19 part-time. *Financial Assistance:* partial scholarships, minority scholarships, government loans, and limited state aid. *Degrees Awarded 1996:* 9.

MONTANA

University of Montana. School of Education, Missoula, MT 59812. (406) 243-5785. Fax (406) 243-4908. E-mail cjlott@selway.umt.edu. Dr. Carolyn Lott, Asst. Prof. of Library/ Media. *Specializations:* Master's and Specialist degrees; K-12 School Library Media specialization with School Library Media Certification endorsement. *Admission Requirements:* letters of recommendation, 2.5 GPA. *Degree Requirements:* Master's: 37 semester credit hours (18 overlap with library media endorsement). Specialist: 28 semester hours (18 overlap). *Faculty:* 2 full-time, 1 part-time. *Students:* 5 full-time, 20 part-time. *Financial Assistance:* assistantships; contact the University of Montana Financial Aid Office. *Degrees Awarded 1996:* 10.

NEBRASKA

University of Nebraska at Kearney. Kearney, NE 68849-1260. (308) 865-8833. Fax (308) 865-8097. E-mail fredrickson@platte.unk.edu. Dr. Scott Fredrickson, Dir. of Instructional Technology. *Specializations:* M.S. in Instructional Technology, M.S. in Educational Media, Specialist in Educational Media. *Admission Requirements:* M.S. and Specialist: GRE, acceptance into graduate school, approval of Instructional Technology Committee. *Degree Requirements:* M.S.: 36 credit hours, Master's comprehensive exam or field study. Specialist: 39 credit hours, field study. *Faculty:* 5 full-time, 10 part-time. *Students:* 57 full-time. *Financial Assistance:* assistantships, grants, student loans. *Degrees Awarded 1996:* M.A., 15; Specialist, 2.

University of Nebraska-Omaha. Department of Teacher Education, College of Education, Kayser Hall 208D, Omaha, NE 68182. (402) 554-2211. Fax (402) 554-3491. E-mail hasel@ cwis.unomaha.edu. Verne Haselwood, Prof., Educational Media Program in Teacher Education. *Specializations:* M.S. in Education, M.A. in Education, both with Educational Media concentration. *Degree Requirements:* 36 semester hours (including 24 in media), practicum; thesis optional. *Faculty:* 2 full-time, 4 part-time. *Students:* 10 full-time, 62 part-time. *Financial Assistance:* Contact Financial Aid Office.

NEVADA

University of Nevada. Counseling and Educational Psychology Dept., College of Education, Reno, NV 89557. (702) 784-6327. Fax (702) 784-6298. E-mail ljohnson@unr.edu. Dr. LaMont Johnson, Program Coord., Information Technology in Education. Marlowe Smaby, Dept. Chair. *Specializations:* M.S. and Ph.D. *Admission Requirements:* Bachelor's degree, 2.75 undergraduate GPA, 750 GRE. *Degree Requirements:* 36 semester credits, optional thesis worth 6 credits, comprehensive exam. *Faculty:* 2 1/2 full-time. *Students:* M.S., 15; Ph.D., 6. *Degrees Awarded 1996:* M.S., 3; Ph.D, 0 (3 anticipated in 1997).

NEW JERSEY

Montclair State College. Department of Reading and Educational Media, Upper Montclair, NJ 07043. Robert R. Ruezinsky, Dir. of Media and Technology. *Specializations:* No degree program exists. Two certification programs, A.M.S. and E.M.S, exist on the graduate level. *Degree Requirements:* 18-21 semester hours of media and technology are required for the A.M.S. program and 30-33 hours for the E.M.S. program. *Faculty:* 7 part-time. *Students:* 32 part-time.

Rutgers-The State University of New Jersey. Ph.D. Program in Communication, Information, and Library Studies, The Graduate School, New Brunswick, NJ 08903. (908) 932-7447. Fax (908) 932-6916. Lea P. Stewart, Prof., Dir., Master's Program, Dept. of Library and Information Studies, School of Communication, Information and Library Studies. (908) 932-9717. Fax (908) 932-2644. Dr. David Carr, Chair. *Specializations:* M.L.S. degree with specializations in Information Retrieval, Technical and Automated Services, Reference, School Media Services, Youth Services, Management and Policy Issues, and Generalist

Studies. Ph.D. programs in Communication; Information Systems, Structures, and Users; Information and Communication Policy and Technology; and Library and Information Services. The school also offers a six-year specialist certificate program. *Features:* Ph.D Program provides doctoral-level course work for students seeking theoretical and research skills for scholarly and professional leadership in the information and communication fields. A course on multimedia structure, organization, access, and production is being offered. *Admission Requirements:* Ph.D.: Master's degree in Information Studies, Communication, Library Science, or related field; 3.0 undergraduate GPA; GRE scores; TOEFL (for applicants whose native language is not English). *Degree Requirements:* M.L.S.: 36 semester hours, in which the hours for media vary for individual students; practicum of 150 hours. *Faculty:* M.L.S., 16 full-time, 10 adjunct; Ph.D., 43. *Students:* M.L.S., 108 full-time, 214 part-time; Ph.D., 104. *Financial Assistance:* M.L.S.: scholarships, fellowships, and graduate assistantships. Ph.D.: assistantships and Title II-B fellowships. *Degrees Awarded 1996:* Master's, 131; Ph.D., 11.

William Paterson College. School of Education, 300 Pompton Rd., Wayne, NJ 07470. (201) 595-2140. Fax (201) 595-2585. Dr. Amy G. Job, Librarian, Assoc. Prof., Coord., Program in Library/Media, Curriculum and Instruction Dept. *Specializations:* M.Ed. for Educational Media Specialist, Associate Media Specialist, Ed.S. *Degree Requirements:* M.Ed.: 33 semester hours, including research projects and practicum. *Faculty:* 6 full-time, 2 part-time. *Students:* 30 part-time. *Financial Assistance:* limited. *Degrees Awarded 1996:* M.Ed., 2; Ed.S., 1.

NEW YORK

Buffalo State College. 1300 Elmwood Ave., Buffalo, NY 14222-1095. (716) 878-4923. Fax (716) 878-6677. E-mail nowakoaj@snybufaa.cs.snybuf.edu. Dr. Anthony J. Nowakowski, Program Coord. *Specializations:* M.S. in Education in Educational Computing. *Admission Requirements:* Bachelor's degree from accredited institution, 3.0 GPA in last 60 hours, 3 letters of recommendation. *Degree Requirements:* 33 semester hours (15 hours in computers, 12-15 hours in education, 3-6 electives); thesis or project. *Faculty:* 7 part-time. *Students:* 3 full-time, 76 part-time. *Degrees Awarded 1996:* 17.

Ithaca College. School of Communications, Ithaca, NY 14850. (607) 274-1025. Fax (607) 274-1664. E-mail Herndon@Ithaca.edu. Sandra L. Herndon, Prof., Chair, Graduate Corporate Communications; Roy H. Park, School of Communications. *Specialization:* M.S. in Corporate Communications. Students in this program find employment in such areas as instructional design, multimedia, public relations and marketing, and employee communication. The program can be tailored to individual career goals. *Degree Requirements:* 36 semester hours, seminar. *Faculty:* 8 full-time. *Students:* approx. 25 full-time, 15 part-time. *Financial Assistance:* full- and part-time research assistantships. *Degrees Awarded 1996:* 25.

New York Institute of Technology. Dept. of Instructional Technology, Tower House, Old Westbury, NY 11568. (516) 686-7777. Fax (516) 686-7655. E-mail plumer@vidar.nyit.edu. Web site http://www.nyit.edu. Davenport Plumer, Chair, Depts. of Instructional Technology and Elementary Education. *Specializations:* Master's in Instructional Technology; Master's in Elementary Education; Specialist Certificates in Computers in Education, Distance Learning, and Multimedia (not degrees, but are earned after the first 18 credits of the Master's degree). *Features:* computer integration in virtually all courses; online courses; evening, weekend, and summer courses. *Admission Requirements:* Bachelor's degree from accredited college with 2.75 cumulative average. *Degree Requirements:* 36 credits with 3.0 GPA for Master's degree, 18 credits with 3.0 GPA for certificates. *Faculty:* 7 full-time, 42 part-time. *Students:* 80 full-time, 720 part-time. *Financial Assistance:* graduate assistantships, institutional and alumni scholarships, student loans. *Degrees Awarded 1996:* Master's, 31; Specialist, 40.

New York University. Educational Communication and Technology Program, School of Education, 239 Greene St., Suite 300, New York, NY 10003. (212) 998-5520. Fax (212) 995-4041. Francine Shuchat Shaw, Assoc. Prof., Dir.; Donald T. Payne, Assoc. Prof., Doctoral Advisor. *Specializations:* M.A., Ed.D., and Ph.D. in Education for the preparation of individuals to perform as instructional media designers, developers, producers, and researchers in education, business and industry, health and medicine, community services, government, museums, and other cultural institutions; and to teach in educational communications and instructional technology programs in higher education, including instructional television, microcomputers, multimedia, and telecommunications. The school also offers a post-M.A. 30-point Certificate of Advanced Study in Education. *Features:* emphasizes theoretical foundations, especially a cognitive perspective of learning and instruction and their implications for designing media-based learning environments. All efforts focus on multimedia, instructional television, and telecommunications; participation in special research and production projects and field internships. *Admission Requirements:* M.A.: 3.0 undergraduate GPA, responses to essay questions, interview related to academic and professional goals. Ph.D.: 1000 GRE, responses to essay questions, interview related to academic or professional preparation and career goals. *Degree Requirements:* M.A.: 36 semester hours including specialization, elective courses, thesis. Ph.D.: 57 semester hours including specialization, foundations, research, content seminar, and elective course work; candidacy papers; dissertation; English Essay Examination. *Faculty:* 2 full-time, 10 part-time. *Students:* M.A.: 30 full-time, 35 part-time. Ph.D.: 14 full-time, 30 part-time. *Financial Assistance:* graduate and research assistantships, student loans, scholarships, and work assistance programs. *Degrees Awarded 1996:* M.A., 18.

Pace University. Westchester Dept, School of Education, Bedford Road, Pleasantville, NY 10570. (914) 773-3829, (914) 773-3979. Fax (914) 773-3521. Web site http://www.pace.edu. E-mail keyes@pacevm.dac.pace.edu. Dr. Carol Keyes, Chair. *Specialization:* M.S.E. in Curriculum and Instruction with a concentration in Computers. *Admission Requirements:* GPA 3.0, interview. *Degree Requirements:* 33-34 semester hours (15 in computers, 18 in educational administration). *Faculty:* 8 full-time, 50 part-time. *Students:* 60-70 part-time. *Financial Assistance:* assistantships, scholarships.

St. John's University. Division of Library and Information Science, 8000 Utopia Parkway, Jamaica, NY 11439. (718) 990-6200. Fax (718) 380-0353. E-mail libis@sjmusic.stjohns.edu. James Benson, Dir. *Specializations:* M.L.S. with specialization in School Media. The school also offers a 24-credit Advanced Certificate program. *Admission Requirements:* 3.0 GPA, 2 letters of reference, statement of professional goals. *Degree Requirements:* 36 semester hours, comprehensive exam, practicum. *Faculty:* 6 full-time, 15 part-time. *Students:* 21 full-time, 110 part-time. *Financial Assistance:* 15 assistantships and 4 grants. *Degrees Awarded 1996:* Master's, 52.

*State University College of Arts and Science at Potsdam. School of Education, 204 Satterlee Hall, Potsdam, NY 13676. (315) 267-2527. Fax (315) 267-2771. E-mail lichtnc@potsdam.edu. Dr. Norman Licht, Coord., Instructional Technology and Media Management; Dr. Charles Mlynarczyk, Chair, Education Department. *Specializations:* M.S. in Education with concentration in Instructional Technology and Media Management with Educational Computing concentration. *Degree Requirements:* 30 semester hours (15 in computers, 18 in education, 0 outside education); internship or practicum; thesis not required. *Faculty:* 7 full-time, 2 part-time. *Students:* 102 full-time, 34 part-time. *Financial Assistance:* assistantships, student loans. *Degrees Awarded 1995:* 42.

State University of New York at Albany. School of Education, 1400 Washington Ave., Albany, NY 12222. (518) 442-5032. Fax (518) 442-5008. E-mail swan@cnsunix.albany.edu. Karen Swan (ED114A), contact person. *Specialization:* M.Ed. and Ph.D. in Curriculum and Instruction with specializations in Instructional Theory, Design, and Technology. *Admission Requirements:* Bachelor's degree, GPA close to 3.0; transcript, three letters of recommendation. Students desiring New York State permanent teaching certification should possess preliminary certification. *Degree Requirements:* M.Ed.: 30 semester hours with 15-18 credits in specialization. Ph.D.: 78 semester hours, internship, portfolio certification, thesis. *Faculty:* 13 full-time, 7 part-time. *Students:* 100 full-time, 350 part-time. *Financial Assistance:* fellowships, assistantships, grants, student loans, minority fellowships. *Degrees Awarded 1996:* M.Ed., 97; Ph.D., 3.

State University of New York at Stony Brook. Technology & Society, College of Engineering & Applied Sciences, SUNY at Stony Brook, Stony Brook, NY 11794-2250. (516) 632-8763. (516) 632-7809. E-mail dferguson@dts.tns.sunysb.edu. Prof. David L. Ferguson, Contact Person. *Specializations:* Master's Degree in Technological Systems Management with concentration in Educational Computing. *Features:* emphasis on courseware design, multimedia and modeling, applications, and problem-solving. *Admission Requirements:* 3.0 undergraduate GPA, experience with computer applications or computer programming. *Degree Requirements:* Bachelor's degree in any discipline (science or engineering preferred.) *Faculty:* 4 full-time, 3 part-time. *Students:* 10 full-time, 15 part-time. *Financial Assistance:* assistantships, grants, student loans. *Degrees Awarded 1996:* 6.

Syracuse University. Instructional Design, Development, and Evaluation Program, School of Education, 330 Huntington Hall, Syracuse, NY 13244-2340. (315) 443-3703. Fax (315) 443-5732. Philip L. Doughty, Prof., Chair. *Specializations:* M.S., Ed.D., and Ph.D. degree programs for Instructional Design of programs and materials, Educational Evaluation, Human Issues in Instructional Development, Media Production (including computers and multimedia), and Educational Research and Theory (learning theory, application of theory, and educational and media research). Graduates are prepared to serve as curriculum developers, instructional developers, program and product evaluators, researchers, resource center administrators, communications coordinators, trainers in human resource development, and higher education instructors. The school also offers an advanced certificate program. *Features:* field work and internships, special topics and special issues seminar, student- and faculty-initiated mini-courses, seminars and guest lecturers, faculty-student formulation of department policies, and multiple international perspectives. *Admission Requirements:* doctoral: Master's degree from accredited institution, GRE (3 tests required) scores. *Faculty:* 2 full-time, 4 part-time. *Degree Requirements:* M.S.: 36 semester hours, comprehensive and intensive exam or portfolio required. *Students:* M.S., 18 full-time, 22 part-time; doctoral, 25 full-time, 30 part-time. *Financial Assistance:* some fellowships, scholarships, and graduate assistantships entailing either research or administrative duties in instructional technology. *Degrees Awarded 1996:* M.S., 50; doctorate, 5.

NORTH CAROLINA

Appalachian State University. Department of Library Science and Educational Foundations, Boone, NC 28608. (704) 262-2243. Fax (704) 262-2128. E-mail Webbbh@appstate.edu. Web site http://www.ced.appstate.edu/ltl.html. John H. Tashner, Prof., Coord. *Specialization:* M.A. in Educational Media and Technology with three areas of concentration: Computers, Telecommunications, and Media Production. *Features:* IMPACT NC (business, university, and public school) partnership offers unusual opportunities. *Degree Requirements:* 36 semester hours (including 15 in Computer Education), internship; thesis optional. *Faculty:* 2 full-time, 1 part-time. *Students:* 6 full-time, 25 part-time. *Financial Assistance:* assistantships, grants, student loans. *Degrees Awarded 1996:* 6.

East Carolina University. Department of Library Studies and Educational Technology, Greenville, NC 27858-4353. (919) 328-6621. Fax (919) 328-4368. E-mail lsauld@ecuvm.cis.ecu.edu. Lawrence Auld, Assoc. Prof., Chair. *Specializations:* Master of Library Science; Certificate of Advanced Study (Library Science); Master of Arts in Education (Instructional Technology Computers). *Features:* M.L.S. graduates are eligible for North Carolina School Media Coord. certification; C.A.S. graduates are eligible for North Carolina School Media Supervisor certification; M.A.Ed. graduates are eligible for North Carolina Instructional Technology-Computers certification. *Admission Requirements:* Master's: Bachelor's degree; C.A.S.: M.L.S. or equivalent degree. *Degree Requirements:* M.L.S.: 38 semester hours; M.A.Ed.: 36 semester hours; C.A.S.: 30 semester hours. *Faculty:* 9 full-time. *Students:* 5 full-time, 70 part-time. *Financial Assistance:* assistantships. *Degrees Awarded 1996:* M.L.S., 24; M.A.Ed., 7; C.A.S., 3.

North Carolina Central University. School of Education, 1801 Fayetteville St., Durham, NC 27707. (919) 560-6218. Fax (919) 560-5366. Dr. Marvin E. Duncan, Prof., Dir., Graduate Program in Educational Technology. *Specialization:* M.A. with special emphasis on Instructional Development/Design. *Features:* Graduates are prepared to implement and utilize a variety of technologies applicable to many professional ventures, including institutions of higher education (college resource centers), business, industry, and professional schools such as medicine, law, dentistry, and nursing. *Admission Requirements:* undergraduate degree with at least 6 hours in education. *Degree Requirements:* 33 semester hours (including project or thesis). *Faculty:* 2 full-time, 1 part-time. *Students:* 25 full-time, 30 part-time. *Financial Assistance:* assistantships, grants, student loans. *Degrees Awarded 1996:* 11.

North Carolina State University. Department of Curriculum and Instruction, P.O. Box 7801, Raleigh, NC 27695-7801. (919) 515-1779. Fax (919) 515-6978. E-mail esvasu@unity. ncsu.edu. Dr. Ellen Vasu, Assoc. Prof. *Specializations:* M.Ed. and M.S. in Instructional Technology-Computers (program track within one Master's in Curriculum and Instruction). Ph.D. in Curriculum and Instruction with focus on Instructional Technology as well as other areas. *Degree Requirements:* Master's: 36 semester hours, practicum, thesis optional; Ph.D.: 60 hours beyond Master's (minimum 33 in Curriculum and Instruction core, 27 in Research); other information available upon request. *Faculty:* 3 full-time. *Students:* Master's, 13 part-time; Ph.D., 7 part-time.

University of North Carolina. School of Information and Library Science (CB#3360), Chapel Hill, NC 27599. (919) 962-8062, 962-8366. Fax (919) 962-8071. E-mail daniel@ils.unc.edu. Web site http://www.ils.unc.edu/. Evelyn H. Daniel, Prof., Coord., School Media Program. *Specialization:* Master of Science Degree in Library Science with specialization in school library media work. *Features:* rigorous academic program plus teaching practicum requirement; excellent placement record. *Admission Requirements:* competitive admission based on all three GRE components, undergraduate GPA, letters of recommendation, and student statement of career interest. *Degree Requirements:* 48 semester hours, comprehensive exam, Master's paper. *Faculty:* 16 full-time, 10 part-time. *Students:* 35 full-time, 15 part-time. *Financial Assistance:* grants, assistantships, student loans. *Degrees Awarded 1996* (School Media Certification): 22.

NORTH DAKOTA

Minot State University. 500 University Ave. W., Minot, ND 58707. (701) 858-3817. Fax (701) 839-6933. Dr. David Williams, Dir., Graduate School. *Specializations:* Master's in Education (including work in educational computing); M.S. in Management; M.S. in Math and Computer Science; M.S. in Early Childhood Special Education; M.S. in Special Education Specialization in Severe Multiple-Handicaps; M.S. in Communication Disorders, Specializations in Audiology and Speech Language Pathology. *Features:* All programs include involvement in computer applications appropriate to the area of study, including assistive technologies for handicapped persons. Computer laboratories are available for student use in the library and the Department of Education, and a computer course is worked into all graduate programs. Some courses will be offered through the North Dakota Wide Area Network, which currently has four sites. A special laboratory with assistive devices for use by hearing and visually impaired students and a program in audiology are planned for the future. *Admission Requirements:* $25 fee, three letters of recommendation, 300-word autobiography, transcripts, GRE in Communication Disorders or GMAT for M.S. in Management. *Degree Requirements:* 30 semester hours (hours in computers, education, and outside education vary according to program); written comprehensive exams; oral exams; thesis or project. *Faculty:* 14 full-time. *Students:* 61 full-time, 63 part-time. *Financial Assistance:* loans, assistantships, scholarships. *Degrees Awarded 1996:* M.S.: Elementary Education, 32; Math and Computer Science, 6; S.P.Ed., Severe Multiple Handicaps, 4; S.P.Ed. Early Childhood Special Education, 4; Communication Disorders, 30.

OHIO

Kent State University. 405 White Hall, Kent, OH 44242. (330) 672-2294. Fax (330) 672-2512. E-mail tchandler@emerald.edu.kent.edu. Web site http://amethyst.educ.kent./edu/itec/. Dr. Theodore Chandler, Coord., Instructional Technology Program. *Specializations:* M.Ed. or M.A. in Instructional Technology, Instructional Computing, and Library/Media Specialist; Ph.D. in Educational Psychology with emphasis in Instructional Technology. *Features:* Programs are planned individually to prepare students for careers in elementary, secondary, or higher education, business, industry, government agencies, or health facilities. Students may take advantage of independent research, individual study, practica, and internships. *Admission Requirements:* Master's: Bachelor's degree with 2.75 undergraduate GPA. *Degree Requirements:* Master's: 34 semester hours; thesis required for M.A. *Faculty:* 5 full-time, 7 part-time. Students: 39. *Financial Assistance:* 6 graduate assistantships, John Mitchell and Marie McMahan Awards, 4 teaching fellowships. *Degrees Awarded 1996:* Master's, 14.

*The Ohio State University. College of the Arts, Dept. of Art Education, 340 Hopkins Hall, 128 North Oval Mall, Columbus, OH 43210. (614) 292-0235, (614) 292-7183. Fax (614) 292-1674. E-mail carol@cgrg.ohio-state.edu. Dr. Carol Gigliotti, contact person. *Specializations:* M.A. and Ph.D. in Art Education with specializations in the teaching and learning of computer graphics and computer-mediated art; multimedia production and its curricular applications; telecommunications in the arts; and ethical, aesthetic, and cultural aspects of interactive technologies. *Features:* Specialization at the Advanced Computer Center for the Arts and Design (ACCAD). *Faculty:* 1 full-time, 1 part-time in specialty. *Students:* 15 full-time, 3 part-time in specialty. *Financial Assistance:* assistantships, grants, student loans, and scholarships. *Degrees Awarded 1995:* M.A., 8.

*Ohio University. School of Curriculum and Instruction, 248 McCracken Hall, Athens, OH 45701-2979. (614) 593-4457. Fax (614) 593-0177. John McCutcheon, contact person. *Specialization:* M.Ed. in Computer Education and Technology. *Admission Requirements:* Bachelor's degree, 2.5 undergraduate GPA, 35 MAT, 420 GRE (verbal), 400 GRE (quantitative), 550 TOEFL, three letters of recommendation. *Degree Requirements:* 54 qtr. credits, optional thesis worth 2-10 credits or alternative seminar and paper. Students may earn two graduate degrees simultaneously in education and in any other field. *Faculty:* 1 full-time, 4 part-time. *Students:* 24 full-time, 5 part-time. *Financial Assistance:* assistantships. *Degrees Awarded 1995:* 24.

University of Cincinnati. College of Education, 401 Teachers College, ML002, Cincinnati, OH 45221-0002. (513) 556-3577. Fax (513) 556-2483. Web site http://uc.edu/. Randall Nichols and Janet Bohren, Div. of Teacher Education. *Specialization:* M.A. or Ed.D. in Curriculum and Instruction with an emphasis on Instructional Design and Technology; Educational Technology degree programs for current professional, technical, critical, and personal knowledge. *Admission Requirements:* Bachelor's degree from accredited institution, 2.8 undergraduate GPA; conditional admission for candidates not meeting first two criteria possible. *Degree Requirements:* 54 qtr. hours, written exam, thesis or research project. *Faculty:* 3 full-time. *Students:* 20 full-time. *Financial Assistance:* scholarships, assistantships, grants. *Degrees Awarded 1996:* M.A., 12.

University of Toledo. Department of Educational Technology, College of Education and Allied Professions, 2801 West Bancroft, Toledo, OH 43606. (419) 530-6176. Fax (419) 530-7719. E-mail APATTER@UTNET.UTOLEDO.EDU. Dr. Amos C. Patterson, Dir. *Specializations:* Master's, Specialist, doctorate degrees in Instructional Development, Library/Media Education, Instructional Computing, and Human Resources Development. *Admission Requirements:* Master's: 3.0 undergraduate GPA, GRE, recommendations; Specialist: Master's Degree, GRE, recommendations; doctorate: Master's degree, GRE, TOEFL, recommendations, entrance writing sample, and interview. *Degree Requirements:* Master's: 36 semester hours, Master's project; Specialist: 32 semester hours, internship; doctorate: 84 semester hours, dissertation. *Faculty:* 6 full-time, 2 part-time. *Students:* Master's, 9 full-time, 89 part-time;

Specialist, 4 full-time, 27 part-time; doctoral, 13 full-time, 66 part-time. *Financial Assistance:* assistantships, student loans, scholarships, work assistance program. *Degrees Awarded 1996:* Master's, 29; Specialist, 3; doctoral, 2.

Wright State University. College of Education and Human Services, Dept. of Educational Leadership, 244 Millett Hall, Dayton, OH 45435. (513) 873-2509 or (513) 873-2182. Fax (513) 873-4485. E-mail bmathies@desire.wright.edu or bonniekwsu@aol.com. Web site http:// www.ed.wright.edu. Dr. Bonnie K. Mathies, Asst. Dean, Communication and Technology. *Specializations:* M.Ed. in Educational Media or Computer Education, or for Media Supervisor or Computer Coord.; M.A. in Educational Media or Computer Education; Specialist degree in Curriculum and Instruction with a focus on Educational Technology; Specialist degree in Higher Education with a focus on Educational Technology. *Admission Requirements:* completed application with nonrefundable application fee, Bachelor's degree from accredited institution, official transcripts, 2.7 overall GPA for regular status (conditional acceptance possible), statement of purpose, satisfactory scores on MAT or GRE. *Degree Requirements:* M.Ed. requires a comprehensive exam that includes a portfolio with videotaped presentation to the faculty. M.A. requires a 9-hour thesis. *Faculty:* 2 full-time, 12 part-time, including other university full-time faculty and staff. *Students:* approx. 75. *Financial Assistance:* 3 graduate assistantships in the College's Educational Resource Center; limited number of small graduate scholarships. *Degrees Awarded 1996:* Master's, 8.

OKLAHOMA

Southwestern Oklahoma State University. School of Education, 100 Campus Drive, Weatherford, OK 73096. (405) 774-3140. Fax (405) 774-7043. E-mail mossg@swosu.edu. Gregory Moss, Asst. Prof., Chair, Dept. of School Service Programs. *Specialization:* M.Ed. in Library/Media Education. *Admission Requirements:* 2.5 GPA, GRE or GMAT scores, letter of recommendation, GPA x 150 + GRE = 1100. *Degree Requirements:* 32 semester hours (including 24 in library media). *Faculty:* 1 full-time, 4 part-time. *Students:* 21. *Degrees Awarded 1996:* 10.

The University of Oklahoma. Instructional Psychology and Technology, Department of Educational Psychology, 321 Collings Hall, Norman, OK 73019. (405) 325-2882. Fax (405) 325-6655. E-mail psmith@ou.edu. Web site http://www.uoknor.edu/education/iptwww/. Dr. Patricia L. Smith, Chair. *Specializations:* Master's degree with emphases in Educational Technology Generalist, Educational Technology, Computer Application, Instructional Design, Teaching with Technology; Dual Master's Educational Technology and Library and Information Systems. Doctoral degree in Instructional Psychology and Technology. *Features:* strong interweaving of principles of instructional psychology with design and development of Instructional Technology. Application of IP&T in K-12, vocational education, higher education, business and industry, and governmental agencies. *Admission Requirements:* Master's: acceptance by IPT program and Graduate College based on minimum 3.00 GPA for last 60 hours of undergraduate work or last 12 hours of graduate work; written statement that indicates goals and interests compatible with program goals. Doctoral: 3.0 in last 60 hours undergraduate, 3.25 GPA, GRE scores, written statement of background and goals. *Degree Requirements:* Master's: approx. 39 hours course work (specific number of hours dependent upon emphasis) with 3.0 GPA; successful completion of thesis or comprehensive exam. Doctorate: see program description from institution or http://www.ou.education.iptwww. *Faculty:* 10 full-time. *Students:* Master's, 10 full-time, 200 part-time; doctoral, 10 full-time, 50 part-time. *Financial Assistance:* assistantships, grants, student loans, scholarships. *Degrees Awarded 1996:* Master's, 35; doctoral, 4.

OREGON

Western Oregon State College. 345 N. Monmouth Ave., Monmouth, OR 97361. (503) 838-8471. Fax (503) 838-8228. E-mail engler@fsa.wosc.osshe.edu. Dr. Randall Engle, Chair. *Specialization:* M.S. in Information Technology. *Features:* offers advanced courses in library management, instructional development, multimedia, and computer technology. Additional course offerings in distance delivery of instruction and computer-interactive video instruction. *Admission Requirements:* 3.0 GPA, GRE or MAT. *Degree Requirements:* 45 qtr. hours; thesis optional. *Faculty:* 3 full-time, 6 part-time. *Students:* 6 full-time, 131 part-time. *Financial Assistance:* assistantships, grants, student loans, scholarship, work assistance. *Degrees Awarded 1996:* 12.

PENNSYLVANIA

Bloomsburg University. Institute for Interactive Technologies, 1210 McCormick Bldg., Bloomsburg, PA 17815. (717) 389-4506. Fax (717) 389-4943. E-mail bailey@planetx. bloomu.edu. Dr. Harold J. Bailey, contact person. *Specialization:* M.S. in Instructional Technology with emphasis on preparing for careers as interactive media specialists. The program is closely associated with the Institute for Interactive Technologies. *Features:* instructional design, authoring languages and systems, media integration, managing multimedia projects. *Admission Requirements:* Bachelor's degree. *Degree Requirements:* 33 semester credits (27 credits + 6 credit thesis, or 30 credits + three credit internship). *Faculty:* 3 full-time, 1 part-time. *Students:* 40 full-time, 20 part-time. *Financial Assistance:* assistantships, grants, student loans. *Degrees Awarded 1996:* 55.

Clarion University of Pennsylvania. Becker Hall, Clarion, PA 16214. (814) 226-2328. Fax (814) 226-2444. Carmen S. Felicetti, Chair, Dept. of Communications. *Specialization:* M.S. in Communication with specialization in Training and Development. The curriculum is process and application oriented with basic courses in television and computer applications, Internet, Web, and html authoring. Major projects are team and client oriented with an emphasis on multimedia presentations. *Admission Requirements:* Bachelor's degree; 2.75 undergraduate GPA, MAT score. *Degree Requirements:* 36 semester credits (including 27 specific to Training and Development) with 3.0 GPA, optional thesis worth 6 credits. *Faculty:* 9 full-time. *Financial Assistance:* ten 1/4 time or five 20-hour graduate assistantships.

Drexel University. College of Information Science and Technology, Philadelphia, PA 19104. (215) 895-2474. Fax (215) 895-2494. Richard H. Lytle, Prof. and Dean. Web site http://www. cis.drexel.edu. *Specializations:* M.S. and M.S.I.S. degrees. *Degree Requirements:* 48 qtr. hours taken primarily from six functional groupings: Technology of Information Systems, Principles of Information Systems, Information Organizations, Collection Management, Information Resources and Services, and Research. *Faculty:* 16. *Students:* 800. *Degrees Awarded 1996:* M.S., 66; M.S.I.S, 50.

Lehigh University. College of Education, Bethlehem, PA 18015. (610) 758-3231. Fax (610) 758-6223. E-mail WMC0@LEHIGH.EDU. Web site http://www.lehigh.edu. Ward Mitchell Cates, Coord., Educational Technology Program. *Specializations:* Master's degree with emphasis on design and development of interactive multimedia (both stand-alone and on the Web) for teaching and learning; Ed.D. in Educational Technology. *Admission Requirements:* Master's: competitive; 2.75 undergraduate GPA or 3.0 graduate GPA, GRE recommended, transcripts, at least 2 letters of recommendation, statement of personal and professional goals, application fee. Ed.D.: 3.25 graduate GPA, GRE highly recommended. Deadlines are Jul 15 for fall admission, Dec 1 for spring admission, Apr 30 for summer admission. *Degree Requirements:* Master's: 33 semester hours (including 8 in media); thesis option. *Faculty:* 3 full-time, 2 part-time. Ed.D.: 48 hours past the Master's plus dissertation. *Financial Assistance:* university graduate and research assistantships, graduate student support as participants in R&D projects, employment opportunities in local businesses and schools doing design and development. *Degrees Awarded 1996:* Master's, 12.

Pennsylvania State University. 314 Keller Bldg., University Park, PA 16802. (814) 865-0473. Fax (814) 865-0128. E-mail jonassen@psu.edu. D. Jonassen, Prof. in Charge. *Specializations:* M.Ed., M.S., D.Ed., and Ph.D. in Instructional Systems. Current teaching emphases are on Corporate Training, Emerging Technologies, and Educational Systems Design. Research interests include multimedia, visual learning, educational reform, emerging technologies, and constructivist learning. *Features:* A common thread throughout all programs is that candidates have basic competencies in the understanding of human learning; instructional design, development, and evaluation; and research procedures. Practical experience is available in mediated independent learning, research, instructional development, computer-based education, and dissemination projects. *Admission Requirements:* D.Ed., Ph.D.: GRE, TOEFL, transcript, three letters of recommendation, writing sample, vita or resume, and letter of application detailing reasoning. *Degree Requirements:* Master's: 33 semester hours, including either a thesis or project paper; doctoral: candidacy exam, courses, residency, comprehensives, dissertation. *Faculty:* 9 full-time, 2 affiliate, 2 part-time. *Students:* Master's, approx. 160; doctoral, 25 full-time, 20 part-time. *Financial Assistance:* assistantships, graduate fellowships, student aid loans, internships; assistantships on grants, contracts, and projects. *Degrees Awarded 1996:* doctoral, 8.

Rosemont College. Graduate Studies in Education, 1400 Montgomery Ave., Rosemont, PA 19010-1699. (610) 526-2982; (800) 531-9431 outside 610 area code. Fax (610) 526-2964. E-mail roscolgrad@rosemont.edu. Web site http://techined.rosemont.edu/CSTE/info.html. Dr. Richard Donagher, Dir. *Specializations:* M.Ed. in Technology in Education, Certificate in Professional Study in Technology in Education. *Admission Requirements:* GRE or MAT scores. *Degree Requirements:* Completion of 12 units (36 credits) and comprehensive exam. *Faculty:* 7 full-time, 10 part-time. *Students:* 110 full- and part-time. *Financial Assistance:* graduate student grants, assistantships, internships, Federal Stafford Loan Program. *Degrees Awarded 1996:* 19.

Shippensburg University. Dept. of Communications and Journalism, 1871 Old Main Drive, Shippensburg, PA 17257-2292. (717) 532-1521. Fax (717) 530-4013. E-mail CLNash@ARK. SHIP.EDU. Dr. C. Lynne Nash, Dept. Chair. *Specialization:* Master's degree with specializations in Public Relations, Radio/Television, Communication Theory, Press and Public Affairs. *Admission Requirements:* 2.7 GPA. *Degree Requirements:* between 30 and 36 credits, thesis or professional project or comprehensive exam. *Faculty:* 9 full-time, 1 half-time, 3 adjunct. *Students:* 15 full-time, 15 part-time. *Financial Assistance:* assistantships, grants, student loans, scholarships. *Degrees Awarded 1996:* 9.

RHODE ISLAND

The University of Rhode Island. Graduate School of Library and Information Studies, Rodman Hall, Kingston, RI 02881-0815. (401) 874-2947. Jonathan S. Tryon, Prof. and Dir. *Specializations:* M.L.I.S. degree with specialties in Archives, Law, Health Sciences, Rare Books, and Youth Services Librarianship. *Degree Requirements:* 42 semester-credit program offered in Rhode Island and regionally in Boston and Amherst, MA, and Durham, NH. *Faculty:* 6 full-time, 24 part-time. *Students:* 47 full-time, 188 part-time. *Financial Assistance:* graduate assistantships, some scholarship aid, student loans. *Degrees Awarded 1996:* 49.

SOUTH CAROLINA

University of South Carolina. Educational Psychology Department, Columbia, SC 29208. (803)777-6609. Dr. Margaret Gredler, Prof., Chair. *Specialization*: Master's degree. *Degree Requirements*: 33 semester hours, including instructional theory, computer design, and integrated media. *Faculty:* 3. *Students:* 5.

Winthrop University. Graduate Studies, 209 Tillman, Winthrop University, Rock Hill, SC 29733. (803) 323-2204. Fax (803) 323-2292. E-mail: robinsong@winthropu.edu. Dr. George H. Robinson, Dir., Educational Media Program. *Specializations:* certification program for School Library Media Specialists. *Features:* focus on services and resources for school library media centers. *Admission Requirements:* Bachelor's degree from an accredited institution; current professional teaching certificate; NTE/PRAXIS test score that meets the minimum required by the South Carolina Department of Education for the area of certification or satisfactory GRE scores. *Degree Requirements:* 36-45 semester hours. Students may be given approval to waive certain courses if they can show they have completed course work in previous degree programs. Approval to waive a course will depend on how recently the course work was completed and the degree of equivalency of the course to the required course in the educational media program. *Faculty:* 2 full-time, 2 part-time. *Students:* 7 full-time, 36 part-time. *Financial Assistance:* assistantships, student loans. *Degrees Awarded 1996:* 8.

TENNESSEE

East Tennessee State University. College of Education, Dept. of Curriculum and Instruction., Box 70684, Johnson City, TN 37614-0684. (423) 439-4186. Fax (423) 439-8362. E-mail butlerr@etsu-tn.edu. Dr. Rebecca P. Butler, Asst. Prof., Dir. *Specializations:* M.Ed. in Instructional Media (Library), M.Ed. in Instructional Technology. *Admission Requirements:* Bachelor's degree from accredited institution, transcripts, personal essay; in some cases, GRE and/or interview. *Degree Requirements:* 39 semester hours, including 18 hours in instructional technology. *Faculty:* 3 full-time, 4 part-time. *Students:* 5 full-time, 45 part-time. *Financial Assistance:* Scholarships, assistantships, aid for disabled. *Degrees Awarded 1996:* 15.

University of Tennessee-Knoxville. College of Education, Education in the Sciences, Mathematics, Research, and Technology Unit, 319 Claxton Addition, Knoxville, TN 37996-3400. (423) 974-4222 or (423) 974-3103. Dr. Al Grant, Coord., Instructional Media and Technology Program. *Specializations:* M.S. in Ed., Ed.S., and Ed.D. under Education in Sciences, Mathematics, Research, and Technology; Ed.D. in Curriculum and Instruction, concentration in Instructional Media and Technology; Ph.D. under the College of Education, concentration in Instructional Media and Technology. *Features:* course work in media management, advanced software production, utilization, research, theory, psychology, instructional computing, television, and instructional development. Course work will also meet the requirements for state certification as Instructional Materials Supervisor in the public schools of Tennessee. *Admission Requirements:* Send for Graduate Catalog, The University of Tennessee. *Degree Requirements:* M.S.: 33 semester hours; thesis optional. *Faculty:* 1 full-time, with additional assistance from Curriculum and Instruction and university faculty. *Students:* M.S., 4 part-time; Ed.S., 2 part-time.

TEXAS

Texas A&M University. College of Education, College Station, TX 77843. (409) 845-7276. Fax (409) 845-9663. Ronald D. Zellner, Assoc. Prof., Coord. Educational Technology Program, Dept. of Curriculum & Instruction. E-mail zellner@tamu.edu. *Specializations:* M.Ed. in Educational Technology; EDCI Ph.D. program with specializations in Educational Technology and in Distance Education; Ph.D. in Educational Psychology Foundations: Learning & Technology. The purpose of the Educational Technology Program is to prepare educators with the competencies required to improve the quality and effectiveness of instructional programs at all levels. A major emphasis is placed on multimedia instructional materials development and techniques for effective distance education and communication. Teacher preparation with a focus on field-based instruction and school to university collaboration is also a major component. The program goal is to prepare graduates with a wide range of skills to work as professionals and leaders in a variety of settings, including education, business, industry, and the military. *Features:* Program facilities include laboratories for teaching, resource development, and production. Computer, video, and multimedia development are supported in a number of facilities. The college and university also maintain facilities for distance education materials development and fully equipped classrooms for course delivery to nearby collaborative school districts and sites throughout the state. *Admission Requirements:* M.Ed.: Bachelor's degree, 800 GRE, 550 TOEFL; Ph.D.: 3.0 GPA, 800 GRE. *Degree Requirements:* M.Ed.: 39 semester credits, oral exam; Ph.D.: course work varies with student goals. *Faculty:* 4 full-time. *Students:* M.Ed., 20 full-time, 8 part-time; Ph.D., 2 full-time. *Financial Assistance:* several graduate and teaching assistantships. *Degrees Awarded 1996:* M.Ed., 14; Ph.D., 1.

Texas A&M University-Commerce. Department of Secondary and Higher Education, East Texas Station, Commerce, TX 75429-3011. (903) 886-5607. Fax (903) 886-5603. E-mail mundayb@tenet.edu. Dr. Robert S. Munday, Prof., Head. *Specialization:* Master's degree in Learning Technology and Information Systems with emphases on Educational Micro Computing, Educational Media and Technology, and Library and Information Science. *Admission Requirements:* 700 GRE. *Degree Requirements:* 30 semester hours with thesis, 36 without thesis. M.Ed. (Educational Computing): 30 hours in Educational Technology. M.S. (Educational Media and Technology): 21 hours in Educational Technology. M.S. (Library and Information Science): 15 hours in Library/Information Science, 12 hours in Educational Technology. *Faculty:* 3 full-time, 5 part-time. *Students:* 30 full-time, 150 part-time. *Financial Assistance:* graduate assistantships in teaching and research, scholarships, federal aid program.

Texas Tech University. College of Education, Box 41071, TTU, Lubbock, TX 79409. (806) 742-1997 ext. 299. Fax (806) 742-2179. Dr. Robert Price, Dir., Instructional Technology. *Specializations:* M.Ed. in Instructional Technology (Educational Computing and Distance Education emphasis); Ed.D. in Instructional Technology. *Features:* Program is NCATE accredited and follows ISTE and AECT guidelines. *Admission Requirements:* M.Ed.: 850 GRE, 3.0 GPA on last 30 hours of undergraduate program; Ed.D.: 1050 GRE, 3.0 GPA on last 30 hours. *Degree Requirements:* M.Ed.: 39 hours (24 hours in educational technology, 15 hours in education or outside education); practicum. Ed.D.: 87 hours (45 hours in educational technology, 18 hours in education, 15 hours in resource area or minor); practicum. *Faculty:* 5 full-time. *Students:* M.Ed., 5 full-time, 25 part-time; Ed.D., 10 full-time, 10 part-time. *Financial Assistance:* teaching and research assistantships available ($7,800 for 9 months); small scholarships. *Degrees Awarded 1996:* Ed.D., 2; M.Ed., 5.

University of North Texas. College of Education, Box 13857, Denton, TX 76203-3857. (817) 565-2057. Fax (817) 565-2185. Web site http://www.cecs.unt.edu. Dr. Terry Holcomb, Program Coord., Computer Education and Cognitive Systems. Dr. Jon Young, Chair, Dept. of Technology and Cognition. *Specializations:* M.S. in Computer Education and Instructional Systems. *Admission Requirements:* 1000 GRE (400 verbal and 400 quantitative minimums). *Degree Requirements:* 36 semester hours (including 27 in Instructional Technology and Computer Education), comprehensive exam. *Faculty:* 8. *Students:* 85. *Degrees Awarded 1996:* 25.

The University of Texas. College of Education, Austin, TX 78712. (512) 471-5211. Fax (512) 471-4607. Web site http://www.edb.utexas./coe/depts/ci/c&i.html. DeLayne Hudspeth, Assoc. Prof., Area Coord., Instructional Technology, Dept. of Curriculum and Instruction. *Specializations:* Master's degree. Ph.D. program emphasizes research, design, and development of instructional systems and communications technology. *Features:* The program is interdisciplinary in nature, although certain competencies are required of all students. Programs of study and dissertation research are based on individual needs and career goals. Learning resources include a model Learning Technology Center, computer labs and classrooms, a color television studio, and interactive multimedia lab. Many courses are offered cooperatively by other departments, including Radio-TV Film, Computer Science, and Educational Psychology. *Admission Requirements:* both degrees: 3.5 GPA, 1150 GRE. *Degree Requirements:* Master's: 30-36 semester hours depending on selection of program (21 in Instructional Technology plus research course); thesis option. A 6-hour minor is required outside the department. Ph.D: written comprehensive and specialization exam with oral defense, dissertation with oral defense. *Faculty:* 4 full-time, 3 part-time. *Students:* approx. 35 Master's, 50 doctoral. *Financial*

Assistance: Assistantships may be available to develop instructional materials, teach under-graduate computer literacy, and assist with research projects. There are also some paid internships. *Degrees Awarded 1996:* Master's, 11; doctorate, 6.

UTAH

Brigham Young University. Department of Instructional Psychology and Technology, 201 MCKB, BYU, Provo, UT 84602. (801) 378-5097. Fax (801) 378-8672. E-mail paul_merrill@ byu.edu. Web site http://www.byu.edu/acd1/ed/InSci/InSci.html. Paul F. Merrill, Prof., Chair. *Specializations:* M.S. degrees in Instructional Design, Research and Evaluation, and Multimedia Production. Ph.D. degrees in Instructional Design, and Research and Evaluation. *Features:* Course offerings include principles of learning, instructional design, assessing learning outcomes, evaluation in education, empirical inquiry in education, project management, quantitative reasoning, microcomputer materials production, multimedia production, naturalistic inquiry, and more. Students participate in internships and projects related to development, evaluation, measurement, and research. *Admission Requirements:* both degrees: transcript, 3 letters of recommendation, letter of intent, GRE scores. Apply by February 1. Students agree to live by the BYU Honor Code as a condition for admission. *Degree Requirements:* Master's: 38 semester hours, including prerequisite (3 hours), core courses (14 hours), specialization (12 hours), internship (3 hours), thesis or project (6 hours) with oral defense. Ph.D.: 94 semester hours beyond the Bachelor's degree, including: prerequisite and skill requirements (21 hours), core course (16 hours), specialization (18 hours), internship (12 hours), projects (9 hours), and dissertation (18 hours). The dissertation must be orally defended. Also, at least two consecutive 6-hour semesters must be completed in residence. *Faculty:* 9 full-time, 2 half-time. *Students:* Master's, 25 full-time, 2 part-time; Ph.D, 47 full-time, 3 part-time. *Financial Assistance:* internships, tuition waivers, loans, and travel to present papers. *Degrees Awarded 1995:* Master's, 7; Ph.D., 3.

Utah State University. Department of Instructional Technology, College of Education, Logan, UT 84322-2830. (801) 797-2694. Fax (801) 797-2693. E-mail dsmellie@cc.usu.edu. Dr. Don C. Smellie, Prof., Chair. *Specializations:* M.S. and Ed.S. with concentrations in the areas of Instructional Development, Multimedia, Educational Technology, and Information Technology/School Library Media Administration. Ph.D. in Instructional Technology is offered for individuals seeking to become professionally involved in instructional development in corporate education, public schools, community colleges, and universities. Teaching and research in higher education is another career avenue for graduates of the program. *Features:* M.S. and Ed.S. programs in Information Technology/School Library Media Administration and Educational Technology are also delivered via an electronic distance education system. The doctoral program is built on a strong Master's and Specialist's program in Instructional Technology. All doctoral students complete a core with the remainder of the course selection individualized, based upon career goals. *Admission Requirements:* M.S. and Ed.S.: 3.0 GPA, successful teaching experience or its equivalent, a verbal and quantitative score at the 40th percentile on the GRE or 43 MAT, three written recommendations. Ph.D.: Master's degree in Instructional Technology, 3.0 GPA, successful teaching experience or its equivalent, verbal and quantitative score at the 40th percentile on the GRE, three written recommendations. *Degree Requirements:* M.S.: 60 qtr. hours (including 45 in media); thesis or project option. Ed.S.: 45 qtr. hours if M.S. is in the field, 60 hours if not. *Faculty:* 9 full-time, 7 part-time. *Students:* M.S., 70 full-time, 85 part-time; Ed.S., 6 full-time, 9 part-time; Ph.D., 16 full-time, 16 part-time. *Financial Assistance:* approx. 18 to 26 assistantships (apply by April 1). *Degrees Awarded 1996:* M.S., 35; Ed.S., 3; Ph.D., 2.

VIRGINIA

George Mason University. Center for Interactive Educational Technology, Mail Stop 4B3, 4400 University Dr., Fairfax, VA 22030-4444. (703) 993-2051. Fax (703) 993-2013. E-mail mbehrman@wpgate.gmu.edu. Web site http://gse.gmu.edu/depart/instred.htm. Dr. Michael

Behrmann, Coord. of Instructional Technology Academic Programs. *Specializations:* M.Ed. in Instructional Technology with tracks in Instructional Design and Development, Integration of Technology in Schools, and Assistive/Special Education Technology; M.Ed. in Special Education Technology, Computer Science Educator; Ph.D. with specialization in Instructional Technology or Special Education Technology. Master's program started in 1983 and doctoral in 1984. *Admission Requirements:* teaching or training experience, introductory programming course or equivalent; introductory course in educational technology or equivalent. *Degree Requirements:* M.Ed. in Instructional Technology: 36 hours; practicum, internship, or project. M.Ed. in Special Education Technology: 36-42 hours. Ph.D.: 56-62 hours beyond Master's degree for either specialization. *Faculty:* 6 full-time, 5 part-time. *Students:* M.Ed. in Instructional Technology: 5 full-time, 91 part-time. M.Ed. in Special Education Technology: 10 full-time, 8 part-time. Ph.D.: 19 part-time. *Financial Assistance:* Assistantships and tuition waivers available for full-time graduate students. *Degrees Awarded 1996:* M.Ed. in Instructional Technology, 15; M.Ed. in Special Education Technology, 7; Ph.D., 2.

Radford University. Educational Studies Department, College of Education and Human Development, P.O. Box 6959, Radford, VA 24142. (540) 831-5302. Fax (540) 831-6053. E-mail ljwilson@runet.edu. Web site http://www.radford.edu. Dr. Linda J. Wilson. *Specialization*: M.S. in Education with Educational Media/Technology emphasis. *Features*: School Library Media Specialist licensure. *Admission Requirements*: Bachelor's degree, 2.7 undergraduate GPA. *Degree Requirements*: 36 semester hours, practicum; thesis optional. *Faculty:* 2 full-time, 3 part-time. *Students*: 5 full-time, 22 part-time. *Financial Assistance*: assistantships, grants, student loans, scholarships. *Degrees Awarded 1996*: 3.

University of Virginia. Curry School of Education, Ruffner Hall, Charlottesville, VA 22903. (804) 924-7471. Fax (804) 924-0747. E-mail jbbunch@virginia.edu. Web site http://curry. edschool.Virginia.EDU/curry/dept/edes/instrtech/. John B. Bunch, Assoc. Prof., Coord., Instructional Technology Program, Dept. of Leadership, Foundations and Policy Studies. *Specializations:* M.Ed., Ed.S., Ed.D, and Ph.D. degrees with focal areas in Media Production, Interactive Multimedia, and K-12 Educational Technologies. *Admission Requirements:* undergraduate degree from accredited institution, GRE scores, 2 recommendations, transcripts. Admission application deadline is March 1st of each year for the fall semester for both Master's and doctoral degrees. *Degree Requirements:* For specific degree requirements, see Web site, write to the address above, or refer to the UVA *Graduate Record. Faculty:* 4 full-time, 2 part-time. *Students:* M.Ed. and Ed.S., 20 full-time, 5 part-time; Ed.D and Ph.D., 13 full-time, 4 part-time. *Financial Assistance:* Some graduate assistantships and scholarships are available on a competitive basis. *Degrees Awarded 1996:* Master's, 4; doctorate, 2.

Virginia Polytechnic Institute and State University (Virginia Tech). College of Human Resources and Education, 220 War Memorial Hall, Blacksburg, VA 24061-0341. (540) 231-5587. Fax (540) 231-3717. E-mail moorem@vt.edu. David M. (Mike) Moore, Program Area Leader, Instructional Systems Development, Dept. of Teaching and Learning. *Specializations:* M.A, Ed.D., and Ph.D. in Instructional Technology. Preparation for education, higher education, faculty development, business, and industry. *Features:* Areas of emphasis are Instructional Design, Educational Computing, Evaluation, and Media Management and Development. Facilities include two computer labs (70 IBM and Macintosh computers), plus interactive video, speech synthesis, telecommunication labs, distance education classroom, and computer graphics production areas. *Admission Requirements:* Ed.D. and Ph.D.: 3.3 GPA from Master's degree, GRE scores, interview, three letters of recommendation, transcripts. *Faculty:* 8 full-time, 5 part-time. *Students:* 35 full-time and 10 part-time at the doctoral level. *Financial Assistance:* 10 assistantships, tuition scholarships. *Degrees Awarded 1996:* doctoral, 6.

Virginia State University. School of Liberal Arts & Education, Petersburg, VA 23806. (804) 524-5937. Vykuntapathi Thota, Acting Chair and Program Dir., Dept. of Educational Leadership. *Specializations:* M.S., M.Ed. in Educational Media and Technology. *Features:* Video Conferencing Center and PLATO Laboratory, internship in ABC and NBC channels. *Degree Requirements:* 30 semester hours plus thesis for M.S.; 33 semester hours plus project for

M.Ed.; comprehensive exam. *Faculty:* 1 full-time, 2 part-time. *Students:* 5 full-time, 41 part-time. *Financial Assistance:* scholarships through the School of Graduate Studies.

WASHINGTON

*Eastern Washington University. Department Computer Science, Cheney, WA 99004-2495. (509) 359-7092. Fax (509) 359-2215. Internet dhorner@ewu.edu. Dr. Donald R. Horner, Prof. of Computer Science. *Specializations:* M.Ed. in Computer Education (elementary); M.Ed. in Computer Education (secondary); M.S. in Computer Education (Interdisciplinary). Master's program started in 1983. *Admission Requirements:* GRE scores, 3.0 GPA for last 90 qtr. credits. *Degree Requirements:* M.S.: 52 qtr. hours (30 hours in computers, 0 hours in education, 15 hours outside education; the hours do not total to 52 because of freedom to choose where Methods of Research is taken, where 12 credits of supporting courses are taken, and where additional electives are taken); research project with formal report. M.Ed.: 48 qtr. hours (24 hours in computer science, 16 hours in education, 8 hours outside education). *Features:* Most projects involve the use of high-level authoring systems to develop educational products. *Faculty:* 3 full-time. *Students:* approx. 35. *Financial Assistance:* some research and teaching fellowships. *Degrees Awarded 1995:* 3.

University of Washington. College of Education, 115 Miller Hall, Box 353600 Seattle, WA 98195-3600. (206) 543-1847. Fax (206) 543-8439. E-mail stkerr@u.washington.edu. Stephen T. Kerr, Prof. of Education. *Specializations:* Master's, Ed.D, and Ph.D. for individuals in business, industry, higher education, public schools, and organizations concerned with education or communication (broadly defined). *Features:* emphasis on instructional design as a process of making decisions about the shape of instruction; additional focus on research and development in such areas as message design (especially graphics and diagrams); electronic information systems; interactive instruction via videodisc, multimedia, and computers. *Admission Requirements:* doctoral: GRE scores, letters of reference, transcripts, personal statement, Master's degree or equivalent in field appropriate to the specialization with 3.5 GPA, two years of successful professional experience and/or experience related to program goals. *Degree Requirements:* Master's: 45 qtr. hours (including 24 in media); thesis or project optional. *Faculty:* 2 full-time, 3 part-time. *Students:* 12 full-time, 32 part-time. *Financial Assistance:* assistantships awarded competitively and on basis of program needs; other assistantships available depending on grant activity in any given year. *Degrees Awarded 1996:* Master's, 11; doctorate, 3.

Western Washington University. Woodring College of Education, Instructional Technology, MS 9087, Bellingham, WA 98225-9087. (360) 650-3387. Fax (360) 650-6526. E-mail lblack@wce.wwu.edu. Dr. Les Blackwell, Prof., Program Chair. *Specializations:* M.Ed.with emphasis in Instructional Technology in Adult Education, Special Education, Elementary Education, and Secondary Education. *Admission Requirements:* 3.0 GPA in last 45 qtr. credit hours, GRE or MAT scores, 3 letters of recommendation, and, in some cases, 3 years of teaching experience. *Degree Requirements:* 48-52 qtr. hours (24-28 hours in instructional technology; 24 hours in education-related courses, thesis required; internship and practicum possible). *Faculty:* 4 full-time, 8 part-time. *Students:* 5 full-time, 13 part-time. *Financial Assistance:* assistantships, student loans, scholarships. *Master's Degrees Awarded 1996:* 2. Four graduates have advanced to Ph.D. programs.

WISCONSIN

Edgewood College. Department of Education, 855 Woodrow St., Madison, WI 53711-1997. (608) 257-4861, ext. 2293. Fax (608) 259-6727. E-mail schmied@edgewood.edu. Web site http://www.edgewood.edu. Dr. Joseph E. Schmiedicke, Chair, Dept. of Education. *Specializations:* M.A. in Education with emphasis on Instructional Technology. Master's program started in 1987. *Features:* classes conducted in laboratory setting with emphasis on applications and software. *Admission Requirements:* 2.75 GPA. *Degree Requirements:* 36 semester hours.

Faculty: 2 full-time, 3 part-time. *Students:* 2 full-time, 130 part-time. *Financial Assistance:* grants, student loans. *Degrees Awarded 1996:* 10.

University of Wisconsin-La Crosse. Educational Media Program, Rm. 109, Morris Hall, La Crosse, WI 54601. (608) 785-8121. Fax (608) 785-8119. Dr. Russell Phillips, Dir. *Specializations:* M.S. in Professional Development with specializations in Initial Instructional Library Specialist, License 901; Instructional Library Media Specialist, License 902 (39 credits). *Degree Requirements:* 30 semester hours, including 15 in media; no thesis. *Faculty:* 2 full-time, 4 part-time. *Students:* 21. *Financial Assistance:* guaranteed student loans, graduate assistantships.

University of Wisconsin-Madison. Dept. of Curriculum and Instruction, School of Education, 225 N. Mills St., Madison, WI 53706. (608) 263-4672. Fax (608) 263-9992. E-mail adevaney@ facstaff.wisc.edu. Ann De Vaney, Prof. *Specializations:* M.S. degree and State Instructional Technology License; Ph.D. programs to prepare college and university faculty. *Features:* The program is coordinated with media operations of the university. Traditional instructional technology courses are processed through a social, cultural, and historical frame of reference. Current curriculum emphasizes communication and cognitive theories, critical cultural studies, and theories of textual analysis and instructional development. *Admission Requirements:* Master's and Ph.D.: previous experience in Instructional Technology preferred, previous teaching experience, 3.0 GPA on last 60 undergraduate credits, acceptable scores on GRE, 3.0 GPA on all graduate work. *Degree Requirements:* M.S.: 24 credits plus thesis and exam; Ph.D.: 3 years of residency beyond the Bachelor's (Master's degree counts for one year; one year must be full-time), major, minor, and research requirements, preliminary exam, dissertation, and oral exam. *Faculty:* 3 full-time, 1 part-time. *Students:* M.S., 42; Ph.D., 29. *Financial Assistance:* several stipends of approx. $1000 per month for 20 hours of work per week; other media jobs are also available. *Degrees Awarded 1996:* M.S., 15; Ph.D., 4.

Part Seven
Mediagraphy
Print and Nonprint Resources

Introduction

CONTENTS

This resource lists media-related journals, books, ERIC documents, journal articles, and nonprint media resources of interest to practitioners, researchers, students, and others concerned with educational technology and educational media. The primary goal of this section is to list current publications in the field. The majority of materials cited here were published in 1996 or early 1997. Media-related journals include those listed in past issues of *EMTY* and new entries in the field.

It is not the intention of the authors for this chapter to serve as a specific resource location tool, although it may be used for that purpose in the absence of database access. Rather, readers may peruse the categories of interest in this chapter to gain an idea of recent developments within the field. For archival purposes, this chapter may serve as a snapshot of the field in 1996. Readers must bear in mind that technological developments occur well in advance of publication, and should take that fact into consideration when judging the timeliness of resources listed in this chapter.

SELECTION

Items were selected for the Mediagraphy in several ways. The ERIC (Educational Resources Information Center) Database was the source for ERIC document and journal article citations. Media-related journals were either retained or added to the list when they met one or more of the following criteria: were from a reputable publisher; had a broad circulation; were covered by indexing services; were peer reviewed; and filled a gap in the literature. In keeping with the title and original purpose of this section, we have included listings for a sampling of the wealth of current nonbook media products that are now becoming available. They include CD-ROMs, computer software, courseware, online products and resources, and videotapes. Due to the increasing tendency for media producers to package their products in more that one format and for single titles to contain mixed media, titles are no longer separated by media type. The editors make no claims as to the comprehensiveness of this list. It is, instead, intended to be representative.

OBTAINING RESOURCES

Media-Related Periodicals and Books. Publisher, price, and ordering/subscription address are listed wherever available.

ERIC Documents. ERIC documents can be read and often copied from their microfiche form at any library holding an ERIC microfiche collection. The identification number beginning with ED (for example, ED 332 677) locates the document in the collection. Copies of most ERIC documents can also be ordered from the ERIC Document Reproduction Service. Prices charged depend upon format chosen (microfiche or paper copy), length of the document, and method of shipping. Online orders, fax orders, and expedited delivery are available.

To find the closest library with an ERIC microfiche collection, contact:

ACCESS ERIC
1600 Research Blvd.
Rockville, MD 20850-3172
1-800-LET-ERIC (538-3742)
E-mail: acceric@inet.ed.gov

To order ERIC documents, contact:

ERIC Document Reproduction Service (EDRS)
7420 Fullerton Rd., Suite 110
Springfield, VA 22153-2852
voice: 1-800-443-ERIC (443-3742), 703-440-1400
fax: 703-440-1408
E-mail: edrs@inet.ed.gov

Journal Articles. Photocopies of journal articles can be obtained in one of the following ways: (1) from a library subscribing to the title; (2) through interlibrary loan; (3) through the purchase of a back issue from the journal publisher; or (4) from an article reprint service such as UMI.

UMI Information Store
500 Sansome Street, Suite 400
San Francisco, CA 94111
1-800-248-0360 (toll-free in U.S. and Canada)
(415) 433-5500 (outside U.S. and Canada)
E-mail: orders@infostore.com

Journal articles can also be obtained through the Institute for Scientific Information (ISI).

Genuine Article Service
3501 Market Street
Philadelphia, PA 19104
1-800-523-1850 ext. 1536
(215) 386-1011 ext. 1536
E-mail: tga@isinet.com

ARRANGEMENT

Mediagraphy entries are classified according to major subject emphasis under the following headings:

- Artificial Intelligence, Robotics, and Electronic Performance Support Systems
- Computer-Assisted Instruction
- Distance Education
- Educational Research
- Educational Technology
- Electronic Publishing
- Information Science and Technology
- Instructional Design and Training
- Libraries and Media Centers

- Media Technologies
- Professional Development
- Simulation, Gaming, and Virtual Reality
- Special Education and Disabilities
- Telecommunications and Networking

Mediagraphy

ARTIFICIAL INTELLIGENCE, ROBOTICS, AND ELECTRONIC PERFORMANCE SUPPORT SYSTEMS

Devi, R. (1996). Modeling students' construction of energy models in physics. **Instructional Science, 24** (4), 259-293. Examines students' construction of experimentation models for physics theories in energy storage, transformation, and transfers involving electricity and mechanics. Student problem solving dialogs and artificial intelligence modeling of these processes are analyzed. Construction of models established relations between elements with linear causal reasoning. Computer models may advance the development of modeling in student's cognitive processes.

Hoschka, P., Ed. (1996). **Computers as assistants: A new generation of support systems.** [Book, 320pp., $29.95]. Lawrence Erlbaum, 10 Industrial Ave., Mahwah, NJ 07430-2262, orders@erlbaum.com. Discusses the concepts and methods from artificial intelligence and computer-supported cooperative work, and synthesizes them into a model for work assistance systems.

Intelligent Tutoring Media. Information Today, Inc., 143 Old Marlton Pike, Medford, NJ 08055. [Q., $125]. Concerned with the packaging and communication of knowledge using advanced information technologies. Studies the impact of artificial intelligence, hypertext, interactive video, mass storage devices, and telecommunications networks.

International Journal of Robotics Research. MIT Press, Journals, 55 Hayward St., Cambridge, MA 02142. [Bi-mo., $80 indiv. (foreign $102), $185 inst. (foreign $199), $50 students and retired (foreign $72)]. Interdisciplinary approach to the study of robotics for researchers, scientists, and students.

Journal of Artificial Intelligence in Education. Association for Advancement of Computing in Education, Box 2966, Charlottesville, VA 22902-2966. [Q.; $65 indiv. (foreign, $80), $93 inst., $113 library]. International journal publishes articles on how intelligent computer technologies can be used in education to enhance learning and teaching. Reports on research and developments, integration, and applications of artificial intelligence in education.

Kimmel, S. (1996). Robot-generated databases on the World Wide Web. **Database, 19** (1), 40-43, 46-49. Provides an overview of robots that retrieve Web documents and index data and then store it in a database. Nine robot-generated databases are described, including record content, services, search features, and sample search results; sidebars discuss the controversy about Web robots and other resource discovery tools.

Knowledge-Based Systems. Elsevier Science Inc., P.O. Box 882, Madison Square Station, New York, NY 10159-0882. [Q., $552]. Interdisciplinary applications-oriented journal on fifth-generation computing, expert systems, and knowledge-based methods in system design.

Koschmann, T. (1996). Of Hubert Dreyfus and dead horses: Some thoughts on Dreyfus' "What computers still can't do." **Artificial Intelligence, 80** (129-141). Reviews Dreyfus's writings about human cognition and artificial intelligence (AI), and explains some of the implications of his position, particularly in education. Topics include Dreyfus' critique of AI, representationalism and expertise, technology and its role in instruction, computer-assisted instruction, and intelligent tutoring systems.

Mclachlan, R. (1996). A practical, and lasting, approach to using computers in the university history classroom. **History Computer Review, 12** (1), 15-22. Outlines several realistic, practical, classroom-tested strategies for using computers to augment undergraduate history instruction. These include drawing on databases to provide illustrative examples during class lectures and tutorials centering on research questions to be answered in the computer lab. Describes a class project involving developing a database.

Milton, K., & Spradley, P. (1996). A renaissance of the Renaissance: Using HyperStudio for research projects. **Learning and Leading with Technology, 23** (6), 20-22. Discussion of the use of multimedia programs in writing labs or classrooms focuses on the use of "HyperStudio" in high school sophomore advanced English classes for students' research projects. Highlights include computer writing lab activities, teaching strategies, small group demonstrations, printed instructions, individualized help, and teachers' roles.

Minds and Machines. Kluwer Academic Publishers, Box 358, Accord Station, Hingham, MA 02018-0358. [Q., $351]. Discusses issues concerning machines and mentality, artificial intelligence, epistemology, simulation, and modeling.

Odom, M. D., & Pourjalali, H. (1996). Knowledge transfer from expert systems vs. traditional instruction: Do personality traits make a difference? **Journal of End User Computing, 8** (2), 14-20. Reports on the extension of an experiment in which one of three teaching methods (traditional instruction, expert system, or a combination of both) was used to teach a subject.

Wood, D. (1996). A framework for re-engineering traditional training: Interactive training and electronic performance support. **Performance Improvement, 35** (8), 14-18. A solution to the shortcomings of traditional corporate education and training includes interactive and/or multimedia tutorials and electronic performance support. The easiest way to deliver training at the point of need is by implementing a local area network. Organizational benefits include increased productivity, improved service and product quality, and greater ability to compete.

COMPUTER-ASSISTED INSTRUCTION

Apple Library Users Group Newsletter. Library Users Group, Infinite Way, MS3042A, Cupertino, CA 95014. [4/yr., free]. For people interested in using Apple and Macintosh computers in libraries and information centers.

Bottino, R. M., & Furinghetti, F. (1996). The emerging of teachers' conceptions of new subjects inserted in mathematics programs: The case of Informatics. **Educational Studies in Mathematics, 30** (2), 109-134. Investigates teachers' roles and conceptions by analyzing choices taken by mathematics teachers when faced with curriculum reform induced by introducing informatics, educational technology, in secondary school courses.

BYTE. Box 550, Hightstown, NJ 08520-9886. [Mo., $29.95; $34.95 Canada and Mexico; $50 elsewhere]. Current articles on microcomputers provide technical information as well as information on applications and products for business and professional users.

CALICO Journal. Computer Assisted Language and Instruction Consortium, 014 Language Center, Box 90264, Duke University, Durham, NC 27708-0267. [Q.; $35 indiv., $65 inst., $125 corporations]. Provides information on the applications of technology in teaching and learning languages.

Cognition and Technology Group at Vanderbilt University. (1997). **The Jasper Project: Lessons in curriculum, instruction, and professional development.** [Book, 200pp., $19.95]. Learning, Inc., 10 Industrial Ave., Mahwah, NY 07430. Describes the Jasper Project from a developmental perspective; summarizes the Jasper episodes and addresses issues of curriculum integration.

Coleman, M. (1996). The software scene in science. **Education in Science** (167), 8-10. Reports on what science teachers are doing with instructional technology in science and what software they are using to do it with. Includes examples of teachers using data logging, palmtop computers, word processing, spreadsheets, and CD-ROMs.

Collis, B. A., Knezek, G. A., Lai, K., Miyashita, K. T., Pelgrum, W. J., Plomp, T., & Sakamoto, T. (1996). **Children and computers in school.** [Book, 160pp., $14.95]. Lawrence Erlbaum, 10 Industrial Ave., Mahwah, NJ 07430-2262, orders@erlbaum.com. Converges research findings from 4 countries to describe the impact of educational computing.

Computer Book Review. 735 Ekekela Place, Honolulu, HI 96817. [6/yr., $30]. Provides critical reviews of books on computers and computer-related subjects.

Computers and Education. Elsevier Science, 660 White Plains Rd., Tarrytown, NY 10591-5153. [8/yr., $768]. Presents technical papers covering a broad range of subjects for users of analog, digital, and hybrid computers in all aspects of higher education.

Computers and the Humanities. Kluwer Academic Publishers Group, P.O. Box 358, Accord Station, Hingham, MA 02018-0358. [Bi-mo., $85.50 indiv., $180 inst., members $49]. Contains papers on computer-aided studies, applications, automation, and computer-assisted instruction.

Computers in Human Behavior. Pergamon Press, 660 White Plains Rd., Tarrytown, NY 10591-5153. [Q., $388]. Addresses the psychological impact of computer use on individuals, groups, and society.

Computers in the Schools. Haworth Press, 10 Alice St., Binghamton, NY 13904. [Q., $36 indiv., $75 inst., $115 libraries]. Features articles that combine theory and practical applications of small computers in schools for educators and school administrators.

Cook, C. (1996). **Computers and the collaborative experience of learning.** [Book, 272pp., $18.95 US, $26.95 Canada]. Routledge, 11 Fetter Ln., London EC4P 4EE, England. Considers sociocultural aspects of education as it explores the interactivity allowed by current educational technologies.

Dr. Dobb's Journal. Miller Freeman Inc., 600 Harrison St., San Francisco, CA 94107. [Mo., $29.97 US, $45 Mexico and Canada, $70 elsewhere]. Articles on the latest in operating systems, programming languages, algorithms, hardware design and architecture, data structures, and telecommunications; in-depth hardware and software reviews.

Education Technology News. Business Publishers, Inc., 951 Pershing Dr., Silver Spring, MD 20910-4464. [Bi-w., $286]. For teachers and those interested in educational uses of computers in the classroom. Feature articles on applications and educational software.

Electronic Learning. Scholastic Inc., 555 Broadway, New York, NY 10012-3999. [8/yr., $19.95]. Features articles on applications and advances of technology in education for K-12 and college educators and administrators.

Freeman, E. (1996). Ada and the analytical engine. **Educom Review, 31** (2), 40-43. Presents a brief history of Ada Byron King, Countess of Lovelace, focusing on her primary role in the development of the Analytical Engine (the world's first computer). Describes the Ada Project (TAP), a centralized Web site that serves as a clearinghouse for information related to women in computing, and provides a Web address for accessing TAP.

Goodin, A. (1996). **Computers in the classroom: How teachers and students are using technology to transform learning.** [Book, 224pp., $24]. Jossey-Bass, 350 Sansome St., San Francisco, CA 94104. Describes six case studies of CAI installations.

Gray, C. (1996). Will your NQT use IT? **Language Learning Journal** (13), 58-61. Examines students' views of an Initial Teacher (IT) Training component of a modern language course and their resulting attitudes toward the use of computers in the language classroom. Most of the students developed a positive attitude towards this use of computers and intended to use them in their future posts.

Harvey-Morgan, J. (1996). **Moving forward the software development agenda in adult literacy: A report based on the Adult Literacy Software Development Conference**. Paper presented at Adult Literacy Software Development Conference, Reston, VA, October, 1994. [ED 396 151, 66pp.]. This report describes the Adult Literacy Software Working Conference, which was attended by 52 adult literacy practitioners, software developers, hardware vendors, other educational technology specialists, policymakers, and researchers. The conference participants identified market, program and staff, and design and quality issues related to adult literacy software development and discussed potential roles and actions for each of the major stakeholders in adult literacy software development to achieve necessary changes and improvements in the field.

Hirtle, J. (1996). Constructing a collaborative classroom (Part 1). **Learning and Leading with Technology, 23** (7), 19-21. Describes a process used to develop a constructivist, student-created curriculum. Focuses on how objectives were accomplished by forming an alliance with a computer teacher to carry out a collaborative project for high school and elementary school students.

Home Office Computing. Box 51344, Boulder, CO 80321-1344. [Mo., $19.97, foreign $27.97]. For professionals who use computers and do business at home.

Hoyt, W. B. (1996). Balancing technology with established methodology in the accounting classroom. **Journal of Education for Business, 50** (3), 29-31. Discusses the role of technology in secondary accounting courses. Indicates that students must master the principles and concepts in accounting and must experience the manual preparation of documents before automated procedures are integrated.

InfoWorld. InfoWorld Publishing, 155 Bovet Rd., Suite 800, San Mateo, CA 94402. [W., $130]. News and reviews of PC hardware, software, peripherals, and networking.

Interpersonal Computing and Technology: An Electronic Journal for the 21st Century. [Q., electronic journal]. Center for Teaching and Technology, Academic Computer Center, Georgetown University, Washington, DC 20057, with support from the Center for Academic Computing, The Pennsylvania State University, University Park, PA 16802. Articles may be retrieved from gopher: guvm.ccf.georgetown.edu:70/11/listserv/ipct.

Johnson, J. M., Ed. (1997). **1997 educational software preview guide.** [Book, 128pp., $14.95]. International Society for Technology in Education, University of Oregon, 1787 Agate St., Eugene, OR 97403-1923. Designed for educators seeking software for preview, this guide lists more than 700 titles of favorably reviewed software for K-12 classroom use.

Jonassen, D. (1996). **Computers in the schools: Mindtools for critical thinking.** [Book, 291pp., $38.60]. Merrill/Prentice Hall; available from International Society for Technology in Education, University of Oregon, 1787 Agate St., Eugene, OR 97403-1923. Introduces the concept of MindTools (databases, spreadsheets, semantic networking, expert systems, computer-mediated communication, and multimedia) as an alternative application of computers to engage learners in higher-order thinking skills.

Journal of Computer Assisted Learning. Blackwell Scientific Publications, Journal Subscription Dept., Marstan Book Services, Box 87, Oxford OX2 0DT, England. [Q., $48 indiv., $197 inst.]. Articles and research on the use of computer-assisted learning.

Journal of Educational Computing Research. Baywood Publishing Co., 26 Austin Ave., P.O. Box 337, Amityville, NY 11701. [8/yr. (2 vols., 4 each); $95 indiv. (per vol.), $182 inst. (per vol.)]. Presents original research papers, critical analyses, reports on research in progress, design and development studies, article reviews, and grant award listings.

Journal of Research on Computing in Education. International Society for Technology in Education, University of Oregon, 1787 Agate St., Eugene, OR 97403-1923. [Q., $74 US nonmembers, foreign $84]. Contains articles reporting on the latest research findings related to classroom and administrative uses of technology, including system and project evaluations.

Koschmann, T., Ed. (1996). **CSCL: Theory and practice of an emerging paradigm.** [Book, 360pp., $29.95]. Lawrence Erlbaum, 10 Industrial Ave., Mahwah, NJ 07430-2262, orders@erlbaum.com. Describes current research and defines future directions for work in the field of CSCL (Computer-Supported Collaborative Learning).

Kuman, D. D., & Helgeson, S. L. (1996). Effect of computer interfaces on chemistry problem solving among various ethnic groups: A comparison of Pen-Point and Powerbook computers. **Journal of Science Education and Technology, 5** (2), 121-130. Investigates the effect of Pen-Point and Powerbook computers on solving a multiple-step chemistry problem among white, Afro-American, and Hispanic students. Results suggest that the Pen-Point computer has a more positive effect on the problem-solving performance and attitude of students towards computers than the Powerbook computer.

Land, M., & Turner, S. (1997). **Tools for schools: Applications software for the classroom.** 2nd ed. [Book, 320pp.]. Wadsworth Publishing Co., 10 Davis Dr., Belmont, CA 94002-3098. One-semester text that illustrates computer applications as teaching tools.

Learning and Leading with Technology. The ISTE Journal of Educational Technology Practice and Policy. International Society for Technology in Education, University of Oregon, 1787 Agate St., Eugene, OR 97403-1923. [8/yr., $61 nonmembers, Canada $75.97, internatl. $71, internatl. air $91]. Focuses on the use of technology, coordination, and leadership.

Lee, I. (1996). **Challenges to a learning approach through a global network.** Presented at the Annual Conference of the American Educational Research Association New York. [ED 395 567, 14pp.]. Computer networking is a new educational approach that can well serve the educational needs in a society of dynamic and constant changes. This paper examines effective ways of establishing a computer network-based learning system in the Korean educational system.

MacWorld. MacWorld Communications, Box 54529, Boulder, CO 80322-4529. [Mo., $24.]. Describes hardware, software, tutorials, and applications for users of the Macintosh microcomputer.

McGinnis, J. R. (1996). Beliefs and perceived needs of rural K-12 teachers of science toward the uses of computing technologies. **Journal of Science Education and Technology, 5** (2), 111-120. Explores the accessibility, use, and perceived needs toward computing technologies of elementary and secondary science teachers in two large rural school districts. Data analysis indicates significant differences in many areas between elementary and secondary teachers' responses. Discusses implications for science teacher education and research for rural schools.

Miech, E. J. (1996). **On CALL: A review of computer-assisted language learning in US colleges and universities.** [ED 394 525, 115pp.]. This paper examines 22 empirical computer-assisted language learning (CALL) studies published between 1989 and 1994, and 13 reviews and syntheses published between 1987 and 1992, pertaining to CALL in higher education in the US.

Merrill, P. F., Hammons, K., Vincent, B. R., Reynolds, P. L., & Christensen, L. (1996). **Computers in education.** 3rd ed. [Book, 384pp.]. Allyn & Bacon, 160 Gould St., Needham Heights, MA 02194-2315. Text to help teachers integrate computing into the curriculum with effectiveness and efficiency.

Microcomputer Abstracts. Information Today, Inc., 143 Old Marlton Pike, Medford, NJ 08055-8750. [Bi-mo., $159]. Abstracts of literature on the use of microcomputers in business, education, and the home.

Microcomputer Industry Update. Industry Market Reports, Inc., Box 681, Los Altos, CA 94023. [Mo., $355]. Abstracts of product announcements and reviews of interest appearing in weekly trade press.

Morritt, H. (1996). **Women and computer based technologies: A feminist perspective.** Paper presented at the Annual Meeting of the American Educational Research Association, New York. [ED 394 501]. The use of computer based technologies by professional women in education is examined through a feminist standpoint theory in this paper. The theory is grounded in eight claims which form the basis of the conceptual framework for the study.

Morton, A. (1996). **Factors affecting the integration of computers in Western Sydney secondary schools.** Paper presented at EdTech '96 Biennial Conference of the Australian Society for Educational Technology, Melbourne, July. [ED 396 737, 9pp.]. A study of six schools was conducted to explore the integration of computers across the curriculum in Western Sydney (Australia) secondary schools. Analysis of the data shows fluctuation in the way teachers feel about computers. These feelings manifest themselves within the skill base of teachers and in turn influence teacher intentions to use computers as tools for learning and discovery.

Moursund, D. (1996). Effective practices (Part 4): Problem solving. **Learning and Leading with Technology, 23** (6), 5-6. Discusses the use of computers to help with problem solving. Topics include information science, including effective procedure and procedural thinking; templates; artificially intelligent agents and expert systems; and applications in education, including the goal of computer literacy for all students, and integrated software packages such as ClarisWorks and Microsoft Works.

Oshima, J. (1996). Collaborative learning processes associated with high and low conceptual progress. **Instructional Science, 24** (2), 125-155. Computer-Supported Intentional Learning Environments (CSILE) is a database system in which learners collaboratively construct the knowledge represented in the database. This study examines how students in a grade-five and -six classroom built their database on a science topic, electricity. Differences in cognitive and operative activities between high- and low-conceptual-progress students are compared.

Ostwald, T., & Stulz, K. (1996). Using criteria-based evaluation in computer application courses. **Journal of Education for Business, 50** (3), 33-35. A criterion-based strategy to evaluate student performance in computer application courses requires modification of evaluation tools with each technological change. Students benefit by not competing for grades and there is more consistency in student assessment across courses and semesters.

PC Magazine: The Independent Guide to IBM-Standard Personal Computing. Ziff-Davis Publishing Co., Box 54093, Boulder, CO 80322. [Bi-w., $49.97]. Comparative reviews of computer hardware and general business software programs.

PC Week. Ziff-Davis Publishing Co., 10 Presidents Landing, Medford, MA 02155-5146. [W., $195, Canada and Mexico $250, free to qualified personnel]. Provides current information on the IBM PC, including hardware, software, industry news, business strategies, and reviews of hardware and software.

PC World. PC World Communications, Inc., Box 55029, Boulder, CO 80322-5029. [Mo., $29.90 US, $53.39 Canada, $49.90 Mexico, $75.90 elsewhere]. Presents articles on applications and columns containing news, systems information, product announcements, and hardware updates.

Pennington, M. (1996). **The computer and the non-native writer: A natural partnership.** [Book, 240pp., $21.95]. Hampton Press, Inc., Cresskill, NJ. Synthesizes current research concerning computer educational assistance for ESL learners.

Provenzo, E. F. (1996). **The educator's brief guide to computers in the schools.** [Book, 250pp., $39.95]. Eye on Education, 6 Depot Way West, Suite 106, Larchmont, NY 10538. Demonstrates how teachers and administrators can employ computers to assist them with daily tasks.

Ray, R. D., & Salomon, M. (1996). Teaching the low-performance college student: An inexpensive behavioral technology that works. **Educational Technology, 36** (3), 52-64. Reports on a 10-year investigation of the use of behavioral contingency management technology to improve low-performance students' skills, which was conducted across 17 offerings of a sophomore-level undergraduate course. Findings indicate that behavioral contracting technologies involve very little cost and produce highly effective results.

Simic, M., & Essex, C. (1996). **The computer as an aid to reading instruction.** Rev. ed. [ED 392 024, 56pp.]. One of a series of educational packages designed for implementation either in a workshop atmosphere or through individual study, this Hot Topic guide presents a variety of materials to assist educators in designing and implementing classroom projects and activities centering on the topic of the computer as an aid to reading instruction.

Simonson, M. R., & Thompson, A. (1997). **Educational computing foundations.** 3rd ed. [Book, 512pp.]. Merrill/Prentice Hall, 445 Hutchinson Ave., Columbus, OH 43235-5677. Provides fundamental principles of classroom computer use. The 3rd edition adds sections addressing the Web, hypermedia, and statistical software.

Smith, I., Yoder, S., & Thomas, R. (1997). **Classroom activities with ClarisWorks 4.0.** [Book, disk, $27.95]. International Society for Technology in Education, University of Oregon, 1787 Agate St., Eugene, OR 97403-1923. Resource for infusing curriculum with features of ClarisWorks 4.0.

Social Science Computer Review. Sage Publications Inc., 2455 Teller Rd., Thousand Oaks, CA 91320. [Q., $52 indiv. ($67 foreign), $105 inst. ($117 foreign)]. Features include software reviews, new product announcements, and tutorials for beginners.

Software Digest Ratings Report. National Software Testing Laboratories Inc., Plymouth Corporate Center, Box 1000, Plymouth Meeting, PA 19462. [Mo., $450]. For IBM personal computer users. Each issue reports the ratings for one category of IBM PC software, based on multiple-user tests.

Software Magazine. Sentry Publishing Co., Inc., 1 Research Dr., Suite 400B, Westborough, MA 01581-3907. [Mo., $65 US, $75 Canada, $125 elsewhere, free to qualified personnel]. Provides information on software and industry developments for business and professional users, and announces new software packages.

Software Reviews on File. Facts on File, 460 Park Ave. S., New York, NY 10016. [Mo., $210]. Condensed software reviews from more than 150 publications. Features software for all major microcomputer systems and programming languages for library, school, home, and business use.

Thomas, M. (1996). Using computers in the mathematics classroom: The role of the teacher. **Mathematics Education Research Journal, 8** (1), 38-57. Interviews, questionnaires, and observation of mathematics teachers in their implementation of computers in their classrooms found that use of computers is unlikely to result in changes in learning or teaching unless the personal philosophy of classroom practice held by each teacher undergoes a major transformation.

Wagner, C. (1996). Creative behavior through basic inferences: Evidence from person-computer interactions. **Journal of Creative Behavior, 30** (2), 105-125. This article argues that, if creativity is measured by outcomes, then basic forms of reasoning (deduction, induction, abduction, specialization/generalization, and elementary memory associations) can be considered mildly creative. The claim is backed by references to computer programs that have generated creative outcomes. Limitations of this approach to creativity are also discussed.

DISTANCE EDUCATION

American Journal of Distance Education. Pennsylvania State University, School of Education, 403 S. Allen St., Suite 206, University Park, PA 16801-5202. [3/yr.; $30 indiv. ($36 Canada and Mexico, $45 elsewhere); $55 inst. (Canada and Mexico $61, $70 elsewhere)]. Focuses on the professional trainer, adult educator, college teacher, and others interested in the latest developments in methods and systems for delivering education to adults.

Bisman, J. (1996). **Occasional papers in open and distance learning, No. 19.** [ED 395 561, 50pp.]. This document is a collection of four papers dealing with issues of technology in higher education, distance education, and assessment practices.

Development Communication Report. Clearinghouse on Development Communication, 1815 N. Ft. Myer Dr., Suite 600, Arlington, VA 22209. [Q., $10 (free to readers in developing countries)]. Applications of communications technology to international development problems such as agriculture, health, and nutrition.

Distance Education. University College of Southern Queensland Publications, Darling Heights, Toowoomba, Queensland 4350, Australia. [Semi-ann., $A48 in Australia, $67 airmail overseas]. Papers on the history, politics, and administration of distance education.

Distance Education Report. Magna Publications, Inc., 2718 Dryden Dr., Madison, WI 53704. [Mo., $299]. Digests periodical, Internet, and conference information into monthly reports.

Ely, D. P. (1996). **Distance education: By design or default?** [ED 396 715, 12pp.]. Technology is often the driving force in the distance education movement, rather than the needs or educational problems that exist and need to be addressed. This paper considers the questions that should be asked before deciding that distance education is an appropriate solution to an education or training problem.

Evans, T., & Nation, D. (1996). **Opening education: Policies and practices from open and distance education.** [Book, 224pp., $19.95]. Routledge, 11 Fetter Ln., London EC4P 4EE, England. Collection of articles about current concerns in distance education from an international perspective.

Hobbs, V., & Christianson, J. S. (1997). **Educational opportunity through two-way interactive television.** [Book, 300pp., $49.95]. Technomic Publishing Co., Inc., Lancaster, PA. Reviews use of two-way interactive television as a distance learning technology in rural community development settings.

Journal of Distance Education. Canadian Association for Distance Education, Secretariat, One Stewart St., Suite 205, Ottawa, ON K1N 6H7, Canada. (Text in English and French.) [2/yr., $40, add $5 outside Canada]. Aims to promote and encourage scholarly work of empirical and theoretical nature relating to distance education in Canada and throughout the world.

Keegan, D. (1996). **Foundations of distance education.** 3rd ed. [Book, 240pp., $18.95 US, $26.95 Canada]. Routledge, 11 Fetter Ln., London EC4P 4EE, England. Introductory text has been updated to include recent technological developments with examples from Eastern Europe and China.

Lane, C. (1996). **TEAMS evaluation summary, 1992-1996.** [ED 394 505, 11pp.]. TEAMS Distance Learning is an Educational Telecommunications Network service of the Los Angeles County Office of Education (California). It provides live, interactive instructional telecasts for students in grades 2-6 and their teachers and parents across the US and Canada. This evaluation summary consists of an overview of the evaluation design and products of the evaluation.

Lane, C., & Cassidy, S. (1996). **Star Schools project: Distance learning model practices.** [ED 394 506, 16pp.]. This document describes model practices of the Star Schools Program, whose purpose is to provide quality, cost-effective instruction and training through distance education technologies.

Ljutic, A. (1996). Learning to telecommunicate: Distance learning projects in less-developed countries. **Learning and Leading with Technology, 23** (8), 65-67. Discusses worldwide efforts to use technology as a distance learning tool, particularly in less-developed countries. Topics include transfer of knowledge, subject matter, pedagogy employed, use of appropriate technology; and examples of three projects currently underway in less-developed countries.

Martens, R. (1996). Functions, use and effects of embedded support devices in printed distance learning materials. **Learning and Instruction, 6** (1), 77-93. To support distance learning, printed materials for the course are enriched with embedded support devices (ESD) such as schemes, illustrations, examples, questions, or margin texts. Results of 3 studies involving 900 Dutch university students indicated that students used and appreciated ESD, and that they led to better study results.

Martin, B. L., & Bramble, W. J. (1996). Designing effective video teletraining instruction: The Florida Teletraining Project. **Educational Technology Research and Development, 44** (1), 85-99. Evaluates the effectiveness of the Florida Teletraining Project, a project that used video teletraining to provide distance education courses to US military personnel. Describes the instructional methods and strategies used and reports results of performance tests and reactions of students and instructional personnel. Findings indicate that the learning methods were useful and effective.

Moore, M. G., & Kearsley, G. (1996). **Distance education: A systems view.** [Book, 304pp.]. International Thomson Publishing. Covers distance learning technology from a systems approach.

Murphy, T. H. (1996). Agricultural education and distance education. **Agricultural Education Magazine, 68** (11), 3-18, 21-23. Includes "The Time Is Now" (Murphy); "Technological Solution in Search of an Instructional Problem" (Willis, Touchstone); "Principles of Distance Education" (Peasley); "A Star Is Born!" (Swan); "Enrichment in the Classroom" (Blume, Talbert); "Practical Applications for Distance Education Technologies in Remote and Rural Areas" (Davis, Frick); "Future Farmers of America, Agricultural Education, and the World Wide Web" (Holton, Newman); "Distance Education Classroom Design" (Anderson).

Oliver, R., & McLoughlin, C. (1996). **An investigation of the nature and form of interactions in live interactive television.** Paper presented at EdTech '96 Biennial Conference of the Australian Society for Educational Technology, Melbourne. [ED 396 738, 9pp.]. This paper describes a study that investigated LIT (Live Interactive Television) teaching strategies to determine the ways instructors used the interactive capabilities of the technology in their lesson delivery. The study found that instructors tend to use the interactive elements more to create a supportive and stimulating learning environment than for instructional support.

Open Learning. Pearson Professional, Subscriptions Dept., P.O. Box 77, Harlow, Essex CM19 5BQ, England. [3/yr., £59 UK, £60 Europe, $76 US]. Academic, scholarly publication on aspects of open and distance learning anywhere in the world. Includes issues for debate and research notes.

Open Praxis. International Council for Distance Education, National Extension College, 18 Brooklands Ave., Cambridge CB2 2HN, England. [2/yr., $65 indiv., $50 libraries]. Reports on activities and programs of the ICDE.

Pamerleau, N. A. (1996). Attitude in the electronic classroom: A second look at the interactive television system of instruction. **Michigan Community College Journal: Research and Practice, 2** (1), 55-77. Describes a study of 84 high school students taking classes on a 2-way interactive televised system of instruction to determine their perceptions toward the class and the technology. Indicates that students were generally positive toward the system and that there were no differences by gender or on-site and off-site students.

Pietras, J. J. (1996). **Connecticut's evolving interactive distance learning network in the cable and telecommunications industries.** Paper presented at the National Regulatory Research Institute/Biennial Regulatory Information Conference, Columbus, OH, Sep. [ED 398 898, 38pp.]. This paper describes the state of interactive distance learning in Connecticut, particularly the current and future provision of these services by the telecommunications and cable television industries.

RMI Media. (1996). **Interactive learning environments.** [Video, 30min., $79.95]. AECT, 1025 Vermont Ave., NW, Suite 820, Washington, DC 20005-3547. Covers new roles teachers and students experience in the distance learning environment.

RMI Media. (1996). **An introduction to distance education.** [Video, 30min., $79.95]. AECT, 1025 Vermont Ave., NW, Suite 820, Washington, DC 20005-3547. Explores changes taking place in the global community affecting the educational system today.

RMI Media. (1996). **Methods and mediums.** [Video, 30min., $79.95]. AECT, 1025 Vermont Ave., NW, Suite 820, Washington, DC 20005-3547. Introduces a variety of delivery methods and mediums associated with learning at a distance.

RMI Media. (1996). **Telecourse techniques.** [Video, 30min., $79.95]. AECT, 1025 Vermont Ave., NW, Suite 820, Washington, DC 20005-3547. Features teaching strategies using one- and two-way interactive video and audio technology.

Schlosser, C., & Anderson, M. (1997). **Distance education: A review of the literature.** 2nd ed. [Book, 64pp., $15]. AECT, 1025 Vermont Ave., NW, Suite 820, Washington, DC 20005-3547. Provides brief but comprehensive literature review. Defines distance education, discusses major theories, summarizes history and current issues.

Schrum, L. (1996). Teaching at a distance: Strategies for successful planning and development. **Learning and Leading with Technology, 23** (6), 30-33. Describes practical aspects to teaching using distance learning technology, specifically in creating collaborative environments, building pedagogically sound activities, and interacting with students off and on campus.

Schrum, L, with Luetkehans, L. (1997). **A primer on distance education considerations for decision makers.** [Book, approx. 100pp., $7.95]. AECT, 1025 Vermont Ave., NW, Suite 820, Washington, DC 20005-3547. Provides an introduction to the field of distance education; describes concepts, vocabulary, current status, and issues involved in the understanding of this current field.

Sener, J. (1996). **Delivering an A.S. Engineering degree program through home study distance education.** [ED 393 493, 20pp.]. Reports Northern Virginia Community College (NVCC) and the Extended Learning Institute (ELI) project to develop the mathematics, science, and engineering courses required to complete an entire Associate of Science degree in Engineering through home study distance education.

Slade, A. L., & Kascus, M. A. (1996). **Library services for off-campus and distance education: Second annotated bibliography.** [Book, 325pp., $65]. Libraries Unlimited, P.O. Box 6633, Englewood, CO 80155-6633. Focuses on library services and how libraries can meet new demands and take advantage of opportunities resulting from distance learning technology.

Sorensen, C. K. (1996). **Students near and far: Differences in perceptions of community college students taking interactive television at origination and remote sites.** [ED 393 509, 25pp.]. In 1992, the state of Iowa received the first of three grants to implement courses using the Iowa Communications Network (ICN), a fiber optic network that delivers live, full-motion instruction allowing two-way interaction between students and instructors. This survey research evaluates the effectiveness of the ICN courses and makes recommendations.

Telg, R. W. (1996). The roles of television production specialists in distance education programming. **American Journal of Distance Education, 10** (1), 50-61. Twelve full-time production specialists employed at universities were studied to determine the role they play in the development of live, interactive, video-based distance education programs. Data collection consisted of qualitative methods: interviews, observation, and concept maps. Findings show that television production specialists fill multiple roles, many of which go beyond their training.

Terrell, S. (1996). **From teaching to learning: Transition in distance education.** Paper presented at Intercom 96, Miami. [ED 391 978, 8pp.]. Describes how Nova Southeastern University (NSU) in Florida is attempting to improve their distance education programs by creating a more student-centered environment.

Williams, H. M. (1996). **Curriculum conceptions of open learning: Theory, intention and student experience in the Australian Open Learning Initiative.** [Dissertation, ED 394 504, 393pp.]. This thesis seeks to clarify the meaning of the open learning concept by examining it in alternative ways: as an element of social theory, as an intended curriculum, and as a perceived student learning experience. The three curriculum conceptions of open learning are applied to the Australian Open Learning Initiative.

Williams, M. (1996). **The egghead and the TV eye.** [ED 398 870, 16pp.]. This paper describes the first venture of the author (a professor at Kentucky's Morehead State University) into the world of distance learning technology, specifically interactive television.

EDUCATIONAL RESEARCH

American Educational Research Journal. American Educational Research Association, 1230 17th St., NW, Washington, DC 20036-3078. [Q., $39 indiv., $51 inst.]. Reports original research, both empirical and theoretical, and brief synopses of research.

Belland, J. C., Section Ed. (1996). Foundations for research in educational communications and technology. In D. H. Jonassen (Ed.), **Handbook of research for educational communications and technology,** pp. 3-295. New York: Macmillan. Section includes chapters on foundations, behaviorism, systems, communication, cognition, sociology, constructivism, learning environments, critical theory, and postmodernism.

Current Index to Journals in Education (CIJE). Oryx Press, 4041 N. Central at Indian School Rd., Phoenix, AZ 85012-3397. [Mo., $245 ($280 outside North America); semi-ann. cumulations $250 ($285 foreign); combination $475]. A guide to articles published in some 830 education and education-related journals. Includes complete bibliographic information, annotations, and indexes. Semiannual cumulations available. Contents are produced by the ERIC (Educational Resources Information Center) system, Office of Educational Research and Improvement, US Department of Education.

Education Index. H. W. Wilson, 950 University Ave., Bronx, NY 10452. [Mo., except July and August; variable costs]. Author-subject index to educational publications in the English language. Cumulated quarterly and annually.

Educational Research. Routledge, 11 Fetter Ln., London EC4P 4EE, England. [3/yr., £30 indiv. ($55 US and Canada, £33 elsewhere); £68 inst. (£72 foreign)]. Reports on current educational research, evaluation, and applications.

Educational Researcher. American Educational Research Association, 1230 17th St., NW, Washington, DC 20036-3078. [9/yr., $39 indiv., $51 inst.]. Contains news and features of general significance in educational research.

English, R. E., & Reigeluth, C. M. (1996). Formative research on sequencing instruction with the elaboration theory. **Educational Technology Research and Development, 44** (1), 23-42. Examines elaboration theory of instruction (ETI), a theory that prescribes different patterns of sequencing for different kinds of learning. Presents results of surveying undergraduate students who have undergone ETI sequencing. Results identify the strengths and weaknesses of the instruction and ways of improving it. Student debriefing questions are appended.

Research in Science & Technological Education. Carfax Publishing Co., 875-81 Massachusetts Ave., Cambridge, MA 02139. [2/yr., £48 indiv., £178 inst.]. Publication of original research in the science and technological fields. Includes articles on psychological, sociological, economic, and organizational aspects.

Resources in Education (RIE). Superintendent of Documents, US Government Printing Office, P.O. Box 371954, Pittsburgh, PA 15250-7954. [Mo., $77 US, $96.25 elsewhere]. Announcement of research reports and other documents in education, including abstracts and indexes by subject, author, and institution. Contents produced by the ERIC (Educational Resources Information Center) system, Office of Educational Research and Improvement, US Department of Education.

Robinson, R., Assoc. Ed. (1996). Research methodologies in educational communications and technology. In D. H. Jonassen (Ed.), **Handbook of research for educational communications and technology,** pp. 1137-1245. New York: Macmillan. Section includes chapters about philosophy, experimental methods, qualitative methods, descriptive methods, and developmental research.

Ross, S. M., & Morrison, G. R. (1997). **Getting started in instructional technology research.** 2nd ed. [Monograph, 31pp., $9.95]. AECT, 1025 Vermont Ave., NW, Suite 820, Washington, DC 20005-3547. Summarizes authors' ideas and experiences related to performing research in the field. Seeks to motivate new professionals to begin an active research program, and to guide experienced researchers in refining their skills.

EDUCATIONAL TECHNOLOGY

Anderson, L. S. (1996). **K-12 technology planning at state, district, and local levels.** [ED 393 448, 4pp.]. Describes principles to engage the services, creativity, and assistance of all stakeholders in technology planning efforts.

Appropriate Technology. Intermediate Technology Publications, Ltd., 103-105 Southampton Row, London, WC1B 4HH, England. [Q., $28 indiv., $37 inst.]. Articles on less technologically advanced, but more environmentally sustainable, solutions to problems in developing countries.

Barron, A. E., & Orwig, G. W. (1997). **New technologies for education: A beginner's guide.** 3rd ed. [Book, 295pp., $32.50]. Libraries Unlimited, P.O. Box 6633, Englewood, CO 80155-6633. Offers an updated look at the technologies that are affecting education, including LANs, the Internet, and multimedia.

Bazeli, M. J., & Heintz, J. L. (1997). **Technology across the curriculum: Activities and ideas.** [Book, 207pp., $24.50]. Libraries Unlimited, P.O. Box 6633, Englewood, CO 80155-6633. Contains 75 activities focusing on curriculum application and integration.

Bell, C., Bowden, M., & Trout, A., eds. (1997). **Aspects of educational and training technology,** Vol. XXIX. [Book, $59.95]. Stylus Publishing, Inc. Presents papers from the Association for Education and Training Technology International 1995 Conference.

Belynne-Buvia, K. (1996). **The mission to Mars drawing lesson: A Schools for Thought pilot study.** Paper presented at the Annual Meeting of the American Educational Research Association, New York. [ED 398 265, 9pp.]. Community is an essential aspect of the Schools for Thought program, an educational reform project designed to bring educational technology to many public school classrooms. The experimental groups outscored control groups on discrete assessments measuring student content learning about telescopes. On an open-ended assessment, students from the experimental groups were able to explain how a telescope works more often than control students could. Students in the experimental groups were more likely to draw an accurate picture of a telescope than were students in the control group.

Bernauer, J. A. (1996). **Technology and leadership.** Paper presented at the Annual Meeting of the American Educational Research Association, New York. [ED 394 503, 25pp.]. This paper describes how technology has been successfully integrated into a school's curriculum, the leadership decisions leading to this success, and the impact that technology has had on students and the school organization.

Bodilly, S., & Mitchell, K. J. (1997). **Evaluating Challenge Grants for Technology in Education: A sourcebook.** [Book, 206pp., $9]. Rand, Santa Monica, CA. Provides strategies for the evaluation of grant programs, and addresses evaluation issues. Contains instruments.

Branch, P., & Durran, J. (1996). **PC based video on demand trials.** Paper presented at EdTech '96 Biennial Conference of the Australian Society for Educational Technology, Melbourne, July. [ED 396 722, 5pp.]. To gain insight into the issues involved in using this technology in an educational environment that relies heavily on video, a simple, low cost video on demand system was installed in the Visual Arts Library at Monash University, Clayton (Australia). Qualitative trials were then carried out involving staff and students from the film and television studies section of the Visual Arts Department.

British Journal of Educational Technology. National Council for Educational Technology, Millburn Hill Rd., Science Park, Coventry CV4 7JJ, England. [3/yr., £60 inst. U.K., £70 overseas airmail; personal subscriptions £32 U.K., £42 overseas]. Published by the National Council for Educational Technology, this journal includes articles on education and training, especially theory, applications, and development of educational technology and communications.

Burchfield, D. (1996). Technology with a vision: The Ottobine story. **Technology Teacher, 55** (8), 18-21. Describes the transformation of Ottobine Elementary School in Rockingham County, Virginia, from a "little country school" into a model of rural elementary technology education for the 21st century.

CLL Journal. International Society for Technology in Education, University of Oregon, 1787 Agate St., Eugene, OR 97403-1923. [Q., $25]. Focuses on current issues facing computer-using language teachers; covers trends, products, applications, research, and program evaluation.

Canadian Journal of Educational Communication. Association for Media and Technology in Education in Canada, AMTEC-CJEC Subscription, 3-1750 The Queensway, Suite 1318, Etobicoke, ON, M9C 5H5, Canada. [3/yr., $45]. Articles, research reports, and literature reviews on all areas of educational communication and technology.

CCA Consulting Inc. (1996). **Understanding information technology in kindergarten through grade 12, 1994-1995.** [ED 392 391, 12pp.]. This report is the third annual edition of a syndicated study which focuses on developing an understanding of the major issues and events which give shape to computing and information technology across K-12 education in the US.

Cifuentes, L. (1996). **From sages to guides: A professional development study.** Paper presented at the Annual Meeting of the American Educational Research Association, New York. [ED 397 036, 17pp.]. This study examined teachers' transformations from "sages on the stage to guides on the side" through a survey of preservice secondary school teachers (N=73) over time to identify their envisioned preferred teaching methods; a survey of inservice master teachers (N=24) in professional development schools to identify their choices of teaching methods; and an evaluation of the effectiveness of an educational technology course in changing preservice teachers' envisioned preferred methods.

Community College League of California. (1996). **Preparing to serve the student of the future: A planning resource report.** [ED 395 606, 21pp.]. Describes findings and guidelines developed by approximately 600 California community college practitioners participating in forums. Contains specific technology recommendations.

Cradler, J., & Cordon-Cradler, R. (1997). **The technology planning and funding guide.** [Book, 155pp., $39]. Educational Support Systems; available through International Society for Technology in Education, University of Oregon, 1787 Agate St., Eugene, OR 97403-1923. Designed for teachers and administrators who want a practical step-by-step guide for developing grant proposals.

Cummins, Jim. (1996). Multicultural education and technology: Promise and pitfalls. **Multicultural Education, 3** (3), 4-10. Addresses the implications of technology for multicultural education by examining the potential for global learning networks to promote intercultural literacy and critical thinking. The authors argue that computer and telecommunications technology has the potential to act as a positive catalyst in both areas through linkages of distant classrooms focusing on collaborative projects.

Downes, T., & Fatouros, C. (1996). **Learning in an electronic world: Computers and the language arts classroom.** [Book, 154pp., $21]. Heinemann, Portsmouth, NH, (800) 541-2086. Helps elementary teachers build language and literacy around information technology.

Educational Software Evaluation Consortium. (1996). **The 1996 educational software preview guide.** [Annual book, $16.45]. International Society for Technology in Education, University of Oregon, 1787 Agate St., Eugene, OR 97403-1923. Lists titles of favorably reviewed software for K-12 classroom use for assistance in locating software for preview.

Educational Technology. Educational Technology Publications, Inc., 700 Palisade Ave., Englewood Cliffs, NJ 07632-0564. [Bi-mo., $119 US, $139 elsewhere]. Covers telecommunications, computer-aided instruction, information retrieval, educational television, and electronic media in the classroom.

Educational Technology Abstracts. Carfax Publishing Co., 875-81 Massachusetts Ave., Cambridge, MA 02139. [6/yr., $218 indiv., $582 inst.]. An international publication of abstracts of recently published material in the field of educational and training technology.

Educational Technology Research and Development. AECT, 1025 Vermont Ave., NW, Suite 820, Washington, DC 20005-3516. [Q., $55 US, $63 foreign]. Focuses on research and instructional development in the field of educational technology.

Edwards, S., & Morton, A. (1996). **Profiling computing coordinators.** Paper presented at EdTech '96 Biennial Conference of the Australian Society for Educational Technology, Melbourne, July. [ED 396 725, 13pp.]. The people responsible for managing school computing resources in Australia have become known as Computing Coordinators. To date there has been no large systematic study of the role, responsibilities and characteristics of this position. This paper represents a first attempt to provide information on the functions and attributes of the Computing Coordinators in New South Wales (Australia) secondary schools.

Ely, D. P., Assoc. Ed. (1996). Issues of organization and change in educational communications and technology. In D. H. Jonassen (Ed.), **Handbook of research for educational communications and technology**, pp. 1107-1133. New York: Macmillan. Analyzes and critiques current trends in diffusion research.

Ely, D. P. (1996). **Trends in educational technology 1995.** [ED 396 717, 68pp.]. Based on the findings of a content analysis of representative literature on educational technology, this report examines trends in educational technology from October 1, 1994 through September 30, 1995.

Ely, D. P., & Plomp, T. (1996). **Classic writings on instructional technology.** [Book, 225pp., $45]. Libraries Unlimited, P.O. Box 6633, Englewood, CO 80155-6633. Includes 32 previously unpublished articles contributing to the conceptual underpinnings of the field.

EPIE Institute. (1996). **TESS: The educational software selector** (updated version). [Book and cross-platform CD-ROM, $79.95]. International Society for Technology in Education, University of Oregon, 1787 Agate St., Eugene, OR 97403-1923. Contains information on more than 18,000 pre-school through college instructional and administrative software programs.

Farrell, A. M. (1996). Roles and behaviors in technology-integrated precalculus classrooms. **Journal of Mathematical Behavior, 15** (1), 35-53. Analysis of observations in precalculus classrooms in which graphing calculators were integrated with the curriculum found evidence that students and teachers shifted their roles when technology was in use.

Fisher, C., Dwyer, D. C., & Yocam, K. (1996). **Education and technology: Reflections on computing in classrooms.** [Book, 346pp., $28.95]. Jossey-Bass, 350 Sansome St., San Francisco, CA 94104. Examines learning in the technology age, describes change, and suggests integration ideas.

Glennan, T. K, & Melamed, A. (1996). **Fostering the use of educational technology: Elements of a national strategy.** [Book, 120pp., $15]. Rand, Santa Monica, CA. Argues that the US's most prominent educational goals must be to prepare students for future lives which will require critical thinking and information skills. Asserts that technology is not being used effectively today and proposes strategies to remedy this problem.

Grabe, M., & Grabe, C. (1996). **Integrating technology for meaningful learning.** [Book, 384pp.]. Houghton Mifflin, 181 Ballardvale St., Wilmington, MA 01887-7050. Enthusiastically describes how technology can supplement classroom learning.

Green, E. E. (1996). Fitting new technologies into traditional classrooms: Two case studies in the design of improved learning facilities. **Educational Technology, 36** (4), 27-38. Examines research on the influence of classroom design on student learning attitudes and behavior and presents two case studies on the remodeling of five classrooms in two high schools to accommodate new instructional technology for teaching algebra. Highlights include lighting, color, surface materials, noise, climate control, and seating.

Green, K. C. (1996). **Campus computing, 1995: The Sixth National Survey of Desktop Computing in Higher Education.** [ED 394 383, 37pp.]. This monograph reports findings of a Fall, 1995 survey of computing officials at approximately 650 two- and four-year colleges and universities across the US concerning increasing use of technology on college campuses.

Haas, C. (1996). **Writing technology: Studies on the materiality of literacy.** [Book, 296pp., $27.50]. Lawrence Erlbaum, 10 Industrial Ave., Mahwah, NJ 07430-2262. Addresses the relationship of writing to its technologies.

Hackbarth, S. (1996). **The educational technology handbook: A comprehensive guide— process and products for learning.** [Book, 351pp., $46.95]. Educational Technology Publications, 700 Palisade Ave., Englewood Cliffs, NJ 07632-0564. Introduces the total field of educational technology, beginning with the instructional processes involved.

Hairston, E. (1996). A picaresque journey: Corporate change, technological tidal waves, and Webby worldviews. **Change, 28** (2), 32-37. Business and industrial leaders in America believe that higher education is now in the same position business found itself in 15 years ago regarding the technological revolution. While the pressures are from different sources, needs to increase productivity and create more flexible structures are parallel for both higher education and business.

Haugland, S. W., & Wright, J. L. (1997). **Young children and computers: A world of discovery.** [Book, 304pp.]. Allyn & Bacon, 160 Gould St., Needham Heights, MA 02194-2315. Considers educational computing from an early childhood perspective.

Hoffman, R., & Rossett, A. (1997). **School technology planner (STP) software.** [Software: dual platform CD-ROM]. Allyn & Bacon, 160 Gould St., Needham Heights, MA 02194-2315. Assists school technology leaders to draft Technology Use Plans (TUPs); reviews literature on success factors for technology integration.

Infomart Magazine. Covers technology trends and companies at http://www.loc.gov.

Innovations in Education and Training International (formerly *Educational and Training Technology International*). Kogan Page, FREEPOST 1, 120 Pentonville Road, London N1 9JN. [Q., £56, $102 US]. The international journal of the Association for Educational and Training Technology emphasizes developing trends in and the efficient use of educational technology. It is now extending its interest to include the field of staff and educational development.

International Journal of Technology and Design Education. Kluwer Academic Publishers, Order Dept., P.O. Box 358, Accord Station, Hingham, MA 02018-0358. [3/yr., $74]. Publishes research reports and scholarly writing about aspects of technology and design education.

Journal of Instruction Delivery Systems. Learning Technology Institute, 50 Culpeper St., Warrenton, VA 22186. [Q., $60 indiv., $75 inst., add $15 postage for countries outside North America]. Devoted to the issues and applications of technology to enhance productivity in education, training, and job performance.

Jukes, I. (1996). The essential steps of technology planning. **School Administrator, 53** (4), 8-14. An educational technology program needs a conceptual foundation with several critical pillars, including shared leadership, collective vision, a holistic approach, relevant curricula, new pedagogies, staff training, noncomputer technologies, software and technical supports, flexible facilities, multilevel support, long-term commitment, and ongoing evaluation. Allen Hall's sidebar describes an Illinois superintendent's modest plan.

Keltner, B., & Ross, R. L. (1996). **The cost of school-based educational technology programs.** [Book, 104pp., $9]. Rand, Santa Monica, CA. Uses 8 case studies of installations to illustrate costs, helpful in planning cost effectiveness research projects.

Kennedy, E. M. (1996). Realizing the promise of technology in America's schools. **TECHNOS, 5** (2), 9-13. The US senator describes NetDay events, fast-spreading celebrations of educational partnerships committed to technological advancement in schools. Three attitude shifts help technology improve education: (1) educators and software developers creating instructional tools that help all students; (2) policymakers ensuring universal access to technology; and (3) bringing teachers, parents, communities, and businesses into planning for technology.

Kerr, S. T. (1996). **Technology and the future of schooling in America.** [Book, 275pp., $14.95]. University of Chicago Press, Box 37005, Chicago, IL 60637. Admitting that technology does not necessarily improve education, this book discusses the broad impact of technology and suggests adaptations to particular needs.

Kershaw, A. (1996). People, planning, and process: The acceptance of technological innovation in post-secondary organizations. **Educational Technology, 36** (5), 44-48. Discusses the effects of change brought about by technology integration in postsecondary institutions. Strategies are provided for managing the change process, focusing on articulating a vision; developing a plan; creating organizational structures; providing adequate training and support; and promoting technology use.

Kimbell, R. (1997). **Assessing technology: International trends in curriculum and assessment.** [Book, 192pp., $26.95]. Open University Press, Bristol, PA. Applies assessment of existing installations to planning. Draws upon examples from the UK, USA, German, Taiwan, and Australia.

Knapp, L. R., & Glenn, A. D. (1996). **Restructuring schools with technology.** [Book, 208pp.]. Allyn & Bacon, 160 Gould St., Needham Heights, MA 02194-2315. Advocates change through technology and presents steps in the process.

Lamb, A. (1996). **Building treehouses for learning technology in today's classroom.** [Book, 300pp., $39.95]. AECT, 1025 Vermont Ave., NW, Suite 820, Washington, DC 20005-3547. Focuses on the integration of traditional and emerging technologies into today's classrooms.

Land, M., & Turner, S. (1997). **Tools for schools.** 2nd ed. [Book, 320pp.]. International Thomson Publishing. Details specific uses for various computer applications for teachers.

Lehman, J. D., & Brickner, D. (1996). Teachers' uses and perceptions of interactive videodiscs in the science classroom. **Journal of Computers in Mathematics and Science Teaching, 15** (1-2), 85-102. Examined (n=36) teachers' perceptions and use of interactive videodiscs (IVD) in the teaching of science. Perceptions tended to be positive. Major barriers to IVD usage were limited equipment availability and lack of time to develop and implement IVD-based lessons.

Levonen, J. J., & Tukiainen, M. (1996). **Complex learning in computer environments: A special issue of *Machine-Mediated Learning*.** [Book, 96pp., $20]. Lawrence Erlbaum, 10 Industrial Ave., Mahwah, NJ 07430-2262, orders@erlbaum.com. Approaches computer environment learning from interdisciplinary perspective in series of 8 articles.

Logo Exchange. International Society for Technology in Education, University of Oregon, 1787 Agate St., Eugene, OR 97403-1923. [Q., for members of ISTE's SIG for Logo Education]. Brings ideas from Logo educators throughout the world, with current information on Logo research, resources, and methods.

Maddux, C. D., Johnson, D. L., & Willis, J. W. (1997). **Educational computing: Learning with tomorrow's technologies.** 2nd ed. [Book, 351pp.]. Allyn & Bacon, 160 Gould St., Needham Heights, MA 02194-2315. Covers theory, applications, and evaluation of educational computing. Targeted at courses for educators with basic computing skills.

Martorella, P. H., ed. (1996). **Interactive technologies and the social studies: emerging issues and applications.** [Book, 128pp., $12.95]. State University of New York Press, State University Plaza, Albany, NY 12246-0001. Discusses interactive technologies (distance learning, Internet, multimedia, intelligent tutors) from a social perspective.

Mehlinger, H. D. (1996). School reform in the information age. **Phi Delta Kappan, 77** (6), 400-407. Although educational uses of computers and video seem to be increasing, no one knows exactly what kind of technology is used; what is available to teachers; or what is broken, worn out, or in unopened boxes. The technology revolution is proceeding slowly in schools, due to insufficient time, money, and taxpayer commitment.

Michael, S. O. (1996). Financial constraints in higher education: Using a case-study approach. **Studies in Higher Education, 21** (2), 233-239. A survey of 70 faculty at 1 public research university investigated faculty perceptions of the impact of financial constraints on curriculum development, faculty development, and instructional technology at the institution.

Moursund, D. (1996). **Increasing your expertise as a problem solver: Some roles of computers.** 2nd ed. [Book, 130pp., $16.95]. International Society for Technology in Education, University of Oregon, 1787 Agate St., Eugene, OR 97403-1923. Summarizes and synthesizes current thinking on problem solving, incorporating how this domain is affected by computers.

Moursund, D. (1996). **Obtaining resources for technology in education: A how-to guide for writing proposals, forming partnerships, and raising funds.** [Book, 190pp., $34.95]. International Society for Technology in Education, University of Oregon, 1787 Agate St., Eugene, OR 97403-1923. Focuses on how to obtain money, hardware, software, staff development, curriculum materials, and consulting for educational technology.

National Governors' Association. (1996). **Technology and education standards: Issue brief.** [ED 394 518, 8pp.]. Describes how policymakers and educators must coordinate technology purchases and uses with articulated learning standards and curriculum goals.

Owens, E. W., & Waxman, H. C. (1995-96). Differences among urban, suburban, and rural schools on technology access and use in eighth-grade mathematics classrooms. **Journal of Educational Technology Systems, 24** (1), 83-92. Examines technology access and use in urban, suburban, and rural schools by using data from the eighth-grade cohort of the 1988 National Educational Longitudinal Survey. Results indicate significant differences in the use of mathematics technology in school settings, and that inequalities in educational opportunity still need to be addressed.

Plomp, T., & Ely, D. P., eds. (1996). **International encyclopedia of educational technology.** 2nd ed. [Book, approx. 700pp.]. Pergamon Press, 660 White Plains Rd., Tarrytown, NY 10591-5153. Compendium of scholarly writings and research on all aspects of educational technology.

Plotnick, E. (1996). **Trends in educational technology 1995.** [ED 398 861, 4pp.]. Content analysis performed to determine the trends in the field of educational technology for the period Oct 1, 1994 through Sep 30, 1995. Sources for the analysis included five leading professional journals in educational technology, papers given at annual conventions of three professional associations, dissertations from five universities that have a high level of doctoral productivity, and the educational technology documents that have been entered into the ERIC database.

Ralph, C. L. (1996). The illusion of the instructional biology laboratory. **American Biology Teacher, 58** (3), 142-146. Argues that the changing informational content of biology, tightening cost constraints, improving electronic media, increasing pressures from advocates of animal rights, and the growing evidence of the effectiveness of electronic modes of instruction are undermining the traditional belief that all students in biology should have the benefit of exposure to a hands-on laboratory experience.

Reynolds, K. E., & Barba, R. H. (1997). **Technology for the teaching and learning of science.** [Book, 269pp.]. Allyn & Bacon, 160 Gould St., Needham Heights, MA 02194-2315. Consolidates information about current issues such as systemic reform, multiculturalism, and National Standards for Science Education into a text for preservice and inservice teachers. Uses reflectivism as a learning technique.

Rhodes, L. A. (1996). Seeking new connections: Learning, technology, and systemic change. **Learning and Leading with Technology, 23** (8), 45-48. This fourth and concluding article in a series on information technology in the schools explores how a complete educational organization can function when using already-available information technologies to take advantage of the natural independence of individuals' roles in the schools and communities.

Rieseberg, R. (1996). Keeping up on the weather in the Walla Walla Valley. **TECHNOS, 5** (2), 14-15. Describes investments made by Garrison Middle School (Walla Walla, WA) in video and computer technology with which the school's sixth graders produced daily video news broadcasts. The "electronic evolution" there has resulted in a schoolwide computer network which aids activities such as writing and library use. Future plans include remote access.

Roblyer, M. D. (1996). Technology and multicultural education: The "uneasy alliance." **Educational Technology, 36** (3), 5-12. Presents issues related to technology and multicultural education. Examines problems with multicultural education and current uses of technology, including telecommunications, applications for ESL students, and multimedia. Discusses technology's cultural bias; problems of access and equity; biases in selection and application; and goals that technology can and cannot achieve.

Roblyer, M. D., Edwards, J., & Havriluk, M. A. (1997). **Integrating educational technology into teaching.** [Book, 503pp.]. Merrill/Prentice Hall, 445 Hutchinson Ave., Columbus, OH 43235-5677. Provides strategies, examples, and leading-edge developments for use in junior to graduate-level methods classes.

Russell, T. L. (1996). Point of view: Technology's threat to the traditional institution—real or imagined? **Journal of Continuing Higher Education, 44** (1), 22-24. Instruction must be excellent whether technology is present or not. Students perceive that technology will make learning easier, more enjoyable, more accessible, and more flexible without eliminating student-teacher contact. Without those elements, students will elect a traditional classroom.

Salisbury, D. F. (1996). **Five technologies for educational change.** [Book, 247pp., $42.95]. AECT, 1025 Vermont Ave., NW, Suite 820, Washington, DC 20005-3547. Increased competition, choice, and consumer demands are affecting education today in the same way that these factors have affected American business and industry during the past two decades. This new book examines the five essential knowledges or disciplines that can and should have a profound impact on education.

Sammons, M. C. (1996). **Multimedia presentations on the go: An introduction and buyer's guide.** [Book, 200pp., $30]. Libraries Unlimited, P.O. Box 6633, Englewood, CO 80155-6633. Helps educators and presenters decide which hardware and software to purchase for portable computer multimedia presentations that use graphics, animation, video, or sound.

Sandholtz, J. H., Ringstaff, C., & Dwyer, D. C. (1997). **Teaching with technology: Creating student-centered classrooms.** [Book, 240pp., $18.95]. Teachers College Press, Columbia University, 1234 Amsterdam Ave., New York, NY 10027-6694. Based on 20,000 cases described in the Apple Classrooms of Tomorrow database..

Science Communication (formerly *Knowledge: Creation, Diffusion, Utilization*). Sage Publications, Inc., 2455 Teller Rd., Thousand Oaks, CA 91320. [Q., $58 indiv., $172 inst.]. An international, interdisciplinary journal examining the nature of expertise and the translation of knowledge into practice and policy.

Sharpe, D. B. (1996). Out with the old, in with the new: Transition to technology education issues in North America. **Journal of Design and Technology Education, 1** (1), 24-36. Reviews the development of technology education in North America and discusses its emerging replacement of industrial arts. Highlights some of the trends and issues defining curriculum development and classroom instruction. Details various approaches to curriculum design, program implementation, and administration. Examines differences between programs in Canada and the US.

SIGTC Connections. International Society for Technology in Education, University of Oregon, 1787 Agate St., Eugene, OR 97403-1923. [Q., for members of ISTE's SIGTC]. Provides forum to identify problems and solutions, and to share information on issues facing technology coordinators.

Saltrick, S. (1996). A campus of our own: Thoughts of a reluctant conservative. **Change, 28** (2), 58-62. A discussion of technological advancement in the context of the traditions of higher education considers what may be sacrificed if higher education is too readily seduced by new technology, particularly if it is treated as a replacement for real experience and physical environment. A moderated approach that blends the best of both virtual and real educational worlds is recommended.

Slavit, D. (1996). Graphing calculators in a "hybrid" Algebra II classroom. **For the Learning of Mathematics, 16** (1), 9-14. Observations focusing on classroom discourse, uses of graphing calculators, nature of instructional tasks, and instructor-questioning patterns in a high school algebra course found that the teacher modified his teaching strategies and curriculum to accommodate the teaching strategies and topics that arose from the use of the graphing calculator.

Software Publishers Association & ISTE Private Sector Council. (1996). **Education technology promotion guide.** [Book, CD-ROM, $9]. International Society for Technology in Education, University of Oregon, 1787 Agate St., Eugene, OR 97403-1923. Delivers advice for promoting school technology programs.

Sorensen, R. J. (1996). **Designing schools to accommodate technology.** [ED 398 902, 55pp.]. This guide provides the layperson with a concise overview of factors to consider when making plans to outfit elementary and secondary schools with technology inexpensively. The guide draws on the knowledge of consultants, architects, electronics engineers, and the experiences of educators who have been involved in the process of designing schools that allow for efficient and cost-effective use of new technologies.

Strickland, J. (1997). **From disk to hard copy: Teaching writing with computers.** [Book, 136pp., $18.50]. Heinemann, Portsmouth, NH, (800) 541-2086. Takes advantage of the word processor's affordances for the writing process and explains how to implement these educationally.

SyllabusWeb. From the publishers of *Syllabus* magazine. It features news, case studies, product reviews and announcements of interest to technology users in high schools and higher education at http://www.syllabus.com.

Technology and Learning. Peter Li Education Group, P.O. Box 49727, Dayton, OH 45449-0727. [8/yr., $24, $32 foreign]. Publishes features, reviews, news, and announcements of educational activities and opportunities in programming, software development, and hardware configurations.

TECHNOS. Agency for Instructional Technology, Box A, 1111 W. 17th St., Bloomington, IN 47402-0120. [Q., $20 indiv., $16 libr., $24 foreign]. A forum for discussion of ideas about the use of technology in education, with a focus on reform.

TechTrends. Association for Educational Communications and Technology, 1025 Vermont Ave., NW, Suite 820, Washington, DC 20005-3516. [6/yr., $40 US, $44 elsewhere, $6 single copy]. Features authoritative, practical articles about technology and its integration into the learning environment.

T.H.E. Journal (Technological Horizons in Education). T.H.E. Journal, 150 El Camino Real, Suite 112, Tustin, CA 92680-3670. [11/yr., $29 US and Canada, free to qualified educators]. For educators of all levels. Focuses on a specific topic for each issue, as well as technological innovations as they apply to education.

Thode, T. (1996). Technology education and the elementary school. **Technology Teacher, 55** (5), 7-9. In the technology education program at Hemingway School in Ketchum, Idaho, students are involved in hands-on activities that encourage the use of critical thinking skills, tools, and high-tech equipment to solve problems related to real world situations.

Thompson, A. D., Simonson, M. R., & Hargrove, C. P. (1996). **Educational technology: A review of the research.** 2nd ed. [Book, 96pp., $22]. AECT, 1025 Vermont Ave., NW, Suite 820, Washington, DC 20005-3547. Provides an overview of the theories and research that support technology in teaching and learning.

Topp, N. (1996). Preparation to use technology in the classroom: Opinions by recent graduates. **Journal of Computing in Teacher Education, 12** (4), 24-27. Reports on results of a survey completed by Iowa teachers who had recently graduated from a large midwestern university. Most believed that a computer-specific course in preservice teaching programs was essential, especially one on developing strategies to integrate computers into all disciplines. Respondents considered their preservice computer technology preparation inadequate.

Turner, J. (1996). Technology and change of mind: An interview with Robert Ornstein. **Montessori Life, 8** (1), 22-24. Expert on the relationship between human nature and the problems of the world humans have created, Ornstein responds to questions about technology's impact on the shaping of tomorrow's world. Possessing a holistic view of life, he predicts the nature of education and the functions of teachers and schools will be very different in the future.

Vosniadou, S., De Corte, E., Glaser, R., & Mandl, H., eds. (1996). **International perspectives on the design of technology-supported learning environments.** [Book, 408pp., $36]. Lawrence Erlbaum, 10 Industrial Ave., Mahwah, NJ 07430-2262, orders@erlbaum.com. Attempts to reassert the need for thorough theoretical instructional design basis for educational technology installations and environments.

Willis, J., Stephens, E. C., & Matthew, K. I. (1996). **Technology, reading and language arts.** [Book, 256pp.]. Allyn & Bacon, 160 Gould St., Needham Heights, MA 02194-2315. Suggests uses for technology in reading instruction.

ELECTRONIC PUBLISHING

Berge, Z. L., & Collins, M. P. (1996). "IPCT Journal" readership survey. **Journal of the American Society for Information Science, 47** (9), 701-710. Discusses results of a survey of "Interpersonal Computing and Technology: An Electronic Journal for the 21st Century" (IPCT Journal) readers. The survey gathered information on electronic publishing, including authorship, reading, credibility, availability, permanence, and limitations of electronic journals. Use of electronic surveys is discussed, and a copy of the survey is appended.

Brody, H. (1996). Wired science. **Technology Review, 99** (7), 42-51. Examines how the Internet serves the scientific research community. Highlights include collaboration and large group communication via e-mail; USENET discussion groups; advantages of the Web and software-based simulations; changes in information storage; and benefits and problems of electronic publishing and online journals.

Bryce, B. K. (1996). Using newsletters in the library's communication strategy. **Library Administration & Management, 10** (4), 246-251. Examines the practical aspects of publishing a newsletter as a communication tool for libraries. Both internal and external newsletters are discussed, along with ones concerned with fundraising or ones in electronic format. Other topics include editorship, staffing, content decisions, production techniques, distribution, and organizational support.

Desktop Communications. International Desktop Communications, Ltd., 342 Madison Ave., Suite 622, New York, NY 10173-0002. [Bi-mo., $24]. Helps small business, corporate, and individual computer users to design and implement innovative and effective newsletters, reports, presentations, and other business communications.

Electronic Publishing: Origination, Dissemination, and Design. John Wiley, Inc., 605 Third Ave., New York, NY 10158. [Q., $375]. Covers structured editors, authoring tools, hypermedia, document bases, electronic documents over networks, and text integration.

Gardner, S., Ed. (1996). Missouri: Libraries and technology. **Library Hi Tech, 14** (2-3), 185-196. This overview of the use of technology in Missouri libraries describes the statewide bibliographic union database; elementary and secondary school projects using the Internet; full-text magazine database; remote electronic access; state depository program for digitizing resources; networks; electronic publishing; interlibrary loan; public and academic library technology activities; and the University of Missouri library system.

Guhlin, J. M. (1996). The writing technology connection. **Technology Connection, 2** (9), 12-13. Discusses use of multimedia software in a Mt. Pleasant, Texas elementary school, and asserts that the key to writing success is "postwriting," which means publication of the work in some form. Suggests online forums for the publication of children's writing, and provides brief descriptions of four online student publishers, including their Web addresses.

James, F. (1996). Electronic publication: Does it count? **Interpersonal Computing and Technology, 4** (1), 34-56. Describes the modernization of the administrative building of the Sacred Heart College Senior School in Adelaide, South Australia. Reviews one professor's personal experiences of writing an article for publication in an electronic journal. Discusses the concept that electronic publishing allows interaction via electronic mail between an author and readers of the author's work.

Kibirige, H. M. (1996). **Foundations of full text electronic information delivery systems: Implications for information professionals.** [Book, 221pp., $45]. Covers the following topics: open systems, connectivity, and information access in cyberspace; institutional networks in information access and consumption; transparent gateway interfaces in full-text information delivery; U.S. national information policy initiatives for cyberspace; international interfaces and data flow in cyberspace; the human side of information access; and harnessing the electronic full-text superflow in cyberspace. The book contains a glossary of terms, index, and selected bibliography of 138 sources.

MacEwan, B., & Geffner, M. (1996). The Committee on Institutional Cooperation Electronic Journals Collection (CIC-EJC): A new model for library management of scholarly journals published on the Internet. **Public-Access Computer Systems Review, 7** (4), 5-15. Describes the development of an electronic journal collection placed on the Internet by the Committee on Institutional Cooperation. Topics include publisher approval, archiving and preservation, Web home page design, cataloging standardization, and staffing. Concludes with a discussion on the future of the resource and the responsibilities of electronic materials management.

Machovec, G. S. (1996). Telecommunications Act of 1996: Goals and impacts. **Online Libraries and Microcomputers, 14** (2), 1-4. Discusses the effects the Telecommunications Act of 1996 will have on telephone services, telephone and cable mergers and buyouts, cable television rates, alarm monitoring services, satellite services, broadcasting and media ownership, electronic publishing, the television industry, and the Internet. Describes the impacts the act may have on libraries and other consumers of telecommunications services.

Machovec, G. S., Ed. (1996). Electronic journals: Trends in World Wide Web (WWW) Internet access. **Online Libraries and Microcomputers, 14** (4), 1-6. Examines issues surrounding the publication of electronic journals and describes publisher solutions to these issues. Topics include pricing, security, electronic page layout, copyright, backfile availability, and reliability and accessibility of data. Describes some electronic journal projects and lists electronic journal services available via WWW access.

Mason, M. G. (1996). The future revisited. **Library Journal, 121** (12), 70-72. Reviews earlier predictions about technological change in libraries, finds that providing equal access to information remains the library's mission, and forecasts the future. Topics include ownership versus access, electronic resources, information infrastructure, users, levels of service fees, circulation, librarians as "information specialists," collection building, organization of digital resources, preservation, electronic publishing, copyright, training, and measurement.

Monty, V. (1996). Due north: Issues in access to government information, a view from Canada. **Journal of Government Information, 23** (4), 491-497. Describes access to Canadian government information and compares it to the U.S. depository library system. Topics include the Canadian Depository Service Program, privatization, electronic publications, departmental autonomy, cost recovery for information, government policies, and future possibilities.

Peters, M., & Lankshear, C. (1996). Critical literacy and digital texts. **Educational Theory, 46** (1), 51-70. Explores some possibilities for enlarging and enhancing conceptions and practices of critical literacy via reflective appropriation of electronic technologies, advancing a generic account of critical literacy, investigating how modernist enclosures of the text may be thrown into question in cyberspace, and considering implications for critical literacy in cyberspace.

Phillips, M. (1996). The future of the book? **inCite, 17** (8), 10-14, 16-18. Includes five articles that focus on the theme of "the future of the book" in Australia. Topics are library acquisitions and the impact of electronic publishing, censorship of networked communications in public libraries, copyright law reform in the digital environment, technology's implications for library facility design, and preserving digital objects.

Publish! Integrated Media, Inc., Publish!, Box 51967, Boulder, CO 80322-5415. [Mo., $23.95]. A how-to magazine for desktop publishing.

Quinlan, L. A. (1996). Customizing Web documents for the classroom: An example from Lakeville High School's advanced composition class. **TechTrends, 41** (2), 27-30. Discusses how to build customized Web documents; uses examples from an Advanced Composition class at Lakeville High School (Minnesota). Highlights four steps: (1) assessing student needs; (2) developing instructional goals and activities; (3) deciding on content; and (4) organizing and arranging the information into Web pages.

Ratcliffe, F. W. (1996). The Follett report: A blueprint for library/information provision in British universities. **Reference Librarian,** (54), 163-183. Describes a report (published in 1993) on British university libraries. The report addresses funding problems, the growth in desktop and electronic publishing and resulting archiving and preservation issues, the increased number of university students, the impact of information technology on the transmission and storage of information, and the future of the library profession.

Rowland, F. (1996). ELVYN: The delivery of an electronic version of a journal from the publisher to libraries. **Journal of the American Society for Information Science, 47** (9), 690-700. Describes the ELVYN project in the United Kingdom that investigated the scenario of dual publishing (in electronic and print formats) of journals in the physical sciences by delivery of the electronic file from the publisher to academic libraries. Topics include implementation, use of the Web and electronic mail, usage data, and cost data.

Scheid, B. (1996). VTLS proceedings. **Information Technology and Libraries, 15** (1), 34-52. Includes five papers presented at the 1995 VTLS Inc. Fifth Annual Director's Conference in Roanoke (Virginia), entitled "Back to Basics: Rethinking Libraries." Topics include libraries' use of high technology, collection management and electronic publishing, public services and telecommuting clientele, what to expect of library school graduates, and retraining librarians for virtual libraries.

Schamber, L. (1996). What is a document? Rethinking the concept in uneasy times. **Journal of the American Society for Information Science, 47** (9), 669-671. Describes the challenge of redefining the fundamental concept of a "document," focusing on information professionals' apprehensions about changes in information generation, control, and access, and the future of the information professions. Topics include bibliographic control, professional roles in electronic publishing, intellectual ownership, and redefining the concept of "document" to encompass electronic documents.

Tenopir, C., & King, D. W. (1996). Setting the record straight on journal publishing: Myth vs. reality. **Library Journal, 21** (5), 32-35. Dispels misconceptions about print journal publishing so electronic publishing will not be based on old myths. Explains the truth behind 10 myths that have arisen in the publishing community over the past 20 years. Finds that scientists are using more library-provided journals, and that libraries are reducing journal collections by relying on interlibrary loan and document delivery.

Willett, P. (1996). The Victorian women writers project: The library as a creator and publisher of electronic texts. **Public Access Computer Systems Review, 7** (6), 5-16. Describes the Victorian Women Writers Project, a full-text poetry database created and published on the Web by Indiana University Libraries. Electronic formats such as graphical, character-based, and proprietary files are discussed, along with standards for formatting, including ASCII, HTML, and Text Encoding Initiatives. Decisions must consider archival nature and accessibility.

INFORMATION SCIENCE AND TECHNOLOGY

Akyurekoglu, H. (1996). A critical perspective on using communication and information technologies in adult and continuing education. **Journal of Continuing Higher Education, 44** (1), 25-30. Discusses critical aspects of using communication and information technology in adult and continuing education and offers suggestions to maximize the benefits of using these technologies.

Batson, T., & Bass, R. (1996). Primacy of process: Teaching and learning in the computer age. **Change, 28** (2), 42-47. The growth in information technology will bring to higher education hybrid forms of teaching and learning, a blurring of boundaries, different literacies, and changes in the way knowledge is constructed. Comparisons between the print and digital culture are made for the parameters of knowledge, teaching, collaboration, publication authority, thinking, and the classroom.

Bell, S. (1996). **Learning with information systems: Analysis and design in developing countries.** [Book, 248pp., $79.95 US, $111.95 Canada]. Routledge, 11 Fetter Ln., London EC4P 4EE, England. Uses cased-based approach to information systems evaluation in an international context to draw conclusions about effective designs. Addresses issues of sustainability, participation in design, and user ownership.

Bulletin of the American Society for Information Science. ASIS, 8720 Georgia Ave., Suite 501, Silver Spring, MD 20910-3602. [Bi-mo., $60 North America, $70 elsewhere, $10 single copy]. Newsmagazine concentrating on issues affecting the information field, management reports, opinion, and news of people and events in ASIS and the information community.

Canadian Journal of Information and Library Science/Revue canadienne des sciences de l'information et de bibliothèconomie. CAIS, University of Toronto Press, Journals Dept., 5201 Dufferin St., Downsview, ON M3H 5T8, Canada. [Q., nonmembers $95]. Published by the Canadian Association for Information Science to contribute to the advancement of library and information science in Canada.

CD-ROM Databases. Worldwide Videotex, Box 3273, Boynton Beach, FL 33424-3273. [Mo., $150 US, $190 elsewhere]. Descriptive listing of all databases being marketed on CD-ROM with vendor and system information.

CD-ROM Professional. Online, Inc., 462 Danbury Rd., Wilton, CT 06897. [Bi-mo., $55, indiv. and school libraries; $98, inst.]. Assists publishers, librarians, and other information professionals in the selection, evaluation, purchase, and operation of CD-ROM systems and titles.

Coutts, D. (1996). Plugging in: The changing face of technology. **School Business Affairs, 62** (4), 21-24. Like many businesses, public schools are not ready to move into the electronic data storage and transaction mode. Technological improvements such as keyboard alternatives (voice recognition software, electric pens, and optical scanners) will speed this paradigm shift. Increased speed, pocket-sized desktop computers, distance learning, and the expanding Internet are promising developments.

Crawford, R. (1997). **Managing information technology.** [Book, 272pp., $22.95 US, $31.95 Canada]. Routledge, 11 Fetter Ln., London EC4P 4EE, England. Discusses multiple aspects of information technology in secondary school contexts.

Data Sources. Ziff-Davis Publishing Co., One Park Ave., New York, NY 10016. [2/yr., $440]. Comprehensive guide to the information-processing industry. Covers equipment, software, services, and systems, and includes profiles of 10,000 companies.

Database. Online, Inc. 462 Danbury Rd., Wilton, CT 06897. [Bi-mo., $110 US and Canada, $132 Mexico, $145 foreign airmail]. Features articles on topics of interest to online database users; includes database search aids.

Datamation. Cahners Publishing Co., 8773 S. Ridgeline Blvd., Highlands Ranch, CO 80126. [24/yr.; $75; $110 Canada, Mexico; $195 Japan, Australia, New Zealand; $165 elsewhere (free to qualified personnel)]. Covers semi-technical news and views on hardware, software, and databases, for data- and information-processing professionals.

Dholakia, R. R., Mundorf, N., & Dholakia, N., eds. (1996). **New infotainment technologies in the home: Demand-side perspectives.** [Book, 296pp., $59.95]. Presents papers addressing business influences on home information access, information consumer issues, international issues, and policy issues.

Dowler, L, & Farwell, L. (1996). The gateway: A bridge to the library of the future. **RSR: Reference Services Review, 24** (2), 7-11. Describes factors behind a 1993 proposal at Harvard College (Massachusetts) to renovate its undergraduate library to a gateway library to change from print to digital information. Summarizes findings from a national conference sponsored by Harvard College Library and based on a position paper entitled "Gateways to Knowledge: A New Direction for the Harvard College Library."

Durham Technical Community College. (1996). **Strategic plan for information and communication technology.** [ED 394 519, 198pp.]. This report describes a strategic self-study focusing upon the development of an information and communication technology plan at Durham Technical Community College .

Gale Directory of Databases (in 2 vols: Vol. 1, **Online Databases**; Vol 2, **CD-ROM, Diskette, Magnetic Tape Batch Access, and Handheld Database Products**). Gale Research Inc., 835 Penobscot Building, Detroit, MI 48226. [Annual plus semi-annual update $280; Vol. 1, $199; Vol. 2, $119]. Contains information on database selection and database descriptions, including producers and their addresses.

Green, K. C. (1996). The coming ubiquity of information technology. **Change, 28** (2), 24-31. Data from a 1995 survey on campus computing indicate a major gain in the proportion of colleges and universities using information technology as an instructional resource. Four educators respond to this news and examine possible trends and issues to be addressed.

Guidelines for the Accreditation of Programs in Educational Communications and Information Technologies. (1996). [Book, 74pp., $23.95]. AECT, 1025 Vermont Ave., NW, Suite 820, Washington, DC 20005-3547. Officially-approved standards to be met by programs seeking NCATE accreditation.

Information Processing and Management. Pergamon Journals, Inc., 660 White Plains Rd., Tarrytown, NY 10591-5153. [Bi-mo., $152 indiv. whose inst. subscribes, $559 inst.]. International journal covering data processing, database building, and retrieval.

Information Retrieval and Library Automation. Lomond Publications, Inc., Box 88, Mt. Airy, MD 21771. [Mo., $66 US, foreign $79.50]. News, articles, and announcements on new techniques, equipment, and software in information services.

Information Services & Use. I.O.S. Press, Box 10558, Burke, VA 22009-0558. [4/yr., $220]. An international journal for those in the information management field. Includes online and offline systems, library automation, micrographics, videotex, and telecommunications.

The Information Society. Taylor and Francis, 1900 Frost Rd., Suite 101, Bristol, PA 19007-1598. [Q., $110]. Provides a forum for discussion of the world of information, including transborder data flow, regulatory issues, and the impact of the information industry.

Information Technology and Libraries. American Library Association, Library and Information Technology Association, 50 E. Huron St., Chicago, IL 60611-2795. [Q., $50 US, $55 Canada, Mexico, and Spain; $60 elsewhere]. Articles on library automation, communication technology, cable systems, computerized information processing, and video technologies.

Information Today. Information Today, Inc., 143 Old Marlton Pike, Medford, NJ 08055. [11/yr., $39.95]. Newspaper for users and producers of electronic information services. Articles and news about the industry, calendar of events, and product information.

Journal of Database Management. Idea Group Publishing, 4811 Jonestown Rd., Suite 230, Harrisburg, PA 17109-1751. [Q., $65 indiv., $110 inst.]. Provides state-of-the-art research to those who design, develop, and administer DBMS-based information systems.

Journal of the American Society for Information Science. Subscription Department, 605 3rd Ave., New York, NY 10158-0012. [10/yr., $550 US nonmembers, $650 Canada and Mexico, $687.50 elsewhere]. Publishes research articles in the area of information science.

Journal of Documentation. Aslib (Association for Information Management). Subsc. US, Learned Information, 143 Old Marlton Pike, Medford, NJ 08055-8750. [£60 members, £90 nonmembers]. Describes how technical, scientific, and other specialized knowledge is recorded, organized, and disseminated.

Kelly, J., & Robbins, K. (1996). Changing roles for references librarians. **Journal of Library Administration, 22** (2-3), 111-121. Discusses the future outlook for reference librarians, with topics including: "Technology as the Source of Change"; "Impact of the Internet"; "Defining the Virtual Library"; "Rethinking Reference"; "Out of the Library and into the Streets"; "Asking Users About Their Needs"; "Standardization and Artificial Intelligence"; "The Financial Future"; and "Personnel Matters."

Norris, D. M., & Dolence, M. G. (1996). IT leadership is key to transformation. **CAUSEEFFECT, 19** (1), 12-20. This article argues that, if colleges and universities are to capitalize on opportunities presented by the growth of the learning industry, they must transform themselves from Industrial Age educational institutions into Information Age learning enterprises. Leadership strategies, planning challenges, vendor roles, and economic paradigms necessary for these transitions are examined, and emerging models of information technology leadership are discussed.

Oliver, R. (1996). Measuring users' performance with interactive information systems. **Journal of Computer Assisted Learning, 12** (2), 89-102. The discrete forms of knowledge required for successful use of interactive information systems are investigated. Achievement of three forms of knowledge among novice users of a CD-ROM encyclopedia was examined. Tasks measured users' knowledge and skills in managing/controlling the system, navigating between information nodes, and selecting appropriate search strategies given information-related problems.

Oliver, R., & Oliver, H. (1996). Information access and retrieval with hypermedia information systems. **British Journal of Educational Technology, 27** (1), 33-44. Describes an investigation of the search strategies employed by novice users of an interactive information system. A class of 12-year-old students was instructed in use of an electronic encyclopedia, which they used as an information source for projects and to complete skills tests. Students employed inefficient search strategies and had difficulty creating search requests for information-related problems.

Online and CD-ROM Review. Information Today, Inc., 143 Old Marlton Pike, Medford, NJ 08055-8750. [Bi-mo., $115, Canada and Mexico, $125]. An international journal of online information systems featuring articles on using and managing online and optical information systems, training and educating online users, developing search aids, creating and marketing databases, policy affecting the continued development of systems and networks, and the development of new professional standards.

Rakes, G. (1996). Using the Internet as a tool in a resource-based learning environment. **Educational Technology, 36** (5), 52-56. This article describes the concepts of information literacy and resource-based learning as they relate to the Inquiry Training Model of instruction. It also provides guidelines for designing lesson plans using the Internet as a resource and assesses learning outcomes.

Resource Sharing and Information Networks. Haworth Press, 10 Alice St., Binghamton, NY 13904. [Semi-ann., $42 indiv., $115 inst. and libraries]. A forum for ideas on the basic theoretical and practical problems faced by planners, practitioners, and users of network services.

Seedhouse, P. (1996). Using newspapers on CD-ROM as a resource. **Language Learning Journal** (13), 65-66. Presents the advantages of using newspapers stored on CD-ROM as a resource for teaching current topics in civilization, culture and current affairs in the foreign-language class. Articles on CD-ROM can be used for vocabulary exercises and comprehension tests, and on-screen text can be altered as desired to create classroom activities.

Slavin, P. (1996). The information age and the civil society: An interview with Jeremy Rifkin. **Phi Delta Kappan, 77** (9), 607-609. For over a century, American education's mission has centered on preparing future workers to enter the marketplace. Just as the Industrial Age ended slave labor, the Information Age will end mass wage labor, freeing up millions for shortened work weeks and work in the civil society or nonprofit sector. Service learning helps by creating social capital.

Somekh, B., & Davis, N. (1997). **Using information technology effectively in teaching and learning: Studies in pre-service and in-service teacher education.** [Book, 288pp., $22.95 US, $31.95 Canada]. Routledge, 11 Fetter Ln., London EC4P 4EE, England. Incorporates information technology into instructional strategies.

Zabezhailo, M. I., & Finn, V. K. (1996). Intelligent information systems. **International Forum on Information and Documentation, 21** (2), 21-31. An Intelligent Information System (IIS) uses data warehouse technology to facilitate the cycle of data and knowledge processing, including input, standardization, storage, representation, retrieval, calculation, and delivery. This article provides an overview of IIS products and artificial intelligence systems, illustrates examples of IIS applications in ecology, and identifies paths of research and development.

INSTRUCTIONAL DESIGN AND DEVELOPMENT

Allen, M. (1996). A profile of instructional designers in Australia. **Distance Education, 17** (1), 7-32. Reports the findings of a questionnaire that elicited information from 99 instructional designers in Australia about their qualifications, activities they undertake, and perceptions of their role. Variations based on place of employment are discussed, and confusion and negative perceptions regarding instructional designers' roles are examined.

Casey, C. (1996). A model for peer review in instructional design. **Performance Improvement Quarterly, 9** (3), 32-51. Describes an instructional design review process in which peers offer feedback through "structured walkthroughs." Discusses types of reviews, guidelines, and success factors, and summarizes a formal peer review structure developed and tested at Hewlett-Packard Company. Two tables present advantages and disadvantages of types of design reviews and the action plan.

Cennamo, K. S. (1996). A "layers of negotiation" model for designing constructivist learning materials. **Educational Technology, 36** (4), 39-48. Discusses the process of designing a series of case-based interactive videodiscs to be used within a constructivist learning environment for elementary school science. Topics include assumptions about learners and learning, implications for learning materials, and implications for the instructional design process, including process-based versus procedure-based design models.

Dijkstra, S., Schott, F., Seel, N., & Tennyson, R. D., Eds. (1997). **Instructional design: International perspectives.** 2 vols. [Book, 456pp. & 376pp.]. Lawrence Erlbaum, 10 Industrial Ave., Mahwah, NJ 07430-2262, orders@erlbaum.com. Strives to bridge the gap between instructional design principles and practice and define theoretical foundations.

Driscoll, M. P., Assoc. Ed. (1996). Instructional strategies research. In D. H. Jonassen (Ed.), **Handbook of research for educational communications and technology,** pp. 879-1104. New York: Macmillan. Section includes chapters about math, generative learning, feedback research, learner control, attitudes, cooperation, and ergonomics.

Dwyer, F. M., Assoc. Ed. (1996). Instructional message design research. In D. H. Jonassen (Ed.), **Handbook of research for educational communications and technology**, pp. 755-875. New York: Macmillan. Section includes chapters about visual message design, text design, auditory presentations, and multiple-channel communication.

Frank, D. (1997). **Terrific training materials.** [Book, 200pp., $39.95]. Training Express, 11358 Aurora Ave., Des Moines, IA 50322. Provides hands-on, business-perspective approach to graphic design of manuals, handouts, and job aids.

Human-Computer Interaction. Lawrence Erlbaum Associates, 365 Broadway, Hillsdale, NJ 07642. [Q., $39 indiv. US and Canada, $69 elsewhere, $215 inst., $245 elsewhere]. A journal of theoretical, empirical, and methodological issues of user science and of system design.

Instructional Science. Kluwer Academic Publishers, P.O. Box 358 Accord Station, Hingham, MA 02018-0358. [Bi-mo., $345 inst.]. Aimed to promote a deeper understanding of the nature, theory, and practice of the instructional process and the learning resulting from this process.

Journal of Educational Multimedia and Hypermedia. Association for the Advancement of Computing in Education, Box 2966, Charlottesville, VA 22902-2966. [Q., $65 indiv., $83 inst.]. A multidisciplinary information source presenting research and applications on multi-media and hypermedia tools that allow the integration of images, sounds, text, and data in learning and teaching.

Journal of Educational Technology Systems. Baywood Publishing Co., 26 Austin Ave., Box 337, Amityville, NY 11701. [Q., $127 inst. plus $5.50 postage US and Canada, $11.25 postage elsewhere]. In-depth articles on completed and ongoing research in all phases of educational technology and its application and future within the teaching profession.

Journal of Interactive Instruction Development. Learning Technology Institute, Society for Applied Learning Technology, 50 Culpeper St., Warrenton, VA 22186. [Q., $60 indiv., $75 inst.; add $15 postage outside North America]. A showcase of successful programs that will give awareness of innovative, creative, and effective approaches to courseware development for interactive technology.

Journal of Technical Writing and Communication. Baywood Publishing Co., 26 Austin Ave., Box 337, Amityville, NY 11701. [Q., $121 inst.]. Essays on oral and written communi-cation, for purposes ranging from pure research to needs of business and industry.

Journal of Visual Literacy. International Visual Literacy Association, c/o John C. Belland, 122 Ramseyer Hall, 29 West Woodruff Ave., Ohio State University, Columbus, OH 43210. [Semi-ann., $12 indiv., $18 libraries]. Interdisciplinary forum on all aspects of visual/verbal languaging.

Kafai, Y. B., & Resnick, M. (1996). **Constructionism in practice: Designing, thinking, and learning in a digital world.** [Book, 352pp., $34.50]. Lawrence Erlbaum, 10 Industrial Ave., Mahwah, NJ 07430-2262, orders@erlbaum.com. Describes research projects at the MIT Media Laboratory which explore changes in learning modes due to new technologies.

Kimbell, R., Stables, K., & Green, R. (1996). **Understanding practice in design and technology.** [Book, 128pp., $24.95]. Open University Press, Bristol, PA. Discusses research which describes learning experiences in classrooms, studios, and workshops where design and technology are taught.

Kirby, A. (1997). **A compendium of icebreakers, energizers, and introductions.** [Book, 196pp., $69.95]. Training Express, 11358 Aurora Ave., Des Mones, IA 50322. Contains 75 activities designed to capture attention, motivate participants, and prepare participants for training.

Land, S., & Hannafin, M. J. (1996). A conceptual framework for the development of theories in action with open learning environments. **Educational Technology Research and Devel-opment, 44** (3), 37-53. Provides model for learning process of students encountering physics problems through software.

Le Maistre, K., & Weston, C. (1996). The priorities established among data sources when instructional designers revise written materials. **Educational Technology Research and Development, 44** (1), 61-70. Examines the revision practices of 8 experienced instructional designers who were given the task of revising written instructional materials. Findings show that when the designers were provided with the commonly recommended sources of feedback data, they preferred to use their own knowledge as the primary data source for making revisions.

Merrill, M. D. (1996). Reclaiming instructional design. **Educational Technology, 36** (5), 5-7. Identifies some of the assumptions underlying the technology of instructional design and clarifies its role in the larger context of education and social change. Discusses instructional design, learner characteristics, individual learning, knowledge and skill acquisition, and instructional principles.

Performance and Instruction. International Society for Performance Improvement, 1300 L St. NW, Suite 1250, Washington, DC 20005. [10/yr., $69]. Journal of ISPI, intended to promote the advantage of performance science and technology. Contains articles, research, and case studies relating to improving human performance.

Performance Improvement Quarterly. International Society for Performance Improvement, 1300 L St. NW, Suite 1250, Washington, DC 20005. [Q., $20]. Represents the cutting edge in research and theory in performance technology.

Rakes, G. C. (1996). Visuals in instructional design. **Performance and Instruction, 35** (3), 30-32. Using computer graphics such as drawings, charts, and figures in textual instruction can enhance learning by providing a spatial concept of what is being read. It is important for instructional designers to determine the specific instructional objectives to be met, what level of comprehension they want learners to achieve, and how to use the appropriate graphics to obtain that outcome.

Reigeluth, C. M., Ed. (1996). A new paradigm of ISD? **Educational Technology, 36** (3), 13-20. Examines changes in the "supersystem" of instructional systems design (ISD) that indicate the need for a paradigm of training and education based on learning instead of sorting students. Emphasizes the necessity of developing initiative, teamwork, thinking skills, and diversity, as well as new learning-focused instructional theories and user-designer approaches to the ISD process.

Scandura, J. M. (1996). Role of instructional theory in authoring effective and efficient learning technologies. **Computers in Human Behavior, 12** (2), 313-328. Major issues in instructional theory and the advantages of structural analysis for building instructional systems are discussed. Building on core technology and the structural learning theory, a research program is proposed which will enable efficient development of effective learning systems for industry and schools.

Shambaugh, R. N., & Magliaro, S. G. (1997). **Mastering the possibilities: A process approach to instructional design.** [Book, 308pp.; instructor's manual available]. Allyn & Bacon, 160 Gould St., Needham Heights, MA 02194-2315. Uses learner-centered approach in designing instruction with integrated experiences.

Tennyson, R. D., Assoc. Ed. (1996). Soft technologies: Instructional and informational design research. In D. H. Jonassen (Ed.), **Handbook of research for educational communications and technology,** pp. 491-752. New York: Macmillan. Section includes chapters about visual literacy, gaming, instructional design, intelligent tutoring, cognitive teaching models, hypertext, adaptive systems, rich environments, cognitive tools, and information access.

Training. Lakewood Publications, Inc., 50 S. Ninth, Minneapolis, MN 55402. [Mo., $68 US, $78 Canada, $89 elsewhere]. Covers all aspects of training, management, and organizational development, motivation, and performance improvement.

Training Media Database. (1996). National Information Center for Educational Media (NICEM), P.O. Box 8640, Albuquerque, NM 87198-8640. (505) 265-3591, (800) 926-8328. Fax (505) 256-1080. E-mail: nicem@nicem.com. The portion of the NICEM database that deals with human resource issues is now being offered by the Human Resource Information Network Corporation (HRIN). It comprises approximately 100,000 records describing non-print media materials appropriate for corporate and industrial training, staff development, and personnel management. For additional information, contact HRIN Corp., 7200 Wisconsin Ave., Suite 601, Bethesda, MD 20814. (800) 638-8094, (301) 961-6749. Fax (301) 961-6720.

Training Research Journal: The Science and Practice of Training. [Annual issue, $60]. Educational Technology Publications, 700 Palisade Ave., Englewood Cliffs, NJ 07632-0564. An international, peer-reviewed publication providing a forum for theoretical and empirical work relevant to training. Includes empirical studies, theoretical reviews, meta-analyses, and articles of a conceptual nature that contribute to an understanding of the theory, research, and practice of the training of adult learners.

Wild, M. (1996). Mental models and computer modeling. **Journal of Computer Assisted Learning, 12** (10) 10-21. Examines the place of mental models in the process of knowledge construction, particularly by the relationship between mental models and computer models in that process. Analyzes and discusses children's use of spreadsheets to build their own computer models. Suggests that the process of building models on a computer may provide direct support to the cognitive processes of constructing mental models.

Wilson, B. G., Ed. (1996). **Constructivist learning environments: Case studies in instructional design.** [Book, 252pp., $48.95]. Educational Technology Publications, 700 Palisade Ave., Englewood Cliffs, NJ 07632-0564. Provides comprehensive look at the variety of tools and information that can be used in pursuit of learning goals and problem-solving activities.

Winek, G. (1996). Rapid prototyping enters mainstream manufacturing. **Journal of Technology Studies, 22** (1), 2-9. Explains rapid prototyping, a process that uses computer-assisted design files to create a three-dimensional object automatically, speeding the industrial design process. Five commercially available systems and two emerging types—the 3-D printing process and repetitive masking and depositing—are described.

Yelon, S. (1996). **Powerful principles of instruction.** Addison Wesley/Longman. [Book, 299 pp., $28.50]. Explains 10 principles which are basic to all instruction; contains examples and practical guidelines.

INTERACTIVE MULTIMEDIA

Abrams, A. H. (1996). **Multimedia magic: Exploring the power of multimedia production.** [Book, 304pp.]. Allyn & Bacon, 160 Gould St., Needham Heights, MA 02194-2315. Discusses multimedia as an educational presentation medium and as an authoring tool with tutorials featuring specific software packages.

Agnew, P. W., Kellerman, A. S., & Meyer, J. (1996). **Multimedia in the classroom.** [Book, 456pp., $36]. Allyn & Bacon; available from International Society for Technology in Education, University of Oregon, 1787 Agate St., Eugene, OR 97403-1923. Provides preservice and inservice teachers a process for directing student multimedia projects.

Alber, A. F. (1996). **Multimedia: A management perspective.** [Book, 672pp.]. Wadsworth. Intended for introductory multimedia courses in diverse fields.

Allen, C. M., & Boelzner, D. E. (1996). An overview of multimedia and the law. **Journal of Instruction Delivery Systems, 10** (1), 28-31. Reviews the areas of intellectual property law (patent, copyright, and trademark) and discusses how multimedia raises legal issues in each area. The scope of available protection and the concerns involved in negotiating licensing and publishing agreements for multimedia are discussed, as well as issues related to online material.

Bailey, C., & Chambers, J. (1996). Interactive learning and technology in the US science and mathematics reform movement. **British Journal of Educational Technology, 27** (2), 123-133. Presents an overview of the science and mathematics reform movement in elementary, secondary, and higher education institutions, emphasizing the roles of interactive learning and technology. Describes a distance learning project at Florida Community College at Jacksonville where five faculty plus a learning theorist developed and taught two basic integrated science/mathematics courses using multimedia.

Barron, T. (1996). Getting friendly with authoring tools. **Training and Development, 50** (5), 36-46. This primer on authoring tools for training provides tips on selecting software, questions to assess whether to use it, and a directory of companies selling multimedia authoring products.

Bigelow, B., Ed. (1996). On the road to cultural bias. **Social Studies and the Young Learner, 8** (3), 26-29. Assesses the strengths and weaknesses of the interactive CD-ROM "The Oregon Trail." Maintains that, although the program offers a sympathetic portrayal of Native Americans, it is still rife with cultural bias. The simulation's structure accentuates the white male experience at the expense of others.

Burbules, N. C., & Callister, T. A. (1996). Knowledge at the crossroads: Some alternative futures of hypertext learning environments. **Educational Theory, 46** (1), 23-50. Discusses possibilities and dangers involved with using hypertext for learning; explains how it is similar to and different from other forms of information generation, organization, storage, and retrieval; examines its influence on the information it organizes; and explores problematic issues (including the potential for bias and distortion within hypertexts).

Casey, C. (1996). Incorporating cognitive apprenticeship in multi-media. **Educational Technology Research and Development, 44** (1), 71-84. Examines the use of cognitive apprenticeships as a framework for instructional design to help address the needs of a distributed learning environment. Describes the applications of a multimedia training course that helps weather forecasters interpret radar. Findings indicate that cognitive apprenticeships can be implemented in multimedia to meet the cognitive demands of diverse learners.

CD-ROM World. PC World Communication Inc., 501 Second St., Suite 600, San Francisco, CA 94107. [10/yr., $29]. Articles and reviews for CD-ROM users.

Chun, D. M., & Plass, J. L. (1996). Effects of multimedia annotations on vocabulary acquisition. **Modern Language Journal, 80** (2), 183-198. Discusses studies of German students using "CyberBuch," a hypermedia application for reading German texts that contains annotations for words in the form of text, pictures, and video. The article examines incidental vocabulary learning, the effectiveness of different types of annotations for vocabulary acquisition, and the effect of look-up behavior on performance on vocabulary tests.

Coyne, M. S. (1996). A cartoon history of soil microbiology. **Journal of Natural Resources and Life Sciences Education, 25** (1), 30-36. Describes the use of cartoons in presenting a historical perspective of soil microbiology that makes this information more entertaining to introductory students. Presents basic historical facts and major accomplishments of the pioneering soil microbiologists in a factual but tongue-in-cheek survey.

Dalziel, C. (1996). Copyright, fair use, and the Information Superhighway. **Community College Journal, 67** (1), 23-27. Describes the work of the Conference on Fair Use, a national effort to update copyright guidelines to reflect the new technologies of multimedia materials, distance learning, visual archives, and digital libraries. Reviews concerns of users and producers and requirements for maintaining fair use of materials. Provides guidelines for each area of new technology.

Desmarais, N. (1996). Behind the scenes of multimedia publishing: Dream or nightmare? **Computers in Libraries, 16** (4), 61-65. Discusses the processes and difficulties involved in the creation of a multimedia CD-ROM. Topics include searching for a publisher, how deadlines affect creativity, the editorial process, use of politically correct terminology and its influence on content and historical representation, obtaining rights to reproduce images, working with photographs and files, audio and video, and the creation of hypertext links.

Emerging Technology Consultants. (1996). **1997 multimedia and videodisc compendium for education and training.** [Book, 192pp., $45]. International Society for Technology in Education, University of Oregon, 1787 Agate St., Eugene, OR 97403-1923. Lists laserdiscs, CD-ROMS, and multimedia software for education, health, and training industries.

Florio, C., & Murie, M. (1996). Authoritative authoring: Software that makes multimedia happen. **NewMedia, 6** (12), 67-70, 72-75. Compares seven mid- to high-end multimedia authoring software systems that combine graphics, sound, animation, video, and text for Windows and Macintosh platforms. A run-time project was created with each program using video, animation, graphics, sound, formatted text, hypertext, and buttons.

Garrett, M., & Ezzo, M. (1996). Edutainment: The challenge. **Journal of Interactive Instruction Development, 8** (3), 3-7. Education and entertainment both seek to create memorable events. This article explores memory enhancement techniques in each field, the potential role of multimedia in these techniques, determining appropriate and inappropriate merging of education with the emotionalism of entertainment, and assessing one's options for edutainment purchases.

Hall, D. W. (1996). Computer-based animations in large-enrollment lectures: Visual reinforcement of biological concepts. **Journal of College Science Teaching, 25** (6), 421-425. Describes the use of computer-based animations in demonstrating and enlivening scientific principles. Discusses frame-based animation, cell-based animation, object animation, the creation of simple animations, and the use of animation software.

Holt, D. M. (1996). Lone Star 2000: Documenting successful school or university teaching and learning. **T.H.E. Journal, 24** (3), 77-81. Describes a partnership between University of North Florida and Duval County Public Schools which led to Lone Star 2000. The project involved teachers and interns producing a method for multimedia electronic portfolios and assisting students in their creation. Much of the discussion focuses on the courseware used and outcomes of the program.

HyperNexus: Journal of Hypermedia and Multimedia Studies. International Society for Technology in Education, University of Oregon, 1787 Agate St., Eugene, OR 97403-1923. [Q., for members of the SIGHyper of ISTE]. Features articles on projects, lesson plans, and theoretical issues, as well as reviews of products, software, and books.

Jones, K. S. (1996). Experiments in spoken document retrieval. **Information Processing & Management, 32** (4), 399-417. Describes experiments in the retrieval of spoken documents in multimedia systems. Problems in spoken document retrieval are discussed, and a voice mail application is explained that combines state-of-the-art speech recognition with established document retrieval technologies to provide an effective and efficient retrieval tool.

Josephson, H., & Gorman, T. (1996). **Careers in multimedia: Roles and resources.** [Book, 304pp.]. Thomson. Describes multimedia industry for introductory multimedia courses in technology, education, business, and communications.

Kao, M. T. (1996). **Scaffolding in hypermedia assisted instruction: An example of integration.** Proceedings of selected research and development presentations at the 1996 National AECT Convention, Indianapolis. [ED 397 803, 22pp.]. A 3-D contingent scaffolding model of a hypermedia system is proposed which gradually weans learners off the technical support of instructors or more knowledgeable peers as they master certain skills. The model permits the instructor to vary his or her support in response to the learner's performance in a learning task consisting of a sequence of steps.

Kommers, P. A. M., Grabinger, S., & Dunlap, J. C., Eds. (1996). **Hypermedia learning environments: Instructional design and integration.** [Book, 288pp., $24.50]. Lawrence Erlbaum, 10 Industrial Ave., Mahwah, NJ 07430-2262, orders@erlbaum.com. Suggests practical approaches for applying multimedia products to learning tasks for a practicing audience.

Korolenko, M. (1997). **Writing for multimedia: A guide and source book for the digital writer.** [Book, 400pp.]. Thomson. Covers the style of writing required for nonlinear text.

Large, A. (1996). Computer animation in an instructional environment. **Library & Information Science Research, 18** (1), 3-23. Reviews the effectiveness of animation in enhancing textual information for instructional purposes and identifies factors that determine effectiveness. Outlines methodological problems in the research and summarizes design criteria for multimedia instructional products.

Leader, L. F., & Klein, J. D. (1996). The effects of search tool type and cognitive style on performance during hypermedia database searches. **Educational Technology Research and Development, 44** (2), 5-15. Describes a study that investigated the effects of search tools and learner cognitive styles on performance in searches for information within a hypermedia database. Students in a university ESL program were assigned to one of four treatment groups, and results show a significant interaction between search tool and cognitive style.

Lookatch, R. P. (1996). Collaborative learning and multimedia: Are two heads still better than one? **TechTrends, 41** (4), 27-31. Discusses factors for authentic collaborative learning with computers. Highlights include software design, social environment, preparatory activities, accountability structures, and group assignment rationale. Discussion highlights advantages of collaborative learning and the alternatives of individual and large group computer-based environments.

Misanchuk, E. R., & Schwier, R. A. (1996). Benefits and pitfalls of using HTML as a CD-ROM development tool. **Journal of Interactive Instruction Development, 8** (4), 3-14. Discussion of HTML (HyperText Markup Language) focuses on its use for developing CD-ROMs. Topics include the Web; cross-platform compatibility; the incorporation of text, graphics, audio, and video; learner control over display characteristics; and limitations of HTML for designing instructional materials.

Munro, R. K., & Hillis, P. L. M. (1996). Bright ideas, creative people, teamwork, and money: Developing courseware for teaching Scottish history. **History Computer Review, 12** (1), 23-34. Describes three hypermedia databases designed to support secondary education classes in Scottish history. The databases contain mostly 19th-century census information with links to subjects such as fashion, education, and entertainment. Interactive interfaces allow students to create original research applications.

Nicholls, P., & Ridley, J. (1996). A context for evaluating multimedia. **Computers in Libraries, 16** (4), 34-39. Defines multimedia and briefly discusses its history, and details the elements comprising information systems and products. Asserts that the context for evaluating multimedia materials is based in the various layers of the system, and that multimedia materials will be more complex to evaluate than earlier generations of electronic information tools.

Nicholson, A. Y., & Ngai, J. Y. (1995-1996). Converting a traditional multimedia kit into an interactive video CD-ROM. **Journal of Educational Technology Systems, 24** (3), 235-248. Reports on the development of an interactive multimedia project in which an educational television program and supporting instructional materials were converted into digital data, integrated into courseware, and stored on a CD-ROM. Examines benefits and problems of using multimedia technology in the educational environment.

Nicolo, E., & Sapio, B. (1996). Structural analysis of the global multimedia scenario: Techno-logical, market, environmental, and regulatory issues. **Journal of Instruction Delivery Systems, 10** (1), 17-27. Presents a strategic evaluation of the global multimedia scenario, considering both stand-alone workstations and distributed multimedia in the worldwide interactive network, including educational databases on the Internet. Discusses 50 technological, market, environmental, and regulatory factors and estimates their impacts on each other using WISE (Weighted Impact Structured Evaluation).

Parker, A. (1996). **Cool multimedia lesson plans.** [Book, CD-ROM, $29.95]. Published by Pierian Spring. International Society for Technology in Education, University of Oregon, 1787 Agate St., Eugene, OR 97403-1923. Describes 100 classroom-ready lesson plans designed by an educator.

Peck, D. D. (1997). **Multimedia: A hands-on introduction.** [Book with CD-ROM, 320pp.]. Thomson. Written for multimedia and graphics arts courses; covers history, technique, current technology, and resources.

Plowman, L. (1996). Narrative, linearity, and interactivity: Making sense of interactive multimedia. **British Journal of Educational Technology, 27** (2), 92-105. Students ages 11-16 using 4 different educational multimedia packages were observed to determine how children make sense of interactive media. Design implications include the need to create a dynamic narrative which is motivating and absorbing by integrating the rhetoric with strong mythical elements. The interrelationship of narrative, linearity, and interactivity is important for helping learners make sense of interactive multimedia.

Rasmussen, J. L. (1996). ANOVA MultiMedia: A program for teaching ANOVA designs. **Teaching of Psychology, 23** (1), 55-56. Describes a multimedia program for teaching analysis of variance (ANOVA) designs. The program uses colorful images, brief animations, interactive tasks, and immediate feedback. It consists of 10 story problems that tests students' understanding of independent groups and repeated measures variables. Provides information about availability.

Roberts, M. R. (1996). A curriculum using interactive media. **Technology Teacher, 56** (2), 13-15. Learning potential in the technology classroom can be increased by using multimedia techniques that can be used to create a variety of interactive learning environments. Advantages of screen-based text include spontaneity of update, potential for interactivity and reactivity, and the opportunity for incorporating special effects.

Rouet, J., Levonen, J. J., Dillon, A., & Spiro, R. J., Eds. (1996). **Hypertext and cognition.** [Book, 184pp., $19.95]. Lawrence Erlbaum, 10 Industrial Ave., Mahwah, NJ 07430-2262, orders@erlbaum.com. Addresses questions about learner-hypertext interactions, such as selecting relevant information, overload, system facilitation, and effective cognitive strategies.

Schwier, R. A., & Misanchuk, E. R. (1996). Designing multimedia for the hypertext markup language. **Journal of Interactive Instruction Development, 8** (4), 15-25. Discusses the use of HTML (HyperText Markup Language) to create a Web page for multimedia documents and concludes that at present, the limitations argue against its use for interactive multimedia projects. Highlights include studies conducted at the University of Saskatchewan (Canada); file management; and text display and layout.

Speitel, T. (1996). Digital documentation: Using computers to create multimedia reports. **Science Teacher, 63** (3), 40-43. Describes methods for creating integrated multimedia documents using recent advances in print, audio, and video digitization that bring added usefulness to computers as data acquisition, processing, and presentation tools. Discusses advantages of digital documentation.

Thomson Technology Services Group. (1996). **Thomson multimedia resource, 1996 ed.** [Book, 256pp.]. Thomson. Discusses information harvesting, evaluation, development, DVD, interactive television, and other topics for introductory multimedia courses.

Wild, M. (1996). **Perspectives on the place of educational theory in multimedia.** [ED 396 746]. A number of themes and issues emerge in any discussion about educational theory, learning and instruction. Interactive multimedia provides another vehicle to consider and reconsider the place of educational theory, and particularly theories centered on student learning, in the design of multimedia. This paper discusses some of the prevalent issues that emerged as part of the educational theory strand to the Mini-conference for Practitioners of Educational Interactive Multimedia (Curtin University, Australia, July 7-9, 1995).

Zemke, R., & Armstrong, J. (1996). A bluffer's guide to multimedia. **Training, 33** (6), 36-44. Suggests that it is impossible to keep up with the explosion of information about multimedia training. Looks at the history of computers in education, offers a list of experts in the computer industry, and gives information that will increase trainers' familiarity with hardware and software terminology.

Zemke, R., & Armstrong, J. (1996). Evaluating multimedia. **Training, 33** (8), 48-52. In evaluating and selecting multimedia materials to be used in training programs, criteria to consider include content propriety, technology fit, instructional effectiveness, and administrative handiness.

LIBRARIES AND MEDIA CENTERS

Book Report. Linworth Publishing, 480 E. Wilson Bridge Rd., Suite L, Worthington, OH 43085-2372. [5/school yr., $39 US, $47 Canada, $9 single copy]. Journal for junior and senior high school librarians provides articles, tips, and ideas for day-to-day school library management, as well as reviews of audiovisuals and software, all written by school librarians.

Byrne, D. J. (1997). **MARC Manual: Understanding and using MARC records.** [Book, 300pp., $34]. Libraries Unlimited, P.O. Box 6633, Englewood, CO 80155-6633. Explains the three types of MARC records, along with considerations and specifications for MARC database processing.

California Media & Library Education Association. (1997). **From library skills to information literacy: A handbook for the 21st century.** 2nd ed. Hi Willow Research & Publishing. Covers information skills through curricular integration; provides models and strategies. Outlines the adaptation of these principles for ESL students.

Clyde, L. A., Ed. (1996). **Sustaining the vision: A collection of articles and papers on research in school librarianship.** [Book, $35]. Hi Willow Research & Publishing. Contains current international research reports.

Collection Building. M.C.B. University Press Ltd., 60-62 Toller Ln., Bradford, W. Yorks. BD8 9BY, England. [Q., $89]. Focuses on all aspects of collection building, ranging from microcomputers to business collections to popular topics and censorship.

College and Research Libraries. Association of College and Research Libraries, 50 E. Huron St., Chicago, IL 60611.[Bi-mo., $50 US nonmembers, $55 Canada and Spain, $60 elsewhere, $14 single copy]. Publishes articles of interest to college and research librarians.

Computers in Libraries. Information Today, Inc. (formerly Learned Information, Inc.), 143 Old Marlton Pike, Medford, NJ 08055-8750. [10/yr., $87.95 US, $97.95 Canada, Mexico; £68 Europe; $105.95 outside Europe]. Covers practical applications of microcomputers to library situations and recent news items.

Danner, R. A. (1996). Facing the millenium: Law schools, law librarians, and information technology. **Journal of Legal Education, 46** (1), 43-58. Discussion of the role of advancing technology in legal education looks at the administrative and organizational questions it poses, solutions developed at the Duke University (North Carolina) law school, and new possible roles for library directors in managing and planning the growing integration of information technology into all aspects of legal education. Creative institutional responses are seen as essential.

Electronic Library. Learned Information Europe Ltd., Woodside, Hinksey Hill, Oxford OX1 5BE, UK. [6/yr., £95, $106 North America only]. For librarians and information center managers interested in microcomputer and library automation. Features industry news and product announcements.

Emergency Librarian. Box 34069, Dept. 284, Seattle, WA 98124-1069. eml@rockland.com. [Bi-mo. except July-August, $49]. Articles, review columns, and critical analyses of management and programming issues for children's and young adult librarians.

Government Information Quarterly. JAI Press, 55 Old Post Rd., No. 2, P.O. Box 1678, Greenwich, CT 06836-1678. [Q., $70 indiv., $90 foreign; $145 inst., $165 foreign]. International journal of resources, services, policies, and practices.

ICONnect. American Association of School Librarians (AASL), American Library Association (ALA), 50 East Huron St., Chicago, IL 60611. Gopher address: ericir.syr.edu 7070. Gopher URL: gopher://ericir.syr.edu:7070/. Home page address: http://ericir.syr.edu/ICONN/ ihome.html. A technology initiative of AASL and ALA, ICONnect is designed to get students, library media specialists, and teachers connected to learning using the Internet. Its resources are designed to help students develop information and visual literacy skills, and to train teachers and library media specialists to effectively navigate the Internet and to develop and use meaningful curriculum connections.

Information Services and Use. Elsevier Science Publishers, Box 10558, Burke, VA 22009-0558. [4/yr., $220]. Contains data on international developments in information management and its applications. Articles cover online systems, library automation, word processing, micrographics, videotex, and telecommunications.

Journal of Academic Librarianship. JAI Press, 55 Old Post Rd., No. 2, Box 1678, Greenwich, CT 06836-1678. [Bi-mo., $50 indiv., $80 foreign; $145 inst., $165 foreign]. Results of significant research, issues and problems facing academic libraries, book reviews, and innovations in academic libraries.

Journal of Government Information (formerly *Government Publications Review*). Elsevier Science Ltd., Journals Division, 660 White Plains Rd., Tarrytown, NY 10591-5153. [Bi-mo., £251, $400 US]. An international journal covering production, distribution, bibliographic control, accessibility, and use of government information in all formats and at all levels.

Journal of Librarianship and Information Science. Worldwide Subscription Service Ltd., Unit 4, Gibbs Reed Farm, Ticehurst, E. Sussex TN5 7HE, England. [Q., $125. Deals with all aspects of library and information work in the United Kingdom and reviews literature from international sources.

Journal of Library Administration. Haworth Press, 10 Alice St., Binghamton, NY 13904-1580. [Q., $36 indiv., $94.50 inst.]. Provides information on all aspects of effective library management, with emphasis on practical applications.

Krausse, E. B. & Tassia, M. R. (1996). **New games for information skills: Ready, set, go...** [Book, $18.]. Hi Willow Research & Publishing. Describes an approach to the information skills of need identification, access and location, information analysis, utilization, and synthesis.

Kuhlthau, C. C., Ed.; Goodin, M. E. & McNally, M. J., Assoc. Eds. (1996). **The virtual school library: Gateways to the information superhighway.** [Book, 161pp., $24]. Libraries Unlimited, P.O. Box 6633, Englewood, CO 80155-6633. Covers current theory, field success, thinking skills, information curriculum, and distance education.

LeBaron, J. F., Collier, C., & Friel, L. (1996). **A travel agent in cyberschool: The Internet and the library media program.** [Book, 171pp. plus disks, $25]. Libraries Unlimited, P.O. Box 6633, Englewood, CO 80155-6633. Examines how technology-enhanced education improvements fit in with the library media program.

Library Hi Tech. Pierian Press, Box 1808, Ann Arbor, MI 48106. [Q., $45 indiv., $75 inst.]. Concentrates on reporting on the selection, installation, maintenance, and integration of systems and hardware.

Library and Information Science Research. Ablex Publishing Corp., 355 Chestnut St., Norwood, NJ 07648. [Q., $45 indiv., $95 inst.]. Research articles, dissertation reviews, and book reviews on issues concerning information resources management.

Library Journal. Box 59690, Boulder, CO 80322-9690. [20/yr., $94.50 US, $116 Canada, $159 elsewhere]. A professional periodical for librarians, with current issues and news, professional reading, lengthy book review section, and classifieds.

Library Quarterly. University of Chicago Press, Journals Division, Box 37005, Chicago, IL 60637. [Q., $32 indiv., $58 inst.]. Scholarly articles of interest to librarians.

Library Resources and Technical Services. Association for Library Collections and Technical Services, 50 E. Huron St., Chicago, IL 60611-2795. [Q., $55 nonmembers US, Canada, and Mexico; $65 elsewhere]. Scholarly papers on bibliographic access and control, preservation, conservation, and reproduction of library materials.

Library Software Review. Sage Publications, Inc., 2455 Teller Rd., Thousand Oaks, CA 91320. [Q., $49 indiv., $152 US inst.; foreign add $8]. Emphasizes practical aspects of library computing for libraries of all types, including reviews of automated systems ranging from large-scale mainframe-based systems to microcomputer-based systems, and both library-specific and general-purpose software used in libraries.

Library Trends. University of Illinois Press, Journals Dept., 1325 S. Oak St., Champaign, IL 61820. [Q., $50 indiv.; $75 inst.; add $7 elsewhere]. Each issue is concerned with one aspect of library and information science, analyzing current thought and practice and examining ideas that hold the greatest potential for the field.

LISA: Library and Information Science Abstracts. Bowker-Saur Ltd., Maypole House, Maypole Rd., E. Grinsted, W. Sussex, RH19 1HH, England. [Mo., $675 US, £380 elsewhere]. More than 500 abstracts per issue from more than 500 periodicals, reports, books, and conference proceedings.

Loertscher, D. V. (1996). **Collection mapping in the LMC: Building library media center collections in the age of technology.** [Book, $20]. Hi Willow Research & Publishing. Provides an updated approach to collection mapping, including topics such as technology access and reassessing collections in the light of technology. Includes disk with planning tools.

Meghabghab, D. B. (1997). **Automating media centers and small libraries.** [Book, 200pp., $30]. Libraries Unlimited, P.O. Box 6633, Englewood, CO 80155-6633. Covers the entire spectrum of activities involved in automating media centers and small libraries.

Microcomputers for Information Management. Ablex Publishing, 355 Chestnut St., Norwood, NJ 07648. [Q., $40 indiv., $120 inst.]. Focuses on new developments with microcomputer technology in libraries and in information science in the US and abroad.

Naumer, J. N., & Thurman, G. B. (1997). **The works for library and media center management.** [Book, 200pp., DOS/Windows disk, $32.50]. Libraries Unlimited, P.O. Box 6633, Englewood, CO 80155-6633. Demonstrates how media specialists can use integrated software packages to analyze and meet management needs. Disk contains templates. [See Thurman & Naumer for similar book in Macintosh version.]

The Public-Access Computer Systems Review. An electronic journal published on an irregular basis by the University Libraries, University of Houston, Houston, TX 77204-2091. Free to libraries. E-mail: LThompson@uh.edu. Contains articles about all types of computer systems that libraries make available to their patrons and technologies to implement these systems.

Public Libraries. Public Library Association, American Library Association, 50 E. Huron St., Chicago, IL 60611-2795. [Bi-mo., $50 US nonmembers, $60 elsewhere, $10 single copy]. News and articles of interest to public librarians.

Public Library Quarterly. Haworth Press, 10 Alice St., Binghamton, NY 13904. [Q., $40 indiv., $90 inst.]. Addresses the major administrative challenges and opportunities that face the nation's public libraries.

Reference Librarian. Haworth Press, 10 Alice St., Binghamton, NY 13904-9981. [2 vols./yr.; $60 indiv., $120 inst. per vol.; 2 issues per vol.]. Each issue focuses on a topic of current concern, interest, or practical value to reference librarians.

RQ. Reference and Adult Services Division, American Library Association, 50 E. Huron St., Chicago, IL 60611-2795. [Q., $42 nonmembers North America, $52 elsewhere, $12 single copy]. Covers all aspects of library service to adults, and reference service and collection development at every level and for all types of libraries.

Salmon, S., Goldfarb, E. K., Greenblatt, M., & Strauss, A. P. (1996). **Power up your library: Creating the new school library program.** [Book, 292pp., $32.50]. Libraries Unlimited, P.O. Box 6633, Englewood, CO 80155-6633. Based on the methods of the New York City Library Power Program; integrates concepts of flexible scheduling, collaborative planning, and innovation.

Schement, J. R. (1996). A 21st-century strategy for librarians. **Library Journal, 121** (8), 34-36. Discusses the impact of home use of electronic information sources, such as the Internet, on traditional library services. Suggests that librarians should devote themselves to how people seek, organize, and consume information. Describes 21st century strategies to help libraries use traditional information services combined with computer technology to fulfill the information needs of their communities.

Schene, C. (1996). **The development of a strategic plan for networking the kindergarten to grade eight school library media centers in the Taunton School System.** [Descriptive report, ED 398 910, 84pp.]. The purpose of this paper is to determine the current status of the Taunton Public School's (Massachusetts) kindergarten to grade eight library program in terms of networking and resource sharing. A strategic plan as designed to incorporate various networking strategies and resource sharing options for the K-8 library media centers.

School Library Journal. Box 57599, Boulder, CO 80322-7559. [Mo., $79.50 US, $105 Canada, $125 elsewhere]. For school and youth service librarians. Contains about 2,500 critical book reviews annually.

School Library Media Activities Monthly. LMS Associates, 17 E. Henrietta St., Baltimore, MD 21230. [10/yr., $49 US, $54 elsewhere]. A vehicle for distributing ideas for teaching library media skills and for the development and implementation of library media skills programs.

School Library Media Quarterly. American Association of School Librarians, American Library Association, 50 E. Huron St., Chicago, IL 60611-2795. [Q., $40 nonmembers US, $50 elsewhere, $12 single copy]. For library media specialists, district supervisors, and others concerned with the selection and purchase of print and nonprint media and with the development of programs and services for preschool through high school libraries.

Special Libraries. Special Libraries Association, 1700 18th St., NW, Washington, DC 20009-2508. [Q., $60 nonmembers (foreign $65), $10 single copy]. Discusses administration, organization, and operations. Includes reports on research, technology, and professional standards.

Summers, S. L. (1997). **Media alert!: 200 activities to create media-savvy kids.** [Book, $15]. Hi Willow Research & Publishing. Contains an updated approach to media literacy, including such concepts as reality vs fantasy, fact vs opinion, violence, and commercialism.

Sykes, J. A. (1997). **Library centers: Teaching information literacy in elementary schools.** [Book, 280pp., $30]. Libraries Unlimited, P.O. Box 6633, Englewood, CO 80155-6633. Documents a continuous library center program with a series of mini-lessons covering a variety of curricular topics.

Thurman, G. B., & Naumer, J. N. (1997). **The works for library and media center management.** [Book, 200pp., Macintosh disk, $33]. Libraries Unlimited, P.O. Box 6633, Englewood, CO 80155-6633. Demonstrates how media specialists can use integrated software packages to analyze and meet management needs. Disk contains templates. [See Naumer & Thurman for similar book in DOS/Windows version.]

The Unabashed Librarian. Box 2631, New York, NY 10116. [Q., $30 US, $36 elsewhere]. Down-to-earth library items: procedures, forms, programs, cataloging, booklists, software reviews.

Valauskas, E. J., & Ertel, M. (1996). **The Internet for teachers and school library media specialists: Today's applications, tomorrow's prospects.** [Book, 231pp., $35]. This book is a collection of "success stories" written by teachers, media specialists, and school administrators who have developed their own facilities to bring the Internet to their students.

Voice of Youth Advocates. Scarecrow Press, 52 Liberty St., Box 4167, Metuchen, NJ 08840. [Bi-mo., $38.50 US, $43.50 elsewhere]. Contains articles, bibliographies, and media reviews of materials for or about adolescents.

Wilson Library Bulletin. H. W. Wilson Co., 950 University Ave., Bronx, NY 10452. [10/yr., $52 US, $58 elsewhere]. Print edition ceased June 1995. Now available URL:http://www.hwwilson.com/default.html. Also available in microform from UMI, PMC. Significant articles on librarianship, news, and reviews of films, books, and professional literature.

Woolls, B. (1996). **Ideas for school library media centers: Focus on the curriculum.** 2nd ed. [Book, $25]. Hi Willow Research & Publishing. Adds new educational trends such as restructuring and portfolio assessment to best-selling curriculum integration ideas of the first edition.

MEDIA TECHNOLOGIES

Appleman, R. (1996). **Video editing the pictorial sequence.** [Book, 64pp., $7.50]. AECT, 1025 Vermont Ave., NW, Suite 820, Washington, DC 20005-3547. Designed for the beginning teacher or student who is venturing into the process of video editing with a specific task in hand, but who has not had any formal training in video production.

A-V ONLINE. Knight-Ridder Information (formerly *Dialog*), 2440 El Camino Real, Mountain View, CA 94040. (DIALOG File 46; CompuServe KI046. For information on a tape lease agreement, contact Access Innovations, Inc., P.O. Box 40130, Albuquerque, NM 87196.) Updated quarterly, this NICEM database provides information on nonprint media covering all levels of education and instruction. Nonprint formats covered are 16mm films, videos, audiocassettes, CD-ROMs, software, laserdisc, filmstrips, slides, transparencies, motion cartridges, kits, models, and realia. Entries date from 1964 to the present, with approximately 420,000 records as of January 1995.

Berg, M. H., & Smith, J. P. (1996). Using videotapes to improve teaching. **Music Educators Journal, 82** (4), 31-37. Recommends school music departments forming video clubs where teachers can view and constructively criticize videotapes of their classroom performance. Provides a thoughtful and thorough discussion of what to include in a video portfolio and how to conduct viewing sessions. Addresses possible limitations and advantages to this system.

Broadcasting and Cable (formerly *Broadcasting*). Box 6399, Torrence, CA 90504. [W., $117 US, $320 elsewhere]. All-inclusive newsweekly for radio, television, cable, and allied business.

CableVision. Cablevision Magazine, Box 7698, Riverton, NJ 08077-7698. [26/yr.; $55 US, $85 Canada, $165 elsewhere]. A newsmagazine for the cable television industry. Covers programming, marketing, advertising, business, and other topics.

Communication Abstracts. Sage Publications, Inc., 2455 Teller Rd., Thousand Oaks, CA 91320. [Bi-mo., $147 indiv., $474 inst.]. Abstracts communication-related articles, reports, and books. Cumulated annually.

Communication Booknotes. Center for Advanced Study in Telecommunications (CAST), Ohio State University, 210 E. Baker Systems, 1971 Neil Ave., Columbus, OH 43210-1971. [Bi-mo., $45 indiv., $95 inst., add $5 elsewhere]. Newsletter that reviews books and periodicals about mass media, telecommunications, and information policy.

Communications News. Nelson Publishing Co., 2504 N. Tamiami Trail, Nokomis, FL 34275. [Mo., $50, free to qualified personnel]. Up-to-date information from around the world regarding voice, video, and data communications.

Davies, J. (1996). **Educating students in a media saturated culture.** [Book, 316pp., $39.95]. Technomic Publishing Co., Inc., Lancaster, PA. Updates media literacy from current perspective; suggests media literacy curriculum.

Document and Image Automation (formerly *Optical Information Systems Magazine*). Meckler Publishing Corp., 11 Ferry Lane W., Westport, CT 06880-5808. [Bi-mo., $125]. Features articles on the applications of videodisc, optical disc, and teletext systems; future implications; system and software compatibilities; and cost comparisons. Also tracks videodisc projects and covers world news.

Document and Image Automation Update (formerly *Optical Information Systems Update*). Meckler Publishing Corp., 11 Ferry Lane W., Westport, CT 06880-5808. [12/yr., $297]. News and facts about technology, software, courseware developments, calendar, conference reports, and job listings.

Educational Media International. Turpin Distribution Services Ltd., Blackhorse Road, Letchworth, Herts. SG6 1HN, England. [Q., £45, $85 US]. The official journal of the International Council for Educational Media.

Federal Communications Commission Reports. Superintendent of Documents, Government Printing Office, Box 371954, Pittsburgh, PA 15250-7954. [Irreg., price varies]. Decisions, public notices, and other documents pertaining to FCC activities.

Gotfredson, D., & Engstrom, E. (1996). **Teaching with a learning from the video essay.** Paper presented at the Annual Meeting of the Broadcast Education Association Convention, Las Vegas. [ED 394 508, 12pp.]. The merits of the video photo essay as a broadcast production teaching tool and as a genre of television news are examined in this paper.

Historical Journal of Film, Radio, and Television. Carfax Publishing Co., 875-81 Massachusetts Ave., Cambridge, MA 02139. [Q., £60 indiv., £208 inst.]. Articles by international experts in the field, news and notices, and book reviews.

International Journal of Instructional Media. Westwood Press, Inc., 23 E. 22nd St., 4th floor, New York, NY 10010. [Q., $105 per vol.]. Articles discuss specific applications and techniques for bringing the advantages of a particular instructional medium to bear on a complete curriculum system or program.

Journal of Broadcasting and Electronic Media. Broadcast Education Association, 1771 N St., NW, Washington, DC 20036. [Q., $75 US, $90 elsewhere]. Includes articles, book reviews, research reports, and analyses. Provides a forum for research relating to telecommunications and related fields.

Journal of Educational Media. Carfax Publishing Co., 875-81 Massachusetts Ave., Cambridge, MA 02139. [3/yr., $164 personal, $484 inst.]. Forum for discussion of issues concerning educational television and related media.

Journal of Educational Television. Carfax Publishing Co., 875-81 Massachusetts Ave., Cambridge, MA 02139. [3/yr., $128 indiv., $352 inst.]. This journal of the Educational Television Association serves as an international forum for discussions and reports on developments in the field of television and related media in teaching, learning, and training.

Journal of Popular Film and Television. Heldref Publications, 1319 Eighteenth St., NW, Washington, DC 20036-1802. [Q., $34 indiv., $66 inst.]. Articles on film and television, book reviews, and theory.

Kozma, R. B., Assoc. Ed. (1996). Hard technologies: Media-related research. In D. H. Jonassen (Ed.), **Handbook of research for educational communications and technology,** pp. 299-489. New York: Macmillan. Section includes chapters about television, emerging technology, distance education, computer-mediated communication, and virtual reality.

Macciocca, J. (1996). Approaches to media management. **Media & Methods, 32** (5), 6, 8. Describes how media technology specialists organize and monitor instructional resources in schools. Topics include technology coordinators, decentralization of resources, media specialists in each school, and media retrieval systems to schedule the use of media and technology in classrooms. (LRW)

Media International. Oakfield House, Perrymount Rd., Haywoods Heath, W. Sussex RH16 3BR, England. [Mo., £42 Europe, £76 elsewhere]. Contains features on the major media developments and regional news reports from the international media scene.

Multimedia Monitor (formerly *Multimedia and Videodisc Monitor*). Future Systems, Inc., Box 26, Falls Church, VA 22040. [Mo., $395 indiv., $150 educational inst.]. Describes current events in the videodisc marketplace and in training and development.

Multimedia Schools. Online, Inc., Subscription Dept., 462 Danbury Rd., Wilton, CT 06897-2126. [5/yr., $38 US and Canada, $51 Mexico, $60 elsewhere]. Reviews new titles, evaluates hardware and software, offers technical advice and troubleshooting tips, and profiles high-tech installations.

NICEM (National Information Center for Educational Media) EZ. NICEM, P.O. Box 8640, Albuquerque, NM 87198-8640. (505) 265-3591, (800) 926-8328. Fax (505) 256-1080. E-mail nicem@nicem.com. For more than 25 years, NICEM has been serving the education and research communities with quality indexes to educational media. NICEM now offers a custom search service—NICEM EZ—to help those without access to the existing NICEM products tap the resources of this specialized database. Fees are $50 per hour search time plus $.20 for each unit identified.

NICEM (National Information Center for Educational Media) Masterfile. NICEM, P.O. Box 8640, Albuquerque, NM 87198-8640. (505) 265-3591, (800) 926-8328. Fax (505) 256-1080. E-mail nicem@nicem.com. NlightN (a division of The Library Corporation). (800) 654-4486, (703) 904-1010. E-mail info@nlightn.com. Web site: http://www.nlightn.com. NlightN, an Internet online service, widens the accessibility of information in the NICEM database to users of the Internet. The NICEM masterfile provides information on non-print media for all levels of education and instruction in all academic areas.

Technology Connection. Linworth Publishing, Inc., 480 E. Wilson Bridge Rd., Suite L, Worthington, OH 43085-9918. [10/yr., $39]. A forum for K-12 educators who use technology as an educational resource, this journal includes information on what works and what does not, new product reviews, tips and pointers, and emerging technology training.

Telematics and Informatics. Elsevier Science, Journals Division, 660 White Plains Rd., Tarrytown, NY 10591-5153. [Q., £395]. Contains information on applied telecommunications and information technology, and policy and legislation resource management; examines socioeconomic implications.

Video Systems. Intertec Publishing Corp., 9800 Metcalf, Overland Park, KS 66212-2215. [Mo., $45, free to qualified professionals]. For video professionals. Contains state-of-the-art audio and video technology reports.

Videography. Miller Freeman, PSN Publications, 2 Park Ave., 18th floor, New York, NY 10016. [Mo., $30]. For the video professional; covers techniques, applications, equipment, technology, and video art.

PROFESSIONAL DEVELOPMENT

Alley, L. R., & Repp, P. C. (1996). Technology precipitates reflective teaching: An instructional epiphany and the evolution of a red square. **Change, 28** (2), 48-54, 56-67. Two college educators offer their personal stories of adopting technology for college teaching in different disciplinary contexts (a physics course for nonmajors and a design course for interior designers and architects), and the process of redesigning curricula, rethinking instructional techniques, and revising student assessment accordingly. Both found the experience personally, professionally, and intellectually rewarding.

Balli, S. J., & Diggs, L. L. (1996). Learning to teach with technology: A pilot project with preservice teachers. **Educational Technology, 36** (1), 56-61. Describes a pilot project with 11 undergraduate preservice teachers who taught technology-based lessons in elementary school classrooms. Participants indicated that teaching technology was a good way to learn how theory is applied in practice, and field experience enhanced their knowledge.

Brandon, B. (1996). **Computer trainer's personal training guide.** [Book, 312pp., $49.99]. Que/Macmillan; available from AECT Publication Sales, 1025 Vermont Ave., NW, Suite 820, Washington, DC 20005. Describes experiences of working trainers and relates advice, practical tips, and strategies for the experienced trainer or beginner.

Cannon, J. R. (1996). The infusion of telecommunications and word processing educational technologies in the primary preservice teacher's science teaching methods course: An action research project. **Interpersonal Computing and Technology, 4** (1), 9-19. Examines the need for pre- and inservice training programs to educate teachers about educational technology and teaching methods. Describes the use of telecommunications and word processing in a college course and assesses student perceptions of using technology. Course evaluations found that 204 of 213 students did not report any negative comments about using technology.

Faison, C. (1996). Modeling instructional technology use in teacher preparation: Why we can't wait. **Educational Technology, 36**(5), 57-59. The K-12 and higher education communities have already voiced the need for technologically literate teachers. Standards movements and licensing agencies are stressing the importance of technology skills for beginning teachers and legislation is being passed which provides the impetus for change. Teacher preparation programs must have goals for technology infusion and provide consistent modeling of effective uses of technology in the classroom and curriculum.

Faseyitan, S. (1996). An inservice model for enhancing faculty computer self-efficacy. **British Journal of Educational Technology, 27** (3), 214-226. To improve instructional computer use by university faculty, an inservice program consisting of showcases, seminars, and workshops was funded, designed, and implemented. The program proved to be a cost-effective way for administrators to promote classroom use of computers by fostering faculty's confidence and computer self-efficacy. Seminar topics and workshop activities are described.

Gan, S. (1996). Modeling teaching with a computer-based concordancer in TESL preservice teacher education program. **Journal of Computing in Teacher Education, 12** (4), 28-32. This study modeled teaching with a computer-based concordancer in a Teaching English-as-a-Second-Language program. Preservice teachers were randomly assigned to work with computer concordancing software or vocabulary exercises to develop word attack skills. Pretesting and posttesting indicated that computer concordancing was more effective in teaching vocabulary skills.

George, G., & Camarata, M. R. (1996). Managing instructor cyberanxiety: The role of self-efficacy in decreasing resistance to change. **Educational Technology, 36** (4), 49-54. Discussion of educational technology innovations focuses on some of the behavioral challenges facing the drive toward multimedia instruction and suggests a method by which instructor resistance to technological change can be lessened or eliminated based on the concept of self-efficacy. A typology of instructors is explained.

Heinrich, V. (1996). Professional development using the Internet. **Adult Learning, 7** (3), 9-10. Use of the Internet can ensure educators a place in the new world of information resources. The Internet has a unique ability to break down barriers to professional development opportunities by expanding professional networks and sharing resources.

Hirumi, A., & Grau, I. (1996). A review of computer-related state standards, textbooks, and journal articles: Implications for preservice teacher education and professional development. **Journal of Computing in Teacher Education, 12** (4), 6-17. This study examined what educators should know and be able to do with computer technology. Content analyses of state standards, textbooks, and journal articles identified 60 computer-related proficiencies relevant to K-12 educators that were grouped into 10 categories. Results indicate little consensus among information sources on essential computer proficiencies for teachers.

Journal of Technology and Teacher Education. Association for the Advancement of Computing in Education (AACE), P.O. Box 2966, Charlottesville, VA 22901-2966. [Q., $65 indiv. US, $80 foreign, $83 US inst., $103 foreign inst.]. Serves as an international forum to report research and applications of technology in preservice, inservice, and graduate teacher education.

Kahn, J. (1996). **NCATE Standards for educational technology: One college meets the challenge.** Paper presented at the Annual Meeting of the American Association of Colleges for Teacher Education, Chicago. [ED 393 806, 12pp.]. Describes the teacher education unit at Chestnut Hill College (Pennsylvania) working to incorporate National Council for the Accreditation of Teacher Education Standards.

Multer, M., Ed. (1996). **Training in business and industry: Selected research papers.** Paper presented at the Annual Meeting of the American Educational Research Association, San Francisco, April, 1995. [ED 391 946, 137pp.]. This document contains 7 of the 10 papers presented at the 1995 program of the American Educational Research Association's special interest group, Training in Business and Industry.

Journal of Computing in Teacher Education. International Society for Technology in Education, University of Oregon, 1787 Agate St., Eugene, OR 97403-1923. [Q., for members of ISTE's SIGTE]. Contains refereed articles on preservices and inservice training, research in computer education and certification issues, and reviews of training materials and texts.

Sharp, V. (1996). **Computer education for teachers.** 2nd ed. [Book, 438pp., $48.55]. Times Mirror Higher Education Group; International Society for Technology in Education, University of Oregon, 1787 Agate St., Eugene, OR 97403-1923. Provides the computer-novice educator with a current, readable, practical, and concise introduction to computers.

Sheffield, C. J. (1996). An examination of self-reported computer literacy skills of preservice teachers. **Action in Teacher Education, 17** (4), 45-52. Reports a study that examined entering preservice teachers' prior experience in word processing, database, and spreadsheet software, based on self-reported information. Factors that influenced students' entering skills (for example, gender and computer experience) were noted. Survey data indicated that the subjects had little prior knowledge of educational technology.

Wild, M. (1996). Technology refusal: Rationalising the failure of student and beginning teachers to use computers. **British Journal of Educational Technology, 27**(2), 134-143. Discusses the apparent failure of information technology (IT) education in preservice teacher education courses. Offers a conceptual framework for investigating and analyzing this failure.

Suggests that IT outcomes are likely to be diverse and variable for any one student teacher population and these outcomes need to be considered in the context of individual students' constructions of IT meaning.

SIMULATION, GAMING, AND VIRTUAL REALITY

Aspects of Educational and Training Technology Series. Kogan Page Ltd., 120 Pentonville Rd., London N1 9JN, England. [ann. £35]. Covers the proceedings of the annual conference of the Association of Educational and Training Technology.

Eylon, B. (1996). Computer simulations as tools for teaching and learning: Using a simulation environment in optics. **Journal of Science Education and Technology, 5** (2), 93-110. Explores the potential of the RAY learning environment in improving learning about optics. Results indicate that this environment, which includes a flexible ray-tracing simulation, had a significant effect on the spontaneous and correct use of the model by students in solving problems and a limited effect on conceptual understanding, but promoted student understanding when used individually.

Kirby, A. (1997). **The encyclopedia of games for trainers.** [Book, 444pp., $99.95]. Training Express, 11358 Aurora Ave., Des Mones, IA 50322. Contains over 145 group games to encourage participation, motivation, and enjoyment for adults in business training contexts.

Kirby, A. (1997). **Great games for trainers.** [Book, 200pp., $69.95]. Training Express, 11358 Aurora Ave., Des Mones, IA 50322. Contains over 75 educational adult games on topics such as team building, stress management, leadership, creativity, assertiveness, and corporate ethics.

Newstrom, J. W., & Scannell, E. E. (1997). **Games trainers play.** [Book, 301pp., $29.95]. Training Express, 11358 Aurora Ave., Des Mones, IA 50322. Contains games to develop leadership ability, self-confidence, problem-solving, cooperation, and communication in business training contexts.

Rieber, L. P. (1996). Animation as feedback in a computer-based simulation: Representation matters. **Educational Technology Research & Development, 44**(1), 5-22. Explores how users interact and learn during computer-based simulations given graphical and textual forms of feedback. Graduate students were randomly assigned computer simulations with graphical feedback, textual feedback, or graphical plus textual feedback. Findings indicate that graphical feedback provides experiential learning, but that these experiences may not lead to reflective learning.

Rieber, L. P. (1996). **Getting interactive with Authorware: Building simulations and games.** [On-line book]. Available http://itech1.coe.uga.edu/Faculty/lprieber/authorwareinfo.html. Text that describes designing instruction with Authorware.

Rieber, L. P. (1996). Seriously considering play: Designing interactive learning environments based on the blending of microworlds, simulations, and games. **Educational Technology Research & Development, 44** (2), 43-58. Provides a brief overview of the history, research, and theory related to play. Research from education, psychology, and anthropology suggests that play is a powerful mediator for lifelong learning, and the design of hybrid learning environments is suggested based on the constructivist concept of microworlds and supported with games and simulations.

Sanger, J., with Wilson, J., Davies, B., & Whittaker, R. (1997). **Young children, videos and computer games: Issues for teachers and parents.** [Book, 192pp.]. Falmer Press, c/o Taylor & Francis, 1900 Frost Rd., Suite 101, Bristol, PA 19007-1598. Frames debate over effects on young children of computer games, video games, and videos.

Scannell, E. E., & Newstrom, J. W. (1997). **More games trainers play.** [Book, 302pp., $29.95]. Training Express, 11358 Aurora Ave., Des Moines, IA 50322. Second volume in series which contains games, activities, and exercises deigned to help trainers teach vital business skills.

Scannell, E. E., & Newstrom, J. W. (1997). **Still more games trainers play.** [Book, 311pp., $29.95]. Training Express, 11358 Aurora Ave., Des Moines, IA 50322. Third volume in series in business through games.

Simulation and Gaming. Sage Publications, Inc., 2455 Teller Rd., Thousand Oaks, CA 91359. [Q., $59 indiv., $200 inst.]. An international journal of theory, design, and research published by the Association for Business Simulation and Experiential Learning.

Virtual Reality Report. Cobb Group, Inc., 9420 Bunsen Pkwy., Suite 300, Louisville, KY 40220. [12/yr., $327]. Covers developments in the field of virtual reality and cyberspace.

SPECIAL EDUCATION AND DISABILITIES

Bender, R. L., & Bender, W. N. (1996). **Computer-assisted instruction for students at risk for ADHD, mild disabilities, or academic problems.** [Book, 240pp.]. Allyn & Bacon, 160 Gould St., Needham Heights, MA 02194-2315. Considers teacher's perspective with computer applications in special situations.

Burke, J. C. (1996). **Preparing school systems to deliver a hybrid education program for students with autism via distance learning classrooms, in-class teleconferencing, and listserv technology.** [ED 394 755, 18pp.]. Describes a model for teaching autistic students that integrates technology-based instructional and behavioral supports into existing curriculum at the Center for Technology in Education (CTE), a partnership between Johns Hopkins University and the Maryland state department of education.

Cahill, H. (1996). Blind and partially sighted students' access to mathematics and computer technology in Ireland and Belgium. **Journal of Visual Impairment and Blindness, 90** (2), 105-114. A survey of 42 Irish and Belgian blind and partially sighted students (ages 12 to 18) and interviews with 6 Irish and Belgian mathematics teachers found that few of the students took higher-level mathematics examinations, due primarily to mathematical-access difficulties. A computer-based system providing both menu and command (keyboard and voice) input was supported.

Cavalier, A. R., & Ferretti, R. P. (1996). Talking instead of typing: Alternate access to computers via speech recognition technology. **Focus on Autism and Other Developmental Disabilities, 11** (2), 79-85. The importance of alternative access to computers for persons with developmental disabilities and the ways in which speech recognition technology has been used to reach this goal are discussed. Illustrative studies of the use of speech recognition by persons with disabilities are reviewed, and implications for the effective application of this technology are described.

Deines-Jones, C. (1996). Access to library Internet services for patrons with disabilities: Pragmatic considerations for developers. **Library Hi Tech, 14** (1), 57-64, 68. Libraries should seek to serve the disabled by accommodating special needs in physical and intellectual access to the Internet. Some possible enhancements include (1) screen magnifiers; (2) voice interfaces; (3) braille displays; (4) alternative keyboard options; (5) spacious and adjustable workstation areas; (6) provision of remote access; and (7) availability of multimedia Web sites.

Howell, R. (1996). Technological aids for inclusive classrooms. **Theory into Practice, 35** (1), 58-65. This article explores some of the relevant features of the integration of technological tools into both regular and special education, seeking to determine those positive and negative features that would impact the usefulness of new technologies as aids to the inclusion of students with disabilities in general education classes.

Hutinger, P. L. (1996). **Activating children through technology.** [ED 395 411, 41pp.]. This report describes accomplishments and activities of the 3-year Activating Children Through Technology (ACTT) Outreach program at Western Illinois University, which focused on the integration of assistive technology into early childhood services for children (ages birth to 8) with disabilities.

Male, M. (1997). **Technology for inclusion: Meeting the special needs of all students.** 3rd ed. [Book, 198pp.]. Allyn & Bacon, 160 Gould St., Needham Heights, MA 02194-2315. Targets practicioners (either novice or advanced technology users) and suggests affordances of technology for special populations. Topics include mainstreaming, cooperative learning, multiple intelligences, and access.

McGregor, G., & Pachuski, P. (1996). Assistive technology in schools: Are teachers, ready, able, and supported? **Journal of Special Education Technology, 13** (1), 4-15. Analysis of 366 surveys completed by Pennsylvania teachers with educational responsibility for students using assistive technology found teachers were informed and experienced in the use of computers and assistive technology utilization, and training and maintenance were identified as needed supports.

Siegel, J. (1996). Integrating technology into educating preservice special education teachers. **Action in Teacher Education, 17** (4), 53-63. Preservice special educators were introduced to computer-aided instruction and technology in their classes. In some cases, technology was discussed or demonstrated, while in others, students completed projects using computers. Pretesting and posttesting indicated that participation improved students' attitudes toward using computers in the classroom.

Wittenstein, S. H., & Pardee, M. L. (1996). Teacher's voices: Comments on Braille and literacy from the field. **Journal of Visual Impairment and Blindness, 90** (3), 201-209. A survey of 1,663 teachers of students with blindness examined their attitudes about braille literacy. This article summarizes their comments concerning teaching braille, making the print-braille decision, use of technological devices, the importance of braille as a learning medium, use of slate and stylus, teachers' braille skills, legislation, and the possible decline in braille literacy.

TELECOMMUNICATIONS, NETWORKING, AND THE INTERNET

Barron, A. E., & Ivers, K. S. (1996). **Internet and instruction: Activities and ideas.** [Book, 160pp., $31]. Libraries Unlimited, P.O. Box 6633, Englewood, CO 80155-6633. Demystifies the technology of telecommunications and the Internet; provides relevant and feasible ideas and activities for the classroom.

Berge, Z. L., & Collins, M. P., Eds. (1997). **Wired together: The online classroom in K-12. Vol. 1: Perspectives and instructional design.** [Book, 272pp., $22.95]. Hampton Press, Inc., Cresskill, NJ. Collection of articles addressing models for implementation, perspectives, and instructional design.

Berge, Z. L., & Collins, M. P., eds. (1997). **Wired together: The online classroom in K-12. Vol. 2: Case studies.** [Book, 224pp., $21.95]. Hampton Press, Inc., Cresskill, NJ. Collection of examples of networked education for curricular subject areas, special education, and library media centers.

Berge, Z. L., & Collins, M. P., Eds. (1997). **Wired together: The online classroom in K-12. Vol. 3: Teacher education and professional development.** [Book, 224pp., $21.95]. Hampton Press, Inc., Cresskill, NJ. Collection of articles addressing CMC use with preservice teachers, changing classroom roles, and professional development.

Berge, Z. L., & Collins, M. P., Eds. (1997). **Wired together: The online classroom in K-12. Vol. 4: Writing, reading and language acquisition.** [Book, 256pp., $22.95]. Hampton Press, Inc., Cresskill, NJ. Collection of articles describing writing, reading, student publishing, correspondence projects, foreign language learning, and audiographics in second language learning.

Bix, C., with Petrillo, M. A., Morgan, T., & Miller, J. (1996). **Kids do the Web.** [Book, 208pp., $25]. Adobe/Macmillan; available through AECT Publication Sales, 1025 Vermont Ave., NW, Suite 820, Washington, DC 20005. Explores sites created by and for kids and teens.

Blansfield, K. C. (1996). High-tech connections. **Currents, 22** (3), 34-38. Ways in which college alumni officers are using emerging technology to enhance regional programming and distance communication are described, including Web sites, electronic mail, and satellite and video technologies. Suggestions are made for getting started: defining goals, doing research, offering inexpensive connections, and establishing guidelines for Web sites.

Byer, D., & Eckhardt, S. (1996). **Teaching Internet basics.** [Book, $15]. Hi Willow Research & Publishing. Presents Internet basics to teachers new to telecommunications. Contains sections on resource evaluation and ethics.

Cafolla, R., Kauffman, D., & Knee, R. (1997). **World Wide Web for teachers: An interactive guide.** [Book, 231pp.]. Allyn & Bacon, 160 Gould St., Needham Heights, MA 02194-2315. Features four interactive tutorials and a Web site for updating resources mentioned in the book.

Canadian Journal of Educational Communication. Association for Media and Technology in Education in Canada, 3-1750 The Queensway, Suite 1318, Etobicoke, ON M9C 5H5, Canada. [3/yr., $45]. Concerned with all aspects of educational systems and technology.

Clark, D. (1996). **Student's guide to the Internet.** 2nd ed. [Book, 334pp., $14.99]. Que/Macmillan; available through International Society for Technology in Education, University of Oregon, 1787 Agate St., Eugene, OR 97403-1923. With their specific interests and needs in mind, this book ushers in a more productive and profitable Internet experience for novice and casual student users.

Classroom Connect: Your Practical Monthly Guide to Using the Internet and Commercial Online Services. Wentworth Worldwide Media, P.O. Box 10488, Lancaster, PA 17605-0488. [9/yr., $39]. Provides pointers to sources of lesson plans for K-12 educators as well as descriptions of new Web sites, addresses for online "keypals," Internet basics for new users, classroom management tips for using the Internet, and online global projects. Each 20-page issue offers Internet adventures for every grade and subject.

Clearinghouse for Subject-Oriented Internet Resource Guides. Jointly sponsored by the University of Michigan's University Library and School of Information and Library Studies. It can be accessed by: anonymous FTP (host: una.hh.lib.umich.edu, path:/inetdirsstacks); Gopher (gopher.lib.umich.edu, under the menus Other Gophers/University of Michigan); and Web/Mosaic (URL:http://www.lib.umich.edu/chhome.html). WAIS indexing allows full-text searching of the guides. This clearinghouse serves as a central location for a collection of subject-oriented Internet resource guides compiled by individuals throughout the Internet. Volunteers publicize and market the service, process newly submitted guides, obtain updated versions of existing guides, create and label menu items for new guides, answer users' questions, and reindex the collection for full-text searching.

CompuServe Magazine. CompuServe, Inc., 5000 Arlington Centre Blvd., Columbus, OH 43220. [Mo., $30, $40 foreign]. Gives current information on fundamentals of micro-based communications, computer and information industry news, coverage of CompuServe services, commentary, and computer product reviews.

Computer Communications. Elsevier Science, Inc., P.O. Box 882, Madison Square Station, New York, NY 10159-0882. [14/yr., $835]. Focuses on networking and distributed computing techniques, communications hardware and software, and standardization.

Cooper, G., & Cooper, G. (1996). **Gopher it! An Internet resource guide for K-12 educators.** [Book, 122pp., $23]. Libraries Unlimited, P.O. Box 6633, Englewood, CO 80155-6633. Focusing on gopher sites, this directory will help locate lesson plans, teaching materials, current educational research, conference information, and details on grants and funding opportunities.

Cooper, G., & Cooper, G. (1997). **Virtual field trips.** [Book, 160pp., $24]. Libraries Unlimited, P.O. Box 6633, Englewood, CO 80155-6633. Lists Internet resources by subject and cross-referenced.

Cowan, G. (1996). How the Web works. **Social Education, 60** (2), 113. Explains the technical operation of the Web in four simple steps. Includes a glossary of Web-related terms and an explanation of the components making up a universal resource locator (URL) address. Neatly contained on one page, this would make a perfect handout or flyer for a computer lab.

Crotchett, K. R. (1997). **A teacher's project guide to the Internet.** [Book, 184pp., $26.50]. Heinemann, Portsmouth, NH, (800) 541-2086. Guides teachers through Internet with suggestions for student projects.

Data Communications. Box 473, Hightstown, NJ 08520. [Mo., $125 US, $130 Canada]. Provides users with news and analysis of changing technology for the networking of computers.

de Heer, C., with Backstrand, J.,, Murphy, A., & Kaufman, M. (1996). **NetDay96 How-to guide.** [Book and video, $19.95]. International Society for Technology in Education, University of Oregon, 1787 Agate St., Eugene, OR 97403-1923. This guide tells the story of California's successful wiring effort and provides detailed instructions for organizing and executing the process.

Edgar, C., & Wood, S. N. (1996). **The nearness of you.** [Book, 290pp., $16.95]. International Society for Technology in Education, University of Oregon, 1787 Agate St., Eugene, OR 97403-1923. Discusses the dynamic and inventive applications of computer conferencing and interactive technology to student writing, revision, peer editing, and publishing by 24 teachers.

EDUCOM Review. EDUCOM, 1112 Sixteenth St., NW, Suite 600, Washington, DC 20036-4823. [Bi-mo., $18 US, $24 Canada, $43 elsewhere]. Features articles on current issues and applications of computing and communications technology in higher education. Reports of EDUCOM consortium activities.

EMMS (Electronic Mail & Micro Systems). Telecommunications Reports, 1333 H Street NW, 11th Floor-W., Washington, DC 20005. [Semi-mo., $595 US, $655 elsewhere]. Covers technology, user, product, and legislative trends in graphic, record, and microcomputer applications.

Flanagan, P. (1996). The 10 hottest technologies in telecom. **Telecommunications, 30** (5), 29-30, 32, 35-36, 38. Synthesizes opinions of experts regarding technologies deemed most likely to enter the telecommunications mainstream by 1998, including: (1) the Java programming language; (2) voice- over frame relay; (3) virtual local area networks (LANs); (4) cable modems; (5) gigabit LANs; (6) Internet appliances; (7) personal satellite phones; (8) intranets; (9) automated network management; and (10) data mining.

Freedman, K., & Liu, M. (1996). The importance of computer experience, learning processes, and communication patterns in multicultural networking. **Educational Technology Research and Development, 44** (1), 43-59. Investigates issues fundamental to computer-assisted, multicultural education. Studied Asian American middle school students who corresponded electronically with culturally dissimilar students. Findings indicate that students of different ethnic backgrounds may have different attitudes about and knowledge of computers, cross-cultural communication patterns, and learning processes when working with computers.

Freud, R. (1996). **Community colleges and the virtual community.** [ED 397 871, 16pp.]. Community colleges should consider the advantages of providing Internet access to students, faculty, and non-teaching staff. Drawbacks of Internet access are the potential of plagiarism among students and the costs of upgrades.

Giagnocavo, G., McLain, T., DiStefano, V., & Sturm, C. N. (1996). **Educator's Internet companion: Classroom Connect's complete guide to educational resources on the Internet.** [Book with cross-platform CD-ROM, 274pp., $29.95]. International Society for Technology in Education, University of Oregon, 1787 Agate St., Eugene, OR 97403-1923. Contains 30 lesson plans for all major subject areas and grade levels and tips for locating more lesson plans and resources.

Harrison, T. M., & Stephen, T., Eds. (1996). **Computer networking and scholarly communication in the twenty-first-century university.** [Book, 480pp., $19.95]. State University of New York Press, State University Plaza, Albany, NY 12246-0001. Describes the effects of networking and telecommunications on academic scholarship.

Internet Research (previously *Electronic Networking: Research, Applications, and Policy*). MCB University Press Ltd., 60-62 Toller Ln., Bradford, W. Yorks. BD8 9BY, England. [Q., $239]. A cross-disciplinary journal presenting research findings related to electronic networks, analyses of policy issues related to networking, and descriptions of current and potential applications of electronic networking for communication, computation, and provision of information services.

Garner, R., & Gillingham, M. G. (1996). **Internet communication in six classrooms.** [Book, 168pp., $16.50]. Lawrence Erlbaum, 10 Industrial Ave., Mahwah, NJ 07430-2262, orders@erlbaum.com. Relates 6 episodes of Internet use in classrooms.

Hawley, C. (1996). **Electronic mail: An examination of high-end users.** Proceedings of Selected Research and Development Presentations at the 1996 AECT National Convention, Indianapolis. [ED 397 798, 7pp.]. This study examined what high-end users (those who use e-mail many times during the day) do with e-mail and how they feel about it. Three major categories of usage emerged: personal communication, class-related communication, and collaboration with colleagues. The following conclusions were drawn from this study: (1) there is a problem with a deluge of e-mail; (2) there is a cost and time efficiency benefit to using e-mail; and (3) subjects reported that their feelings about using e-mail have changed over time from viewing it as being fun and exciting to viewing it as strictly a communications medium.

Heide, A., & Stilborne, L. (1996). **The teacher's complete & easy guide to the Internet.** [Book, 320pp., $24.95]. Trifolium Books. Discusses exploration of the Internet from a teacher's point of view.

Internet World. Mecklermedia Corporation. Orders for North and South America, Internet World, P.O. Box 713, Mt. Morris, IL 61054; elsewhere, Mecklermedia Ltd., Artillery House, Artillery Row, London SW1P 1RT, UK. [M., $29 U.S]. Analyzes development with National Research and Education Network, Internet, electronic networking, publishing, and scholarly communication, as well as other network issues of interest to a wide range of network users.

Jody, M., & Saccardi, M. (1996). **Computer conversations: Readers and books online.** [Book, 194pp., $12.95]. National Council of Teachers of English, Urbana, IL. Illustrates how students can use computer-mediated communication to discuss literature with each other without geographical constraints.

Kinzie, M. B. (1996). Frog dissection via the World Wide Web: Implications for widespread delivery of instruction. **Educational Technology Research and Development, 44** (2), 59-69. Describes the development of a set of Internet-based instructional materials on frog dissection and anatomy for high schools, and reports on the effectiveness of Internet delivery for encouraging high levels of use and user satisfaction. The importance of the Web for distribution and use of educational materials is discussed.

Kurland, D. J., Sharp, R. M., & Sharp, V. F. (1997). **Internet guide for education.** [Book, 128pp.]. Wadsworth Publishing Co., 10 Davis Dr., Belmont, CA 94002-3098. Introductory educational telecommunications guide, with list of top Internet sites.

Lamb, A. (1997). **Exploring Internet resources.** [Video, 60min., $59.95]. AECT Publication Sales, 1025 Vermont Ave., NW, Suite 820, Washington, DC 20005. Explores implications for teachers and students using the Web; examines basics of utilization.

Lamb, A. (1997). **Integrating Internet resources.** [Video, 60min., $59.95]. AECT Publication Sales, 1025 Vermont Ave., NW, Suite 820, Washington, DC 20005. Illustrates the evaluation, selection, and integration of Internet resources into the classroom.

Lamb, A. (1997). **Creating Internet resources.** [Video, 60min., $59.95]. AECT Publication Sales, 1025 Vermont Ave., NW, Suite 820, Washington, DC 20005. Explores Web sites created by students and teachers; explains Web authoring.

Lamb, A., Smith, N., & Johnson, L. (1996). **Surfin' the Internet: Practical ideas from A to Z.** [Book, 330pp., $30.95]. AECT, 1025 Vermont Ave., NW, Suite 820, Washington, DC 20005-3547. A practical guide for integrating Internet technology into the classroom.

Laughon, S., Kurshan, B. (1996). A monster of a job! **MultiMedia Schools, 3** (1), 12-18. Describes how some K-12 teachers became moderators of educational telecommunication projects, and presents results of a survey of 100 moderators about their roles. Reviews types of networks that provide online learning environments: electronic bulletin boards, Internet lists, Web, and networks.

Leshin, C. B. (1997). **Internet adventures: Step-by-step guide to finding and using educational resources, version 1.2.** [Book, 321pp., $24.95]. Allyn & Bacon; available through International Society for Technology in Education, University of Oregon, 1787 Agate St., Eugene, OR 97403-1923. Written for educators; directs readers to substantial educational resources.

Leshin, C. B. (1996). **Management on the World Wide Web.** [Book, 265pp., $19.95]. AECT, 1025 Vermont Ave., NW, Suite 820, Washington, DC 20005-3547. Teaches the management student about the Web, using *Netscape Navigator* and *Microsoft Internet Explorer.*

Leu, D. J., & Leu, D. D. (1997). **Teaching with the Internet: Lessons from the classroom.** [Book, 200pp., $24.95]. Christopher-Gordon Publishers, Inc., 480 Washington St., Norwood, MA 02062. Explains in teacher-friendly terms how to integrate telecommunications experiences into classroom learning.

Link-Up. Information Today, Inc., 143 Old Marlton Pike, Medford, NJ 08055. [Bi-mo., $25 US, $48 elsewhere]. Newsmagazine for individuals interested in small computer communications covers hardware, software, communications services, and search methods.

Lopata, C. L., & McClure, C. R. (1996). **Assessing the academic networked environment.** [ED 398 876, 162pp.]. This investigation attempts to characterize the current state of networking in academic institutions and to identify and develop tools and approaches to assess academic networking.

Maxymuk, J. (1996). Riding the technology waves in search of electronic access: CD-ROM, gophers, the WWW and beyond. **Journal of Government Information, 23** (3), 327-334. A strong commitment to network resources is the best route for depositories to take in providing access to government information. The Government Printing Office needs to assume a leadership role in the advances of technology, phasing out federal CD-ROMs and replacing them with Internet sources via gophers and the Web.

McCain, T. D. E., & Ekelund, M. (1996). **Computer networking for educators.** 2nd ed. [Book, 188pp., $30.95]. International Society for Technology in Education, University of Oregon, 1787 Agate St., Eugene, OR 97403-1923. Describes the general trends of the computer industry that can serve as a guide to ensure wise investments of time and money.

McConville, D. (1996). So wide a Web, so little time. **Educom Review, 31** (3), 44-48. Discusses new trends in the Web. Highlights include multimedia; digitized audio-visual files; compression technology; telephony; virtual reality modeling language (VRML); open architecture; and advantages of Java, an object-oriented programming language, including platform independence, distributed development, and pay-per-use software.

McEwan, B. (1996). **It is as much the how as the what: Examining my own practices for teaching classroom management.** Paper presented at the Annual Meeting of the American Educational Research Association, New York. [ED 397 011, 33pp.]. This study explored the potential of videotape and E-mail technology for developing a course delivery system encouraging personal reflection on the topic of classroom management. The nature of student-professor E-mail discourse is discussed in detail, and while the process of continuing E-mail contact with students was found to be time consuming, numerous benefits for students and their instructor were noted.

Mende, R. (1996). **Building global learning communities through the Internet.** Paper presented at the Annual Conference of the Association of Canadian Community Colleges, Toronto, May. [ED 397 928, 11pp.]. From Spring 1995 to Spring 1996, Cambrian College, in Ontario, undertook a project to develop Canada's first full program using Internet technology. The major challenges accomplished included the selection of the program; adaptation of materials for digital delivery; selection of a delivery technology; faculty training; and program marketing, delivery, and evaluation.

Miller, E. B. (1997). **The Internet resource directory for K-12 teachers and librarians, 97/98 edition.** [Book, 342pp., $25]. Libraries Unlimited, P.O. Box 6633, Englewood, CO 80155-6622. Designed for educators who are beginners on the Internet; specifies what's out there and demonstrates how to find it.

Morgan, N. A. (1996). **An Introduction to Internet resources for K-12 educators.** [ED 391 460 and ED 391 461]. First document (Part 1) lists information resources; second document (Part 2) addresses question answering, listservs, and discussion groups.

Ohio State Legislative Office of Education Oversight. (1996). **Ohio SchoolNet initiatives: School readiness for computers and networks.** [ED 398 859, 45pp.]. This report examines the readiness of Ohio's schools to use the computers and network wiring provided by SchoolNet and SchoolNet Plus.

Online. Online, Inc., 462 Danbury Rd., Wilton, CT 06897. [6/yr., $110 US and Canada, $132 Mexico, $145 foreign airmail]. For online information system users. Articles cover a variety of online applications for general and business use.

Perritt, H. H. (1996). The information highway: On ramps, checkpoints, and tollbooths. **Government Information Quarterly, 13** (2), 143-158. Discusses how open computer network architecture, along with the browsing capabilities of the Web, facilitates the dissemination of public information. Competitive markets will be created as those from the private sector package electronic information with value added. Copyright law and information pricing policies are outlined, and speculations are made on prospects for an "electronic government."

Peters, P. E. (1996). Are you ready for that thing called "change"? **Educom Review, 31** (2), 16-17. Suggests that there is danger in focusing too much on developing new features for relatively stable Internet hardware and software platforms, and not enough attention to creating new value for networked information users. Criteria for networked information systems functions and performance factors must be developed, and it is necessary to plan and evaluate development efforts with user-centered standards in mind.

Powell, W. W. (1996). Interorganization collaboration and the locus of innovation: Networks of learning in biotechnology. **Administrative Science Quarterly, 41** (1), 116-145. Develops a network approach to organizational learning and derives firm-level longitudinal hypotheses that link research-and-development alliances, interfirm management experiences, network position, and other factors, using a sample of dedicated biotechnology firms. Collaborative networks provide entry to a field with widely distributed relevant knowledge not easily manufactured or obtainable through market transactions.

Proctor, L. F. (1996). **Speedbumps on the Information Highway.** Paper presented at the Annual Conference of AECT, Indianapolis. [ED 393 449, 7pp.]. The topic for this paper developed as a result of observations made during the course of a joint Internet pilot project with K-12 teachers and administrators in the city of Saskatoon (Canada); the project was designed to determine the amount of professional development time the participants needed to become functional Internet users and to explore ways of integrating network resources into classroom instruction.

Provenzo, E. F. (1997). **The educator's brief guide to the Internet and the World Wide Web.** [Book, 200pp., $29.95]. Eye on Education, 6 Depot Way West, Suite 106, Larchmont, NY 10538. Demonstrates access, integration, planning, and resources for the beginning educational telecommunicator.

Risinger, C. F. (1996). Webbing the social studies. **Social Education, 60** (2), 111-112. Provides some basic and rudimentary information on using the Internet and the World Wide Web. Includes a list of recommended Web sites for general coverage of social studies.

Rosen, D. J. (1996). **How easy is it for adult educators to use the Information Superhighway?** [ED 392 964, 10pp.]. In November 1995, an online survey was conducted of 113 adult literacy practitioners who were actively using the Internet. Respondents reported difficulties encountered in learning to use the Internet, kinds of supports and training helpful in overcoming these difficulties, and ways the Internet was used for adult education activities.

Ryder, R. J., & Hughes, T. (1997). **Internet for educators.** [Book, 240pp.]. Merrill/Prentice Hall, 445 Hutchinson Ave., Columbus, OH 43235-5677. Guides teachers through Internet explorations with an interactive approach. Contains appendices with sample Acceptable Use Polices (AUPs).

Schrum, L., & Berenfeld, B. (1997). **Teaching and learning in the information age: A guide to educational telecommunications.** [Book, 179pp.]. Allyn & Bacon, 160 Gould St., Needham Heights, MA 02194-2315. Offers introduction to using telecommunications for educators and others within authentic curricular activities in educational settings, placed in the context of professional development, research, and compelling issues.

Schrum, L., & Solomon, G. (1996). **Connect online! A telecommunications simulation.** Thomson Learning Tools, Cincinnati OH. Simulates online environments for learners (grades 4-10 and staff development) using telecommunications for curricular activities, presenting vocabulary practice in electronic searching, email, conferencing, and using real networks.

Serim, F., & Koch, M. (1996). **NetLearning: Why teachers use the Internet.** [Book and Windows CD-ROM, 292pp., $24.95]. International Society for Technology in Education, University of Oregon, 1787 Agate St., Eugene, OR 97403-1923. Presents practical approach to telecommunications from an optimistic perspective.

Sharp, R. M., Levine, M. G., & Sharp, V. F. (1997). **The best math and science Web sites for teachers.** [Book, 125pp., $18.95]. International Society for Technology in Education, University of Oregon, 1787 Agate St., Eugene, OR 97403-1923. Lists and describes appropriate Web sites alphabetically, and by curriculum area and grade level.

Sharp, V. F., Levine, M. G., & Sharp, R. M. (1996). **The best Web sites for teachers.** [Book, 374pp., $22.95]. International Society for Technology in Education, University of Oregon, 1787 Agate St., Eugene, OR 97403-1923. Lists 700 outstanding Web sites organized alphabetically by curriculum area.

Slough, S. W. (1996). **Area under constructivism: A pilot study using a World Wide Web home page to assess professional development.** Paper presented at the Annual Meeting of the National Association for Research in Science Teaching, St. Louis. [ED 396 919, 16pp.]. The purpose of this study was to evaluate the potential of Web Home Page construction as a way for teachers to demonstrate their professional development as they construct new professional knowledge and networks.

Starr, R., & Milheim, R. (1996). Educational uses of the Internet: An exploratory survey. **Educational Technology, 36** (5), 19-28. To determine how the Internet is being used in education, researchers surveyed newsgroup participants. Questions concerned demographics and usage. Responses totaled 147. Results indicate that there is a solid foundation of users who are optimistic about the future despite hardware and software problems and concerns about offensive material. Seven graphs depict results. The questionnaire is appended.

Telecommunications. (North American Edition.) Horizon House Publications, Inc., 685 Canton St., Norwood, MA 02062. [Mo., $75 US, $135 elsewhere, free to qualified individuals]. Feature articles and news for the field of telecommunications.

Tennat, R., Ober, J., & Lipgow, A. G. (1996). **Crossing the Internet threshold: An instructional handbook,** 2nd ed. [Book, 169pp., $50]. AECT, 1025 Vermont Ave., NW, Suite 820, Washington, DC 20005-3547. Covers the three Internet services: mail, telnet, and file transfer.

Thornburg, D. D. (1996). **Putting the Web to work: Transforming education for the next century.** [Book, 201pp., $24.95]. Proposes that computers offer schools a compelling and irresistible opportunity to be much more than places where teachers teach and students are taught.

T.I.E. News (Telecommunications in Education). International Society for Technology in Education, 1787 Agate St., Eugene, OR 97403-1923. [Q., $20 members, $29 nonmembers, $31.40 Canadian members, $41.33 Canadian nonmembers]. Contains articles on all aspects of educational telecommunications.

Trahant, M. N. (1996). The power of stories: Native words and images on the Internet. **Native Americans, 13** (1), 14-21. Traces changes in the nature of storytelling from oral tradition to books, newspapers, television, and now, the Internet, which presents information in a nonlinear multilayered format more similar to traditional storytelling than are other media. Discusses Native American participation on the Internet and problems of access. Lists native Web sites and other Internet options.

Watson, O. (1996). A networked learning environment: Toward new teaching strategies in secondary education. **Educational Technology, 36** (5), 40-43. This article discusses telecommunications infrastructure and instructional innovation at Townview, a college preparatory school in Dallas, Texas. Topics include connectivity, Internet access, the multimedia center, videoconferencing and student-directed curricula, resource sharing, cooperative learning activities, advanced science learning and information sharing, digital tutors, and teacher training.

Weiss, J. (1996). The wiring of our children. **NewMedia, 6** (8), 36-37, 39. Examines developments in Internet usage in the nation's schools. Discusses educational benefits of the Web, including cost-effectiveness, child-friendly browser software, and possibilities for multimedia lesson plans and materials. Describes options for collaboration on Computer Curriculum Corporation's CCCNet, the GLOBE (Global Learning and Observations to Benefit the Environment) program, and the CoVis (Collaborative Visualization) project.

Wilson, B. (1996). **Cultural assimilation of the Internet: A case study.** Proceedings of Selected Research and Development Presentations at the 1996 National AECT Convention, Indianapolis [ED 397 848, 12pp.]. Despite enormous growth of the Internet and its proliferation of tools, resources, and on-line communities, the connection between local learning environments and virtual learning environments remains tenuous. This paper examines this relationship, based upon a case study of an academic unit at the University of Colorado at Denver.

Index

This index lists names of associations, organizations, articles and papers, authors, and titles. Graduate programs in instructional technology of individual states are listed in boldface type. In addition, acronyms for all organizations and associations are cross-referenced to the full name. Please note that a classified list of U.S. organizations and associations appears on pages 113-17.

AACC. *See* American Association of Community Colleges (AACC)
AACE. *See* Association for the Advancement of Computing in Education (AACE)
AAP, 3. *See also* Association of American Publishers (AAP)
AASCU. *See* American Association of State Colleges and Universities (AASCU)
AASL. *See* American Association of School Librarians (AASL)
Abraham, Michael R., 62, 68-69, 73, 74
Abrams, A. H., 240
"Academic publishing and new technologies: Protecting intellectual property is the key," 22
Academic publishing on the Internet, 16-23
described, 16-18
potentials and pitfalls of, 20-22
as process, 18-19
Academy of Motion Picture Arts and Sciences, 118
Access ERIC, 96-97, 133
ACCESS NETWORK, 164
"Access to library Internet services for patrons with disabilities: Pragmatic considerations for developers," 255
ACEI. *See* Association for Childhood Education International (ACEI)
ACHE. *See* Association for Continuing Higher Education (ACHE)
ACRL. *See* Association of College and Research Libraries (ACRL)
Acts of meaning, 77
"Ada and the analytical engine," 213
Adams, D. M., 77, 79
ADJ/CH1. *See* Adjunct ERIC Clearinghouse on Chapter 1 (Compensatory Education) (ADJ/CHP1)
ADJ/CL. *See* Adjunct ERIC Clearinghouse on Clinical Schools (ADJ/CL)
ADJ/CN. *See* Adjunct ERIC Clearinghouse for Consumer Education (ADJ/CN)
ADJ/JS. *See* Adjunct ERIC Clearinghouse for United States-Japan Studies (ADJ/JS)
ADJ/LE. *See* Adjunct ERIC Clearinghouse for ESL Literacy Education (ADJ/LE)

ADJ/LR. *See* Adjunct ERIC Clearinghouse for Law-Related Education (ADJ/LR)
Adjunct ERIC Clearinghouse for Art Education, 134
Adjunct ERIC Clearinghouse for Consumer Education (ADJ/CN), 134
Adjunct ERIC Clearinghouse for ESL Literacy Education (ADJ/LE), 136
Adjunct ERIC Clearinghouse for Law-Related Education (ADJ/LR), 134
Adjunct ERIC Clearinghouse for United States-Japan Studies, Adjunct to the ERIC Clearinghouse for Social Studies/Social, 134
Adjunct ERIC Clearinghouse on Chapter 1 (Compensatory Education) (ADJ/CHP1), 138
Adjunct ERIC Clearinghouse on Clinical Schools (ADJ/CL), 137
Advanced Telecommunications in U.S. Public Elementary and Secondary Schools, Fall 1996, 2, 5
"Advantages of a theory-based curriculum in instructional technology," 30, 33
AECT. *See* Association for Educational Communications and Technology (AECT)
AECT Archives, 125
AECT Division of Learning and Performance Environments (DLPE), 17, 21
AEE. *See* Association for Experiential Education (AEE)
AEL. *See* Appalachia Educational Laboratory, Inc. (AEL)
AERA. *See* American Educational Research Association (AERA)
AFB. *See* American Foundation for the Blind (AFB)
AFC. *See* Anthropology Film Center (AFC)
"The affective dimension in curriculum improvement," 77
Agency for Instructional Technology (AIT), 118
"Agenda-building and its implications for theory construction," 33
Agnew, P. W., 240
"Agricultural education and distance education," 219
AI (Artificial intelligence), 44

"Using newspapers on CD-ROM as a resource,"
236
"Using the Internet as a tool in a resource-based
learning environment," 236
"Using videotapes to improve teaching," 249
Utah
**graduate programs in instructional
technology, 205**
Utah State University, 205

Vacca, J. A. L., 77, 80
Vacca, R. T., 77, 80
Valauskas, E. J., 249
Valdosta State University, 183
"Validating instructional design in schools: A
teacher planning inventory," 35
Van Allsburg, C., 80
"The Victorian women writers project: The
library as a creator and publisher of
electronic texts," 233
Video editing the pictorial sequence, 249
Video Systems, 252
Videography, 252
"Viewing film and television as whole language
instruction," 79
Vincent, B. R., 215
Virginia
**graduate programs in instructional
technology, 205**
Virginia Polytechnic Institute and State Univer-
sity (Virginia Tech), 206
Virginia State University, 206
*The virtual community: Homesteading on the
electronic frontier*, 20
Virtual field trips, 257
"Virtual publication and the fair use concept," 22
"Virtual realities," 5
Virtual reality (VR), 5, 6
Virtual Reality Report, 255
*The virtual school library: Gateways to the infor-
mation superhighway*, 246
Visual communication: Images with messages,
78, 79
Visual literacy: Image mind and reality, 78
*Visual literacy connections to thinking reading
and writing*, 77, 78, 79
"Visual literacy in education - A semiotic
perspective," 78
*Visual messages: Integrating imagery into
instruction*, 77, 78, 79
"Visuals in instructional design," 239
Voice of Youth Advocates, 249
Vosniadou, S., 230
VR (Virtual reality). *See* Virtual reality (VR)
"VTLS proceedings," 233
Vygotsky, L. S., 77

Wagner, C., 217
Walberg, Herbert J., 46, 47-48, 50, 56
Walden University, 192
Wang, Feng, 62, 69-71, 73, 74
Washington
**graduate programs in instructional
technology, 207**
Watson, O., 263
Watts Pailliotet, Ann, 76-93
Waxman, H. C., 227
Wayne State University, 192
*Ways with words: Language life and work in
communities and classrooms*, 77
*We teach with technology: New visions for
education*, 79
Weaver, D., 77
Web, 66, 97
The web of meaning, 77
"Webbing the social studies," 262
webCATS, 96
Webster University, 193
Webster's third new international dictionary, 36
Wedman, J. F., 33
Weiss, J., 263
WestEd, 163
Western Illinois University, 185
Western Maryland College, 189
Western Oregon State College, 201
Western Public Radio (WPR), 164
Western Washington University, 207
Weston, C., 238
Weston, Mark, 7
WFS. *See* World Future Society (WFS)
"What can research on teacher thinking
contribute to teacher preparation?
A second opinion," 31
"What is a document? Rethinking the concept in
uneasy times," 233
"What is instructional-design theory and how is
it changing?," 8
"What is media literacy? Two leading
proponents offer an overview," 78
Whatley, M., 12
"What's in a plan? Stated and unstated plans for
lessons," 32
Whittaker, R., 254
"The why of cognition: Emotion and the writing
process," 77
"Why schools can't improve: The upper-limit
hypothesis," 34
Wiggins, G., 77
Wild, M., 240, 244, 253
Wilkinson, Gene L., 16-23
"Will your NQT use IT?," 213
Willett, P., 233
William Paterson College, 195
Williams, H. M., 221